FORWARD WITH PATTON

AMERICAN WARRIORS

Throughout the nation's history, numerous men and women of all ranks
and branches of the U.S. military have served their country with honor
and distinction. During times of war and peace, there are individuals
whose exemplary achievements embody the highest standards of
the U.S. armed forces. The aim of the American Warriors series is to
examine the unique historical contributions of these individuals, whose
legacies serve as enduring examples for soldiers and citizens alike. The
series will promote a deeper and more comprehensive understanding of
the U.S. armed forces.

SERIES EDITOR: Roger Cirillo

An AUSA Book

FORWARD WITH
PATTON

THE WORLD WAR II DIARY OF
COLONEL ROBERT S. ALLEN

ROBERT S. ALLEN

EDITED BY
JOHN NELSON RICKARD

UNIVERSITY PRESS OF KENTUCKY

Scholarly publisher for the Commonwealth,
serving Bellarmine University, Berea College, Centre College of Kentucky,
Eastern Kentucky University, The Filson Historical Society, Georgetown
College, Kentucky Historical Society, Kentucky State University, Morehead
State University, Murray State University, Northern Kentucky University,
Transylvania University, University of Kentucky, University of Louisville,
and Western Kentucky University.
All rights reserved.

Editorial and Sales Offices: The University Press of Kentucky
663 South Limestone Street, Lexington, Kentucky 40508-4008
www.kentuckypress.com

Unless otherwise noted, maps are by John Nelson Rickard.

Library of Congress Cataloging-in-Publication Data

Names: Allen, Robert S. (Robert Sharon), 1900–1981, author. | Rickard, John
   Nelson, 1969– editor.
Title: Forward with Patton : the World War II diary of Colonel Robert S.
   Allen / Robert S. Allen ; edited by John Nelson Rickard.
Description: Lexington, Kentucky : University Press of Kentucky, 2017. |
   Series: American warriors | Includes bibliographical references and index.
Identifiers: LCCN 2017019632| ISBN 9780813169125 (hardcover : alk. paper) |
   ISBN 9780813169132 (pdf) | ISBN 9780813169149 (epub)
Subjects: LCSH: Allen, Robert S. (Robert Sharon), 1900–1981—Diaries. |
World War, 1939–1945—Personal narratives, American. | United States. Army.
   Army, 3rd—History—World War, 1939–1945—Sources. | World War,
   1939–1945—Campaigns—Western Front—Sources. | Patton, George S.
(George Smith), 1885–1945. | Soldiers—United States—Diaries.
Classification: LCC D769.26 3rd .A53 2017 | DDC 940.54/1273092 [B] —dc23
LC record available at https://lccn.loc.gov/2017019632

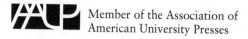

Contents

Photographs follow page 162

Editor's Preface

Colonel Robert S. Allen was a key member of Colonel Oscar Koch's G-2 Section in Lieutenant General George S. Patton Jr.'s Third Army headquarters. Allen served as chief of the Situation (Combat Intelligence) subsection and as executive officer for Operations. Like many American officers during the war, Allen kept a personal journal to record what was important to him. Although his full wartime journal covers the period from July 26, 1942, to June 3, 1945, this book includes only the portion from February 1944 to June 1945, the period during which he was associated with Patton.

Allen wrote his journal entries in small booklets. The original handwritten journal and a typed transcript are currently held in the Allen Papers in the Archives Division of the Wisconsin Historical Society. A transcript of the journal was also held for many years in the Patton Museum of Cavalry and Armor at Fort Knox, Kentucky. In 2011 this transcript was moved to the new Armor Museum at Fort Benning, Georgia. It is not known when or where the handwritten journal was transcribed or who performed the task. In a few places British spellings are used, such as *centre* instead of the American *center,* leading one to suspect the work of a British transcriber. It is possible that one of the several British enlisted men who served in Third Army's Special Liaison Unit (SLU) to handle Ultra intelligence transcribed Allen's penciled notes during the war. However, there is no proof of this.

Very small portions of Allen's journal have been published before. George F. Hofmann used a few entries for his 2006 study *Through Mobility We Conquer: The Mechanization of U.S. Cavalry,* and I quoted from the journal in my 2011 work *Advance and Destroy: Patton as Commander in the Bulge.*[1] The journal edited here is a different manuscript from Allen's 1947 book *Lucky Forward: The History of Patton's Third U.S. Army,* which contains none of Allen's vitriol and obviously includes no mention of Ultra.[2]

Allen's journal is of historical significance for several reasons. First, it reflects his private thoughts on his wartime experiences. He consistently condemned the Regular Army politics that prevented his earlier promotion based on merit. The journal also provides insight into the employment of the Third Army staff and the strengths and weaknesses of its individual members. The tone of the writing reveals Allen's character. He was petty and vindictive and was drawn to rumors of a personal nature, mirroring his prewar journalism career characterized by an obsession for gossipy political stories. Critics of his journalistic style emphasized his proclivity for character assassination and sensationalism, often at the expense of the facts.

Allen was stinging in his criticism of many of his fellow staff officers in terms of character and competence, but he held Oscar Koch, the G-2; Halley Maddox, the G-3; and Walter Muller, the G-4, in high regard. He was less charitable to Hugh J. Gaffey, the chief of staff, and Hobart R. Gay, the deputy chief of staff. Allen reserved special contempt for Major Generals Wade Haislip, Walton Walker, and Manton Eddy, commanding generals of XV, XX, and XII Corps, respectively. None of them met Allen's standards of physical appearance and persona, derived from his admiration of Patton.

Third Army's SLU officer, Major Melvin C. Helfers, did not think much of Allen. Once, when Helfers requested G-2 supplies, Allen asked him what the supplies were for. When Helfers replied that he could not tell him, Allen stated that his response was not good enough and refused to give him any. Helfers reflected, "After he started attending the small early Ultra briefings, Colonel Allen tried to become very friendly with me. Even if I had liked him, I could not have stood him. Not only was he the most foul-mouthed person I ever met but he also had the worst case of halitosis I have ever come across."[3] Major John Cheadle, who served under Allen in the Situation subsection, also had a low opinion of him, noting, "He was a character, that Allen. He wasn't too good an Officer."[4]

Allen was grossly biased in favor of Patton and Third Army. Allen's entire perspective of strategy on the Western Front was, perhaps inevitably, filtered through a Third Army lens. Third Army was the hammer and the other Allied armies were a series of anvils on which Patton's army would destroy the Germans. The hypersensitivity to any real or perceived slight against Third Army produced an intense Anglophobia in Allen. The primary object of his distain was Field Marshal Bernard Montgomery, commander of Twenty-First Army Group. Allen regularly eviscerated Montgomery's character, describing him as a coward, a criminal, and a glory seeker, and he judged him to be a pedestrian commander. Every thwarting of Patton's will had its origins in Montgomery's machinations.

Allen's "circle the Third Army wagon" mentality ensured a wide canvas for his vitriol. General Dwight D. Eisenhower, the Supreme Allied Commander; General Omar N. Bradley, commander of Twelfth Army Group; and Lieutenant General Courtney Hodges, commander of First United States Army, all suffered Allen's cutting indictments. He also expressed particular contempt for Major General Kenneth Strong, Brigadier General Edwin Sibert, and Colonel Benjamin Dickson, the G-2s of Supreme Headquarters Allied Expeditionary Forces, Twelfth Army Group, and First Army, respectively.

Despite Allen's obvious bias, his journal offers some insightful observations on Patton's operational and command techniques and his interactions with staff. Patton's keen interest in intelligence processes and products is apparent, as is his handling of subordinate commanders, particularly the cautious Eddy. Especially revealing are Patton's efforts to maintain momentum and the extent to which he prepared to sell his ideas to Bradley or withhold information about his intentions.

The journal is also important for its illumination of a controversy that followed Patton from Sicily and involved the killing of prisoners. On several occasions, Allen offers evidence that Patton conditioned Third Army not to take Gestapo or SS prisoners. For instance, Allen mentions a time in early November when Patton declared to everyone that he was going up to XII Corps to tell the troops not to take prisoners. Allen notes, "He shot a hard look at me, standing off to one side near the door. I said nothing, and neither did he."

Allen's frequent reference to Ultra adds to the journal's historical significance. In late May 1944 Allen attended the British Secret Intelligence Service (SIS) school in London. On July 11 he wrote in his journal, "*ULTRA*—I am inducted." According to Helfers, Allen was ultimately indoctrinated into Ultra because Koch was routinely sick in his quarters and could not fully execute the G-2 functions. A "high-ranking" British officer from Bletchley Park came over to France and briefed Allen. Although Allen does not specifically state that it was Royal Air Force Group Captain Frederick W. Winterbotham who briefed him, Winterbotham is mentioned.

By referring to Ultra at all, Allen clearly violated the security protocols established by the Government Code and Cypher School at Bletchley Park to protect the source. Near the very end of the war, Patton allowed Allen to go on a dangerous intelligence mission, knowing full well that Allen had been indoctrinated into Ultra. Allen's capture demonstrated the correctness of Bletchley Park's concerns about placing such individuals in harm's way. Patton no doubt considered the risk low so late in the war.

Allen's comments on Ultra give the reader a sense of the importance and utility of this intelligence at various times. Allen first refers to the possibility of a German spoiling attack in the Ardennes on November 3, but on November 12 he noted that there was "not one hint" from Ultra of the German buildup opposite Third Army following the start of its new offensive on November 8. Yet he heavily criticized Sibert and Dixon for not using Ultra evidence to predict the Ardennes counteroffensive. Allen clearly doubted Ultra's utility at times, and overall, one gets the sense that, at Patton's level, it was no more valuable than the whole range of non-Ultra intelligence-gathering capabilities, from prisoner of war interrogation to air reconnaissance.

Allen personally wrote the majority of Third Army's intelligence estimates and target area analyses, regularly gave Patton the daily G-2 briefing at 1100 hours, and frequently referred to these intelligence products in his journal. I have included appendix B containing two estimates, one from August and one from November, to give the reader some insight into Allen's approach to intelligence analysis. The estimates also allow the reader to judge Allen's accuracy against actual events.

The editing of Allen's journal posed certain challenges. He often wrote in shorthand, with many acronyms and incomplete sentences. I have spelled out military acronyms and abbreviations the first time they appear and employ the acronyms and abbreviations thereafter; for non-military abbreviations, I have used the unabbreviated terms throughout (e.g., *yards* for *yds* and *feet* for *ft*). Allen widely employed standard army capitalization. For example, he capitalized compass directions, and I have maintained the integrity of his capitalization to demonstrate his contemporary writing style.

My silent corrections consist of three types. First, I have inserted minor words such as *to, the,* and *or* to improve the readability of the original text. Significant words that assist in readability but that Allen did not actually use are placed in brackets. Second, Allen sometimes forgot to add a unit designator such as *Division* or *Army,* and he usually referred to Patton as *P* and Koch as *K.* I have added unit designators where appropriate and spelled out the names Patton and Koch throughout. Third, I have corrected obvious spelling mistakes (e.g., changing *speher* to *sphere*). Allen was particularly sloppy when it came to personal names and places. These have been corrected in brackets the first time they are encountered, and the proper spelling is employed thereafter.

My editorial comments are of two types. First, I have identified the individuals mentioned by Allen, providing basic biographical information for as many of them as possible. This includes full name, dates of birth and death, and a brief description of their assignments immediately preceding their duty with Third Army or the date of their first mention in the journal. In some cases, identification has proved impossible, such as for those individuals referred to by last name only; in addition, some officers who served in Third Army prior to Patton's arrival were difficult to identify. West Pointers are listed in the *Register of Graduates* of the Association of Graduates, United States Military Academy, West Point.

The second type of editorial comment concerns Allen's gross bias and frequently inaccurate information. I have inserted editorial comments directly into the text to address some of the most blatantly biased statements, and I have corrected as many significant factual errors as possible by inserting editorial comments in the text or in an endnote. Readers should consult *Third U.S. Army After Action Report,* volume 1, *Operations, 1 August 1944–9 May 1945,* and volume 2, *Staff Section Reports.* These volumes contain a massive amount of information that both complements and corrects Allen's journal. Koch's *G-2: Intelligence for Patton,* published in 1971, contains good material on Allen's role in the G-2 Section.

I would like to thank Dr. Robert S. Cameron, historian at the Armor School in Fort Benning, for tracking down and providing Allen's typescript journal. Justin Batt of the Maneuver Center of Excellence graciously provided Allen's 201 File and copies of his handwritten journal. Lee Grady of the Wisconsin Historical Society assisted with photographs and permissions to publish the material. Leo Barron, Colonel (Retired) Don Patton, Hal Winton, and Major General Bradford Swedo assisted with the difficult task of identifying some of the lesser-known individuals in the text. Allison Webster of the University Press of Kentucky was invaluable in guiding this book through to final production. Finally, I would like to thank Dr. Roger Cirillo, director of AUSA's Book Program, for his support in the preparation of this work.

Introduction

A Biographical Sketch of Colonel Robert Sharon Allen

Robert Sharon Allen was born in Latonia, Kentucky, on July 14, 1900. When he was sixteen, he lied about his age and enlisted in Troop F in the U.S. Cavalry. He served in Mexico in 1916–1917 and took part in the pursuit of Pancho Villa; he later served in France during World War I. He was commissioned as a second lieutenant in June 1918 and spent time with the 17th U.S. Cavalry in Douglas, Arizona. Allen was honorably discharged from the army in January 1919. He quickly obtained a commission as a captain in the Wisconsin National Guard Reserve in April 1920, and in September he was commissioned as a second lieutenant in the Wisconsin National Guard. He graduated from the National Guard Troop Officers' Course at the Cavalry School at Fort Riley, Kansas, in 1924. He resigned from the Wisconsin National Guard and was honorably discharged in December 1926. From 1928 to July 1941 he was a captain in the Cavalry Reserve.[1]

After World War I Allen also pursued a career in journalism. He graduated from the University of Wisconsin School of Journalism in 1923 and completed postgraduate work at the University of Munich in 1924. He witnessed Hitler's beer-hall putsch speech and wrote about it for the *Christian Science Monitor*.[2] In 1928 Allen graduated from George Washington University, and the next year he married Ruth Finney, a correspondent for the Scripps-Howard Newspaper Alliance since 1923.

In 1931 Allen was the Washington bureau chief for the *Christian Science Monitor*. He wrote anonymous articles about government officials for *American Mercury*. Allen and Drew Pearson of the *Baltimore Sun* anonymously published *Washington Merry-Go-Round* in the summer of 1931. It was a scathing indictment of President Herbert Hoover's administration, and when their identities were discovered, both men were fired

1

that year. Columbia Pictures purchased the rights to the book's name only and released *Washington Merry-Go-Round* in October 1932.

In 1932 Allen and Pearson published *More Merry-Go-Round*, and late that year they started working for United Features Syndicate to produce a syndicated "Washington Merry-Go-Round" column that appeared in hundreds of papers nationwide. In 1936 Allen and Pearson published *Nine Old Men*, an unflattering portrayal of the Supreme Court justices that made it to the best-seller list. Reviewer Thomas Reed Powell stated that it was "vulgar in language, vulgar in tone and innuendo, and guilty of enough inaccuracies to be unreliable in general." The authors were "gossips at second hand."[3] Allen, a political liberal at the time, was demonstrably malicious toward Republicans.

On December 7, 1941, Allen and Pearson were on NBC Radio describing the events at Pearl Harbor.[4] Allen joined the Regular Army in July 1942 and was immediately promoted to major. He was attached to Lieutenant General Walter Krueger's Third Army headquarters and served as assistant to Third Army's public relations officer from July to December 1942. Allen attended the Command and Staff School Special Course No. 10 for G-2s at Fort Leavenworth, Kansas, and graduated in February 1943 with the rating of "excellent."

Allen returned to Third Army headquarters at Fort Sam Houston, Texas, in March 1943 and assumed the duties of assistant chief of staff, G-2, chief of training and operations. In May he was promoted to lieutenant colonel to fill the position of assistant chief of staff, G-2, on the recommendation of the new commanding general of Third Army, Lieutenant General Courtney H. Hodges. Allen served as the G-2 of XXI Provisional Corps during the Louisiana maneuvers in October–November 1943 and organized, directed, and conducted three courses for Third Army's G-2s and S-2s from July to November 1943.

With Patton's arrival in January 1944, the staff sections underwent a thorough reorganization, and Allen served as executive officer of the Situation subsection under Colonel Oscar W. Koch, Patton's assistant chief of staff, G-2. During the course of the war, Allen regularly filled in for his ailing boss. Koch recommended Allen for promotion to full colonel in August 1944, but this request was denied in September. Koch resubmitted the paperwork in November, and Allen was finally promoted to colonel on March 11, 1945.

In early April Patton selected Allen to lead an intelligence team to test the credibility of information obtained from prisoners of war indicating that the German high command intended to establish a series of communications centers. At Apfelstadt, Allen became involved in a firefight and was wounded and taken prisoner. As a result of his injuries, his right forearm was amputated in a German military hospital in Erfurt. Four days later, he was liberated from Erfurt by 1st Battalion, 318th Infantry, 80th Infantry Division, and flown to a hospital near Third Army's command post at Hersfeld, accompanied by Charles B. Odom, Patton's personal physician. When Patton visited him, Allen requested permission to stay with Third Army until the end of the war. Patton acquiesced, and after missing only seventeen days due to his wound, Allen was, in Koch's words, "back at his desk doing full military duty, asking no favours and receiving none."[5] For the next year, Allen recovered at Walter Reed Army Hospital in Washington, DC, and left the army in December 1946.

In the postwar period, Allen's relationship with Pearson deteriorated over the issue of royalty payments from their column. In 1947 Allen, having taught himself to type with his left hand, published *Lucky Forward: The History of Patton's Third U.S. Army*. Allen clearly leveraged his journal and other G-2 material to write the book. He started writing a syndicated column with Paul Scott called "The Allen and Scott Report" in the late 1940s and edited *Our Sovereign State* in 1949, a critique of state politics. Allen's career as a columnist, however, experienced a steady decline in the postwar period, possibly due in part to his growing fascination with the UFO craze of the early 1950s, prompting him to write several columns on the subject.[6]

As Allen's career faded, his political views shifted to the center and right as the Cold War developed, and he spent much of the 1960s expressing conservative views on national security issues. In 1963 Attorney General Robert F. Kennedy and Secretary of Defense Robert S. McNamara pressured CIA Director John McCone to wiretap the phones of Allen and Scott, based on the allegation that classified material continually turned up in their columns. The operation was called Project Mockingbird.[7] By 1968, Allen had teamed up with John A. Goldsmith of United Press International to write a column called "Inside Washington," which was the last of Allen's journalistic collaborations.

In the early 1960s Allen was hired by Twentieth Century Fox to develop a script for a motion picture about Patton. Allen's script, entitled "Bright Flash of War," was never used, apparently because of resistance from Patton's family. In November 1961 Allen wrote a short piece titled "Patton: A Profile" for General Frank McCarthy, who was collecting material for a possible film treatment of Patton.[8] In 1965 Allen initiated a plagiarism lawsuit against Ladislas Farago, whose 1964 biography

Patton: Ordeal and Triumph eventually served as the basis for Twentieth Century Fox's 1970 box-office hit *Patton*.[9] The lawsuit was settled out of court, and Allen received a small sum of money. Farago mentioned Allen in the biography and called him "as great a soldier as he is a newspaperman."[10]

The most intriguing aspect of Allen's story is that he was apparently in the pay of the People's Commissariat for Internal Affairs (NKVD) in the early 1930s. Alexander Vassiliev's recent research in the KGB archives reveals that Allen was referred to as source "Sh/147" and that his cover name was George Parker.[11] The duration of Allen's involvement with the KGB is unclear, but according to a 1967 CIA report, "Allen has a record of favoring Communist causes during the 1930's and possibly into the 1940's."[12] Some of Allen's statements about the Russians in his journal can be interpreted as being sympathetic to communism, and in one place he refers to Russia as "a sensible country."

Following the death of his wife in 1979, Allen married his former secretary Adeline Sunday. She published her memoirs, *Come Live with Me and the Colonel,* in 2009, and Allen figures prominently in her story.[13] By the time Allen remarried, he had been diagnosed with cancer. On February 23, 1981, he shot himself in his Georgetown home in Washington, DC. He was eighty years old.

1

From New Jersey to England

Editor's note: Third Army headquarters was alerted for overseas move-ment on January 1, 1944. The advance party departed on January 22. Patton assumed command of Third Army on January 26 by secret order and greeted the advance party at Glasgow, Scotland, on January 29.

Friday, February 18, 1944: Arrived Camp Shanks, near Nyack, N.J., after 5-day trip across country via NO [New Orleans]. [Lieutenant General Courtney H.] Hodges[1] still not with us and no word about or from him. Shanks is a miserable hole. Filthy little temporary shacks, coal stoves that pour forth gaseous smoke, cold greasy mess—in brief, one busy [lousy] place for a POE [port of embarkation].

Friday, February 25, 1944: Sensation—Colonel [Frederick H.] Kel-ley[2]—Hq Comdt [headquarters commandant]—showed me letter deliv-ered to him addressed to Lt Genl George S. Patton, Jr., and bearing our APO [Army Post Office] No.—403. Letter written by Mrs. Patton[3]—obviously means Patton now CO [commanding officer] Third Army—and that means [Brigadier General George A.] Davis[4] and some of the staff are going to get rolled because Patton must have some of his own staff.

Monday, February 28, 1944: Story of Patton has gotten around Army GS [General Staff]. Great excitement. Running around, asking me ques-tions, awkwardly trying to pump me—very funny to watch them running around like chickens with heads cut off. Serves them right—Davis high-handed—[Colonel Richard G.] Dick McKee,[5] G-3, is weak, incompetent, petty. [Colonel] Fred Matthews[6] even weaker—congenitally incapable of making a decision—total loss.

Wednesday, March 1, 1944: Supposed to sail today—but nothing happened. Informed our priority on [HMS] *Queen Mary*[7] given to some Air outfit—that's how high we rate.

Friday, March 3, 1944: Got one hell of a cold—sick as poisoned pup.

Friday, March 10, 1944: Still sick. This cold—or whatever the hell it developed into—has really laid me out. Still no news about sailing. However, several more letters for Patton, and his C/S [chief of staff]—clear now he is the new C/G [commanding general] Third Army.

Saturday, March 11, 1944: Suddenly alerted for sailing—at last. Still feel like poisoned pup. This goddamned camp will kill me, with the cold, smoke, if I stay much longer. Colonel [George Albert] Hadd[8]—AG [adjutant general]—operated on for ulcers. Perkins[9] and Weeks[10]—in hospital with severe colds—at least 60% of the outfit sick with colds.

Sunday, March 12, 1944: Major Adelbert Zwrick,[11] pilot for Hodges, is a rare specimen. Tubby, pot gut—far from handsome, yet apparently a very successful cassanova—very frank about conquests. One—old friend of his wife. Another—wife of a Brooklyn undertaker, who sent him pictures of herself in the nude. Zwrick explained various techniques he worked out after long study and experience. One—he calls tit technique. Another—indifferent. Third—hard to get.

Sailed for England today. On *Ile de France.*[12] In tiny stateroom on boat deck with seven other Lt Cols—among them [Lieutenant Colonel William A.] Bill Borders[13]—my roommate across country and at Shanks. Over 10,000 troops packed on the ship. Crowded to the gills—sailed without escort. On board—asked by Lt Col Grover Davis,[14] Deputy Troop Commander on ship, whose wife is Betty Jesse Jones he says, to broadcast news every afternoon—gave me something to do and also a little practice at my old profession—apparently broadcasts went over very good—lot of compliments—some from Davis. 300 Army nurses on board. Much skirt chasing. Amusing to see old dogs like Colonel [Arthur] Pulsifer,[15] Sig O [signals officer]; William A. Borders, who married Tommy Thompkin's daughter, chasing those babes after only a few weeks from home.

Tuesday, March 21, 1944: Landed at Gourock, Scotland—about 25 miles from Glasgow on Clyde River. Things happened fast. Learned Patton is our Third Army L/G [lieutenant general]. Hodges, at least temporarily, is deputy commander of First Army, commanded by Omar Bradley,[16] whom amicably Hodges mocks. Also Col Tim Andring [James G. Anding],[17] G-4, and McKee, G-3, were greeted with orders relieving them and ordering them to VII Corps, which is in First Army—apparently Matthews and [Colonel John C.] Macdonald[18] stay on for present and same for rest of staff till they are looked over—but Anding and McKee fired right off. Also Davis not expected with our party and much surprise expressed that he is with us. Obviously he too is rolled.

Wednesday, March 22, 1944: Debarked at Gourock and entrained for Chelford about 18 miles from Manchester where our CP [command post] is located. Told fired officers they would be billeted in a private home. Spent night at Camp Toft, just outside Knutsford where HQ Third Army is located. Camp Toft is the rear echelon. Advance echelon at Peover, about 3 miles from Knutsford. Peover is an old manor place—said to have been the home of the Peels once. Our part of the home is very old— over door is shield bearing date 1585. Big main part of the house is much newer, probably built in 1800s. Little church adjoining house has tiny chapel built originally by Rauhl Wainwright in 1456. Another chapel on other side of the church has several Wainwrights buried dated 1672 and 1702. In both chapels are life-sized figures in marble of a knight in armor and his lady. Churchyard practically all graveyard. House apparently unused for years. Grounds, however, well kept for us and the large estate is under cultivation. Huge trees, some of them encumbered with rockeries. The big house is where General Patton lives—on second floor— where his personal HQ are and where War Room is located.

Thursday, March 23, 1944: Reported for duty and informed I'd be Chief of Situation—or Combat Intelligence—subsection with following staff—Major George Swanson,[19] Major Joe McDowell,[20] Major John Cheadle,[21] Lieutenant William Goolrick[22] and 4 EM [enlisted men] headed by S/Sgt [Staff Sergeant] Martin Reitman. Also informed that Col Oscar S. [W.] Koch[23] (G-2 of 7th Army) would be G-2 of Third Army Hq, and that Colonel Macdonald was to be the Provost Marshal. Terrific blow to him, but he is taking it chin up.

Friday, March 24, 1944: Patton addressed Officers and EM of Hq assembled in large plaza before the big house. Very smartly attired— every stitch of him obviously tailored—from overseas cap to boots and combat jacket. West Point ring on left hand—two rings on right and riding crop. Very trim in stature, but somewhat heavy around middle. Voice not raucous, but he was very profane—goddamn and SOB used repeatedly. Little talk not bad. Very adroitly brought out that he had FDR [Franklin Delano Roosevelt][24] support—said great men backing me because they believe in me. Said he was given command of Third Army for reasons which would become clearer later. Reason we are fighting over there—defeat and crush Nazis; save our liberties; and because men like to fight.

Saturday, March 25, 1944: Told our role and general invasion plan. First Army, under Bradley, goes in first in Cotentin Peninsula area. Third Army follows—cuts off Breton Peninsula, then turns West. If First Army is dormant, it will establish a beachhead—then Third Army will try one. With First Army—a British and Canadian Army will simultaneously also launch invasions.

Also I was put in charge of the War Room under great cloak of Top Secrecy. MP [military police] guard outside War Room 24 hours a day. *Editor's note: The G-2 planning staff assembled for the first time on this date.*

Sunday, March 26, 1944: After long day of hard work preparing for big staff conference tomorrow, attended evening song service at little church behind the Big House. Saw in church framed list of Priests and Vicars dating from 1556 to 1943. Gave up my billet in Knutsford. Nice people, but place is too "primitive," no heat, no hot water—toilet not in washroom. Returned to Peover Camp where I am living in hutment but close to office and can have a hot shower in the morning and be near the mess.

Monday, March 27, 1944: Began to read myself into the problem. Masses of "top secret" material from TIS [Theater Intelligence Section][25]—First U.S. Army ETO [European Theater of Operations]—and British. Told target area is Normandy and Brittany Peninsula from Honfleur to Nantes. OVERLORD[26]—code name for invasion of Continent. NEPTUNE[27]—code for 21st Army Group made up of the 1st U.S. Army, 2d British Army.[28] FUSAG[29]—First U.S. Army Group presumably made up of 1st and 3d U.S. Armies. C/G—right now? Probably General Bradley. SHAEF[30]—Supreme Headquarters Allied Expeditionary Forces, commanded by [General Dwight D.] Eisenhower.[31] ETOUSA [European Theater of Operations United States Army][32]—administrative organization commanded by [Lieutenant General J. C. H.] Lee.[33]

Tuesday, March 28, 1944: Capt Dups[34]—from TIS—told us today they have a printer in Holland who makes all the maps for the Germans and our copy for TIS. Also in Amsterdam, is a man who makes up the German Order of Battle and slips a copy each week to TIS. Also TIS has regular plane service between France and England. Dups very confidentially claimed no leaks from England to the Continent but I have my doubts.

Wednesday, March 29, 1944: Big scramble by G-2, G-3 and G-4 to get cream of special staff personnel—later told the special staff was top-heavy and over-manned, and the three G sections will be greatly expanded at their expense. Looks like the organization of Hq Third Army is being ripped apart and recast. Also heard that General Davis was to be made Asst Div Comdr [assistant division commander] in First Army in the Div

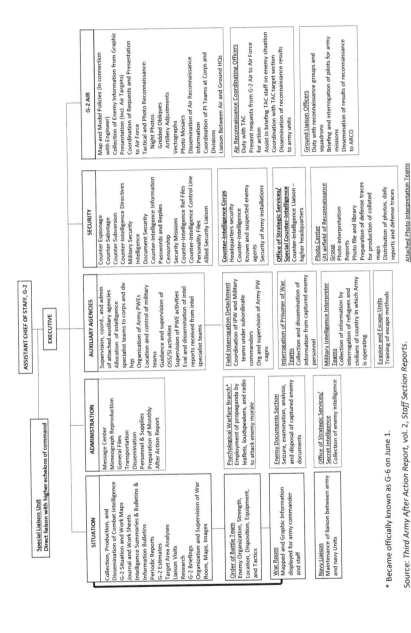

ASSISTANT CHIEF OF STAFF, G-2

Special Liaison Unit
Direct liaison with higher echelons of command

EXECUTIVE

SITUATION

Collection, Production, and Dissemination of Combat Intelligence
G-2 Situation and Work Maps
Journal and Work Sheets
Intelligence Summaries & Bulletins &
Information Bulletins
Periodic Reports
G-2 Estimates
Target Area Analyses
Liaison Visits
Research
G-2 Briefings
Organization and Supervision of War Room, Maps, Images

Order of Battle Team
Enemy Organization, Strength, Location, Disposition, Equipment, and Tactics

War Room
Mapped and Graphic Information displayed for army commander and staff

Navy Liaison
Maintenance of liaison between army and navy Units

ADMINISTRATION

Message Center
Mimeograph Reproduction
General Files
Transportation
Dissemination
Personnel & Supplies
Preparation of Monthly
After Action Report

Psychological Warfare Branch*
Employment of propaganda by leaflets, loudspeakers, and radio to attack enemy morale

Enemy Documents Section
Seizure, examination, analysis, and disposal of captured enemy documents

**Office of Strategic Services/
Secret Intelligence**
Collection of enemy intelligence

AUXILIARY AGENCIES

Supervision, coord., and admin of attached auxiliary agencies
Allocation of intelligence specialist teams to corps and div hqs
Organization of Army PWEs
Location and control of military teams
Guidance and supervision of OSS/SI activities
Supervision of PWE activities
Eval and dissemination of intel reports received from intel specialist teams

Field Interrogation Detachment
Coordination of IPW and Military teams under subordinate commanders
Org and supervision of Army PW cages

Interrogation of Prisoner of War Teams
Collection and dissemination of information from captured enemy personnel

Military Intelligence Interpreter Teams
Collection of information by interrogation of refugees and civilians of country in which Army is operating

Evasion and Escape Units
Training of escape methods

SECURITY

Counter Espionage
Counter Sabotage
Counter Subversion
Counter-Intelligence Directives
Military Security
Intelligence
Document Security
Counter-Intelligence Information
Passwords and Replies
Censorship
Security Missions
Counter-Intelligence Ref Files
Counter-Intelligence Control Line
Personality Files
Allied Security Liaison

Counter-Intelligence Corps
Headquarters security
Counter-Intelligence
Known and suspected enemy agents
Security of Army installations

**Office of Strategic Services/
Special Counter-Intelligence**
Counter-Intelligence Liaison – higher headquarters

Photo Center
(At airfield of Reconnaissance Group
Photo interpretation
Reports
Photo file and library
Preparation of defense traces for production of collated maps
Distribution of photos, daily reports and defense traces

Attached Photo Interpretation Teams

G-2 AIR

Map and Model Policies (In connection with Engineer)
Collection of Enemy Information from Graphic Presentation (Incl. Air Targets)
Coordination of Requests and Presentation to Air Force
Tactical and Photo Reconnaissance:
    Night Photos
    Gridded Obliques
    Artillery Adjustments
Vectographs
Photo Mosaics
Dissemination of Air Reconnaissance Information
Coordination of PI Teams at Corps and Divisions
Liaison Between Air and Ground HQs

Air Reconnaissance Coordinating Officers
Duty with TAC
Present requests from G-2 Air to Air Force for action
Assist in briefing TAC staff on enemy situation
Coordination with TAC target section
Dissemination of reconnaissance results to army units

Ground Liaison Officers
Duty with reconnaissance groups and squadrons
Briefing and interrogation of pilots for army missions
Dissemination of results of reconnaissance to ARCO

* Became officially known as G-6 on June 1.

Source: *Third Army After Action Report*, vol. 2, *Staff Section Reports*.

Organizational and Functional Chart

that participates in first move of assault. He is obviously out of the picture as far as Third Army is concerned. Hodges' whereabouts and role are still a mystery.

Thursday, March 30, 1944: Put on briefing for G-2 Section on situation in target area—sort of dry-run performance to show Col Koch what I and Situation Section can do.

Friday, March 31, 1944: Story on General Patton. During time Advance Party was here—he walked into downstairs part of manor house where in one corner Lieutenant-Colonel [Lorraine L.] Manly[35] was sitting with several junior officers. Manly is a Regular Army NCO [noncommissioned officer] who got a reserve commission and is a Lt Col in AG Section. Around 35, sordid marriage and sex life. Wife Hazel lived with Madelon in apartment next to one Paul and I occupied on Hillyer Court and I never liked him—punk, and although he saw Patton, Manly did not get up. Patton walked through the place several times and the third time, he suddenly wheeled, walked over to where Manly was and said—"I should think that an officer who has been in army long enough to be a Lt Col would know enough to get to his feet when his C/G enters room." Patton then turned on his heel and walked away.

Cy Long[36] told me Davis is to be made Asst Div Comdr of 28th Inf Div [Infantry Division], a former P[ennsylvani]a NG [National Guard] division and Bradley's old outfit. He was made C/G to clean it up. Div is rife with politics and GOP [Grand Old Party] politicos and sour as hell. There is an Asst Div Comdr now but Cy says Davis will replace him. 28th to be in initial assault, which Cy says is very imminent. Also said that [Major William C.] Bill Sylvan,[37] Hodges' aide, told Townsend, Davis' aide, that when Hodges went to AG and enroute to England, they raised hell with him about Davis—for keeping a whore in San Antonio, etc,— and that Hodges took the attitude that Davis let him down. However, Hodges still considers him very able and is going to use him in combat. Hodges is Deputy Comdr First U.S. Army.

Zwrick, his pilot, has to learn to fly a Cub as that is the only plane generals use in front areas.

Saturday, April 1, 1944: Extracts from "Letter of Instruction No. 1" issued by Lt General George S. Patton to Corps, Division and separate unit commanders of Third U.S. Army: "Each, in his appropriate sphere, will lead in person. Any commander who fails to obtain his objective and who is not dead or severely wounded, has not done his full duty.

"The function of staff officers is to observe, not to meddle.

"Staff personnel, commissioned or enlisted, who do not rest, do not last.

"You can never have too much reconnaissance.

"Information is like eggs. The fresher the better.

"Keep troops informed. Use every means before and after combat to tell the troops what they are going to do and what they have done.

"The desperate determination to succeed is just as vital to supply as it is to the firing line.

"Replacements are *spare parts*. They must be asked for in time by the front line. An educated guess is just as accurate and far faster than compiled errors.

"Visit the wounded personally.

"Decorations are for the purpose of raising the fighting value of troops, therefore they must be awarded promptly.

"There is only one kind of discipline—perfect discipline.

"If you do not enforce and maintain discipline, you are potential murderers. You must set the example.

"There are more tired Corps and division commanders than there are tired Corps and divisions.

"Fatigue makes cowards of us all. Men in condition do not tire. High physical condition is vital to victory.

"Do not take counsel of your fears."

At his introductory conference with Third Army Hq Staff, Patton told us: "Despite some similarities in speech, English and Americans are not the same. English are foreigners to us, and we to them. General [Bernard] Montgomery[38] told me that once himself."

Sunday, April 2, 1944: McDowell told me today the story of how the Advance Party learned Patton was Third Army C/G—Day ship *Queen Mary* landed Col [Edward T.] Williams,[39] Actg [acting] Officer, told them not to be surprised at anything that may happen and not to say or write a word. Very perplexed, but never dreamed of a change in C/G. Next day were assembled in dining room and suddenly Patton came in—still did not suspect anything. Thought he came to welcome troops. He knocked them for loop by saying, "I am your new L/G. I am the C/G of Third Army." Mouths dropped and eyes bulged despite admonition from Williams not to show surprise. Patton then shook hands with each, and they debarked and entrained on a special train he had.

Illustration of the way the Army personnel system operates: Patton group didn't want Col Dick McKee, Hodges' bumbling and incompetent G-3. First Army asked for Col Macdonald, Hodges' very able G-2. But Patton wouldn't let him go. So McKee, the discard, goes to VII Corps, where he is made C/S, the job they wanted Macdonald for, and he is kept by Patton and eased out of G-2 and bumped down to Provost Marshal!

Heard that [Lieutenant Colonel Charles] Brehner,[40] snide punk whom Macdonald rolled last December before we were alerted, is in London as a copy pusher in the office of the historian of the ETO, seems not very happy about it, and is looking for something else. Also heard that Maj General [Willis Dale] Crittenberger[41] has been relieved as C/G of XIX Corps, which he commanded since its inception and brought over, and has been sent to North Africa or Italy. Seems he lost the Corps on the claim it was too late for him to work into the situation—sounds fishy to me.

Col Koch, returning from visit to SHAEF, London, told me he learned there that the Allies have suffered 100,000 casualties in Italy, of which 25,000 were at Reggio beachhead. *Editor's note: Allen's information here is inaccurate. The British landing in the Reggio di Calabria area during Operation Baytown on September 3, 1943, was virtually unopposed. The Allies started to take significant casualties during the amphibious landings at Salerno on September 9 during Operation Avalanche.* Also that highway across interior rocky hill mass of Brittany, from Brest to Rennes, has been given first maintenance priority by Germans. Could mean they got some wind of NEPTUNE operation—or may be merely a general preventing measure.

Tuesday, April 4, 1944: First G-2 briefing of staff in War Room at Peover Hall—1100 hrs. Every one of Section Chiefs present—Maj Gen [Hugh J.] Gaffey,[42] C/S; Brig General [Hobart R.] Gay,[43] Deputy C/S. Not Patton—away from camp. Show went off very well—many compliments.

Wednesday, April 5, 1944: Saw odd sight from window of War Room this evening as it was beginning to get dark. Group of men and women very industriously scrubbing tombstones in little churchyard and of tiny old church behind Peover Hall. Must be for Easter—which is Sunday.

Thursday, April 6, 1944: NEPTUNE supplement #5. 20 Jan '44. Under title of FLAK: Latest news of the French Railway Anti Aircraft units (401 and 402 Regts [Regiments]) is that they are to be dissolved or, at least, reorganized. This development is not altogether surprising. From the earliest days of the new force, relations between the Germans and the French have been noticeably lacking in mutual confidence and sympathy. Since the first batteries have been operating in northern France, five German aircraft have been shot down. Moreover, desertions have been frequent.

Patton has a personal physician—Lt Col Charles Odom[44] of New Orleans. Seems Patton took a fancy to him and carries him along as "house" physician.

Col Macdonald told me we had first white-black trouble last night at Norwich—near Chester. White and negro troops got to brawling and for a while local MPs had hands full—called for help and emergency Platoons that the Col had set up at various places for just this sort of thing were alerted, but a reconnaissance by one of his Officers showed they didn't have to call them. Things quieted down. Vicinity filling up with troops. Ten Inf Divs coming into area and numerous other outfits.

Patton keeps a diary. Also complete file of all letters he received and sends. Two other operations at least—AXEHEAD[45]—SWORDHILT.[46] Patton has long, thin, well-kept hands. On left, 2 rings—one on little finger; on right, West Point class ring.

Friday, April 7, 1944: From the sublime to the ridiculous; from the mansion to the outhouse—for Davis, who a few weeks ago was the all-mighty C/S of TUSA [Third United States Army]. Today he is Deputy Asst C/G of 28th Division—assistant. The NG 28th was to be in first assault but found "wanting" and exchanged for 2d Inf Div[47]—which stank in '42 maneuvers.[48]

So the 28th is back in TUSA with Davis an asst to an asst Div C/G in TUSA. What a come down. Learned from Borders today that Patton was given command of TUSA Jan 26. We didn't leave San Antonio until Feb 15. Six weeks before we sailed, Eisenhower took command of TUSA from Hodges and gave it to Patton. Explains why Hodges left sitting in San Antonio without any work—why he didn't go with us and all the other things that transpired.

At G-2 presentation we had to put on suddenly this evening, Patton, Gaffey, Gay and another general were present. During discussion that followed, Patton, referring to big London conference he attended last week, remarked apropos NEPTUNE operation, "Churchill made most pertinent remark of all. He said, 'I don't want this to become another defensive lodgement.'" Obvious a crack at Italy. *Editor's note: Churchill was referring to Operation Shingle, the invasion of Anzio on January 22, 1944, that almost ended in disaster.*[49]

Saturday, April 8, 1944: Getting lots of information. Germans using tens of thousands of foreigners in Reich[s]wehr.[50] Russian PW [prisoners of war],[51] Poles, Czechs, etc. Most coast defense Divs have these elements—some as much as 60%. Nazis so hard up for manpower, even using foreigners in SS Waffen[52] units—those once Nazi-party elite—extra

Army units—now they are being diluted. Also Inf Divs being reorganized into 3 regts—each of 2 bns [battalions]—due to manpower shortage.

Easter, April 9, 1944: Beautiful day, which I spent reading the Joint Plan[53] and Annexes 1 to 10 for Operation OVERLORD. In conversation with Col Koch I discovered he is from Milwaukee; was Troop Commanding Officer of Cav Sq [cavalry squadron] there and went into RA [Regular Army] as 2d Lt in 1920 from there.

FUSAG Mission: Under supervision of 21 Army Group, to coordinate the movement of FUSA [First U.S. Army], Ninth Air Force[54] and Com Z [Communications Zone][55] (being _____ by ETOUSA) as continuation of the FUSA movement and to plan for operations in two stages: (1) Open ports St. Nazaire and Nantes and commence operation on Brittany Peninsula. (2) Concentrate TUSA astride Loire River. Facing East. Complete reduction of Brittany Peninsula and its organization as part Com Z. FUSA consists of:

4 Corps (1 attached from TUSA)
9 Inf Divs (2 attached TUSA)
2 Armd [Armored] Divs
2 Airborne Divs
TUSA: 3 Corps
5 Inf Divs
4 Armd Divs
XV, XX, XII plus VIII Corps, initially with FUSA.

ETOUSA—Monty is in control of Operation. Operation is the responsibility of ETOUSA. FUSA—Stage 1—After capture of Cherbourg, drive to South and South East to cut Brittany Peninsula and secure ports North and South. VIII Corps turns to West to clean up resistance on Peninsula. VIII Corps to report to command TUSA when its Hq becomes operational on Continent. Stage 2—FUSA will advance to the line of the UPPER SEINE prepared for further action to North East and assume command of British corps southwest of Paris. (U.S. units are to capture Paris, but British Corps attached. FUSAG actually to occupy it for "political reasons"). TUSA—Land on Continent. (1) Through Cherbourg, or over beaches between Varreville and Colleville-sur-Mer and beaches and minor ports North & East of St. Malo. (2) Through the Loire ports North & St. Nazaire, if they're opened. (3) Through Brittany Peninsula ports or beach installations. After clearing Brittany Peninsula & concentrating on right, FUSA, TUSA will place one Armd Div in FUSAG Reserve near

Le Mans. Alternative Plan—paragraph 12: May develop that FUSA and TUSA will be contained and unable to secure either Brest or the Loire ports. A plan for securing Brest with two airborne Divs is being considered (25 March 44).

Battle Casualties—Annex 1 (G-1)
Annex 10 (G-4)

Type of Org[anization]	"Light" Battle Day (%)	"Severe" Battle Day (%)	"Maximum" Battle Day (%)
Bn or Regt	2.5	15	25
Div	1	8	15
Corps	0.5	3	5
Army	0.35	1	2.5
L[ine] of C[ommunications], SOS [Services of Supply*], and service units not incl[uded] in other est	0.25	0.6	1
	Daily Average (%)		
	D + 15–29	D + 30–59	D + 60–90	Thereafter
Entire "effective force"	0.35	0.25	0.20	0.15

Average[s] apply only to Army as a whole. Average[s] above divided as follows:

	K, C or Missing	Wounded
D to D + 1	30%	70%
D + 2 and thereafter	25%	70%

Wounded divided [into]:
Litter cases   50%
Walking cases   50%

* *Editor's note: The Services of Supply was established in May 1942 to achieve the intent of Bolero, the great buildup of American forces in Britain. See Roland G. Ruppenthal, U.S. Army in World War II: Logistical Support of the Armies, vol. 1, May 1941–September 1944 (Washington, DC: Center of Military History, 1989), 32–41.*

Artificial port: An artificial port will be constructed at St. Laurent which will have an estimated average capacity of 5,000 tons per day after completion. Evacuation policy of casualties for planning purposes:

D to D + 18—All
D + 19–39—7 days
D + 40–59—15 days
D + 60–90—30 days

(Hold casualties there a number of days before evacuating them to UK.)

Annex 3 (Civil Affairs)[56]

Planning for civil affairs will proceed on the assumption that full control will pass to French National Authority as soon as military necessity permits. Military control over civil administration will be exercised through appropriate indigenous officials.

Annex 11 (Med[ical])

Venereal diseases: These diseases, especially gonorrhea, and to a less extent syphilis, are highly prevalent. Adequate supplies of approved prophylactic materials will be made available to all troops. Unremitting efforts will be made to control prostitution.

Nutrition: Recent investigations have shown that "C," "R" and "10 to 1" rations to be low in calories and inadequate in vitamin content for long continued use. An energy supplement and some nutrients are provided by the use of the "O" bar. However, if troops are to be on this diet for longer than 15 days, it will be necessary to supply multi-vitamin capsules. Troops subsisting entirely on B rations for long periods (30 days or more) lose weight and their efficiency is decreased. Ration should be reinforced as early as possible with fresh bread, butter and fresh vegetables (cooked). Close attention to the adequacy of rations is a responsibility of command.

Monday, April 10, 1944: SHAEF order freezing all U.S. troops in UK from 0001 to 2400—in their camps. First thought _____ big show. Col Macdonald told me there was an all-UK showdown on AWOLs [those absent without leave]. Said there were thousands of soldiers roving around without passes or furloughs.

Tuesday, April 11, 1944: Swiss and Sweden only go through motions of interning fliers who land there. Keep for awhile when they are forced to "escape." Doubtless do same with Germans. Air people tell me our boys not anxious to "escape" as they have a grand time as "PW."

Saturday, April 15, 1944: New H Plan—U.S. forces for Op OVER-LORD rescind—no important changes from original.

Sunday, April 16, 1944: SOE [Special Operations Executive],[57] SO [Special Operations], OSS [Office of Strategic Services][58]—estimate that potentially in Western Europe one million men available for clandestine operations against Nazis.

Op OVERLORD divided into Phase I, assault and capture of beachhead known as NEPTUNE, and Phase II, enlargement there to include the area West of Seine River. And North of the Loire River.

Phase I:
21st Army Group
TUSA
2d British Army
Phase II:
FUSAG
TUSA and FUSA plus British Army Group
2d British Army and a Canadian Army[59]
Assisting Op also:
Western Naval Task Force[60]
Ninth Air Force
Com Z (ETOUSA)

One change in new H Plan: FUSA drives South to Loire, secures St. Nazaire and Nantes, and then reduces Brittany Peninsula—with elements of TUSA (VIII Corps). TUSA then enters area, then Cherbourg and Brittany Peninsula and Loire ports as required and places itself astride Loire on South flank of FUSA. Com Z organizes. Brittany Peninsula to accept forces direct from U.S. at rate of 4 Divs per month with necessary supporting troops. Completion of Stage I estimated as D + 50—Stage II as D + 90.

Op OVERLORD Cos (43) *Editor's note: Cos is most likely an abbreviation for COSSAC—Chief of Staff Supreme Allied Command.*

416 (o) dated 30 Feb '43
NEPTUNE—Initial Joint Plan, 21 Army Group, NJC [acronym unknown] 1004, dated 1 Feb '43. *Editor's note: The date should be February 1, 1944.*

Object of Op OVERLORD
To secure lodgement area on Continent from which further offensive operations can be developed.
Phase I—The assault and capture of an initial lodgement area, including the development of airfield sites in the Caen area and the capture of Cherbourg.
Phase II—Enlargement of area captured in Phase I to include Brittany Peninsula, all ports South to the Loire River (inclusive) and the area between the Loire and the Seine. Phase I and some parts of Phase II will

be executed by U.S., British and Canadian forces assigned or attached to 21 Army Group.

Joint Plan—Final Draft—8 April 1944
Supporting air forces will be:

Ninth U.S. Air Force [USAF]
2d Tactical Air Force [TAF] (RAF [Royal Air Force])[61]
Eighth U.S. Air Force[62] (both fighters and heavy bombardment)
Air Defence of Great Britain (RAF)
Coastal Command (RAF)
Troop Carriers—both USAAF [United States Army Air Forces]
   and RAF

All under command of Joint Ninth USAF and 2d TAF (RAF) commanders in coordination with AEAF [Allied Expeditionary Air Force].[63]

Mission

Air superiority
Isolation of battlefield
Direct support of ground operations

Patton dropped into War Room—very pleasant. Had ugly white English bulldog with him. Hideous brute but Patton is very fond of him. In odd way, same head conformation as Patton. I was directing a number of changes in various situation maps. Patton very much interested. Joked over German Div symbol McDowell had stuck on Knutsford for fun. Patton remarked: "No question in my mind now that we can establish beachhead. Had some doubts but none now. Only question now is what happens after we get foothold." Entourage feel he should have commanded Italy operation—would have done a lot better than it has turned out.

Tuesday, April 18, 1944: Asst SOW (Secretary of War) [John J.] McCloy[64] accompanied by Lt General [Joseph Taggart] McNarney[65]—thin, dark and scraggly-haired, and Lt General Lee came for visit to TUSA, and Patton put on briefing by G-2, 3, 4 and Sig O. Went off very well. At dry-run the night before, Patton laughingly referred to coming dignitaries as "visiting Elks."

Wednesday, April 19, 1944: Col Koch took me aside this morning, and after praising my work as Chief of Situation Subsection, proposi-tioned me about becoming Ex O [executive officer] of the G-2 Section in place of Lt Col [Johnson P.] Edwards.[66] Present Ex O. Edwards is a very nice guy and easy to get along with, but not very aggressive and appar-ently has not measured up to what Koch wants. He obviously wants someone to take details off his shoulders, and Edwards is not doing it. Told him I had deliberately ducked that when I was in San Antonio because I preferred field soldiering. Col Koch said being Ex O wouldn't interfere with that; that I'd learn more and get a fuller picture, and that I got things done and he would like to have me try it out. However, he didn't press for an immediate decision. Told me to think it over and he would talk to me again next week. I'd hate to hurt Ed. Swell guy and has been very nice to work with—but he clearly isn't the driver needed. One lot of holes to be plugged up. However, I'm not anxious to get a tougher job than I already have—we'll see.

Friday–Saturday, April 21–22, 1944: Attended Air/Ground confer-ence put on by Ninth Air Force—numerous generals, etc, present—most colorful figure was Brig General [Elwood R.] Quesada,[67] Commander 9th U.S. Fighter Command.[68] Among other things, he told us that most of the fighters that will support the assault will be P-47 (Thunderbolts)[69] which were rated as the best fighter-bombers the Allies have. Also they can operate from small and bumpy fields expected in assault area. Also, absolutely confident they can keep GAF [German Air Force] from inter-fering with assault and are hoping GAF will come out in force so they can more easily and quickly annihilate it. Also, that our radar is better than Germans'. We have stuff which enables us to bomb through over-cast and apparently Germans don't have this, as they have not done any of this bombing.

General Walker—C/G 101st AB [Airborne] Div—told us they are going in D–4 hours. *Editor's note: Allen is in error here. Maxwell Tay-lor had assumed command of the division on March 14, 1944.* I also know 82d AB Div also going in by D+24 hours. Attended briefing of P-47 Wing that went off to bomb marshalling center near Calais. All just kids—including Wing Comdr, a Lt Col. Would have liked to have stayed to hear interrogation when they returned, but had to leave to catch plane for return trip.

Sunday, April 23, 1944: Major [Charles W.] Flint,[70] Signals Section, told me we have a cryptograph device that he claims is better than any other in operation. Said he's seen all the British [devices] but they haven't one that we have—that is, this super-super device. I wonder? Also heard of two more Top Secret names: RANKIN[71] and BOLERO.[72] RANKIN is a case or condition. BOLERO apparently is an Op—maybe the British counterpart to NEPTUNE.

First Corps of FUSA scheduled to go in is VII Corps; first Div—4th Infantry Division; first Regt—8th Infantry.

Our build-up calls for 32 Divs by D+50, both U.S. and British. We estimate the Germans have capability of build-up of 52 Divs by that day, but that doesn't necessarily mean superiority because many of their Divs are 3 regt–2 bn units. We'll get a better picture when we break lineup down to bns, which we are working on.

Monday, April 24, 1944: TUSA briefed the first of its Corps, XV, today. C/G—Major General [Wade Hampton] Hazlip [Haislip].[73] Little roly-poly guy. I served under him in DHQ[74] last year for a short time when he was maneuver director before Hodges personally took over in June. Haislip became Director from commanding the 87th Inf Div and was notoriously unfair as Director to the 93rd (negro) Div.[75]

In Allied Force Hq, weekly Intl [Intelligence] Summary #69, Dec 18/43 read: "The Greek is an individualist. This trait has prevented material cooperation between the numerous little cliques which collected soon after the German occupation to work for liberation. Thus since the summer of 1942, when some of them began to raise guerrilla forces and to gain considerable strength, they have striven to ensure that this power would still be theirs after the German withdrawal. The present 'civil war' is largely the outcome of the enemy's clever 'plant' that he was going to withdraw—as neat a piece of deception as the Germans have achieved in this war.

"It was hoped that the agreement of July1943, by which all the Greek guerrillas would cooperate with each other under operational orders of British GHQ in the Middle East would solve their internal differences and enable them to be used to the best effect against the Germans. The agreement has foundered owing to the unscrupulous ambitions of E.A.M., abetted perhaps by German propaganda. E.A.M.—Ethinken Afaelenthrotikru Metopan—National Liberation Front[76]—Directed by committee presided over by Secretary of Greek Communist Party."

Tuesday, April 25, 1944: XV and VIII Corps briefed at 3-hour show. Everything went off very well. Patton very pleased. Wound up proceedings with brief statement: "I have won in battle and I'm going to win again. But I've won because I had good commanders and staff officers, and today's presentation [is] further evidence of that."

After G-1 talk, Patton remarked two things he wanted noted—(1) "That Grave Registration Service always did its burying along roads so that those not buried had a lot of grave markers to look at." (2) That important thing was to get combat troops into combat. Did no good in rear areas.

OMAHA—code for beach North of Caen where V Corps is going in on.

UTAH—code for beach North East of OMAHA where VII Corps is going in on.

Mission of British 2d Army—attacking on Left of FUSA—to capture Bayeaux [Bayeux] and Caen on D-day. Three British Divs will make initial assault between Tracy-sur-Mer and Onisterham [Ouistreham]. Y-day is 1 June '44. D-day is subsequent and will be announced to Cmdrs shortly before embarkation for the assault.

Air people told me one reason for concentrating bombing on German gun installations on French coast was British fear of bad morale effect in England if Germans battered London, etc, severely with long-range rocket guns. People are war weary and it is felt that they are not in the mood to stand heavy artillery mauling. Also attacks to prevent Germans from hammering concentration and marshalling areas.

Patton told Corps Cmdrs he wanted them to see to it that U.S. soldiers stealing money and things from PW stop. Said it was a "national scandal" and wanted none of it in TUSA.

UTAH BEACH—North Westwards from mouth of River Vire.

OMAHA BEACH—from East limit of Utah to West breakwater at Port En Bessin.

Lt Col [Joseph H.] Herve Wright,[77] Operations Chief G-3, just told me they got word from FUSAG that the British were injuriously opposing any attack on Channel Islands because people were British subjects.

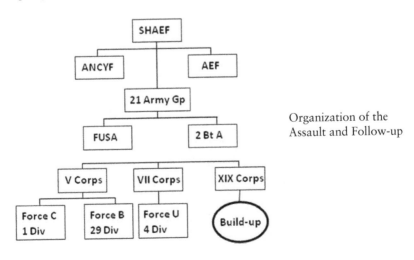

Organization of the Assault and Follow-up

Initial production of maps printed for the invasion amounts to about 116,000 copies. This does not include stocks of large-scale (1/2500) and other special maps printed by Field Survey units. Overall total about four times the quantity of maps produced during the entire 1914–1918 war.

Wednesday, April 26, 1944: We were told today we could sew back on our Third Army shoulder patches—which we took off in San Antonio just about three months ago. Patton's presence in UK rumored but nothing yet about Third Army or his connection with it. BBC[78] broadcast will be used by OSS and SOE to communicate orders and messages to Resistance Groups for invasion operation. Among the equipment to be furnished assault troops in marshalling area are the following:

7 sticks gum
10 sickness prevention capsules
1 can body dusting powder
2 vomit bags
3 prophylactics, medicals

Jap garrison fighting troops on Tarawa[79] on D-day was 2,619 out of a total of 4,836. Remainder Korean labor who did not fight. Jap plan of defense: To destroy attacking force as far as possible before landing. Between reef and shore was high double wire fence which was not destroyed by the preliminary bombardment, but later breached by amphibian tractors. Behind wire Japs had a double lane of anti-boat mines with extra powerful charge. An amphibian truck that struck one was blown 20 feet in air. Found on island after the battle—but missed for some reason—were sniper shields, 1/8 hardened steel, instant mobile rifle pits. Were found new and with paint unscratched. Japs had no organized system of defense in depth. Once elaborate beach defenses breached, they had no positions to fall back to. Jap gun positions stood up better than expected and preliminary "softening up" bombardment did not do the damage hoped for. Japs did not make use of 12 flame throwers they had. One thing preliminary bombardment did do was to knock out most of Jap communications system. This believed responsible for their failure to counterattack until late in the fight. On Makin Island,[80] Japs had naval garrison of about 400 and 150 Jap laborers. Garrison made no attempt to prevent landing. Tried to destroy U.S. force after landing. Many Japs committed hari-kari rather than be taken prisoner.

There is no formation flying in big RAF raids. Each plane flies individually to the target, and precise timing is absolutely essential in order that enemy defenses are saturated by the might of the attack. Pathfinder planes equipped with special navigational apparatus precede the main attacking force and mark route by dropping flares and then the target. In clear weather, ground target indicators are used. In cloudy weather, sky markers are released and bombardiers sight on them.

Thursday, April 27, 1944: Win Booth[81] came up from London. Spent evening and morning. Had him out to camp for breakfast.

Friday, April 28, 1944: While talking to Bill Borders about G-3 plans for the assault, it suddenly struck me that the C/S of VII Corps, scheduled to go in with V Corps in the first FUSA waves, is none other than Dick McKee, ex-G-3 of TUSA, who was rolled before he got off the ship—a stupid, timid, incompetent fumbler. It's unbelievable that such an ass could hold down such a vital post. Wonder how long he will last. Originally McDowell was slated for that place but they wouldn't let him go, and McKee, the moron, got the call.

Saturday, April 29, 1944: General [Jacques Philippe] Le Clerc,[82] French Army, called on Patton. Patton came popping up the steps before Le Clerc arrived saying—"Got to get out that French pronunciation record and brush up on my accent."

Sunday, April 30, 1944: Made Executive Officer of G-2 Section in place of Lt Col J. Edwards—who was rolled and given a place in Provost Marshal Section by Col Macdonald. First thing I learned was that the volume of paperwork on this side was 100 percent greater than in U.S. Fine way to fight a war.

Monday, May 1, 1944: GIs' penchant for souvenirs costs lots of lives. One illustration: At Salerno, a soldier at battalion CP proudly showed G-2 a map he had taken off a dead German. The map was a diagram of all the minefields in the area. Had this soldier turned in the map when he found it, would have saved many lives lost in breaching the minefields.

Tuesday, May 2, 1944: TUSA plans changed and our entry date moved up 11 days—from D+28 to around D+17. Instead of Hq Third Army going in after XV Corps, now goes in after VIII Corps—that is, between VIII and XV.

Wednesday, May 3, 1944: Patton's dog Willie was pet of RAF [pilot] shot down in Europe. Has free run of Hq. Wanders in and out of most secret War Room conferences.

Thursday, May 4, 1944: Major General Gaffey apparently is to be the real C/S and not mere figurehead. Was Patton's C/S in Africa and later made C/G of 4th Armored. Brigadier General Gay becomes Deputy. Both he and Gaffey give me the cold eye. *Editor's note: Gaffey did not become commander of 4th Armored Division until early December 1944. He commanded 2nd Armored Division in Sicily, and this may be what Allen meant. If not, and Allen intended to state 4th Armored, it suggests that he actually wrote this section much later.*

Friday, May 5, 1944: Heard today we have been secretly alerted and may get underway in a couple of weeks. Notice Hq Comdt is very busy rushing around getting Sections to get their stuff ready for moving—crates, equipment, etc. E & E Teams—Escape & Evasion—very hush-hush outfits. Only 25 Officers and 75 EM in entire U.S. forces over here.

Saturday, May 6, 1944: Koch told me he was told topside that a U.S. brigadier general was relieved of his command and placed under charges for violating security control. He indicated he knew the name but did not give it.[83]

Sunday, May 7, 1944: Chemical Warfare Secret Report dated 21 April states reports received from a number of widely scattered districts in France that German units are devoting considerable time and attention to anti-gas training. In Bordeaux and Toulon areas, German service personnel are wearing respirators on an extensive scale. Frequent gas alert practice in Rennes. Staff of Chief of Military Administration in Belgium and France conduct frequent gas chamber drills. Toulouse district—secret circular to troops gave location of decontamination centers and clothing to be worn in event of use of gas. Estimated 50 percent of the population of Germany have respirators; also large firm recently got big order to start production of gas-proof suits. Frederick Strael & Co of Konstanz.

Monday, May 8, 1944: Things warming up. Hq Comdt called for detailed charts for movement of each section by vehicle and boat. Also word received that our next UK Station will be Erlstoke, near Bristol. Couldn't find it on map so it must be a very small spot.

Wednesday, May 10, 1944: [Lieutenant Colonel Harold M.] Forde[84] (Lt Col Hal) appeared today. Cadaverous with slanting brow and handlebar mustache—the only mustache in the entire TUSA Hq. A Regular who has been a Lt Col for nearly two years, which tells the whole story. If he were really any good, as a Reg he would have been a full Col a long time ago. They are making them full Colonels out of the class of '35/'36. Looks like an eccentric to me and I have my fingers crossed on him. Koch told Forde he is to take a week and work around in subsections. Koch still hasn't told me whether I'm to stay on as Ex O or go back to Situation. Has been very effusive in praise of my work as Ex O and the way I've organized things and got things rolling. Also told me he might use

Forde to take hold of Map & Photo subsection which is badly bogged down and to set up Army Photo Center, on which no progress has been made. Said Forde is an expert on this. Personally, my hunch is Forde is going to duck everything he can and grab off the Executive job as the softest and also because he is the ranking Lt Col.

Thursday, May 11, 1944: Things begin to clear up regarding Forde. New TUSA T/O [table of organization] came out today and it provides for two full Colonels for G-2 Section. Two and two makes four. Was he brought up from 2d Armd Div (where Koch said he was having some trouble) to give him a promotion, regardless of capacity? It's an old, old story in the Army these days. Never happened to me before. Macdonald often spoke about evils of doing that; of jumping own officers with senior outsiders. Now it seems in the works, with me on the receiving end.

Friday, May 12, 1944: Koch still said nothing about my returning to Situation and Forde made no move to spend any time in Army Sections. Hangs around G-2 office all the time—even though Situation is working on ESTIMATE No. 2,[85] which I organized with Swanson, in addition to my Ex O work; and Map & Photo continues sour even though Lt Col Kenneth McIntosh,[86] Air Force, has taken over from Capt. John Newman,[87] one of our original group. This McIntosh is another screwy cookie. Says he was school teacher and acts like a flighty spinster. Weird little guy—sparrow-like face, sloppy in attire, and always popping up with some more or less irrelevant remark, usually about his contacts with the British. Forde clearly doesn't propose to get tangled up with any of the Section headaches if he can help it, and Koch is doing nothing to shove him into doing what he told him to do. That seems very funny to me.

Sunday, May 14, 1944: Took things in my own hands. At noon, after putting in furious morning, putting finishing touches on Target Area Analyses,[88] getting Situation news presentation set and racing through a pile of Executive work, all with Forde hanging around over my shoulder, I told Koch I planned to move back to Situation that afternoon. He looked startled for a moment and asked if Forde was ready to step in. I said he had a lot more time to get set than I had. Nothing more was said, and during lunch hour I had my things moved back to the big house.

Monday, May 15, 1944: Major Joseph McDowell, who was put in as Chief, Administration Subsection in place of Captain [John] Birch Mayo,[89] told me he had clashed with Forde over his coming into the section while McDowell was out and bawling out W/O [Warrant Officer] Fred Hose because most of the EM were off. They had worked until

0400 that morning getting out detailed movement report for our Section for Hq Comdt, and McDowell let them off for part of afternoon. Forde hadn't worked overnight since he arrived and McDowell was very sore. Told Forde if he had any bawling out of Administration personnel, to do it through him.

Tuesday, May 16, 1944: Lt Bird,[90] young typographic expert of Engineers, told me interesting story of state of confusion in London. Stories of buck-passing and beating around the bush there are everyday affairs. Everyone who goes down to ETOUSA, SHAEF, TIS returns with tales of being passed from one place and hot-shot to another and getting nowhere. Bird went down to look into rectographs forces [photos] on terrain model we have of OVERLORD area and Belle Isle and also for priority beaches we are working on. This is a project I personally started with idea of distributing blow-up pictures of models in lieu of inability to reproduce models in quantity. Bird had uncovered some rectograph supplies at an air depot near London. When he went down there to see just what they had, he ran into officials bemoaning the fact they were about out of rectograph supplies. Among the moaners was a civilian expert. No one knew that there were 2 sets of supplies in the depot not over 100 yards from their office. Bird says [he] had located them by phone from here through a junior officer friend in the depot; took the officials over and showed them the supplies they didn't know were in the UK, and the depot didn't know anyone was in need of the stuff. Oh, red tape, where is thy sting!

Wednesday, May 17, 1944: TUSA has apparently been assigned a more important role in the invasion. Topside reported after visit by Patton to London that TUSA will go in ahead of D+25, as under present plans. Patton is scrapping hard to elbow more importantly into the picture.

Thursday, May 18, 1944: Wrote G-2 Estimate No. 3,[91] which was approved by Col Koch without a single change. Col Macdonald told me that one thing that is operating against Patton is the charge that in the Sicilian operation he ordered 60 PW shot because they refused to obey some order.[92] Macdonald said facts are known to *international* authorities, but the story has been suppressed so far. (This may be one of the reasons why Patton was the only one of the Generals whose permanent rank was refused confirmation. Also why he is trying so hard to get bigger role in invasion.)

Friday, May 19, 1944: Despite all the pressure and thundering about security, our own Top Secret Section of Army Group pulled one of the goddamnedest lapses conceivable. Sent 75 copies of TUSA plan, containing all details of OVERLORD and NEPTUNE invasion plans, to ETOUSA in London in an unsealed mailbag by a jeep messenger. No other safeguard or protection. London has raised hell, as they should. Personally, I'd try the two Top Secret punks who did this and bust them. It is inconceivable that anyone but the grossest incompetent would do a thing like this. Anywhere along the route to London the copies could have been lost or stolen or examined, and the whole colossal venture exposed. Any one of those copies are worth 1,000,000 men to Hitler. Yet they were allowed to go half the length of England in an unsealed mailbag in a jeep driven by a buck private who didn't know what he was carrying.

Saturday, May 20, 1944: Patton attended our weekly news presentation. Was complimentary. Talked about 10 minutes at conclusion to effect that troops always move in direction of other troops and the predicted German counterattack would come from the South East. Pointed out that rail and road way favored that.

Sunday, May 21, 1944: There are 26 Allied Divs in the new offensive to crack Adolf Hitler line[93] and capture Rome. Two Divs are Polish and there is one French Corps of 4 Divs. Dope here is that the Allied plan is to wind up Italian offensive in time to release a number of Divs for attack on Europe in South France—Operation ANVIL[94]—the operation Seventh Army—Patton—was working on when he was brought to UK to assume command of TUSA. ANVIL would be in conjunction with OVERLORD and be in the nature of a diversion assault to force Nazis to split forces. Also, expected that Russians would resume their offensives. They have been quiescent since capture of Sevastopol several weeks ago. Marshes should be dry by 1 June, and it is believed they will start up again then.

New operations learned about today. CHASTITY[95]—capture of Vannes and Quiberon Bay area with Belle Ile by VIII Corps, commanded by General Miller. *Editor's note: Major General Troy H. Middleton commanded VIII Corps.*[96] VIII part of TUSA, but scheduled to go in on D+19, capture St. Malo and then move South to seize Quiberon Bay. One RCT [regimental combat team] or two Ranger bn, plus parachute forces assigned to take Belle Ile. This is our first real operational plan and I've ordered photo coverage and beach sketches, models, and collated maps. Miller [Middleton] is a regular who resigned in 1928 [1927] as a Colonel, became a dean of an American University [Louisiana State], and then returned to active duty in 1941. [Lieutenant Colonel] Herb Hauge[97] says

[Middleton is] a very able [officer] and nice, with civilian viewpoint. VIII Corps was [Daniel Isom] Sultan's[98] old Corps. He was sent to China as [Joseph Warren] Stillwell's[99] Deputy—C/S was bounced and staff sent here—where given a C/G—[Emil Frederick] Reinhart[100] who was so lousy, he lasted only a couple of months and then replaced by Miller [Middleton] and Eisenhower. Hauge says Reinhart was sent over personally by [George C.] Marshall.[101]

Monday, May 22, 1944: Over 25 percent of German units in West have non-German troops. Estimate 300,000 of which 150,000 are Russians. Also large numbers of Poles, Belgians, Croats, etc. Most are PW who have been impressed in service. Ost [East] region—25,000—in South West France—consists of Cossacks, Georgians, Tartars, etc. Big question: how good they'll fight for Germans. In Italy, Russian battalions not very good. Number of PW first day. On other hand, it was Poles who resisted British raid at Dieppe and fought very well. Germans now diluting 25 units with non-German elements because of dearth of manpower. Some of the limited employment—static type—Divs have as much as 50 percent non-Germans. Lot of Russian troops on West coast of Cherbourg-Cotentin Peninsula and units on Channel Islands—Jersey and Guernsey—reported to be mostly Russian ex-PW. 6,000 British Indians captured at Tobruk—treated badly in PW camp in Germany, then released and put under command of renegade Indian who turned Nazi.

Rolled couple more Section chiefs here. Col [T. F.] Gallagher,[102] Anti-Aircraft—private handed him his orders dated several days before. Nice man—West Pointer—but utter incompetent. Should never have been brought along. Other was Col Brisher [Levi M. Bricker][103]—Ordnance—also a bust. Wonder why in hell they don't roll Col Matthews—G-1—a complete incompetent who has a bunch of incompetents around him. Whole staff is sour on Matthews and his pack because of their failure to produce personnel. We've been trying to get some Officers and EM for weeks without result. Why Matthews is kept, I don't know. Everybody talks only about how lousy he is, yet he is still around. Must have drag somewhere. Maj Gen Gaffey, who was made C/S shortly after we came, thus reducing Brig Gen Gay to Deputy C/S, is Patton's brother-in-law, I was told today—?

Lt Col Bernard "Bunny" Carter,[104] formerly in [J. P.] Morgan & Co. in Paris and now head G-2 Auxiliary Section, told me this story on Patton: One day when he was walking on the main street of Casablanca, passed a Sgt who didn't salute. Stopped him and asked why not. "I don't salute Generals. They don't need it," was reply. "Lock SOB up," bellowed Patton in a voice heard a block away.

Another Operation

RANKIN PLAN—in event Germans collapse. Haven't had time to read it yet, although I've seen a big pile of documents. SUSSEX PLAN[105]—Combined British-American operation developed by British SIS [Secret Intelligence Service][106] and U.S. OSS/SI [Special Intelligence] in collaboration with French SIS for purpose of obtaining information by use of undercover agents in enemy-occupied territory.[107]

Tuesday, May 23, 1944: In London to attend SIS school. London very drab, dirty, overrun with U.S. military—saluting terrible. British never salute under policy that no one sees anyone in London unless talked to. But U.S. units have no such policy and are supposed to salute. Eisenhower issued strongly worded Circular No. 5 on that a few months ago, but military courtesy is very bad.

"Willow Run" *Editor's note: It is not clear what this refers to. Willow Run was a Ford Motor Company assembly plant in Michigan that manufactured arms during the war.*

Senior officers' mess all very good. Reasonable, excellent food. But buck-passing and goldbricking is rampant and as bad as in Washington. Except for looks of town, no war atmosphere among U.S. personnel. Told that a month or so ago, German bombers V-rocketed[108] a number of high Hqs in London, including Whitehall. Bomb landed in adjacent street and one right in front of St. James Palace—leaving huge crater and killing two sentries.

Told that although not announced publically, that Lt Gen Omar Bradley, C/G FUSA, has been made C/G of FUSAG. Also, that 21 Army Group, which makes OVERLORD assault, was derived from 2d British Army and First U.S. Army. 21—21st—seems British idea—that's how 15 Army Group was cooked up.

Heard that Hodges—Lt Gen Courtney—former C/G TUSA—just hanging around doing practically nothing, although supposed to be Deputy C/G FUSA. Has let all aides go except Sullivan,[109] and about the only thing he does is go out now and then to inspect Bns. What a comedown. Another Army—U.S.—over here—4th,[110] which succeeded Third in San Antonio. Has pulled out and those who took over retaining 4th name. First [Lieutenant] General [William Hood] Simpson's[111] (tall, bald, cadaverous) group was to be known as Eighth U.S. Army, but British said it would be confusing with theirs—so renamed Ninth. Also, heard still another U.S. Army—Second[112]—also due to come over. That would make four U.S. Armies—over 1,250,000 men. Also, 2d French Armd Div is being organized in UK. To be directly under SHAEF command. Unit very secret and we got instructions that under no circumstances were we to tell them anything as they "don't know anything."

Wednesday, May 24, 1944: Lot of anti-British feeling among U.S. officers. Kept under cover mostly, but very evident it's there. One reason—British servants, especially in hotels, are very insulting. Ritz headwaiter curtly told me to go downstairs when I said I didn't have a booking. Personally, outside of this, courteous treatment everywhere.

Saturday, May 27, 1944: Patton attended our weekly briefing and was very complimentary. I talked on hitting German Para and Panzer forces in France. Afterwards, Patton talked for a few minutes, expressing belief that the Germans would counterattack from the South East—on grounds that troops always go where other troops are. Said nothing about TUSA plans, or fact that he has written a personal letter to Eisenhower for permission to move the Hq to the South of England. General [Harold P.] Bull,[113] Eisenhower's G-3, turned request down and Patton has gone over his head. [Lieutenant Colonel Coy G.] Eklund[114] showed me the letter in London—military form, but strong appeal.

Tuesday, May 30, 1944: Ninth U.S. Army—NUSA—came up for briefing. Patton handled G-3 presentation and was in fine spirits, although pronunciation of French atrocious—pronounced Ren—Rens; Van—Vannes; Le Man—Le Mans. At conclusion of briefing, Patton complimented Colonel Koch and "his very able assistants." Only one Patton commanded—[Colonel Charles P.] Bixell[115]—Ninth Army G-2, among those present and he sure appeared to be in a daze. He is no more fit to be an Army G-2 than I am to fly a B-24.[116] But—he has the right service number and also right drag at AGF [Army Ground Forces].[117] Was once aide to General [Robert] Beck[118] and that doubtless helps a lot. Wonder if that punk Kirke is still with him and coming over. Probably send him here for us to teach. If that happens, I'll teach him all right—?

Thursday, June 1, 1944: Heard screamingly funny story on Bill Borders—he took out niece of local social czarina. Married, but like Bill, apparently not averse to an evening of entertainment. Bill got to talking about WD [War Department] identification cards and pulled out his billfold to show what it looked like. As he pulled the card out—out popped a condom and fell on the gal's lap. Bill told me the story at the mess and still was blushing over incident.

Friday, June 2, 1944: Some more operations: *POINT BLANK*[119]—Air offensive against Nazi Europe began Jan 1/44. *FORTITUDE*[120]—Cover plan to hide invasion plans by bombing battery, positions, communications centers, storage points and beach defenses in Dieppe and Pas de Calais areas. *SWORDHILT*—Plan to capture Brest by landing at Morlaix, or in St. Brieuc area, and seizing port from land side. XV Corps has this mission tentatively. Week ago we were told tentatively to suspend planning on this operation for present. *CROSSBOW*[121]—British designation for pilotless aircraft installations of Germans on invasion coast. This is the real secret weapon we've been bombing and not rocket-gun positions. Ski-slide sites for these aircraft estimated by TIS as now numbering 53 divided about equally aligned on London and Worthing and Plymouth. Most of the sites in the Pas de Calais and Cherbourg Peninsula. Others under construction with Germans trying to hide and protect them from bombing. According to Ninth Air Force Plan, 3,200 vessels take part in invasion and will be protected by 800 warcraft. Among those listed are:

3 U.S. Battleships
   Nevada—14"
   Texas—14"
   Arkansas—12"
U.S. Cruisers
   Tuscaloosa—8"
   Augusta—8"
   Quincy (?)—8"
HMS Monitor—Erebus—2–15"
Cruisers
   Glasgow—6"
   Enterprise—6"
   Hawkins—7.5"
   Black Prince—5.25"
   Bellona—5.25"
22 U.S. destroyers
135 Landing Craft various type—gun, tank, smoke

Saturday, June 3, 1944: Told that tomorrow morning is D-Day—if tide right. Last few days raw, chilly, wet and cloudy. Prepared 1/100,000 Operation Map in War Room. Today's report in MARTIAN[122] Report (TIS) ups German Divs in West to 60 for total of—316 Inf Bns, 23 Tk [tank] Bns. This does not include General Headquarters units with another

11 Inf Bns, 15 Tk Bns, 23 Arty [artillery] Bns. Estimate about 1,600,000 troops, of which about 300,000 "foreigners," of which 150,000 Russians, Tartars, Georgians, Mongols, etc. Received Eisenhower's first field report Cositintrep [Combined Situation Intelligence Report] No. 1, Part 1. Land. Nothing to report. Heard that if invasion doesn't start in next few days it will be postponed for another month.

Sunday, June 4, 1944: No word of anything started yet. Patton, Gaffey and Gay ordered briefing at 0930. Only ones present with Colonel [Halley G.] Maddox,[123] G-3. Listened to all they had to say and Patton asked only one question—any bombing of bridges over Seine R. Just got report from London—18 out of 23 have been bombed out in last few days—that I read him, hitting bullseye right on the nose. Nodded his head approvingly and said he wanted a daily briefing from now on at 1100. All three generals then went to a service in little old church behind big house. Heard plan now on to move to Redding by 15th. Also heard we won't now, due to lack of transportation. Remain here, but G-2/G-3 may send staffs to FUSAG. That suits me, as we will work closer to source of material, although I've finally sold Col Koch on sending Liaison Officer (Goolrick) to London.

Completed Estimate No. 4[124] and also Target Area Analyses Nos. 4 and 5.[125] No. 4 on Belle Isle and Quiberon Bay area—Operation CHASTITY—VIII Corps—on which we've prepared a lot of material, including air photos that we've had flights made for on Islands.

Sunday, June 5, 1944: No word of anything yet. Weather continues raw, cloudy and stormy. Eisenhower's Cositintrep the same—Nothing to Report. At briefing at 1100 Patton said he was at 21 Army Group Hq Friday night and Montgomery stated both U.S. First Army and British 2d were completely confident they could effect a landing. Also that Germans could put 700 tanks into motion by H+24 hours—150 French Renault 2-man tanks, and by D+3, 1,800 trucks. Also, that unit to watch was 2 Panzer Div[126] located at Amiens. This is the best Panzer Div Germans have in West and the way it will move will indicate which way Germans expect assault. Montgomery said Germans were not sure whether assault would be in Pas de Calais (Dover) or Cherbourg Peninsula area.

2

Watching and Waiting

Tuesday, June 6, 1944: Big show is on. Patton walked into 1100 briefing smiling broadly and exclaimed—"Congratulations, gentlemen, the war is finally on." Put Sit[uation] Sec[tion] on 24-hour basis and issued my first ISUM [intelligence summary]. Invasion actually began at 0200B with issuance of pre-arranged radio silence signal—"ADORATION with effect." Warning Order from ETOUSA 051920B read—Secret with Reference to our Secy. XRay Three One Zero Six Seven dated Third June CMA[1] ADORATION to take effect at Zero Two Zero Zero Baker Hour CMA Six June. 1200 report from FUSAG on assault: Underwater obstacles proved not nearly as difficult as expected. Considerable tactical seafire effected. 2 American Destroyers; 2 British; 1 LST [landing ship, tank] and 1 Corvette lost; 5 German subs destroyed. Out of 915 American planes in AB operation, only 15 lost. Out of 374 British planes in AB operation, only 8 lost. By 1000 hours, 4 Brig [brigades] (Regt) ashore. Patton cautioned at 1100-hour briefing that while secrecy of NEPTUNE very well kept, must continue to be careful about Third Army. Said that Germans still did not know that Third Army was in England, and the secret must be kept.

Wednesday, June 7, 1944: Sour reports from OMAHA beachhead.[2] Shows up only about one mile on our 1/250,000 map. Seems trouble not so much the Germans as bad weather. Gale that has been raging since Saturday still bad, with high seas hampering debarking, especially tanks. Reported number lost in unloading, with result troops unable to push ahead against German forces. Gen Bradley reported to have inquired of British about possibility of coming in over their beaches if high waves continue.

Thursday, June 8, 1944: Situation much better. OMAHA doing a lot better and last night both men and vehicles got on various beaches in big numbers. German air and naval resistance not very effective. British extended their beachheads to beyond Caen and into Bayeux, and east of

Orne River to Bayent and Yaraville. *Editor's note: Allen's information is incorrect. The British and Canadians were not south of Caen at this time. The British 3rd Division had to send a brigade to help the 6th Airborne Division hold the bridgehead east of the Orne River. The 3rd Canadian Infantry Division had been successfully blocked by the 12th SS Panzer Division on D+1 northwest of Caen.* German salient on bridgehead from Caen to Douvre, held by 192 PGR [Panzergrenadier Regiment] of 21 Panzer Div[3] cut down considerably. Navy also last night brought over first MULBERRY tows—artificial harbor. As of last night, beaches about 24 hours behind landing schedules—due to bad weather—but expect to pick up lost time.

At 1100 hour briefing today, Patton cautioned about "being gloomy." "Don't go around looking gloomy. The worse things get, the more cheerful you must look. Also don't spread rumors. Some young men like to get vicarious glory out of saying 'Col. so-and-so told me such-and-such,' and by the time the story gets to the third toilet, it sounds like doom was about to descend on all of us." Concluded with big smile, "Well, gentlemen, we are one day nearer to getting into it." Looked very trim and walked with brisk and firm tread. In afternoon, came in with [Major] Gen [Walton H.] Walker,[4] C/G XX Corps, and I gave them G-2 briefing on situation. Patton very affable and pleasant. Preparations for movement getting underway. Our bedding rolls and valpaks marked. I'm all packed and can move out anytime.

Friday, June 9, 1944: Eisenhower Cositintrep; 091400: Both hospital carriers damaged by mines on June 7, but reached harbor safely and one serviceable in a week. Port-en-Bessin—Gooseberries—progressing rapidly. 2d and 90th Div landing completes initial landing program that included: D+4.

U.S.	British
VII—79, 9, 90, 4 Divs	XII—43, 59, 53 Divs
XIX—3, 31, 2 Divs	XXX—49 Inf, 50 Inf, 7 Armd Divs
V—2, 21, 1 Divs	VIII—Armd Gds, 15 Inf, 11 Armd Divs

Editor's note: Allen's list of divisions in V Corps is incorrect. The 29th, not the 21st Infantry Division, was in the Corps at the time. The Guards Armored Division did not land until June 28. 20 Naval PW captured at harbor Ouistreham, including commandant of the harbor. PW was captured drunk in a shelter to which they retired when landing began. From Bradley—Utah beaches in excellent condition. Omaha situation improving but difficulties still exist. I presented G-2 part at 1100 briefing today. When I finished Patton said, "Thank you very much. Very good."

Saturday, June 10, 1944: D+4: Situation continues to improve. Our delays offset by slowness of German reaction. Their buildup at least two days behind our estimates. By D+4, I had given them capability of 17½ Divs in my last G-2 Estimate No. 4, 5 June—126 Inf Bn, 13 Tk Bn (800/1000 tanks). So far, identification of units employed total only 10½ Divisions—60 Inf Bns, 9 Tk Bns (600/800 tanks). 21 Army Group. Daily Estimate for 9 June attributes delay in German buildup to two factors: Bombing out of bridges from Paris to Seine. The threat to Pas de Calais area that was mounted before invasion by heavy bombing, patrol raids, air Rcn [reconnaissance], propaganda. At FUSAG our AB losses estimated at 60 percent, but not certain.

Finally learned explanation for why all units of 352 Inf Div[5] were so neatly lined up against Omaha. The German Div was having maneuvers in the beachhead area when the landing [was] made. 90th Div was supposed to land on Omaha and was ferried there, but was switched and landed near Utah to close gap between the two beaches. Learned today that all of 2d Armored Div landed last night. Army Cositintrep as of 111409B reports 5,000 casualties evacuated from Utah up to 1100 last night.

At briefing this morning—I again gave G-2 presentation—I pointed out concentration of 17 SS Panzer Div[6] in Foret de Derisy [Forêt de Cerisy], South of Bayeaux [Bayeux], [and] 130 (Lehr) Panzer Div[7]—both near boundary of British and U.S. Armies. Patton listened very intently and when I finished said: "Point made by Col Allen very interesting because Germans always attack at boundaries between units. That is an old story with them."

Apparently another upheaval in the Section is in the works. McIntosh got so in the hair of Air and ETOUSA that they demand his ouster. I warned Col Koch he was a bust and there would be trouble with him. Now it's come to pass. McIntosh is to be bounced and Koch announced at Target Day Conference that Forde would replace McIntosh as G-2 Air,[8] and I would become Operational Executive Officer—*again*. Wonder how long it will last this time?

Sunday, June 11, 1944: Gave G-2 briefing today: Situation continues to improve on beachheads; about 8,500 PW reported as of 2400 last night—4500 U.S.—1st Army [and] 4300 British—2d [Army].

All *Gooseberries* in place. Gooseberries are artificial breakwaters made by sinking COEs, which are small—coasters—loaded with concrete.[9] MULBERRIES—also well underway. Mulberries are artificial docks made of Gooseberries, plus steel and concrete installations that are towed into place. Gooseberries all went off perfectly and in operation.

Monday, June 12, 1944: Gave G-2 briefing today. Germans beginning to shove in Panzer stuff. Four Divs in now—17 SS Pz [Panzer], 130 Pz, 12 SS,[10] 21 Pz. Also 3 and/or 5 Para[chute] Divs[11] on Brittany Peninsula coming in. Germans may be planning to try to keep us from going after Cherbourg from land side—or to bottle us up on neck of Cotentin Peninsula. Their armor so far is between Carentan and Bevant, east of the Orne River.

Tuesday, June 13, 1944: Three more Divs identified in contact—3 Para from Morlaix area; 77 Inf Div from Dinan; and 2 Panzer from Amiens. 2 Panzer rated Germans' best outfit in France. Lodgement sectors appear to be going very well. Reports say Resister operations delaying German troop movements plus Air operations. Continued to give G-2 presentation. Patton asked no questions.

Wednesday, June 14, 1944: First Casualty Reports received:

Casualties	Killed	Wounded	Missing	Total
British—0600 June 10	776	3,233	2,854	6,869
U.S.—2400 June 10	1,042	5,479	4,344	1,120

Editor's note: Allen's totals do not add up, most likely due to a simple error in addition.

Air reported para operations were the most successful we have yet attempted. Losses only 2.2 percent in landing troops. Air also reported that Germans pulled out one of their secret (?) weapons on 12 June—pilotless planes.[12] Allied [intelligence] knows all about them, and we have been bombing launching installations on French coast. Attack was aimed at London, and some got through but damage reported slight.

PW as of 1000 June 13:

British	6,597
U.S.	6,300
[Total]	12,897

Reports state among Russian PW one 12-year-old boy. Russians relate [they were] beaten and even shot by Germans. Most bitterly anti-German—but no offer to fight for Allies. Merely want to get out of the war. Returned today to Ex O job as Operational Ex O. Continued to give

G-2 presentation. Hq preparing for visit by Gen Marshall. Had dry-run rehearsal tonight, attended by Patton and he closely corrected various speakers.

Thursday, June 15, 1944: Reports today on Allied buildup in lodgement area:

U.S.	11 Divs
British	19 Divs
[Total]	30 Divs

(German radio say we have 30 Divs there.)
Total men landed:

U.S.	171,738
British	224,060
Total	395,798
Increase	29,656 over D+5

Germans have 14½ Divs in contact (9½ Inf, 5 Panzer)

Air Ministry Report on result of March/April bombing of Krupp[13]— all but 6 out of 200 buildings damaged. Six unharmed small, unimportant buildings. 125 severely damaged. Report on German pilotless planes (secret ?) weapon: Bombed London—Out of nine, four reached UK. Intimation is that failures due to possible radio interception.

Friday, June 16, 1944: The three Generals, Patton, Gaffey and Gay, have SP [self-propelled] Ordnance repair tr[uc]ks, electrically heated and cooled, fixed up as their individual sleeping trailers. Work benches and metal cabinets ripped out of bunks, and desk, closets of wood fitted in. Make very comfortable lodges. Major Ralph (Tex) Stiller,[14] barrel-chested aide-driver for Patton, former AF [Air Force] Sgt, told this story in War Room bull session: He and Patton were walking on road near Medina when a couple of Arab babes came up and as they passed Patton, propositioned them. Startled, but said nothing. Stiller barked at them, "Get the hell out of here." To which one of the babes, both in flowing robes with gilt shoes, retorted—"Whatsa matta. No like fuckee Arab woman." Patton said nothing, but after the women departed [he] laughed heartily.

Heard from London today—via our Ln Sec [liaison section] there— they had 12-hour Air alert, due to pilotless plane attacks. No information on degree of damage.

Saturday, June 17, 1944: Am continuing to give G-2 daily briefing and wonder how long it will last. Patton says nothing. Listens dourly. Wonder if I'm getting in his hair. More reports from London of increased pilotless plane attacks, via telephone, that they are coming over every half hour. Adv Party left today for our new camp. We are alerted to leave sometime next week.

Sunday, June 18, 1944: Col Macdonald—later confirmed by Borders—told me that TUSA got orders yesterday to send four full Colonels to FUSA as replacements for Regtl Comdrs who have been relieved in the lodgement area as incompetent. Macdonald also said he heard that two Div C/Gs were bounced. Borders said that Lt Col Paul Hamilton,[15] Reg Inf, who came over with us in G-3 Sect[ion], and was sent over as Ln O [liaison officer] with FUSA, has been given a line Bn. Also getting clipping from States that Mike Danby,[16] who was busted by Mark Clark[17] from Corps C/G to Colonel and returned to U.S. for allegedly "losing his head" at Salerno, has been promoted again by Roosevelt to Brig Genl. That is very interesting on two scores: (1) The kick in the teeth at Clark. (2) Reports of Div, Regt and Bn Cmdrs being bounced across the Channel.

Got some official figures today on Allied casualties in Italy as up to 7 June:

Fifth U.S. Army

11,368 Killed
43,487 Wounded
8,723 Missing
63,578 [Total]

Eighth Br[itish] Army

5,017 Killed
23,068 Wounded
9,740 Missing
37,825 [Total]

French Corps

3,943 Killed
15,008 Wounded
1,268 Missing
21,219 [Total]

Out of 24 German Divs in Italy—estimated that only 12 are now battle-worthy. Estimate [that]:

715 Inf Div
71 [Inf Div]
94 [Inf Div]
29 Panzer GR
15 [Panzer GR] have been destroyed

German PW—6 June:

U.S.	20,978
British	5,942
French	5,942
[Total]	32,862

Also received official report today—

84 U.S. Inf Div
88 U.S. Inf Div
45 U.S. Inf Div
3 U.S. Inf Div
34 or 36 U.S. Inf Div
1st Armd Div
2d Algerian Div
4th Moroccan Mt [Mountain] Div [−]

All have been taken out of line for reorganization.

Maj Gen Crittenberger, formerly of XIX Corps, who was rolled when he got to UK, is commanding 4 or 6 Corps in Italy. Also that Major Henry Cabot Lodge[18]—ex-Senator from Mass[achussetts]—was with Crittenberger as PM [provost marshal] or PRO [public relations officer], but got ill and now is back in U.S. He'll probably claim he was wounded in battle—like he claimed he fought in tank action in Africa—a god-damned lie.

21 Army Group Report as of 15 June makes three interesting points.

(1) Est[imate] that the Germans have 300,000 troops in battle area with, however, a combat effectiveness of only 200,000 men. This due to—low morale, non-German elements, equipment

shortages, restricted movement due to Air bombing and Resistance.

(2) Less tanks than estimated. Estimate 15/1800 tanks by 15 June. Estimate actually only 900, of which 450 Mark IV, 150 Mark V, 60 Tiger,[19] 250 French.

(3) Large proportion of non-German elements which do not have high combat efficiency—

709 Inf Div
711 Inf Div
716 Inf Div
352 Inf Div

Also 3 Para Div has not conducted itself well so far.

Monday, June 19, 1944: U.S. Strategic Air Force Report 11 June. 2,362 heavy bomber sorties supported D-Day landings—covered by 1,000 fighters—dropped 4,841 tons of bombs. During first five days of assault, flew more than 12,000 sorties over battle area. Biggest sweep was night 5/6 June—1,321 AC [aircraft] pounded batteries, Rd [Railroad] yards, roads, junctions, troop concentration in Forêt de Cerisy, Carentan, St. Lô, Liseux and others.

Germans have Helicopter Kite for U-Boats that they use for sort of an elevated OP [observation post]. At 450 feet altitude—maximum—Kite has visibility of 25 miles. Made of aluminum—15 feet long. No motor power—towed, which rotates blades. In event of a crash landing, automatic device cuts cable and leaves pilot up in air—with small parachute.

In addition to sleeping van, Patton also has one of the new 6-wheel armored Rcn Cars, a ¼ [ton] equipped with radio—that his driver commandeered from CB [counterbattery?] team—and a big limousine.

SHAEF report on pilotless plane operations [indicate] that between 2300B 15 June and 1600B 16 June—135 made landfall in Southern England, of which 62 hit London. At least 12 were destroyed by tempests.

Tuesday, June 20, 1944: More reports of pilotless planes. First TUSA casualty due to this. Col. Gustav B. Greunther [Guenther],[20] new G-6—P & PW [public relations and psychological warfare]—killed Sunday near St. James Square—which was severely plastered by bombing several months ago. Actually, planes are not radio-controlled. Shot off from ski slides, has 150-mile range, and carries one-ton demolition charge. Official report that as of 18 June, casualties in England from pilotless bombs are—111 Killed, 418 Seriously Wounded, 379 Slightly Wounded, 322 Unclassified—[Total] 1,230.

Ski sites in Seine-Sorne area. Some believed to be in Cherbourg but not operating. Wedge across Cotentin 4/6 miles today—9th Div did job—60th Inf (RCT) took Barneville with 47 RCT on West flank, and 357 RCT took Harve de Portbail on South. Elements of 4 German Divs trapped in envelopment including 709, 77 [and] 319 Divs and 91 AL [Air Landing], between 10/25,000 troops.

Wednesday, June 21, 1944: First day of summer and a glorious day it is—balmy, without being hot or soggy, brilliant sun and with just enough breeze to make it brisk and peppy. It now stays light from about 0430 to 2400, and the countryside is rapturously lovely. It is easy to understand why the English rhapsodize about their little Island. The big cities are grim and grimy, but the countryside is like a great park.

Heard today that the move to South of Salisbury apparently is off, due presumably to the delay on the Continent. The assault is about four days behind schedule, more than in taking Cherbourg. Last official report was that we had it under artillery fire but were about 8/10 miles from city. Up to 18 June—landed 621,986 troops (314,547 British, 307,439 U.S.), 95,750 vehicles, 217,624 tons of stores. All over the beaches, Mulberries and small ports in assault area.

While U.S. cutting off top of Peninsula, British haven't moved in their sector for 10 days now. Lines same since about 10 June with Caen still untaken and St. Lô still untaken—although Caen has been pounded to pieces by shelling.

Latest info on pilotless planes: Actually is a plane with an engine operated by compressed air and low-grade octane oil. Has range of about 130 miles at rate of one gallon per mile. Carries charge equal to 2,000-lb bomb and is operated by compass and gyroscope. It is "shot off" from fixed ski sites. 57 different ones have been plotted; about 12 in Cherbourg tip. Planes fly at about 1,000 feet. 40 were shot down by aircraft Monday. Sunday our one PP [pilotless plane] hit Wellington Barracks Chapel during morning service, killing over 100 and seriously injuring several hundred more. Col Guenther, G-6, first TUSA casualty, killed there. Pilotless plane obviously not a major threat. Irritant and annoyance, and also gives Nazis propaganda hoopla, although that apparently is backfiring, because their broadcasts are beginning to soft-pedal on the effectiveness of this so-called "secret weapon," which is not secret at all, as reports on its design and operation were very complete even before D-day and have been confirmed since by fragments of planes put together from those shot down and that were hit in UK.

From OSS got report today that around 12 June enough arms and ammunition were dropped around Pontiry [Pontivy] and East of Vannes to equip 2 Bns of Resisters. This is the largest concentration of Resister armaments so far dropped in area of this size in France. This armament believed responsible for delay of [2nd] SS Panzer Das Reich Div[21] which reportedly left Montauban on 9 June but not yet reported in Normandy. On 16 June it now reported the Div left Montauban in 15 trains—without its heavy tanks. There is a great and thrilling story being enacted behind the fog of battle in interior France in the warring against the Nazis by the various Resister groups, particularly the *Maquis*,[22] the most aggressive and best organized of them.

Thursday, June 22, 1944: High seas the last three days have seriously hampered landing troops and supplies. Reports state 4 Divs are being held on ships offshore and numerous barges of stores and ammunition. Arty Ln O report I saw stated Arty is limited to 1/5 of a unit of fire per day when full unit needed.

Patton's three aides are an odd collection. Not one a Regular, which is interesting in itself as most high-ranking Generals have at least one Regular as aide. The three are: Lt Col Charles R. Codman,[23] Lt Col Charles B. Odom, Major Alex C. Stiller. Codman is from Boston; socially prominent background; flyer in World War I, real estate business in Boston, which he hated. Knew Patton before the war when he used to go to shore to play polo. Mrs. Patton is Boston girl and old friend of Mrs. Codman. Codman loves theater and has international acquaintance among actors. Mild and soft-spoken, antithesis of Patton. Very pleasant person. Stiller, trucker in Texas and Oklahoma. Big barrelled and chested. Claims New Deal taxation policies put him out of business. Bulky and burly type—loves drink and women of any kind. Actually, he is Patton's driver, although he has an EM driver. Odom not listed as an aide, but carried on staff Medical Section in the Consultant Subsection. Tall, dark and curly haired, well built and good looking. From New Orleans, and is said to be a good doctor. Very pleasant. Actually Patton's personal physician. Casualty figures as of 17 June: 35,000 Killed, Wounded and Missing. PW evacuated to UK as of 19 June: 17,000.

Friday, June 23, 1944: Ninth Air Force report 18 June: 1,080 bomber planes carried out dive bombing and Recn missions in Cherbourg Peninsula. No enemy fighter opposition at all. 18 planes lost due to flak and ground fire. Conferred with OSS/SI (Special Intelligence) and OSS/SO Detachments. SI functions under G-2 and produces enemy information. SO functions under G-3 and directs and supports Resister operations. Lt Col [Robert I.] Powell[24] commands SO Det[achment]. He had overlay on 1/500,000 Map showing extent of Resister activities since D-Day. Very heavy in Toulouse-Bordeaux area—which accounts for 2 SS Panzer Div and 11 Panzer Div[25] not arriving in battle area yet, although they started moving about 8/9 June—east of Paris, in the Vannes area and in the Haute-Savoie. The number of rail, road and bridge cuts in Toulouse-Bordeaux area heaviest of all, and the overall picture was most impressive. Best idea these OSS operations have had yet. Powell said they have dropped several bns of special troops as well as agents. Troops lead Resisters and fight—in uniform—as well. SOE has two elements— RF Circuit[26] and R Circuit. Agents direct areas which have names like Churchman, Rocketeer, Foodman, etc. An RF team consists of a U.S. or British officer, a Frenchman, and a radio operator. SI also drops teams— agent and radio operator—who collect military and other information. I put Powell into the daily briefing as part of the G-2 show, although he is attached to G-3. He has been sitting on this information for a week and they had no idea of it. When I dug it out, they still didn't have enough brains to grab it and I put it on as part of G-2 presentation.

Ninth Air Force report 8/15 June states: "First of anticipated enemy expendable pilotless plane[s] was launched at dawn on 13 June. The attack was on a small scale and only four aircraft, all of which exploded, were located on land. Description—AC is midwing monoplane with single fin and rudder. Length of fuselage—21 feet 10["], Wing span—16 feet. Apart from extreme nose of fuselage and control surfaces, the structure of plane is entirely of steel. 130 Gallon gas. Aircraft of robust construction throughout, and design simplified for rapid production. Launched from ramp with a take-off rocket."

Saturday, June 24, 1944: After today's briefing, exceptionally good with weekly roundup of war fronts, Patton, obviously pleased, rose, pulled down his tight-fitting battle jacket and said: "I've been a general staff officer for seven years now and have seen good staff work. I consider this staff among the best." Then he paused for a few seconds and with smile concluded, "Keep going and don't let up."

Navy reported that on 22 June, owing to high seas, coasters had to be beached in Cherbourg pocket zone in order to meet urgent ammunition needs. Also that considerable damage occurred in Mulberries due to storm and that they are only 30 percent effective.

Sunday, June 25, 1944: C/S Gen Gaffey announced at staff meeting today that the CP would move to new place South of Salisbury next Thursday. SHAEF Weekly Intl Summary No. 14, 24 June—commenting on fact bad weather prevented Germans from evacuating any troops from Cherbourg, said: "The recent weather has prevented him from either reinforcing the port or evacuating by sea—perhaps the only instance when the elements have in any way favored our effort."

Monday, June 26, 1944: This is D+20 when we originally—through VIII Corps—were supposed to have started in. Our line was to have been more or less West/East from Avranches at neck of Cotentin Peninsula. Actually we hold only about half of the Peninsula, with Cherbourg still not completely taken. Our actual line is about D+5. As of 21 June, Allied casualties: 42,000 Killed, Wounded, Missing. PW—19 June—17,000. Troops landed as of 24 June—710,000. 280,000 tons supplies.

Tuesday, June 27, 1944: At briefing today, Ordnance showed film of land mine exploder. Consists of two giant wheels of steel made up of five disks, the whole attached to front of a tank. Weighs about 58,000 lbs and picture showed it cruising through mine fields without danger. It was characterized as indestructible and looked like it. Should be tremendously useful in rapid breaching of lanes through mine fields. Such a simple device, I wonder why it was not conceived and used in Africa.

Col Miller,[27] Air, back from trip, related that V U.S. Corps had complained about being held back in Carentan area last week. This done on orders of Higher Hq at behest of British, who feared advance by V Corps at that time would endanger their positions further East. Miller also stated that as a result of bombing, believe 80 percent of sites for launching new German heavy aerial torpedoes have been destroyed. Believe bombing definitely delayed these attacks. However, also believe Germans have developed type of site that can be put up in 24 hours, which means they can operate these devices from interior if forced off coast. Miller also said a shortage of heavy ammunition had delayed attack on Cherbourg.

Wednesday, June 28, 1944: Started evacuating Poever Hall for new CP—Braemore in south England, near Salisbury. 21 Army Group reported that from a "normally reliable" source, [Field Marshal Erwin] Rommel[28] plans a major counterattack on 29 June and for that purpose—3 Panzer Divs—1 SS [from] Antwerp;[29] 9 and 10 SS[30] of II SS Pz Corps[31] from Russia. 3–4 Inf Divs have been concentrated South of battle area in the Normandy bocage. Estimate Germans have around 875 effective "reserves"—tanks—of which 400 Mark IV; 350 Panthers; 125 Tigers. This is less than 50 percent of what we had estimated they could commit by this time—D+21.

Thursday, June 29, 1944: Up to 12 June, total Allied casualties in Italy—136,441. Fifth U.S. Army[32]—11,588 Killed, 44,384 Wounded, 8,933 Missing; French—4,090 Killed, 16,284 Wounded, 13,032 Missing; British Eighth Army—5,092 Killed, 23,348 Wounded, 9,690 Missing; PW—12 June—U.S. 21,276; French, 6,691, British 5,184: [total] 33,051.

Friday, June 30, 1944: Moved to Braemore—huge 200-room manor house in South England, about 25 miles from Portsmouth and 90+ miles to lodgement area. Set up new CP—with War Room on ground floor. Borders told me that bulk of VIII Corps Hq in move across Channel two nights ago suffered very heavy casualties. About 200 out of 450, of which about 75 were killed. Five LCTs [landing crafts, tank] hit mines and EM down below suffered. Convoy so badly hit it turned back to the Isle of Wight and the staff will have to be reconstituted before it can function.

21 Army Group claims German Panzer Divs have lost 200 tanks totally destroyed since D-Day, with an equal number out of commission under repair. Also—say now no doubt Rommel is the real anti-invasion commander, as a result of impetuous German tactics the last few days, such as committing Panzer Div Res[erves] piecemeal. Characterize Rommel as "Impetuous Div commander, but with more troops to expend." Say—Rommel had planned to build up 7–8 Div striking force in Normandy Bocage, South of battle area, but his impetuosity has forced him to commit elements of 3 Panzer Divs—1 SS, 9 SS, 2 SS. Only elements of these doubtful so far, Inf, that appears to be the Germans' greatest troop need. Say that as of today, Germans now have the 9 Panzer Divs our pre–D-Day Estimate predicted they could bring into employment. That is, they have caught up with Panzer estimates but are still lagging—50 percent—on Infantry—Estimate—32 Inf Divs, Actual—17 Inf Divs.

Pilotless aircraft killing a number of people in London and causing considerable damage. 27–29 June, killed around 100 and wounded several times as many. Also now definitely established that on 25 June, an Me-109[33] flew with a Ju-88[34] attached, which was released at about 500 feet at a warship. Hit water with terrific explosion, slightly damaging nearby small craft.

PICKABACK PLANE

Mine laying from German planes continues to hamper Allied shipping across Channel and unloading in lodgement area—viz VIII Corps report.

Saturday, July 1, 1944: Rainy, raw, chilly. Looks like and feels like early October at home. Borders told me today we were due to move out of here by 11 June.

Three new operations projected today—*LUCKY STRIKE*[35]—Airborne and seaborne blow at St. Malo, to flank German battleline and start drive to force whole German Army into pocket up against Seine River; that is, sweep them across the Normandy Bocage presumably on hinge made by British Army. *HANDS UP*[36]—Seaborne attack on Quiberon Bay area, to open up Loire ports and flank German line. *BENEDICTION*[37]— The Morlaix-Swordhilt[38] operation. LUCKY STRIKE—so far—assigned to XX Corps to plan, under direction of FUSAG and in cooperation with TUSA.

Major Fred Linton,[39] TUSA, G-4 Ln O with 21 Army G[rou]p, reported that on D-Day a strong wind of gale proportions was coming out of North East and a heavy channel sea was running. This general condition continued over Channel up to D+15, greatly hampering troops and unloading of troops and supplies. However, the very bad weather on D-Day operated to lull the Germans and played a big role in effecting surprise.

Sunday, July 2, 1944: As of 30 June, landed in lodgement area, total of 850,000 troops and 710,000 tons of supplies. U.S. Divs landed—101st AB, 82d AB, 1st Inf, 4th Inf, 29th Inf, 90th Inf, 2d Inf, 2d Armored, 9th Inf, 30th Inf, 79th Inf, 3d Armored, 89th Inf: 13 Divs. Total U.S. and British Divs—26 Divs, 224 Inf Bns, 45 Tank Bns. Germans—22 Divs identified in contact, of which at least two—709, 243—destroyed in Cherbourg. Estimate Germans now have 9 Panzer and 15 Inf Divs in battle area, of which only inf elements of 4 SS Panzer Divs have been identified in contact. Their tanks still uncommitted. *Editor's note: Allen's information is incorrect. The tanks of 12th SS Panzer Division had been in contact since June 7. Tanks of 9th and 10th SS Panzer Divisions counterattacked the British during Operation Epsom on June 29. In addition, the Germans have several battle groups from Brittany Divs, but at most not more than 26 Divs in Normandy.*

At 1530B, special staff meeting suddenly called, at which it was announced by Gen Gaffey, C/S, that Hq TUSA would be loaded and packed in barracks by 1800B, 4 July (Tuesday), would embark in Portsmouth area, evening 5 July, and land on UTAH beach 6 July—*exactly two years today I went on active duty.* From UTAH, we go to concentration area to await further orders. Later, I heard reason for moving up our date is desire to set up FUSAG operationally, so as to get out from under 21 Army Group control. Intimation that Gen Montgomery has been getting in the hair of Gen Bradley, who is slated to become C/G FUSAG. Interesting fact—I've met no English officer who [is] very enthusiastic about Monty, and none of ours who served in Africa or Italy are very keen about him either. British seem to consider him a publicity hound, and USA'ers a credit grabber.

Staff meeting was halted for a few minutes to allow Patton to appear. He came in beaming happily exclaiming—"Congratulations, we're going to war. Gentlemen, the Third Army is either going to make big history or there will be a lot of work for the Graves Registration Bureau." Then, with another broad smile and wave of his hand, he left. Well, this showing off is okay with me. From the looks of things—PW and other reports—personally, I don't think the Germans can hold out very long in France. Just haven't got the stuff. Troops inferior; either very young, old, or non-German. Poor and little equipment. Very little Air. Ln Os say they never saw a German plane in the air. Very little Artillery and less than ½ the tanks we estimated they would have. As of today (D+25), have 9 Panzer Divs in line, as we predicted, but instead of these Divs having 1,750–2000 tanks, actually have only from 400 to 900. A PW from 12 SS Panzer Div is reported to have said—"How can we hope to win the war, when our equipment consists of French tanks, with which the French lost the war." There is still plenty of fight in the German Army, and the SS is still a killer, but it's my conviction that once the real pressure is applied the whole West defense will collapse like a house of rotten beams. VIII Corps was to have launched its drive against 84th Corps Sector Friday, then Sunday, then today. Whether it has done so, no word yet.

A report from Major George Swanson, our Ln O with VIII Corps, says Cherbourg not very badly damaged and port scheduled to be in operation by 3–4 July. Also that first objective of VIII Corps is Coutances, on west coast of Cotentin. That is logical, as it is key to communication lines in that area. Next phase is Avranches, at the base of the Peninsula.

Visited old Saxon church—100 yards from Braemore Manor. One old church in England dates back to 10th Century, I believe. Small, neat, cool and soothing.

Tuesday, July 4, 1944: Departed Braemore for Southampton to embark on LST 168 for UTAH Beach. Before leaving, every O[fficer] and EM was issued two day's K-ration, one D-ration and six conduces [condoms] and two prophylactics—such is modern war. Heard today it was Arty Section of VIII Corps that got shot up in Channel crossing. Also, that Gen [Matthew B.] Ridgway,[40] of 82d AB Div, had reported 42 percent of his outfit casualties after first landing. However, lot of missing beginning to return. Our LST is 264 Navy number—168 Army number. Was among the first to land and has made nine trips without mishap. Drove through New Forest—created by King John—enroute to Southampton. Arrived around midnight and spent rest of night in convoy lined up against _____. Slept on trailer top.

Wednesday, July 5, 1944: Embarked around noon but did not sail until midnight. Most slept in their clothes but I undressed in LST. Very comfortable. Senior officers put up four in tiny cabin, junior officers and EM in bunks down below.

Thursday, July 6, 1944: Very quiet passage. Very large convoy of LSTs, Liberty and Victory ships, etc, most with a balloon attached. Spectacular sight, especially when we passed another large convoy returning. Debarked by driving off LST onto beach at low tide, near Radonville. Went to designated area to de-waterproof vehicles and then to another area where the Section reassembled and moved out around 1700 for TUSA bivouac area in vicinity of Ste. Colombe. Enroute saw debris of many LCTs, vehicles, etc., of original landing parties. Also wrecked gun emplacements of Germans and North of UTAH, extensive fields of underwater obstacles—Element C, tetrahedan, hedgehogs, piles, etc, still with mines attached. Bivouacked Section and spent night in a Normandy apple orchard—scraggly little old trees, with white moss-covered branches that are very thin and brittle—break very easily and can be chopped easily. All fields heavily hedgerowed with deep ditches and thorny thickets—lot of blackberry thickets, but all growth still in early stages. Easy to understand as weather similar to that of late October at home—raw, wet, chilly.

Friday, July 7, 1944: Set up War Tent, Sit Sec Tent and Chalson A bivouac. Lot of rain during day. Mess in adjoining field—K-rations out in field. TUSA is not operational and I gather none too welcome as far as FUSA is concerned. They bounced one of our Signal Os who went over to see about communications with them.

Saturday, July 8, 1944: Got big pack of newsmen with us—40-odd with G-5. Went to see VIII Corps. Visited Col [Andrew R.] Reeves,[41] G-2, whose outfit has turned out some very sloppy and inferior Periodic Reports.[42] Reeves opposed us in Louisiana maneuvers last year and we put it all over him. A fuddy-duddy old Reg of run-of-mine caliber.

Sunday, July 9, 1944: Went up to front lines—Hill 131 near La Haye du Puit[s], which VIII Corps [has] been trying to take since last Monday. Apparent 79 and 90th Divs engaged in attack have had tough time of it, despite tremendous artillery concentrations. Almost continuous day and night firing since night we pulled into area—three days ago. On way down from hillcrest, we suddenly discovered unburied German soldier, near what had been an MG [machine gun] nest. Soldiers nearby said lot more dead Germans were unburied couple hundred yards away. On way back, saw graves of two U.S. soldiers near roadside. Saw our Arty fire on enemy lines on ridge ¾ miles distance and they certainly were being pounded. Pont le'Abbe [Pont l'Abbé] badly hammered, although our people say Germans did more damage by firing [at the] places than our Arty. But our guns did plenty, here and in other towns in vicinity. St. Sauveier de Vicomte [St. Sauveur-le-Vicomte], St. Mere Église, Fourcsrville. *Editor's note: Allen cannot be referring to Pont l'Abbé, which is in the southwestern corner of the Brittany Peninsula. Fourcsrville is probably Fougères.*

This countryside may be romantic in music—"Apple Blossom Time in Normandy"—and historic, but doesn't begin to compare with British rural area. Villages are of grim stone buildings, not very clean or picturesque. However, farms all look prosperous and cattle sleek and fat. No starvation around here, although natives very eager to get sugar, soap, shoes, clothing, cigarettes and K-rations, which they consider a great treat. Lot of cider and Calvados—a local White Mule around— some wine and brandy, and plenty of dairy products, but t_____s are out of bounds. Natives don't care for this funny money we have. In fact, they don't want money. They want to trade—barter—eggs, etc., for soap, sugar, candy, etc.

Monday, July 10, 1944: Whole area apparently covered with discarded German ammunition of all kinds. Saw some German anti-gas lotions and smoke grenades, including the deadly Molotov cocktail— anti-tank grenade. Phone rang. Someone asked for me and when I answered, replied—"This is Gen. Patton, Allen. Want exchange name of First Army and VIII Corps." Fortunately I had them—shot them off, and he said "Thanks" and that was that. Why he called me, instead of operator, I don't know. Duke Shoop[43]—*KC Star*—and fat as a hog, showed up, apparently on prowl for some dope. Later Ken Crawford[44]—*Newsweek*—appeared. Apparently told by Shoop I was here. Ken has old lines in his face—of pain, or drink, or something. I told them nothing. They told me press gang met Patton and he told them he was a "military secret." Shoop told me that before press gang left London they were told TUSA was slated to stage the big show of the invasion, after the initial landing; that Patton would be the big story. It may be bull, and then again it may not—certainly Patton will try to make it come true. What I don't get is—if he is a military secret and we are the ace up the sleeve, the KO blow, how come our shoulder patches were not ordered resumed?

Tuesday, July 11, 1944: Colonel Koch recommended I be appointed to General Staff Corps. Be interesting to see what topside does about it. No actual vacancy exists and they'll have to make one if I'm to be appointed.

PW—8 July:

British—13,043
U.S.—45,475

Casualties	Killed	Wounded	Missing	Total
British	3,692	17,471	5,735	26,898
U.S.	6,201	27,559	5,347	39,107
[Total]	9,893	45,030	11,082	66,005

Patton received a Letter of Instruction from General Montgomery[45] to the effect that the plan is to "suck in" German Armor in the British Zone and use them up and then with the British as a pivot to make East-ward and Southward swing by U.S. forces, after reaching Avranches—presumably that is when TUSA enters the picture. Meanwhile, we are marking time, fancying up War Tent, etc. I'm operating now entirely as Opns Ex O.

Heard today that Brig Gen Nelson "Johnny" Walker,[46] Asst C/G 8th Inf Div, was killed when he took over a Bn from its Cmdr and personally led an attack across a hedge-grove field. Walker was with us in maneuvers last summer and we considered him screwy as a hoot owl. Called him the "Wild Indian." He came up when we were at Poever not over a month ago and I got him a couple of maps he asked for. As I got the story—he went down to front lines and criticized a Bn Cmdr for not pushing ahead faster. CO refused to plunge ahead, so Walker told him he was relieved, took command of Bn himself and led a platoon in a rush against a hedge-row. An MG cut him down with some of the men he was leading.

Wing Comd (Lt Col) [F. W.] Winterbottom [Winterbotham][47]

ULTRA[48]—I am inducted. The great Allied secret weapon. Since 1940. High-grade codes, etc. Hitler, High Cmd, operational, sea, air, Army names listed. Must be approved by Winterbotham and London. Roosevelt & Churchill[49] get messages. In messy British hall-type tent on edge of ditch of high hedgerow of a little apple orchard in Normandy near Nehon [Nehou]. Given direct line on everything they have done—orders, movements, complaints, etc. Great cure in use. Cover with Rcn, and other disguises. Monty almost gave away Maradeth Pass—would be attacked in 48 hours. Told Div Comds to rush. Several officers were captured and they boasted they knew of the coming attack. Got very suspicious, but finally threw them off track by casting suspicion on Italian Gen in Rome.[50] Came to me out of clear blue—SLU [Special Liaison Unit].[51] Only Patton, Gaffey, Gay, Koch and I have it.[52]

Wednesday, July 12, 1944: Visited Cherbourg. Like a deserted village, although residents beginning to come back. Harbor and docks badly wrecked; naval station shattered and gutted. The amazing thing was tremendous concrete positions and small-caliber guns mounted in them. Also visited *mysterious* vast concrete construction at Brix, little stone-structured village above Valognes. Certainly a huge pile of concrete. Report that local people say Germans used Russian workmen on construction work. Valognes was a shambles. Heart of town completely destroyed and only outskirts left standing, and they are banged up. The Cotentin Peninsula is becoming the most densely populated area in the world. As of 10 July, a total of 1,096,421 personnel landed, of which 505,781 British 589,540 U.S. plus 221,165 Vehicles. 835,069 tons of supplies.

Friday, July 14, 1944: Visited First Army G-2 Sec[tion]. Very elaborate set-up, with 2½-ton tr[uck] offices with service canvas extensions. Col [Benjamin] Dixon[53] operates differently than Koch. Sits in center of Sit Sec set-up and functions amid all the ying-yanging and clatter. Everything centralized in and around him. Great deal more and higher rank personnel than we have. Four duty-officer teams of two officers each, a Lt Col and a Major, on 8 hours and off 24. Each duty officer supervises an auxiliary agency. That's a very sound idea and I think an improvement on our set-up, where Sit Sec is removed from direct contact with AAs [auxiliary agencies].

Homeward, visited UTAH beach and heard there had been a big fire, started accidently, in ammunition dump last night. Number killed and wounded. Visited some supply dumps. Vast installations out in open. Good thing we have air superiority or it would be just too bad. Brooding sight of beachhead against gray lowering sky, balloons, scores of LSTs, LCTs, MTs [motorized transports], etc, unloading or waiting their turn. Told today that by Sept 1, Cherbourg would be taking in 15,000 tons a day. This would be the maximum, so another port, or ports, have to be opened. After Avranches is taken, dated around middle of August, TUSA becomes operational—VIII Corps out to West and takes St. Malo (BENEFICIARY). XV Corps strikes across Rennes basin to Quiberon Bay (HANDS UP) and a third Corps, possibly XX, protects flank open between them. After this is done, TUSA then makes sweep Eastward

(LUCKY STRIKE) to push Germans up against Seine and crush them. This sweep set for October.

Got a birthday present from Koch today—the announcement that he might make me ARCO—Air Rcn CO [air reconnaissance coordinating officer]. Has all earmarks of combination deal to clear way to promote Bunny Carter to full Colonel (I rank him) and for me to do the work that Forde is too goddamned lazy to do. What I can't understand is that he has so highly praised my work. ___ not asked I be made GSC [General Staff Corps] and had me made ULTRA. After all the work and just when I really feel competent to be a top G-2, to be shunted on to a sidetrack. Some Birthday Gift!

When announcement made at briefing this morning that Brig Gen Theodore Roosevelt [Jr.][54] died in his tent last night—Patton, before he rose to leave, paused for a moment and then with grin remarked, "That shows you the danger of sleeping." TR was known to be a heavy drinker.

Saturday, July 15, 1944: From ULTRA—Msg [message] from LXXXIV Corps[55] (West sector against VIII U.S. Corps) 0200, 14 July— 'Our fighting power so weakened, effective defense no longer guaranteed. High casualties among officers. Impossible for units to hold their ground against extremely heavy enemy Air and Arty operations.'

Captured pay voucher of Field Marshal [Albert] Kesselring,[56] Italy Commanding General for June '44:

Pay for June	2886.60 RM [Reichsmarks]
Deductions	
Income tax	630 RM
Pay tax	894.60
Old age pension	9.31
Rent (no garage)	197.40
Bonds	26.
Air force club	1.50
Welfare organization	5.0
(Munich)	
Bavaria foundation	9.55
Alliance insurance	5.
Total deductions	1,778.36
Balance	1,108.24

Sunday, July 16, 1944: Apparently ARCO move off—for present anyway. Koch told me today he was dropping the matter. Have my fingers crossed.

New Operation: COBRA—VIII and VII Corps—Coutances (Objective).[57] Plan is to slash enemy in flank while VIII Corps holds in its zone. Use two Armd Divs for attempted breakthrough. Bad ground—narrow front—can't get full weight of Armor to bear. Purpose of Operation to attempt to crumple German lines, break out of this vicious Bocage country, with its endless ramparted hedgerows and narrow sunken lanes, and clean up entire Cotentin Peninsula, so as to get more maneuver room for further operations West, East and South. NEPTUNE now more than 30 days behind schedule. Making progress, but very slowly and at heavy cost. Murderous terrain is tremendous ally of Germans and if we don't get out of it soon, they will get another powerful ally in three months— the weather. Fall and winter very soggy and wet here, and entirely possible advances [will] bog down and Germans will be able to further strengthen natural advantages of terrain by building up organized trench and strong points system and fixed position warfare of World War I [will] develop. This [is] exactly what Nazis [are] playing for—stalemate. Drive to jump off 18 July dependent on weather as attack to be preceded by big air bombardment.

Monday, July 17, 1944: OSS/SO—Jedburg[58] Teams—British, French or U.S. officer, plus radio operator, dropped into various places in France to lead Resisters. On July 14 dropped 314—largest drop. Jedburgers operate in uniform of their own Army. Estimate about 30,000 armed Resisters in France as of 15 July. Plan to equip enough to bring total in Brittany up to 30,000 by August 1. Germans using Russians, Poles and Rumanian troops to fight Maquis and other Resistance groups.

Flying (buzz) bombs, 12 June to 11 July	
Launched	3,213
Overland	2,813
London area	1,167
Destroyed by fighters	881
[Destroyed by] AA	385
[Destroyed by] balloons	71
[Total destroyed]	1,337

Visited two Buzz Bomb sites near our camp—one, about 700 yards and other 1½ miles. Built on country lanes, very carefully concealed and camouflaged, and consist of three installations—(1) Concrete house, apparently assembly plant, (2) 200 yards down road, turntable of non-magnetic concrete with groove for tail, where bomb is aimed (gyroscope), set and (3) firing site, where tracks built into concrete for erection of portable ski. Two small concrete dugouts for propelling liquid and firing mechanism. All very cleverly built into terrain and surroundings, and even if spotted, would be difficult to hit from the air. Air military experts say many of these and other versions of the sites found all over the Cotentin. The two near us are sighted on Portsmouth. Also said that reputed V-2 flying bomb supposed to carry 12 tons of explosives, weighs 50 tons and can be shot up into stratosphere vertically and come down by force of gravity.

Tuesday, July 18, 1944: Rain, cold, overcast. COBRA postponed. Heard some reports today of three of our Armd Rcn planes hit by our own troops. Also, some stories of our planes shooting up and strafing our troops. This is an old story that has happened in every theater. One of those things that is inevitable in war, I guess, but it's not funny to those hit.

Wednesday, July 19, 1944: More and worse mean weather. Again COBRA postponed.

Italy—Casualties to 16 July	Killed	Wounded	Missing	Total [Casualties]	PW
U.S.	13,382	51,194	10,900	75,476	28,177
British	12,043	51,144	13,567	76,754	17,725
French	5,169	20,692	1,579	27,440	8,222
Pole	1,042	4,281	502	5,825	1,363
Italian	298	869	562	1,729	33
[Total]	31,934	128,180	27,110	187,224	55,542 [55,520]

Thursday, July 20, 1944: Weather still bad. Major Jeff Foothorap,[59] CO, TUSA, CIC [Counter Intelligence Corps],[60] in report 19 July, stated that following capture of Cherbourg there was looting by O and EM of Provost Marshal, Engr, SOS [Services of Supply] and Navy after combat troops left. Heard [Brig Gen John J.] Bohn,[61] Combat Command CO of 4th Armored Div, was relieved after he lost 50 tanks following attack to straighten out a salient in the line East of St. Lô. *Editor's note: Bohn served in 3rd Armored Division.* Succeeded in this, but instead of pushing on, as would have been possible if he had good Combat Intelligence because there were few enemy in front of him, he stopped. Germans laid down heavy Arty fire and knocked out 50 of Bohn's tanks (54 tanks in Bn). Also heard the C/S of 90th and 79th Divs were relieved.[62] Not surprised about 90th. It was in maneuvers in Feb 1943 and had lousy C/G then—who later was relieved or switched. He should have been reclassified as he wasn't a good Regtl Comdr. Dope around here is that topside is very sour on Haislip, C/G XV Corps. That is not surprising either, as he certainly failed to show any high abilities as Maneuver Director in Louisiana last year and what I've seen of his staff is far from impressive.

Friday, July 21, 1944: Weather still bad. British claim that up to 16 July they have knocked out 582 tanks, of which 250 were totally destroyed. More ULTRA—msgs. Enemy crying for replacements and reinforcements and unable to stand up much longer under terrific Air and Arty pounding. Yet, Germans are holding out and fighting hard, and we [are] finding it very costly to push ahead. Because we are not fighting Germans but terrain and it's murderous. Interesting to conjecture what the situation would be if adequate troops had been used initially in Italy; if overrun quickly and ANVIL—up Rhône Valley—had been the main effort. No hedgerows and natural defense-in-depth terrain for Germans there. With Patton running that show, he might really have run through France in relatively short order.

Saturday, July 22, 1944: Navy Report on Cherbourg. Bringing in Liberty freighters, but have to unload them outside the harbor because of tremendous destruction of dock facilities. Navy expected to be unloading 6,000 tons daily by now. Actually only 2,000 tons. Plans call for 20,000 by Sept 1, but on present basis it will be only about 6–8,000. We may go operational in a few days if COBRA, again postponed, bogs down. Plan would be to put TUSA into line with three Corps to clean out Cotentin, then Brittany and Quiberon Bay. Estimate about 25,000 Inf in Brittany plus 50,000 Navy and Army supply elements. Also, 8/10,000 Russians—altogether not over 90,000 enemy in entire Peninsula.

Sunday, July 23, 1944: At VIII Corps CP near La-Haye-du-Puits—they told us two Bns of 90th Div got across See [Sée] River, but later driven back by Germans—due to heavy Arty and mortar fire. No explanation why our far superior Arty and Air couldn't have squashed enemy fire. Also told us PW knew little about attempt on Hitler's [life][63] and disturbances in Germany. Also, that VIII Corps estimated from 7,200 to 9,500 enemy on their front with 10,000 in immediate Reserve. Against that, VIII Corps has four full U.S. Inf Divs—12,000 each—tremendous Arty and Air superiority—plus this murderous terrain. That is the big thing—this ramparted hedgerow terrain. That is what is nailing us down. Lt Col Herb Hauge, Asst G-2, told me they had made a study of German tactics and terrain, and the method recommended to use in attack [was] as follows:

1 Platoon Inf. 1 Alligator—tank with special, thick frontal piece to push hole through hedgerow.

60 and 81mm mortars. Mortars to blanket hedgerow with white phosphorous, and tank to rake hedgerow with HMG [heavy machine gun]. Then to attack with Platoon while meanwhile mortars lift fire and interdict next hedgerow where enemy mortars usually are located.

Visited Montbourg [Montebourg] which is as flat as La Haye-du-Puits, St. Sauveur-le-Vicomte, Pont l'Abbé, Valognes and others pounded to rubble.

Monday, July 24, 1944: At briefing this morning, apropos 90th Inf attack yesterday, Patton remarked—"That was very bad. Couldn't have been done worse. I understand some people are going to be tried for that. Personally, I think they ought to be shot." Heard that when 4th Armd Div moved into V Corps line last week, their CP was raided by one Co[mpany] of Germans who infiltrated through our lines and inflicted 30 casualties. Weather clearing and COBRA about a week late supposed to start tomorrow.

Editor's note: On July 25 the 2nd Canadian Corps launched Operation Spring to seize Verrières Ridge to keep the panzer divisions from moving against Cobra.

Tuesday, July 25, 1944: Several hundred P-47s with 500-lb bombs went over around 1200B. Heard later they missed the target. Also that there were a number of shorts among our troops—4th Armd—with 50 casualties. Report of Brig Gen W. M. Hoge,[64] Hq E+ of O, OCE [Office of the Chief Engineer] 12 July, transmitted by Lt Col Roger L. Morris,[65] Chief, Info[rmation] Section OCR. Report in nature of an "interview" with Hoge, on OMAHA beach. For initial removal of underwater obstacles had special force under command of Lt Col [John T.] O'Neil,[66] CE [chief engineer], of 146 and 299 Eng[ineer] Combat Bn, plus two Naval Demolition units about same size as an Army [battalion]. Force landed D+3 minutes and in three hours, as per previous schedule, had cleared six lanes. Arty and small arms fire caused 42 percent casualties. Despite this, by D+2, had beach reasonably cleared of mines and obstacles. Much confusion resulted trying to locate ships and specific cargoes. The special Brigade Group brought its manifests for first three days and other manifests were to be brought by fast boats, but they did not arrive. In fact, some manifests were found days later in British area. The Navy had no definite information on where ships were and could not locate them. Craft requested by Army Brigade Group. The plan was for an NOYC [NOIC—naval officer in charge] to be in charge of all naval activities on land, including repair and salvage, placing ships in position and ferry craft. The NOIC did not arrive until D+2 at Genl Hoge's Hq and then

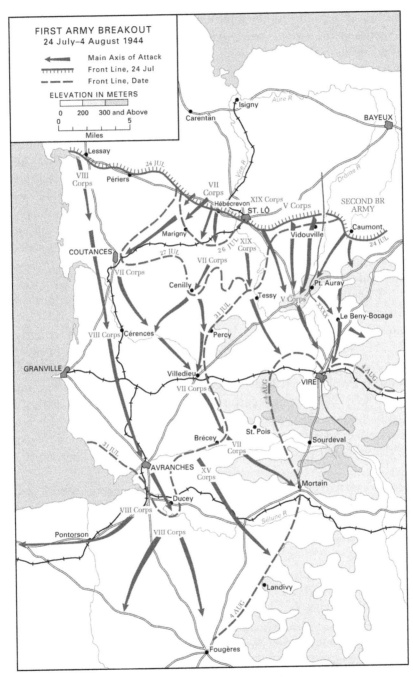

Breakthrough, July 24–August 4, 1944 (Center for Military History, Washington, DC)

was not able to furnish the information needed to coordinate the Navy activities in line with the needs of the Army Brigade Group. Genl Hoge is of the opinion that the division of responsibility between the Army and Navy as it presently operates is unsound. The naval part of the unloading operations was handled in such an unsatisfactory manner from the standpoint of the Army's needs that it was necessary to reorganize the NOIC set-up at about D+3. The failure of the NOIC set-up, and the failure to receive accurate information on ship arrivals and other manifests were most serious shortcomings during the early operations of OMAHA Beach. However, despite difficulties, unusually strong enemy resistance, storms—beach operation was within 20 percent of plans by D+20 with maximum daily tonnage of 15,000 tons. This caustic report confirms reports we heard of chaos and confusion in handling of shipping and unloading. The Navy CO of this Theater—if I am correct—is that drooling old incompetent Admiral [Harold R.] "Batty" Start [Stark],[67] whom they had to kick out when they brought in King.

Wednesday, July 26, 1944: Told us we might go operational in a few days. Zones extending North—Vessay to Carentan; South—Carentan to Mortain; West—_____ below Selune River to south of Avranches. Toughest kind of Bocage country. TUSA to have three Corps of two Inf and one Armored Divs each and to attack with two Corps abreast southward to clean out remainder of Cotentin to line Avranches–Mortain— our original LD [line of departure], which was to have been reached by D+20. It is now D+52 and our line is at about D+15. Worked with Situation Section all night turning out our first Estimate of Situation (No. 6)[68] in the field, EEI [essential elements of information] and a terrain study (tactical) of the area.

Thursday, July 27, 1944: Acting G-2. Koch sick again with stomach ailment. Ordered to Cherbourg for few days rest. Took Carter with him, so I am running the show. Estimate and TTA [tactical terrain analysis] approved. Told that our going operational depends on success of COBRA now underway. If it goes we continue to wait until the Avranches line is reached. If plan bogs down, TUSA moves into the picture. Strictest secrecy enjoined about our plans, as told that TUSA knows nothing about them. TUSA may not, but Bradley does as Patton sent him a letter outlining our plan. Also, Bradley now C/G of Twelfth Army Group, which replaces FUSAG in the field as Hq of First and Third U.S. Armies. Apparently, new FUSAG Staff will be set up in London under [Lieutenant General Lesley James] McNair[69] or someone else. We hear McNair is now over in the UK, either as commanding general of ETOUSA or as commanding general FUSAG. How Twelfth Army Group [was] concocted is still a mystery. Also what [is] in it is unknown—1 and 3 or 3 and 9, or what? Also, not Twelfth U.S. Army Group, but just Twelfth. Also heard CP may move to vicinity La Haye-du-Puits. Also, got details of bombing of our own troops North West vicinity Peries [Périers] yesterday. Over 3,000 heavies took part in a close support of ground attack. First of its kind and highly experimental. Pulled back about one mile but apparently not enough. Two groups dropped their loads—total about 150 tons—on our lines in 9th Armd Div zone and about 150 of our men were killed and 500–600 wounded. Only two out of about 20 groups did this—which they explain was due to practice of heavies of bombing center of impact and smoke line. First bombs created lots of dust and smoke which a wind blew toward our lines. Two groups bombed smoke and as a result unloaded on 9th Armd. Why in hell if this is so experimental, ground officers from 9th did not brief pilots and they were not given more explicit instructions is hard to understand. Anyway, as a result of the casualties, one Regiment had to reorganize and didn't get underway until 1½ hours after schedule.

Friday, July 28, 1944: ULTRA—Fliegerkorps IX[70] complained about German bombers hitting their own troops. Also reported Allied Air had 60–90 jet and/or rocket-propelled planes in operation. Told that the ANVIL Operation is in the works. Scheduled for D+90. That a number of Divs in Italy are being pulled out of the line in preparation for the attack and that large U.S. Naval forces are assembling in the Mediterranean for the operation.

Saturday, July 29, 1944: Informed we would move in a day or so south. COBRA beginning to roll—VIII Corps took Coutances and VII Corps is hammering south of St. Lô. 101st and 82d Airborne Divs now back in UK for reorganization. Counting them, 23 Divs—U.S. and British—landed in Normandy.

Sunday, July 30, 1944: We move south tomorrow and go operational 1200B, 1 August. Mission of TUSA—seize Brittany and capture Brest and other Brittany ports. Two Corps initially—VIII and XV, with XX in reserve. XII not yet in picture—although over here. VIII to go West and take Brest. XIV [XV] South West to seize Quiberon Bay and Nantes. Shifted Major G. Swanson to G-2 Air and made Major Ed[ward J.] Schmuck[71] chief of Situation Section.

Monday, July 31, 1944: Moved to vicinity Coutances—again in apple orchard. Beautiful day but roads very congested and very dusty. COBRA still rolling. Armor has crossings over Selune River south of Avranches,

4th Armored in van. Told that Patton has actually been racing VIII Corps for over a week and is responsible for pushing armored outfits ahead.

After briefing this morning Patton rose and said, "We go operational tomorrow noon. Doubtless will be some complaints about pushing people too hard. I believe in the old and sound axiom that an ounce of sweat is worth a gallon of blood. One thing we must remember: The harder we push, the more Germans we kill and the sooner the war will be over. And we must forget this business of always worrying about flanks. We have to guard our flanks, but not to the extent that we don't do anything else. Some goddamned fool once said you have to protect flanks and some son-of-a-bitch since has been going crazy guarding his flanks. I don't want to get any messages 'I am holding position.' We are not holding anything. Let the Germans do that. We are advancing and are not interested in holding. We have to push to keep advancing and we are going to advance. Frederick the Great said—'Audacious, audacious, always audacious.' That's what we want to be, always audacious." Then with amused smile he concluded: "Want to thank you for your work. You performed very well doing nothing. Want you to do just as good doing something."

What a goddamned habit-ridden institution the army is, after all. Here the U.S. Army is the most mobile and motor minded in the world, yet our CP is in a tent—old behemoths that have to be put up and taken down laboriously by hand every time we move. Takes hours, wears out our clerks and draftsmen, and clogs and delays operations. Whereas, if we had a couple of big vans, we could set up permanent offices, slap up sides and roll without delay and set up in a few minutes without delay. Air has that; but Army, with tens of thousands of every kind of vehicle, including tank, GATOR, trucks, jeeps, etc, doesn't. Screwy, doesn't make sense, but still going on and no one in the Army doing a thing about it. Told Koch about it, and he made no comment.

3

Third Army Enters the Fight

Tuesday, August 1, 1944: TUSA finally entered the war at 1200 noon. Heard Patton told chief of Section this morning, "There is very little in front of us and we must keep going hard. The Germans are groggy and we want to keep them that way. Not give him a chance to catch his breath and balance." We are operational, but no announcement will be made of that. They want Germans to announce that another Army is in the field, headed by Patton. Twelfth Army Group is our next higher Command. Bradley C/G. Don't know yet who C/G of FUSA is. First operation message is a captured map showing defenses of Rennes.

Wednesday, August 2, 1944: VIII Corps outfits 4th & 6th Armored Divs spreading out into Brittany Peninsula. Nearing Rennes. Alerted CP will be moved tomorrow South to Les Meavil de Rouges, just North of Avranches. PW evacuated to UK—29 July—62,695.

Thursday, August 3, 1944: On way to new CP saw scores of German MT and horse drawn transport burned out on the side of roads by our Air when Nazis pushed through Avranches bottleneck. New CP in ferny dell. Hell of a day, tied up on road for hours because of messed up movement order. We were supposed not to move before 90th Div going South had cleared CC 7. Instead, we were ordered to shove off at 0900, and 1½ miles from camp were held up on road for two hours. Hell of a mess that if some non-Reg had committed would have meant his head.

Friday, August 4, 1944: Our troops are South of Rennes and approaching St. Malo. Naval group from Cherbourg, on report from BBC radio that St. Malo had fallen and without authority from TUSA or checking with us, shoved off to enter St. Malo. At dock in St. Malo Peninsula they were ambushed and after two hours were extricated by TD [tank destroyers] which had been summoned to rescue them. Captain [N. S.] Ives,[1] NOIC, CO of group, and a number of others killed and wounded—all wholly and totally unnecessary. Pure stupidity and criminal incompetence. Navy has Ln O with us; could have had the informa-

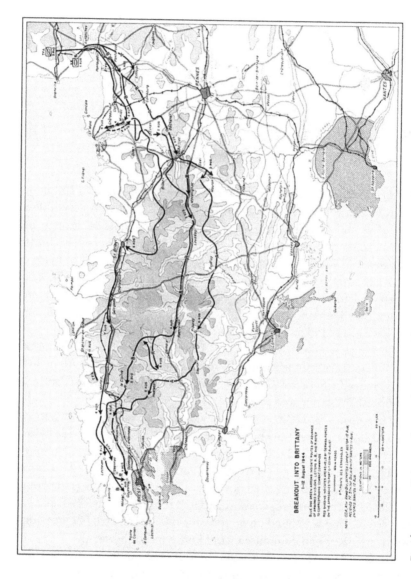

Breakout into Brittany, August 1–12, 1944 (Center for Military History, Washington, DC)

tion in a few minutes by calling us. Instead, barged out on own and a number of men were needlessly killed and wounded.

Saturday, August 5, 1944: Went to Granville on way back from PW cage near Avranches. Little port town; interesting view from hillside down on harbor in dusk, just as it was turning dark and moon beginning to come up. Upon return saw German air attack on Avranches and flaming rocket-like flash across sky into ground—plane shot down in flames.

Sunday, August 6, 1944: At 2400 hours 7 August, major offensive launched by all Allied armies against Germans. Third Army objective—Le Mans-Angers. Then TUSA will occupy Angers and prepare to move East and protect right flank of invasion. Patton was jubilant at the announcement yesterday that Brest had been taken but it turns out to have been quite a bit off. Actually, 6th Armd CCs [Combat Commands] were 15–20 miles from town. Personally, I predict it will be a hard fight to take the town. We now know the missing 2 Para Div[2] went West and not North, and is probably in the city. Also, it is even more heavily fortified than Cherbourg and the garrison is of at least 10,000 Naval troops. Further, it is all to the Germans' advantage that the port be defended and denied to us as long as possible. Same true of Lorient, Nantes, and St. Nazaire.

Spectacular German air raid in the vicinity of our bivouac at around 2400. Dropped numerous flares in strings and clusters, made runs, but not all flares were bombed. Considerable AA fire. At first it looked like they were aiming at us and if they had been and we'd been plastered, may have been some casualties as few slit trenches were dug. But apparently they were after an ammo dump several miles away, which was hit by the last string and set off a bursting fire for hours. Nazis either have Tac Photo or ground agents. Anyway, very exciting show to watch.

Monday, August 7, 1944: Alerted to move CP again south of Avranches, halfway to Fougeres [Fougères]. Nazi planes came back again but not near us. Attacked PW cage near Avranches, killing a number of PW (16) and some (2) of our guards. Cage fully lit up as required by Geneva Convention, but was attacked notwithstanding. Very amazing outrage. Saw the attack from our camp, 10 miles away. Like last night, they dropped flares and then made runs. Lt [John P.] Dieter[3] returned and a Lt [William J.] Dunkerle [Dunkerley],[4] ex–Los Angeles C of C employee, joined Situation Subsection on trial. This ought to help in relieving terrific pressure. Schmuck folded for awhile and I had to run the Sit Sec.

Got out our first International Annex and Weekly Periodic Report. Both very nice looking jobs. St. Malo still holding out. 83rd Inf Div

Reinf[orced] slowly reducing opposition but it is taking time. Tommy[5] doubtless badly mauled by Air and Arty by now. St. Brieuc taken by Task Force A (Genl Earnest[6] group) without trouble, but in Brest, Lorient and Nantes strong opposition appears to be organizing. Lot of snipers and harassing groups of Nazis and OSS troops roving about in interior of Brittany. Mopping up job badly needed but we are moving too fast to stop for that now. Local French doing a considerable job along that line.

Tuesday, August 8, 1944: Moved again to vicinity of Poilley, this time in a sandy and dusty wheat field. Score so far: 2 apple orchards, one ferny dell, one sun-baked dusty wheat field.

ULTRA—22 July—Jap Naval attaché[7] in Berlin reported that London was to continue to be the main flying bomb target. Also still not possible to use V-1 yet against beaches or [Allied] forces. V-2 will be ready operationally in two–three months. Also said he was told V-2 was more accurate than V-1 and would be used against ports.[8] Conferences, Hitler, Kesselring, [Admiral Karl] Doenitz,[9] CO Navy, 9 July—agreed that strategy on all fronts was to gain time. Every kilometer to be defended to the last as a few months may be decisive. Time needed to restore equilibrium of forces, especially Air. Production excellent in tanks and AT [antitank] guns. Assaults expected of flying bombs, long-range rockets and new-type U-boats. 31 July—Doenitz stated that he expected an attack on the Mediterranean coast any time. Four cruisers, many landing craft and concentration of tanks observed in Corsica. Jap Ambassador reported [Joachim von] Ribbentrop[10] told him a counterattack in Brittany would be too costly at this time. Mission (main) was to stabilize East front. Reinforcements were going there and Germany would soon take the offensive there. Jap Ambassador also reported a plan to be considered of attempting a separate peace with Britain or Russia, but Hitler balked on grounds that it would mean Germany admitted defeat. Jap thought Allied attack in Pas de Calais area still likely in August and that defeats in Italy were due to Allied Air superiority. GAF now has production priority. Oil production down 50 percent but will soon be upped to 80–90 percent. On 27 July, Jap Ambassador to Vichy[11] [government] reported that the Allies have 42–43 Divisions in Normandy against 17–18 German.

Wednesday, August 9, 1944: New plan of strategy for campaign. Not going East as originally planned, but turning North, up rear of German Army in Normandy, to destroy it by envelopment or by pushing it into Seine River. More air attacks at night, in Avranches area, where Germans are trying to drive a wedge in the Channel to sever our North and South columns. Have seen Nazi air raids every night now since last Sunday and Jerry planes have been over our CP every night. Have very distinct sound—not continuous like ours, but sort of sawash, sawash, like that.

ULTRA—11 Panzer Div force from Mediterranean coast now North of the Loire.[12] Also 49 Inf Div and 6 Para Div[13] are moving into Normandy against our exposed east flank. Patton at morning briefing said— "We are taking a chance, but will depend on your planes, [Otto P.] Weyland[14] (Brig Genl, C/G XIX TAC [Tactical Air Command]), to keep them off of us if they gang up on our East flank." Heard today that ANVIL now scheduled for 17–19 August. Hope it comes off soon. Help a lot on our front.

Thursday, August 10, 1944: XV Corps—*Hickory*[15]—given mission to drive North on axis Le Mans-Alençon-Sées, with objective area between Carrough [Courtomer]-Sées. Two divisions to make drive—2d French Armored on West, and 5th U.S. Armored on East. Direction of attack North West from Le Mans to West of Argentan. RCT of 79th Inf Div to cover East flank and is to jump off at noon today.

Col Koch told me that he is going to recommend me for promotion to full Colonel. Also "Bunny." He as G-2 Exec O, which he is not, and me as ARCO, which I am not. I am the Exec, and have been for several months now. Bunny has never been and couldn't be, and admits it. Also he has not been one year in grade. But he is a Koch favorite and Koch is pushing him at my expense. Bunny has GSC rating which belongs to me. Koch's recommendation for me on that was turned down on ground that all vacancies in G-2 were filled. Which is true. Bunny is filling one I should have. Koch told me Bunny offered to turn his in but Koch said he would make another try for me. Be interesting to see what happens on the promotion. Yes, sir!!

Saturday, August 12, 1944: More ULTRA—Rushing reinforcements from Pas de Calais and East of Loire into area of our exposed Right flank.[16] Hickory [XV Corps] advanced about 30 miles to within about 10 miles of Alençon. Hard fighting in some spots, with 2d Armored (French) getting its blooding. Crossed Orne River and was counterattacked but beat it off. Alerted for another move—to Haras, about six miles from Laval. First we're going to visit Le Mans.

Sunday, August 13, 1944: At briefing this morning Patton, apropos the forming Argentan-Falaise pocket, answered the question on everyone's mind—why didn't clamp close. Patton remarked, "Once wrote thesis that traps should not be closed. Was a mistake to do that, contrary to popular belief. The wiser course is to leave an opening and then let the sons-of-bitches walk themselves to death."

Visited XV and XX Corps CPs. XX is in the vicinity of Laval; XV vicinity of Alençon. Laval beat up quite a bit. Le Mans is the largest town we have run into so far, little touched. Several bridges out and some houses on outskirts knocked up, but otherwise the town is untouched. Saw a lot of burned up German vehicles on roads, hit by Air, including some tanks. Also above Le Mans, five of our tanks of 2d French Armored Div, which I heard later were knocked out by 88mm when the tanks came up the road in line. Passed French going west and they were stopped at every hamlet being hailed as heroes. At XV Corps, they told me the Div was a terrific supply headache because they were constantly out of gas and rations, which they dished out with open hands to all comers along route of advance. Drove back to our CP—90 miles—blackout through 2 Divs going North and it was some ride—blacker than hell and all sorts of hectic driving.

Monday, August 14, 1944: Alerted to move again. St. Oren—near Le Mans. Hope it isn't another damned forest hole. Patton is some guy. Took off today in L-5 plane to fly to VIII Corps CP at Granville, taking chances of being popped off.

Tuesday, August 15, 1944: Moved to St. Oren. Convoy Comdr. Nice trip. Jerry planes over our CP last night. Report that our patrols are in vicinity of Paris. Third Army certainly making history while British are still PIVOTING ON CAEN and First Army piddling around. Whatever else he is, Patton has the drive and guts to sweep out and hammer away relentlessly at enemy. New CP is a very pleasant place in [a] meadow surrounded by hedgerows. Our set-up is very convenient. *Editor's note: 2nd Canadian Corps launched Operation Totalize on August 8 and Operation Tractable on August 14, all-out efforts to punch through to Falaise.*

Wednesday, August 16, 1944: Borders gave me three cases of liquor— one of Cointreaux, one of Benedictine, one of Martel Cognac. At Angers, once a chief U-boat Hq, we captured 9,000 cases of Cointreaux that was labelled for Wehrmacht use only. Not to be sold commercially. Borders' stuff didn't come from Angers.

Thursday, August 17, 1944: VIII Corps is having a hell of a time taking St. Malo; citadel, rock and reinforced concrete, holding out. [Major] Genl [Troy H.] Middleton, Corps C/G, told Patton he needed more than three Divs to mop up Brittany and to take Brest, Lorient, St. Nazaire, which enemy apparently intends to hold and deny us as long as they can. Heard we had 2,000 casualties trying to take St. Malo. Costly business. Argentan-Falaise pocket closing up as 5th Inf [Div] and 2d French

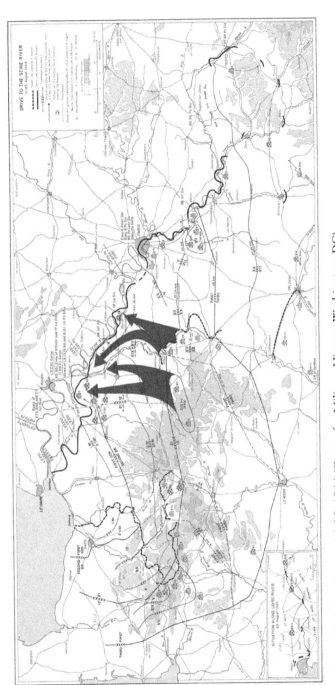

Drive to the Seine, August 16–25, 1944 (Center for Military History, Washington, DC)

Armored push forward toward Sées. Heard Canadians lost a regiment of tanks in vicinity of Falaise in attack toward Argentan.[17]

Friday, August 18, 1944: Genl Spong [Karl Spang],[18] CG 275th [266th] Inf Div,[19] captured in Brittany, brought to CP and interrogated by Patton and Koch. The interpreter was a Jewish Lt Herman, very smart and snappy O. Spang had dinner with Patton, but at a separate table. Asked for sleeping powder. Patton told him he had captured a number of German general Os, but never one under such circumstances—all alone. Spang interpreted this as a reflection on his honor and replied he had fought to last bullet, then bared breast to attack; when unharmed, left car and took to hiking to Brest. Next day was surprised by U.S. Armored (6th) troops and captured. *Our* troops reported in Versailles.

Saturday, August 19, 1944: ANVIL broke today. Ought to be nothing more than premonths [preliminaries] as Germans don't have more than 4–5 Divs down there. New plan—XV Corps to go North up Seine to Mantes, Casicourt—a major enemy bridgehead—after taking it, move up to Louviers and establish a bridgehead for us across river. Purpose is to create another pocket with Seine as restraining wall. Also to prepare for next phase of operations East of Seine. British to move up coast against Pas de Calais.

Heard Genl Montgomery asked for 15 U.S. Divs to reinforce his British & Canadian armies. Same old stuff—British still PIVOTING ON CAEN. Certainly a lot of feeling about them all through U.S. ranks. They are all over our area but won't allow us even to have a Ln O. Heard story that while enroute to this CP, Patton passed British-driven trucks, stopped and demanded—"Who are you, what are you doing, and where are you going?" Told him they were transporting ammunition for U.S. forces, apparently because there is not enough for British to do as they have only a small area to cover while we are so spread out we haven't enough transportation. Montgomery's request for 15 U.S. Divs turned down—because we don't have them to give—and instead Ninth U.S. Army, which is lolling around at Bristol, will become operational with XV Corps. FUSA and TUSA South of Paris, with latter on Loire, but not south of it. 2d French [Armd Div] to pass to First Army. Both XV Corps Hq and 2d French—both good riddance. First is a lousy outfit, from C/G "Ham Haislip" on down, and French are messy. French designated to "take" Paris, although they had no more to do with that than a hoot owl. But will be good politics. Patton remarked when he heard it—"They'll sit in Paris and be no goddamned good after that." Provisional Corps set-up—Gaffey commander—to take Dreux-Chartres line.

Germans hammering away at these points, also Argentan, to keep jaws of gap open. Long Range Plan—Advance on Metz. TUSA objective—three bridges over Seine at Melun, Montereaux, Sens—preliminary to further movement to Z (Germany).

Sunday, August 20, 1944: Moved today to new CP—woods in vicinity of Bron. Bright, sunny, beautiful August day. Just before we pulled out, Patton, bareheaded and hands in pocket, sauntered over to where I was standing watching trucks loading, and with smile said—"Allen, guess you will have lots to write about after this is all over." I evaded the question and asked him one—"Why we didn't take Paris? Why were we held back from pushing across River eastward as nothing to stop us if we moved fast and were given enough troops." Patton replied—"We don't want Paris. Minute we take it, we have to start feeding them and we have our hands full feeding our troops. Supply is one hell of a problem, extended as we are, and with only one port open to us so far. The thing we ought to do is bypass Paris and keep after the German Army, killing as many as we can and running the rest to death. Paris isn't the real capital of France right now and there is no political advantage in our taking it."

Marvelous trip through lovely rolling countryside to new CP. Sunday afternoon and all the people out. Many showered us with delicious pears—wonderful tasting—eggs, apples, and offered drinks of wine and cider. We traded cigarettes for fruit and tomatoes, and I even got a cucumber. Was convoy commander so I took it easy—gave kids a chance to get stuff and enjoy the trip—a very happy interlude that we all needed and enjoyed. Passed through a number of small towns, untouched, prosperous looking. Countryside certainly showed no sign of war or occupation—lot of fine looking cattle and horses. Saw first railroad train coming into Nogent La Rotognes [Nogent-le-Rotrou] west of LaFeste-Bernard [Le Ferté-Bernard]. Apparently was first train over the line for some time as had a U.S. guard detail, although crew seemed to be French. Just [s]ample of engines and several cars, all much used. Depot hit by Air but not badly damaged. New CP in another wood, but not as bad as the Heras (St. Oren) one.

Wednesday, August 23, 1944: ULTRA—Hitler ordered Paris reduced to rubble heap.[20] Awakened early by inquiry of what to do about group that came out of Paris under white flag to negotiate surrender terms, headed by Swedish Consulate. Included in party were several British agents posing as FFI. Also, learned later after partial interview with Patton—there was an Austrian Count, who is adjutant to the German General commanding Paris.[21] He declared Hitler had ordered Paris to be held up to 30 percent casualties and had taken the General's wife and daughter into custody to enforce this order. The General obviously had no stomach for a fight and wanted a show of force so he could quit. Group sent topside to 12 Army Group.

Friday, August 25, 1944: Paris taken, but troops that did it not really there. OSS, PW, press, all spare parts and goldbricks and hangers-on constituted chiefly the conquering columns and enjoyed the numerous delights of the occasion—wine, women and glory. Attack jumped off against Brest—preceded by heavy bomber attack.

Saturday, August 26, 1944: Gay—ended briefing, called attention to fact that crime wave was rampant with negroes heading list with rape, murder and robbery. Directed special staff sections, especially QM [Quartermaster], Engr, Sig, to act to crack down on their units. "You all know who I mean, and act accordingly." *Editor's note: At this point, Allen writes, "(See scrap notes.)," and the journal has a significant gap from August 27 to October 17.*

4

The Lorraine Campaign

Editor's note: Patton initiated operations in Lorraine on September 5. Attempts by XX Corps to capture Metz failed. On September 18 4th Armored Division was attacked by elements of Hasso von Manteuffel's Fifth Panzer Army. On September 25 Eisenhower and Bradley halted Third Army, and Patton passed over to the defensive for almost six weeks. During this period Patton unsuccessfully attacked Fort Driant. He would not begin full-scale offensive operations again until November 8. Allen's G-2 Estimate No. 10, published on August 28, and his Target Area Analysis No. 12, issued on October 5, dealt with routes into Germany.

Wednesday, October 18, 1944: Genl [Hans] Eberbach,[1] one of the PW generals, and son, also PW, brought together and dictaphoned. Eberbach complained bitterly about Hitler's constant interference in the West and put the blame for the debacle on this. Said got so bad, generals got together, got hold of Sepp Dietrich,[2] SS Genl, and persuaded him to undertake a trip to Hitler on the matter. But effort abortive because Hitler met him with big hoopla, promotion and decorations, and Dietrich returned without accomplishing his mission.

Since D-Day dropped: 8,001,682 S, [and] 12,567,245 O.[3]

Thursday, October 19, 1944: Every day since we pulled out of Fort Driant[4] Parks [Patton][5] asks Weyland what about that revenge bombing. Like Cato, he doesn't forget. Weyland says request made to Bomber Command,[6] but not approved yet. Patton tells him to keep after them. Patton in expansive mood at special briefing. Said, "Got another clip holster. Going to keep this one. Makes 14. Gave all others away. One to [His Majesty the] King.[7] Sure is dull bastard. Wasn't for his equery, but completely dumb. Didn't know what to do with holster." Philippine invasion[8] broke today—as Marshall said it would.

Friday, October 20, 1944: Called to Patton's office and gave Estimate of Situation to him and [Major] General [Manton S.] Eddy,[9] XII

71

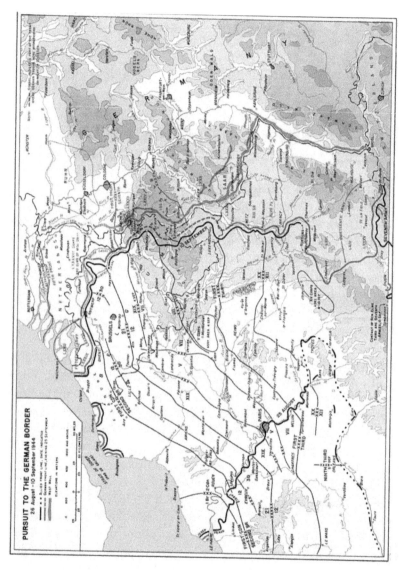

Pursuit to the German Border (Center for Military History, Washington, DC)

Corps CG. Eddy said—"Guess get my PA [Public Affairs] ready to go up on lines in about a week and give Bosche a shot of propaganda." Patton—might be advisable not to wait a week. Decision reached at this meeting to bomb down in the vicinity of the Dienz [Dieuze] dam[10] so the water runs out before we jump off. Also to flood area to keep Germans from using it as troop and tank concentration area, which they are doing. Weyland announced today that Bomber Command approved the Driant show—after personal visit by Major-General [Hoyt S.] Vandenberg[11]— slender, youngish, lean-faced, very handsome.

Sunday, October 22, 1944: Dam successfully bombed. TAC/R [Tactical Reconnaissance] shows water spreading—low gradient so not a flood, but it's moving all right. Lot of AA, showing importance the Germans attached to the dam, but no planes down. First good bombing day, with new bomb never used before in the West—only 1600 lbs, but terrific velocity because it has a rocket device that begins to operate after bomb released. Has 50-foot penetrating power.

III U.S. Corps—from West Coast—commanded by [Major] Genl [John] Milligan [Millikin],[12] reported. Briefed staff and I gave Sig[nificant] facts and capabilities, after which Patton made brief talk: "We have our own staff methods. Don't become desk bound—G-2/G-4 must get out and see what is going on up front. Don't overwork. No good if groggy. Make EM take care of themselves. Watch trench feet. Make dry socks and clothes. If we let them alone, they fall asleep in wet clothes. Got to make them dry. Was up on lines and Regt CO told me had no way to dry men's clothes. We were in a room so goddamned hot it would have dried all clothes in his Regt in a couple hours. Don't tell me it can't be done— always find a way. Cellar of house, couple stores, wires."

95th Inf—[Major] Genl Harry Twaddle[13] and [John E.] Jack Carter,[14] G-2—now in line. Also 26th Inf Div—reliefs for 5th U.S. Inf and 6th Armored Divs. Brig Genl [Benjamin O.] Davis[15]—negro General—visited Patton who brought him to briefing. Then he left while we put on special briefing for III Corps. Stiller later told me a story of an incident a couple days ago on the road. Patton stopped by halted column. Dashed up to front. Found 14-ton van driven by negro down with a bad tire. Told negro to drive the car off the road through a fence, then bawled him out for stopping the vehicle on the road and holding up movement. Two hours later went by on way back. Van neatly parked off road and tire repaired. Stopped and praised driver and wound up—"When you drove through that fence, best piece of driving I'd seen in long time." Old politician—left negro beaming from ear to ear.

First buzz-bomb reported in Third Army area—few miles out of Nancy. Later in day reports of three more further North.

Monday, October 23, 1944: Saw today Twelfth Army Group directive dated 21 October: 21 Army Group—clear Meuse-Venlo area & seaward to Antwerp. Sixth Army Group—seize Belfort and secure crossing over Rhine in vicinity Strasbourg. 12 Army Group—regroup and prepare for an advance by all three armies to Rhine. Target dates—FUSA and NUSA—5 Nov. TUSA—10 Nov—Mainz-Worms.

26th Infantry Div—South sector of XII Corps zone—got very bloody nose in first operation. Apparently all due to incompetence of Bn and Regt COs. Division claiming big victory in its limited objective attack to take Bezange-la-Petite and Moncourt South East of St. Dieuze. Real story is—104th Regt, which conducted operation, got a pasting. CO 2d Bn, which was supposed to take hill dominating Bezange would not order artillery barrage—pre-arranged—because of fear of killing men of platoon that had got to edge of town. Result was that the Platoon was wiped out and the Regt had over 200 casualties because of the failure to get Arty support that was ready and waiting to give it. Finally, as getting dark, called for six tanks, but they wouldn't go up because of the danger of being knocked out. GIs swell in the outfit, but bn and regt leaders, and apparently, Div, too, are very sour.

Hq got an "allotment" of Croix de Guerres and Legion of Honor decorations. G-2 Section allotted two, and Col Koch ruled I was to get one and another to an EM. Arcade[16] was chosen on my recommendation. Allotment of Croix de Guerres is to Divs on basis of so many days of combat and to staffs on something similar. One per 14,000 men. Seems decorations are dished out on that basis—10 percent of an outfit or something like that. Vive le Glorie.

New Units—at Marseilles—100 Inf Div, 103 Inf Div, 14 Armd Div. In UK—99 Inf Div, 11–12 Armd Divs. In U.S.—assigned to ETO: Infantry, 78, 66, 42, 87, 76, 89, 106, 63, 65, 75, 70, 71, 69, 10. Armored, 8, 13, 20, 16. XXI Corps.

Tuesday, October 24, 1944: Today is D+140. Shelled last night by the Germans' 280mm RR [railroad] guns in our zone. Sixteen rounds landed in Nancy on line with XII Corps CP, the RR station, bridge and yards and our compound. Four rounds within a block of THIERS hotel and one close to Patton's villa and broke amber windows. Firing lasted from 0300 to 0500. Line of fire of guns very good as chart we made up shows. Only one round off, and it was not very far. First big shelling since we arrived. Several small ones before. Last Friday night, XX Corps CP at

Conflans got same kind of pasting we had last night. We had no casualties; they had a couple.

MP at Patton's place wounded in the back by splinter of the shell that landed near there. One round a dud, landed in courtyard of 12 Evacuation Hospital, few blocks away from our compound and where Colonel Koch is now with bad throat and his old stomach trouble.

The two German PW captured by 90th Div some weeks ago in civilian clothes—while making a night patrol—have been tried, found guilty of being spies and sentenced to be shot. Papers signed by Patton today.

New dope indicates that big gun shooting last night was aimed at Patton's billet. Develops now one round landed 25 yards from his house, another 35 and third 50. One splinter lodged in the wall of Gay's room, and wall moulding knocked off in Patton's room. Our RI [radio interception] picked up some coordinates from low grade code German Bty [battery] is using. Also sound and flash. XII Corps got 10 digit coordinate as a result of the shooting. Also at 1130 from RI it was known the gun was being set up for firing. Takes 2½ hours to mount gun. Patton very jovial at special briefing. Kidded Weyland, "You'd better get busy or I'll make you change billets." When first shell landed in Patton's billet, MP rushed to his room. He was up. After asking if there was anything he could do, MP said he was going to help people in a nearby house which was hit. Patton said he would go along and did. Blast of shell knocked six MP sentries down, but only one—splinter in back—slightly hurt.

Wednesday, October 25, 1944: Date of TUSA drive moved up to 5 November from 10 November. General Lee, ETOUSA, visited today. Put on a lot of dog for him—band, MP Platoon. They don't like him and he probably knows it, so put on a lot of show. Also to try to work him for more supplies for offensive. Patton asked me to get up a comparison of German casualties in the St. Mihiel and Meuse-Argonne [battles][17] and TUSA campaign in September. "I think you'll find we are just a bunch of amateurs. They were wholesalers. We captured and killed thousands. They tens of thousands." Captain Robinson[18]—former ADC [aide-de-camp]—says Lee loves having a lot of dog and show put on for him. (Marshall won't allow it). Also that Lee is called *Lt. Jesus Christ Himself Lee*. Lee—short, zoot-suited, para boots, went for ceremony in a big way. Inspected MP Guard of Honor, saluted flags, etc. Patton standing off to side under tree, rocked on his heels. Attired in boots and whipcord breeches.

Thursday, October 26, 1944: 761 Tk Bn,[19] one of the few negro tank units, on its way to Third Army. Boys call them "asterisk" or "midnight" fighters. Visited flooded area vicinity of Château Salins and CP 137 Regt,

35 Div. Some firing by SP guns and one of our 240mm guns that has been emplaced to go after German 280mm (11 inch) when it opens up again. Been quiet since it plastered Nancy. We have a number of coordinates and are ready to nail it when it opens up. Russians in Norway in force. Jap fleet badly mauled in Pacific. We continue to sit with very little in our front, and that is junk. My estimate this week is about 30,000 mostly low-grade units. Our front is wide open for an offensive but we are still sitting.

Friday, October 27, 1944: Ninth Army adopted my idea of photo-[graphic] Sit Map and distributing with PR [photo reconnaissance] instead of overlay. Typically, sloppy job of photography and drafting. Col [Thomas H.] Nikson [Nixon],[20] Ord[nance], and Col [John F.] Conklin,[21] Engr—two goddamnedest ball polishers in Hq. Always scurrying to Patton to claim credit and show what they are doing. Conklin claimed all credit this morning for breaking the coordinate code on 280[mm] RR gun OP [observation post]—which are on hill tops within our lines—four of them. Never said a word about the fact that we supplied data from RI and we are the ones who got captured German maps. Or that it was RI code personnel that broke German code. Conklin claimed whole credit.

Patton very interested in weather. "Organize patrols and go up and kill every male on those hills. Kill them all. Wait until get 40 minute alert and then nail them." I suggested it would be desirable to get a few PW from them. Valuable information might be obtained about guns, location, operation. "All right, we'll get you some PW"—with grin. Later to me—"Sit down Allen. You will get flat feet standing so much." Nixon brought in map from Hermann Goering steel plant[22] South of Thionville showing names of local collaborators. Should have gone to us direct. Instead, showed it to Patton, who called me over to handle matter. Said glad to have information, but we had very large lists already prepared and had been working on CI [counterintelligence] matters for months. Nixon didn't like the jab but couldn't say anything.

Saturday, October 28, 1944: V-1 (Buzz-bomb) went over Nancy at 0715 this morning and hit about three miles due south. I reported this to Patton at special briefing. Later, at regular briefing, question was raised and Colonel Nixon, ball-polishing and boot-licking Ord—burped up, "Not V-bomb. Didn't sound like it." Patton and Gay turned around and laughed at him. Patton said—"How would you know? You weren't up then." Captured two renegade Frenchmen who dropped the night before in the vicinity of Étain with radio to report on our tank movements from Verdun. Dropped from plane that departed from field in the vicinity of Aschaffenburg, 40 miles North East of Merzig, that fly at night to supply garrisons on Channel Islands (319) and besieged ports. According to one of the agents, Germans have regular service. Also got report from XX Corps of capture of three pigeons with German messages in code—confirming reports that Germans have pigeon lofts in our rear which are used by agents to send information.

Germans have new sub device called SCHNORBEL [Schnorkel]—an air tube that projects above water like periscope and when erected U-boat is able to charge batteries and ventilate while submerged. Enables subs to remain under water much longer and reduces time to have to be on surface and subject to air attacks. Apparently been very effective, although sub operations have been sharply curbed by loss of French bases. Forced to use Norwegian [bases] now under Russian attack. Germans now putting out pre-fabricated subs in some quantity. Spain border getting increasingly hot. Loyalists in France and Red French (Maquis) raiding Spanish [areas] and had some sharp encounters. ULTRA—report [Francisco] Franco's[23] Ambassador in London asked British to communicate protest to [Charles] De Gaulle.[24] He rejected a demand to allow them to cross the French border. Said would police own border. Here's hoping this is the beginning of the end for Franco's regime.

Sunday, October 29, 1944: Sat in on staff conference in Colonel Maddox's office on Plan of Operations for our new attack. Double envelopment of Metz by XX Corps; smash to Siegfried Line[25] by XII Corps—along routes outlined in my terrain study. 90th Inf Div to make "Demonstration" opposite Metz to nail troops in that area down. Plan is for FUSA to jump off first and we follow one day later. FUSA D-day dependent on 21 Army Group plans. Five days to a week after we go, 6 Army Group jumps off. Preceding our offensive, plan is to beat up two South Metz forts that flank XII Corps. Also 83d Inf Div of FUSA to aid XV [XX] Corps by establishing a bridgehead over Moselle North of Thionville.

Monday, October 30, 1944: Patton talked very sharply to Weyland about his failure to get detailed data to Bomber Command on Metz forts. "That's a big failure. Want that remedied at once." Patton still pressing for REVENGE bombing of Metz forts. Keeps on pressuring for it every day. Great field commander but serious weakness. Lack of strong personal staff—Codman—socialite, goldbrick, lazy, doesn't know anything and interested only in fixing himself up for after the war. Gaffey—incoherent, arbitrary, sputtery. Not a very good tactician or organizer.

Gay—strong, but interested in details like uniforms, billeting, promotions—on which [he] had very old Regular Army views—only seniority. [Colonel Paul D.] Harkins[26]—good tactician and pretty decent. Better organizer and manager than Gay or Gaffey, but still no ball of fire. Average ability. Patton's big weakness—never looks into staff affairs. Lets Gaffey, Gay run it entirely, with result that there is no redress from their unfairness and foibles—except cases where section chiefs have guts to go over their heads and take issue direct to him. Very few dare do that. Koch is one of the last. Result—many unfair things happen. Conklin—got Bronze Star for [Daniel] Kennedy[27] by sounding off about breaking code on 280[mm] RR gun position when we and RI did whole thing. Nixon—a phony and pusher; another who circumvents Gay and Gaffey by sucking up to Patton and bootlicking. Maddox—puts up a fight and as result got for his section: 1 Colonel; 5 Lt Colonels; 3 majors in one month.

Tuesday, October 31, 1944: Last week out of some 20,000 shells we fired—10,700 were captured Germans' as against 10,400 of our own. Plans for our offensive continuing. Numerous conferences. Corps commanders met with Patton for big war council over plans and boundaries. Eddy (XII) and Walker (XX), one big tub of lard and other a little tub, had big row over boundary. Both are mediocrities. From PW and other sources, apparent that the Germans are facing grave oil shortages. Hearing ULTRA report that all training flights to be halted to conserve oil, Patton remarked, "That's what may win the war. Weyland, be sure to impress that on your Air people. Tell them to keep hammering at those bastard's oil supplies." Patton is displaying intense interest in the weather for next month. "If we can get a few good days at the right time, they can't stop us. We'll kill the sons-of-bitches on the run as we did across France."

Wednesday, November 1, 1944:

TUSA casualties 1 August to 1 November	
Killed	5,668
Wounded	28,019
Missing	5,372
Non-combat casualties	23,007
Total	62,066
Light tanks	156
Medium tanks	374
Vehicles, all types	1,656
Arty over 75mm	108
Enemy [casualties]	
PW	102,281
Buried	11,728
Light tanks	824
Medium tanks	445
Vehicles, all types	5,078
Arty over 75mm	751
Total German PW—D-Day to 26 October	633,400

Dope is that Antwerp should be cleared by end of the week and that it's ready to handle 21,000 tons of supplies daily at once and go up to 40,000 in a month. That should solve all supply problems and clear way for big final smash. Worked until 0200 on G-2 Estimate #10.[28] So far I've written every one turned out by us. Felt lousy; cold, sour stomach. Had to lash myself to dictate.

Thursday, November 2, 1944: Sat in on conference on Air targets. Eddy and XII Corps Division CGs. What a big worry wart he is. Most of Div CGs made much better impressions, and they all seem to be disgusted with him. Lot of palaver—with Patton in at end—that we jump off at 0900 hours on 8th, good weather or bad weather. Patton asked what the Heavy Bomber safety range was. When told 3,000 yards, said "Make it 4,000." Same on Mediums, 2,000—"make it 3,000 yards." "Worse effect on morale to bomb our own men than not to bomb at all. Rather attack without bombing if there is any danger of dropping on our men." Finished Estimate, and with practically no changes, Koch told me to have it published. Praised it several times as very superior job.

BIG CHANGE IN PLANS—Bradley here and after conference, we got word that Third Army leads new Allied offensive in West. D-day is November 5 up to November 8, depending on weather. Can jump off any day between 5–8 with full Air support, but regardless of weather, 8th is a must go. Up to 8th we get all Air that was to have gone to FUSA including 8th and 9th TAC. Change due to FUSA not being ready to go before 10th—and it is not ready apparently because its plans are built around British (21 Army Group). Anyway, the order now is—TUSA; FUSA—by 10 November; SIXTH Army Group—by 15 November. Corps CGs and Division CGs meeting on Air targets which I attended was due to this change in plans and our getting all Air up to 8th and possibly 10th Nov. Patton obviously highly elated and exhilarated by change in plans. In very buoyant and jovial mood. "Goddamn it, bet you we have good weather and get the best Air-Ground effort in the world." Chief topic of conference—how to mark targets so Heavies and Medium bombers do not bomb our troops. Patton very emphatic that no chances will be taken. For Heavies—raised minimum from 3,000 to 4,000 yards, and Mediums from 2,000 to 3,000 yards. "I want to make sure that bomb lines are out far enough so as to not hit our troops. I want to kill Germans; that's what we are bombing the SOBs for." Koch went to bat with Gay on my promotion issue on ground that seniority should be based on date of original commission—in my case, 1918—and not current rank. Far as I'm concerned, works out fine for me, although plan still disregards merit and T/O factors. Koch says Gay tentatively approved idea—but we'll see. Wager nothing comes of it. However, at least he is steamed up and I got him to make poll of views of section on promotion policy. At least he knows how we feel. Have heard nothing more on Koch's plan to recommend me for Croix de Guerre. Presumably, it went in. *Editor's note: Koch submitted the recommendation on October 20. See appendix C.* Did hear that G-1 got an allotment and that Matthews and [Lieutenant Colonel William A.] Horn[e][29] put themselves down for one each. Great heroes.

Friday, November 3, 1944: [Major George R.] Pfann[30] also told me that Koch's recommendation for a star has gone up to theater, and Ecklund told me that Maddox's and [Colonel Walter J.] Muller's[31] have been approved by Theater and have gone to Washington. Koch, Maddox and Muller—the three strong men of the staff. All top men and far superior to Gaffey, Gay and Harkins. They should have been Generals long ago. Patton has recommended them repeatedly, but never got by ETOUSA. Also heard that Macdonald's recommendation was sent by Theater.

Patton—at ULTRA briefing, suddenly asked—"How do you spell Gestapo?[32] I'm going to tell the troops to kill the SOBs. No prisoners from them, and we don't give a goddamn what some chicken-hearted people may say." When he said this, he walked up and down Gay-Harkins's office where ULTRA briefing was held, puffing on cigar, and wearing pearl-handled automatic in hip holster. "I'm going down to XII Corps to address the officers and I'm going to tell them to kill every goddamn Gestapo they find. To hell with taking them prisoners." As he said this, he shot a hard look at me, standing off to one side near the door. I said nothing, and neither did he. *Editor's note: Patton's overt declaration that he was willing to kill certain types of prisoners of war is a common theme. Allen returns to it again on December 19 and 22.*

Patton again mentions desire to bomb Metz forts Driant and Jeanne D'Arc.[33] Asked if Bomber Command now had all material for that, and when Weyland assured him they had, he expressed approval: "Now all we need is a day of good weather and then we'll blow those SOBs to hell. I certainly don't want to lose out on that." Good old CATO—here's hoping he gets the weather. Plan is to use the new type bombs on the forts and if they smack them, they'll wreck them. For some reason I haven't heard—though suspect it's FRENCH—we are laying off bombing or even heavily shelling Metz. A General [André Marie François] Doty [Dody][34] has been named by De Gaulle as Military Governor of Metz, and Dody has hot pants to take over the post. Has several times unofficially inquired about the matter. There is no doubt we could take Metz and defending forts if we wanted to concentrate a full effort on it— but cost would be foolish. Merely waste lives and material. Plan is to try and draw Germans out by double envelopment by XX Corps plus 90th Div demonstration, or if that doesn't bring them out, to contain the place by III Corps while we smash ahead.

After ULTRA briefing, Patton went to his office, but came into regular staff briefing shortly before it concluded. Then got up, took stance before big War Map and after taking puff from cigar and looking hard, said—"Third Army has been given the great honor to lead the new offensive. Our D-day starts on the 5th—depending on weather. I don't have to impress on you the vital necessity for complete secrecy. Enemy must not know our plans. Also, despite my talents for bullshit, I am unable to express my complete confidence that we will succeed in breaking through, and except possibly for a skirmish on the Rhine, we will go deep into Germany and end the war. Must make hard hitting and unremitting effort and to kill every German bastard between here and the Rhine. As I said, may be some skirmishing on the Siegfried Line, but we are going to break through to the Rhine and from there into the heart of Germany if that is necessary to win the war. We are going to win (clamping jaws and squinting eyes). Have absolutely no doubt about it. We are going to win and end the war." Then after glowering silence for a moment, relaxed, smiled, took draw of cigar and said—"Also, as a result of my intimate relations with God, I'm sure we'll have the good weather we need for a lucky jump-off." Everyone laughed, and he left smiling and rolling the cigar in his mouth.

General [Edwin] Seibert [Sibert],[35] G-2, 12 Army Group, told us today that he got word that Germans organizing 2 Bns of men who lived in U.S. and talk U.S. for special terroristic operations behind our lines— like blowing up General's quarters, dumps, etc. Plenty of evidence they have that capability. One three-man patrol captured by 5th Infantry Division North of Metz consisted of one *SS* officer, one *Wehrmacht* officer and a sergeant who had lived in Detroit 14 years and talked perfect U.S. Mission to get information on our installations and movements. From dope we got from them and their map, they knew where all our Divisions were—over-estimated the number of Armor Divisions we have (actually we only got three, 6, 4, 10), and they gave us three in each Corps. But otherwise had our outfits marked cold. ULTRA confirmed this, except for one big boner. They believe we have 92nd and 93rd Infantry (negro) Divisions. Neither in France. We do have negro tank battalions and a lot of service, telephone and QM negroes. No doubt Germans getting a lot of information about us and this area is infected with spies and agents. Also from what Sibert and ULTRA reported—apparent it's a race between Allies and Germans over which jumps off first. Germans not capable of much more than a spoiling attack, but every indication they are getting ready to pop one. Two panzer corps have been withdrawn from the line, an indication of an impending operation as these Corps are used for offensive operations.[36]

Germans have gained time needed to organize miscellaneous units into Divs, and rest and refit a number of Panzer (5) and Para (3) Divs, that will be a powerful force for an offensive. Great deficiency is gas, small arms and MT, but have built up GAF and estimated now have 900/1000 SR [short-range] fighters for close ground support.

Obvious to Germans there has been an Allied build-up, and with the clearing of Antwerp, we are about to launch major offensives to deliver knockout blow and finish the war. An effective spoiling attack might disrupt all these preparations and plans, and besides nailing us down for the winter, it would give the Germans time to build up new Army, new Air Weapons, concentrate forces against Russians and—engage in political and diplomatic machinations to try to make a peace deal.

It's a gamble, but they haven't a thing to lose, and everything to gain. If they sit, we are sure to hit them and somewhere break through and overrun them. If they can jump and unbalance us, they might be able to gain the winter's period and that is their last chance to avoid early defeat.

Patton is very LUCKY conscious—anxious to jump off by 8th. That was the day he landed in Sicily with very swell weather, although predictions unfavorable. *Editor's note: Patton landed in Morocco, not Sicily, on November 8, 1942.* Eleven is another number he considers lucky. His birthday is 11 November. He picked TUSA code name *LUCKY* and considers it a very effective talisman.

Germans increasingly using V-bombs and jet planes.[37] In three days around 27 October, 57 [V-weapons] launched against England, of which 18 made low [land] fall and 7 hit London. Also firing them at Antwerp and Brussels from launching sites in Cologne area that ULTRA reported some weeks ago they were surveying. Reports of jet planes now daily occurrence. Also, Sibert told us that XX Corps report of "pink cloud" we got several weeks ago was first confirmation of "something we've been expecting for some time." He did not elucidate further (?).

Saturday, November 4, 1944: (Ike's snappy British WAC [Women's Auxiliary Corps] driver.) At a demonstration near Nancy of new type of flame-throwing tank that has proved very effective—when Lt in charge, after explanation of weapon, said, "Suggest you gentlemen step back to ensure complete safety." Patton, who was present, broke in in his high-pitched voice, "They won't do anything of the kind. You go right ahead with your demonstration, Lt. War is not a safe business, and if they don't know that by now, this is [a] good place to learn it. Goddamn it, it isn't safe for tank crew or the men who attack with these tanks to kill Germans, so we can take a chance at this demonstration. You go ahead, Lt., and we'll all stay right here."—And they did, to the evident distress of a number of high-ranking Rear Echelon goldbricks and paper pushers. Lt Col Potter,[38] G-2 Sec, Com Z, Paris, visiting us at Nancy, told us that apparently at instigation of U.S. perfume industry—the profiteering bastards—ETOUSA is publishing an order that soldier gifts of perfume are subject to a gouging tariff. That's a fine piece of cheap, war-profiteering son-of-bitchery. Only thing kids can send home is [missing text] and now this racketeering perfume business is going to get its pound of flesh out of the kids.

Ln O report by Lt Col J. Alison, Jr.,[39] 12 Army Group, dated 2 Nov, states—"First French Army[40] has assumed a defensive role and is not attempting to advance other than as is necessary to maintain contact. Letter of Instruction No. 2 of Sixth Army Group called for an attack by the French Army on 1 Nov in the vicinity of Gerartmer [Gérardmer]. This attack has been postponed to a date to be announced later." Next para of report—"The Seventh Army (other component of Sixth AG [Army Group]) continues to advance in both XV and VI Corps [sectors]." Casualties—Sixth AG:

Killed & Missing, U.S.	6,233
Wounded	15,457
[Total]	21,690
PW	47,624
[Killed & Missing] French	2,718
[Wounded]	9,699
[Total]	12,417
PW	58,313 (2 Nov)

New policy—and about time—on selection of Div and Corps CGs. None not proved in combat to be appointed. A Brig Genl commanding a Div must prove himself in combat before getting second star. Corps CGs in U.S. without combat experience must give up command if Hq ordered overseas.

New rule missed Major General Millikin of III Corps, but caught Major General [William H. H.] Morris[41] of XVIII [Airborne] Corps, so he stepped down and was given command of 10th Armored, which just closed with us in XX Corps zone. At 2200 hours, we got information from copy of a coded cable reading—"Please report line Third Army troops. Urgent. [General James H.] Doolittle."[42] This apparently for laying on of big Air show tomorrow. Dope so far is it will be fair weather day tomorrow. Here is hoping. Had conference at 2000 hours and told Sit Sec O and EM we are going to war again. All very earnest, but eager. Great bunch of youngsters that I hand-picked myself. Probably best Operation G-2 group as a whole in U.S. Army.

Sunday, November 5, 1944: Patton appeared in blouse, white whipcord riding breaches, highly polished boots, no spurs, and wearing .38 short barrel revolver in hip holster. Appeared in good humor. First thing he asked—"How's weather?"—Told that at 2400 hours, big show laid on for 1,000 Heavies, 1,500 fighters, 600 Mediums, but that by 2430 hours all scrubbed. However, this morning raid on again. Day—mild and Indian summerish. Overcast about 2/3000 feet. All right for fighters and going to operate over our whole front all day burning up everything on and behind German lines. Movements, concentrations, vehicles, dumps, etc. Heavies and Mediums hit two forts on the south flank of Metz and forts Driant and Jeanne D'Arc, long demanded by Patton. Biggest Air show of war in this Theater so far—according to Lt Col Pat Murray,[43] G-3 Air, Patton said—"Want to push this Air operation. Haven't got much time. Only a few days and have to make the most of our opportunities. If we get break today, we will jump off tomorrow." Told weather around Metz will be spotty, with breaks in overcast that would permit Heavy and Medium bombing. All depends on whether breaks are at the time when bombers due over—between 1030/1130 hours. With XIX TAC fighters, means there'll be 2,000 fighters on our front today. Also, good prospect for pretty good weather tomorrow, that gives us another day for all-out Air show to soften the bastards up. Couple days of Air assault of this size in our relatively small zone—about 40 miles by 30 miles to Siegfried Line (Saar)—should really demoralize them.

Looked for a while like bombing program would go through, but around noon called it off and Plan B substituted. Heavies hammered Frankfurt, Mainz, Karlsruhe and Mediums went after Moselle bridges, dumps, depots, concentrations, etc. Fighters out and apparently had pretty good results. One reported weather over Mainz was 10/10—8 flak and 2 cloud. Slap-happy kids. Around midnight AA opened up suddenly. Didn't last long; apparently was only a passing enemy plane. Approaches to Antwerp, Walcheren Island cleared and channel swept to FLUSHING.[44]

Monday, November 6, 1944: Although stars out last night, day broke heavily overcast that developed into showers around 0830 and kept up that way all morning. Bombers going to try to nail Metz forts today, and fighters repeat scourging. All this emphasizes *vital* role Air is playing in this war. If we had a few days clear weather, the amount of Air we got would have hammered the way clear for us to Saar, through the line and then to Rhine in a couple weeks. That's what happened back West of Paris. Air was the way hacker; it demoralized enemy communications, transportation, movements, and if we had a few good days weather now, with the amount of Air that has been made available to us, we could literally overwhelm them—followed by tanks and Mz [Mechanized] Inf. We'd be on the Rhine before they were aware what really hit them.

Patton brisk this morning but silent. Listened but asked no questions and made no comments. Laughed heartily over 8/10 flak and 2/10 cloud crack by Murray at briefing.

Tuesday, November 7, 1944: Rainy, cloudy. Total loss for Air. Patton appeared very cheery. At the briefing rose, and said—"Tomorrow we jump off. No conditions and no doubts. Doubt is a disease. We are not only going to the Rhine but over the Rhine. This is the final beginning of the end of the war. I want to thank each and every one of you for your fine work in preparing this operation. You have worked very hard and effectively, and (with smile) I expect you to keep it up harder than ever."

Wednesday, November 8, 1944: Offensive started. Arty began hammering at around 0530. 26th Infantry Division made good progress right from the start. 80th Infantry Division also did well in establishing bridgeheads over the Seille [River]. By 1300 weather cleared considerably and Mediums considered certain on Metz forts and other targets. Also 10 Groups of fighters—about 350—will be up. No Heavies, but fighters and Med[iums] ought to raise plenty of hell. All indications are that our jump-off was a surprise. Germans expected something, but no idea what, when, where. A XIX TAC [officer] was called into a conference attended by Vandenberg and "Sammy"[45]—another young two-star Air General—on blasting way through dragon's teeth in the Sig [Siegfried] Line. Advised they do it in vicinity of Saarbrücken, as my terrain study showed, and that was tentatively agreed on.

Murray reported—No Heavies and no Med. But P-47s out in force. Used Napalm[46] bombs against German troops with excellent results.

Also beat up large number of reported CPs, dumps, RR, marshalling yards, etc. Patton out early and spent the whole day on the line watching the battle in XII Corps zone. Returned in evening very pleased— good spirits—to attend little gathering to commemorate 2d anniversary of the landing in Morocco. About 21 of Hq with him then. Patton likes these sorts of affairs and does honors very well. Shook hands all around. Expressed high satisfaction with day's progress—"Doing better than I expected. Much better. If we can keep this up for a couple more days, there will be nothing to it. We'll go through them like a dose of salts." In the midst of the party, General Eddy, CG XII Corps, big, fatty, worry wart, called up and apparently put on one of his moan and wail acts. Patton cheered him up. "Don't worry. Everything is going fine. You're doing fine, fine. Keep it up. Good work." (Then getting tough.) "But get those tanks over the River (Seille). Get them over if you have to swim them. You understand." Afterward Patton remarked, "That was Eddy—having a case of evening jitters."

Thursday, November 9, 1944: Colonel Koch told me today he is resubmitting recommendation for my promotion to Colonel. Said I stood 20 in list of Lt Cols in Hq, but he was going to bat on the ground of my seniority in length of service. Nice of him—but we'll see how far he gets with General Hap Gay—who is filling a non-T/O job. *Editor's note: Koch's initial recommendation for Allen's promotion was denied on September 14 and he resubmitted it on November 13.* Heavies and Meds bombed Metz forts this morning. Through the clouds, saw them coming back and they looked mighty good. First we've seen for long time.

Friday, November 10, 1944: Lieutenant Generals [Carl A.] Spaatz[47] and Doolittle spent night with Patton and are attending briefings this morning. At ULTRA hearing when Patton heard that CP of 17 SS and 48 Infantry Divisions had been destroyed by Air the day before, he let out a whoop and yelled to Weyland—"Hot dog. That got them. We'd been laying for them for long time and got the bastards. Good work." Murray reported yesterday was one of the best Air days in a long time. Really beat up Germans all over our zone.

ULTRA—20 October—Jap ambassador in Berlin reported Germans need until April to prepare for offensive. Very precarious position and may not be able to withstand new Allied offensive.

At 101600 railway station at Arnaville shelled by Germans. Three shells, believed 155mm, dropped on station as General Patton's private railway car stopped there. Patton not in car. Only damage—glass in rear car blown out. First I heard Patton had such a car—where, how he got it a mystery. Colonel "Maud" Muller, G-4, made report. Maybe he got the car?

Walcheren Island finally cleared yesterday, 9 November, and should make Antwerp operationally active in matter of a few days now.

Patton had little ceremony in front of his office building this morning. Suspended the sentence for 20 negro service GIs connected with rioting in UK months ago. Given five years by court martial. Patton suspended the sentence. Negroes lined up in front of platform and he addressed them— "I've suspended your sentence because I believe that you will contribute more to war effort doing duty than in a PW cage. But I want to warn you. The first crooked move you make, that sentence will be reimposed and you go to jail for five years with dishonorable discharge. You have a chance to rehabilitate yourselves. I expect you to do that and to be good soldiers."

Saturday, November 11, 1944: Patton's birthday. Very chipper at briefing. Came in wearing fur-collared Air jacket, pearl-handled revolver, and thanked me for a historical map—showing World War I lines November 8—that I dug up. In evening, Patton attended cocktail party given in his honor by Colonel Koch at a ville on Rue Jeanne D'Arc. Patton stayed awhile, drank one Armored Diesel punch cocktail and ate a couple of toasted cheese sandwiches. After he left, Stiller came back and reported Patton said—"Sure would have liked to have stayed and got drunk."

Weather only fair. Fighters up but no bombers. Also weather outlook sour.

Sunday, November 12, 1944: Word from topside now is that sweeping at Antwerp will not be completed until 28 November and port facilities not fully available until then. Also, that a V-2 hit the power plant that operates port facilities and completely destroyed plant—lucky hit, but necessitates new facilities being created—cruiser, battleship, or something similar. Maj Monjay[48]—TUSA Med[ical] Section—told me today he makes special trip to Patton's quarters every day to de-chlorinate a 5-gallon can of drinking water because Patton expressed dislike of heavily chlorinated water we are being given to drink. Weather complete shutout today. Nothing up.

Germans lost a great opportunity to wipe out the 90th Inf Div yesterday. Eight of 9 Infantry Bns were over the Moselle, when record flood cut them off from Artillery, tanks, TDs. 200-yard bridges put over, but unusable because approaches under 54 inches of water. If Germans had attacked in force with tanks, could have wiped out Div. Today, they did attack, but after 3 km penetration, were beaten off by Arty. Inf Bns being supplied by cub plane and a couple motor launchers. Situation very precarious. Meanwhile, German reaction to our offensive beginning. Nailed down 21 Panzer Div, up from Seventh Army zone; also 25 Pz Gren[adier] Div.[49] With 11 Panzer and 17 SS Pz Gren Divs, gives enemy 9 Pz Divs for possible offensive operations. Very exciting watching build-up unfold. Also significant—not one hint of it from ULTRA—all on ground & RI.

Weather certainly making the deciding difference in this offensive. With what we got and what's in front of us, with only a few days good weather we'd go through them like dose of salts. Weather (Air) is the deciding factor. With all the Air we had available to us, we could literally have burned our way to the Saar and through the Siegfried Line. But we don't have the weather—very clear now and unless there is a miracle, won't have it. Despite Patton's belief in his *LUCK*, he has not had any weather breaks so far. Attack going pretty good in XII Corps zone—only be a lot better if we had Air. Be cinch then. Same story as last Aug. Clear now it was Air, burning the way for our tank-Infantry teams and columns that did the trick.

From Dutch source, report that Germans have U-boat that is equipped to make V-weapon attack on N.Y. Sounds plausible—as we are launching planes from subs and Germans now doing all their V-1 bombing of UK from He [Heinkel] 111.[50] Also, it is known that Germans are now concentrating on two types of U-boats—

1) 1500-ton long-range (XII) type
2) 180/250-ton short-range type

60 of (1) and 20 of (2) under construction. (See clipped account of anti–U-boat campaign.)

Apparent Germans still trying to wage Naval warfare and resume undersea attacks with faster and new model U-boats.

Colonel Macdonald told me today that 2 German soldiers caught behind our lines in civilian clothes when we were at Étain were shot Saturday at Toul by MP firing squad.

Monday, November 13, 1944: Heard today that Von Tirpitz[51] bombed and finally sunk. RAF Lancasters caught the bitch yesterday and put her on the bottom with some direct hits with 12,000-lb "earthquake" bombs. One out of 28 planes that made attack was lost.

In an exchange at ULTRA briefing this morning between Patton and Weyland, latter admitted two flights of four planes each of our XIX TAC accidently bombed some 26th Inf troops with some casualties. Patton brought it up by observing that he saw several men with legs off in a hospital train in Nancy depot. "They weren't sore. Seemed to feel it was one of the unavoidable accidents of war."

ULTRA reported that [Field Marshal Gerd] Von Rundstedt[52] very concerned about an Allied airborne operation East of Rhine brought laugh from Patton. "Certainly hope they keep him as CG. He is the best friend we have. Not only dumb son-of-a-bitch, but weak. Hope he stays. Be big help to us, like he was last summer."

Heard how 6th Armored Div captured 40-ton bridge intact over Neid River, our last major stream obstacle in South before Saar. Troops of 25 Engr Bn, Army T[roo]ps, swam down river and working *UNDER* water, found and cut demolition wire, thus blocking destruction of bridge and giving us tremendous local tactical advantage. The lieutenant who commanded the detail was killed by shellfire.

Weather again STINKO and everything scrubbed. Not a combat mission got off the ground. During night we [discovered] that 36th Inf Div,[53] on our North flank in VIII Corps (FUSA) zone had come down into our XII Corps zone. Not only no hint of this from ULTRA, but neither VIII Corps nor FUSA nor Twelfth Army Group know (36) had left and was out of contact. I raised hell about this to Col Koch, who reported it to Patton. That makes three new Divs in our zone in 24 hours with build-up equivalent to eight Divs and all outside of ULTRA.

Latest word now is that FUSA won't jump off until 16th or even later. Plan now is—

XV Corps today
VI Corps on 15th with Saarburg-Strassburg as their objectives
VII Corps was supposed to have jumped off yesterday but was
    delayed (?)
VII Corps in FUSA
V and VIII Corps go after VII Corps, whenever the hell that is.
    Ninth Army also after VII.

In other words, TUSA is the sucker bait. We try to draw them out and others wait to see how we make out and also for *good weather.* Meanwhile, heard FUSA had eight inches of snow in its area. Probably means delay of another week now.

Tuesday, November 14, 1944: Result of my squawk, Patton called Bradley at ULTRA briefing this morning. "Brad, this is George. Say, appreciate it if you talk to *MR.* Middleton (Troy H., CG VIII Corps) and get him to bestir himself and find out what the hell is on his front. We picked up 36th Inf Div last night in our zone, although reported by VIII Corps as still in contact on their front." (Actually, while VIII at fault, FUSA also to blame, and to have been absolutely fair, Patton should also have squawked about Hodges. But never mentioned him or FUSA, which Bradley commanded. Patton put whole blame on VIII and Middleton.) "We're having quite a build-up. Three Divs in 48 hours, two of them panzer-type. When are the others going to do something? We are getting a lot of stuff thrown in our way. Ike called last night. Yes, things coming along, but sure would like to have something started at other points. Yes, weather lousy as hell here, too. Haven't been able to get a thing up in the Air since Saturday. Tough break."

Went out to 4th Armored Div North of Château-Salins—cold, raw, wet, low hovering clouds over the hills; valleys full of water and everything covered with *MUD. MUD, MUD, MUD* everywhere. Scene like movie of what war is like. Gloomy, somber, dead cattle, ambulances rolling back, beat up and deserted towns. Very definite line between French and German beginning vic[inity] Sur-Seille. More and more apparent the crucial decisive role that Air plays in successful modern war. Also, fact that topside bulled in this operation in counting on Air when they knew weather very uncertain. With Air out—or unpredictable—got to increase punching power of ground to make up for lack of Air. Topside failed to do this and as a result, our progress is very, very slow. We are moving, but at walk instead of racing gallop, which would have been [possible] with full power of Air.

Wednesday, November 15, 1944: After ULTRA briefing, Patton turned to Gaffey and said—"Go up there and explain to those goddamn fools about the blankets. It's very simple. I don't care who gets whose blankets. Whether 95th go to 90th, or vice versa. What I want is to get blankets to the infantryman on the line. That is the whole thing, and I want it done right now. Muller's memo is all cockeyed and I want you to go up and straighten it out."

Around noon Eisenhower, in cap and Air Corps fur-lined jacket, rolled in. Inspected MP guard and then posed for pictures with Patton. I heard and saw for first time Ike's snappy and beauteous English driver. Attired in well-fitting slacks, jacket and overseas cap, she is definitely SOME Babe and an extraordinary chauffeur for a field commander to have. Name, I'm told, is Kay. She is a civilian, with status of officer. Been with him for two years, since Africa. (Her full name is Kay Summersby).[54] Also, his bodyguard. Two husky EM, attired in three-buckle

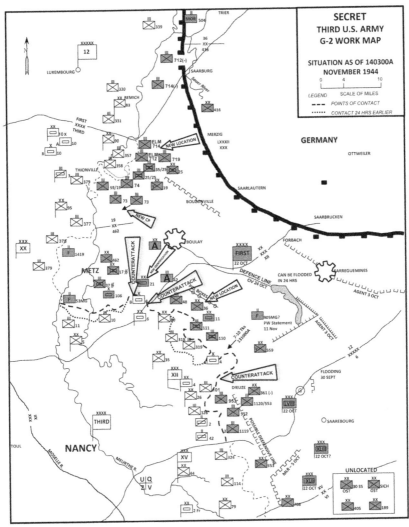

Third Army G-2 Work Map, November 14, 1944

boots, overseas caps, Sam Browne belts and .45 automatics, in special fast-draw hip holsters. Quite an entourage.

Weather still sour, but late in afternoon two missions did get off for some 30 sorties. Beat up convoy, marshalling yard. Not much, but first Air activity since last Saturday.

Thursday, November 16, 1944: Eisenhower attended ULTRA briefing. Afterwards asked some questions—how much [ULTRA] stuff we get.

Said when he visits Chamberlain [Churchill] shows him reams of stuff [he] doesn't see. *Editor's note: Allen clearly means Churchill here. Joseph Chamberlain had not been prime minister since May 1940.* Says Churchill reads all of it every day. Afterwards, attended regular staff briefing and then addressed staff—"Want to take a few moments to say Good Morning and to express my appreciation for the good work you are doing. (Habit of rolling his eyes to ceiling on left side.) The Plan of Battle is this: The enemy is stretched to the breaking point. Straining every nerve to stave off defeat. Our plan is to keep on hitting him at every sensitive point until he cracks. Bound to crack if we keep hammering him without let-up. Strained to limit and if we keep on hitting him, he is through. Not hit him all along whole 600-mile front, but at sensitive points. You are working on him. Then Seventh Army started. Tomorrow, next day First Army and so on. Keep it up all winter if needed. He can't stand winter fighting and we can because our men will be better equipped and armed for winter fighting than Germans. Our men won't be comfortable, but they will be more comfortable than enemy—and that's all important. If our men know they are better clothed, fed, armed and cared for than other guy, they have a sense of superiority that is certain to lead to victory. I want all you G-4s, QM, Ord, Engr, Med, to see to it that nothing will be left undone in having our men better fed, clothed, equipped and armed than other guy. That must be done and I want nothing to interfere with that. Another thing we have the other guy hasn't and which will tell the story is the greatest Air-Ground teamwork in history. Germans thought they had the best in 1940, and it was the best then—the only one then. But we have developed so far, they are now not remotely in our class. The brilliant work of Quesada, FUSA and Weyland, TUSA, is outstanding and they were selected because of the desire to ensure the best in Air-Ground teamwork. I don't care who the guy is that is running Germany—Hitler, [Heinrich] Himmler[55] or some other bird. We can lick them if we keep on pounding them without let-up. And that is what we intend to do all winter without let-up. I need your help, fellows, and I know I can count on you to deliver." Guys, fellows—bit incongruous, coming from him. Pep talk style—campaign harangue; definite pressure spiel, like he had given many times before. Good voice, good line, but some touches out of place.

Afterwards saw the Babe—some cookie. Tall, slender, hana [henna]-haired English. No spring chicken. Seen 30 years. Slacks, fur-collared Air jacket. Bare-headed. Played with black Scotty same as Falla [Fala].[56] (Recalled saw her in F/O [flight officers'] mess in London with BG.) Certainly amazing thing for Supreme Commander floating around battle areas with snazzy red-headed English Babe as chauffeur and Scotty dog. Kay jumped out of the car and opened the door for Patton, who got in on left side. Patton addressed Eisenhower as "General."

Arty Sec reported that in barrage that opened our offensive, fired by XII Corps Arty, 30,000 rounds in 1½ hours. Fifty percent more were fired on entire Army front the whole week before.

Friday, November 17, 1944: Good weather day, and all squadrons of XIX TAC up. Should really burn them up—I hope. More info on Kay— Ike's hot mama chauffeur. She is divorcee and he got her when he was given ETO command. British were using women drivers as ETO staff was very small, he asked for one of the she drivers and Kay was assigned from Transportation Corps. She made a hit and has stayed on since. Is a civilian and according to Capt Robinson, draws pay of Major. Also, according to him, she was engaged to a U.S. Col of Engr who was killed in Africa by a mine.

FUSA jumped off at 1245 yesterday with very fine Air attack. Got good break in weather—about 2 hours—and they poured it on with Heavies, Meds and Bomber-fighters. Caught two German Divs in middle of changing positions (one taking over from another) and plastered the hell out of them. VII Corps did the jumping, finally getting underway.

Third Army made *first inroad into Germany* today. Patrol of 3rd Cavalry entered *Perl*, South West corner boundary between Luxembourg and Germany, but was forced out by Arty fire. Presented special briefing on Metz situation today (see photo and prop) and it seemed to go over very well. Number of commendations.

Here is a hot one—Discovered today that MII [Military Intelligence interpreter] Sgt Walter Ducloux in our Section is a brilliant symphony director and was [Arturo] Toscanini's chief assistant.[57] A Swiss by birth, Ducloux directed leading European symphonies before going to U.S. He can't be over 30 years old and apparently was drafted and put in MII for linguistic skill; speaks French, German, Italian. Very good and brave soldier. Did special duty with 3rd Cav under fire and only a week ago was approved for recommendation for Bronze Star. How I found out about his musical background was—I was told he is to lead Nancy symphony orchestra this Sunday afternoon. The funny thing about all this is—that not only that I knew nothing about it but back in Nehou, when he was directly under me, I used him as an orderly to get us eggs, bread, cheese, wine and laundry. *Boy—that's really Hot.*

ULTRA—German plane shot down enroute to Spain carried an

agent with plans to set up Nazi ring abroad. Plans disappeared and British Secret Service sent out message to be on watch for them. In that connection, ULTRA reports that Germans now have airfields in operation in Lorient and La Rochelle, also Channel Islands, where garrisons still holding out. Planes sent to them at night with mail, some supplies and probably agents. Also indications of planes going to Spain and Portugal, carrying agents, money and possibly big-shot Nazis.

Scene at Pont-a-Musson [Pont-à-Mousson] on Moselle: Higher water forced use of foot bridge. At one end, several hundred rookie replacements waiting to march over to entruck to go to line outfits as battle replacements. At other end of bridge, ambulances lined up with stretcher carriers taking out wounded to carry across bridge for transfer to ambulances on other side. Replacements eying wounded with tense seriousness touching intentness. Very dramatic and heart-rending scene. C'est la guerre.

It sure was a good Air day. Following XIX TAC results for the day:

RN [?] plan	15 on ground
	5 air
MT	135 destroyed
	31 damaged
Loco[motives]	30 destroyed
RR cars	167 destroyed
	44 damaged
Gun pos[itio]n[s]	19 destroyed
	14 damaged
Bridges	17 destroyed
RR cuts	15
Marsh[aling] yards attacked	9
Towns attacked	11

(One train hit with two rockets, knocked clear off tracks).

Saturday, November 18, 1944: Today is the best Air day we've had yet. And XIX TAC went to it—not only during day but throughout night, which was also tops. Long list of claims, including 60 locomotives, 300-plus RR cars, etc. If we had three days of this kind of weather, we could scorch through Siegfried Line, and if we had a week, we could get to the Rhine. No question about it. Enemy in retreat everywhere on our front, and with Air for few days running, we could make it a rout, like last Aug. Metz now completely surrounded and all but a few major forts taken. If we had the Air and Armor they have given First Army, Patton would be on the Rhine now.

FUSA drive definitely limping despite promising start and fact they have three full corps. If we only had another corps—that is, if III Corps had its complement of 2 Inf and 1 Armd Div—we'd be on Rhine in week. Patton snorted about this fact at ULTRA briefing. Told FUSA "bogged down," he remarked sarcastically—"That's strange. That's where all the better people are fighting. Well, if they bog very long, I may get VIII Corps back again and then I'll side slip them in and really kill Germans."

Stiller told me this story: Driving back yesterday, Patton said— "Remember those shark teeth given in Africa. Scientist tells me 1 million years old." Stiller—"That's just about the same as eternity." Patton— "You know what is eternity. If a sparrow were to come to earth once every 10,000 years and carry away one grain of sand, by the time the whole earth had been carted away, it would be time to have breakfast in hell."

Heard story of Eisenhower—visited 26th Infantry Division with Patton, walked up to GI digging foxhole. Looking up and seeing Eisenhower's snazzy Air Corps boots, GI, continuing to shovel, remarked— "Gezus, I'd trade mine and 500 francs for those." "It's a deal, soldier. Give me your boots and dough." GI damn near dropped when he looked up and saw who it was.

Patton told a Platoon about to attack—"You boys cut out being cautious. Nothing to be afraid of as long as you keep going and don't let those bastards have the time to take an aimed shot at you. Don't jump into foxholes when you get shot at. Go out and kill the sons-of-bitches." Platoon killed 40 and captured 73.

From Swiss source through Seventh Army—letter from Allen W. Dulles,[58] U.S. Minister, to Sibert—reporting contact being made with a *certain* German general. No details, etc. From other sources in Switzerland report that July 20 attack on Hitler left him stone deaf. Also rising feeling in Army and Industrialist circles against Himmler. General [Hans] Oschumann [Oschmann],[59] CG 338 Infantry Division opposing 1st French Corps, killed 16 November by Arty preparation. Diary found on him had this—"Very quiet on our front, and no indication of anything going to happen."

Sunday, November 19, 1944: Another good Air day, starting with dawn about 0630 with a *blood red* sky—fine omen to knock off Germans. We have a *Medical* mission to be up [near] Merzig—North East corner of our zone and on Saar around 1030. All XIX TAC groups (4) Airborne by 0750. Patton strode into ULTRA briefing and beaming, said—"Weyland, did your cheeks itch about 0800? Should have, because your planes were over my billet then and I wanted to kiss you." Metz completely encircled at 1000 today—5th and 95th Infantry Divisions closing trap East of bastion. Historic achievement—first time Metz actually captured by force—not siege—since ancient times.

Monday, November 20, 1944: Yesterday was best day we had in Air—407 sorties, largest number in couple months. Beat up lot of stuff. Today, however, not so hot—only three Groups Airborne by 1000; one still weathered in. Later in morning, rain set in. Not so good.

Visited trial of two PW captured in civilian clothes. One, Sgt, cold, calm veteran. Other, callow kid who is just a dupe. The Sgt is polluted stuff and good riddance to shoot him. The kid is just a punk—the kind that made the Nazis what they are. Millions more like both in Germany. Wonder how to get rid of them.

Visited Seventh Army at Épinal. Not in our class, and Épinal a messy-looking place.

Koch told me this story about Patton—addressing group of GIs, said, "You think I am an SOB. I am—to the Germans. And they are SOB to you. And in Germany some are SOBs to other Germans. Everyone is an SOB to someone. Isn't question whether you are an SOB, but what you are doing about it." Greeting Weyland this morning, said—"Have good day yesterday? Fine, then must have killed a lot of Germans."

Heard from Ruth today that [Hamilton] Fish [III],[60] [Gerald Prentice] Nye,[61] [Stephen A.] Day,[62] [John A.] Danaker [Danaher][63]—got knocked off in elections. Really stupendous!

(More CFATK[64] Info—ULTRA report what Germans had ready.)

Tuesday, November 21, 1944: Seventh Army crowd very sour on French. (We sure aren't very joyous about our Allies. No one likes the British and everyone thinks the French soft and Mexicanish.) Get no info from them and had to infiltrate an OB [order of battle] Capt into 1st French Corps to find out what's what. He did so well that he actually became G-2 of Corps. But if not for him, Seventh would get no information. Also say they told French three weeks ago only about 10,000 Germans against them, but French won't move. Claimed 40,000 Germans in their front. Big gains last few days prove they were wrong and Seventh right. Seventh says Germans got only 15,000 on 6th Army Group front right now.

Wednesday, November 22, 1944: Went to Dieuze and Moyenic [Moyenvic] with Col [Edward Maynard] Fickett,[65] CO 6th Cav G[rou]p. Wet, gloomy, lowering skies, mud, abandoned villages and towns badly battered and completely deserted, and water and mud everywhere. Whole area a battlefield, with dead cattle, horses, burned out tanks, gun-positions, dug-outs. Like a book or movie description. Just outside of Dieuze, a vast French Arty barracks that oddly is very little damaged, although town across stream hammered flat. In barracks, caught up with Col [Charles H.] Reed,[66] CO 2d Cav Gp, who informed me he is the husband of Jackie Cannon, black-haired girl I knew at Camp Douglas, Wisconsin, 20 years ago. Odd, after all those years, to meet her husband in that deserted corner of the battlefield as winter dusk began to fall.

Thursday, November 23, 1944: Col Macdonald told me an interesting story about Gaffey: Said that at a staff meeting of Section chiefs not long ago he said number of recommendations for promotion to Colonel received and he was sending them back. "My permanent grade not Colonel. Go slow on such promotions. Full colonelcy something that means something throughout man's entire life. No reason for bestowing such an honor too freely. May be doing good work, but that's their duty. Further, such promotions should go first to officers of Regular Establishment." First I've heard of such an outburst, but I'm not surprised. Gaffey is capable of such stupidity. Certainly that's been his policy so far. Only four colonelcies:

1—[John B.] Coates [Jr.][67]—Reg Medical
1—Odom—Patton's Medical
1—Forde—Reg
1—Borders—whom Gaffey thought was a Reg as result of Borders' slick maneuvering. Macdonald very outraged.

Today D+15 and score sheet as follows:

TUSA		ENEMY	
K	1,234	PW	20,489
W	11,145	Buried	1,153
Miss[ing]	2,360	Total	21,562
Total	15,205	Est. W	30,500
Non-battle	10,520	K	10,300
Total	25,725	Total	62,000*
MATERIAL			
	TUSA**	GERMAN	
Light Tk	37	47	
Med Tk	82	23	
Arty—75 mm & over	7	308	
Vehicles	318	254	

* This figure is highly significant. We began offensive with Est[imated] 32,000 Germans on our front. In 15 days, PW, K, W total of 62,000 or 200 percent of original figure, and today we Est enemy total on our front at 51,000—150 percent of original figure—making 350 percent consumption in 15 days.
** Shows cost of the Adv[ance]—as I saw in visit to Dieuze—burned out tank groups 3/55 dotting landscape.
Editor's note: Some of Allen's totals do not add up.

G-2 Thanksgiving party at Colonel Koch's house. Patton, Gaffey, Gay attended. Nurses. Patton stayed until 10 p.m. and had nice time. Gaffey got nicely oiled and stayed until after 11 p.m., dancing with Red X gal. Party consumed seven turkeys, 60 magnums of champagne and two cases of cognac.

Friday, November 24, 1944: ULTRA [reveals German] appreciation of Allied plans—Montgomery to do nothing until he builds up strong reserves, brought snort from Patton—"Sure got him pegged right." Patton held press conference in War Room. Got same manner as FDR. Told them everything and very smooth answers. When asked whether he knew the Moselle would flood, grinned and said—"Shall I tell I was great strategist or really didn't know. Got caught, just like Germans, but when it did happen we used it to our advantage. They didn't think we would attack and when we did, caught them napping." Characterized 90th Div crossing as outstanding exploit of invasion— covers up for fact that Div damned near got destroyed. If Germans had attacked that Sunday, Div had nothing to stop them and Bns could have been wiped out. Kidded with correspondents; answered all questions; obviously enjoyed occasion and had Gay read German leaflet that described Patton as "Capone and Dillinger" who beat wounded—allusion to exposure story.

Big build-up of GAF. ULTRA reports 175/200 jet-propelled [aircraft] by 1 January.[68] IX Air Force estimates SR fighters in West up to 1500.

Saturday, November 25, 1944: Patton interrogated in his office SS Brigadeführer Anton Dun[c]kern,[69] SS chief of Lorraine, Colonel Konstantin Mayer [Meyer],[70] commandant of Metz, captured at Metz. Dunckern, rat-faced swine in full-length, gray-green leather topcoat, boots. Meyer a short Reg Army officer. Patton gave Dunckern the works. Made him stand at attention and barked at him, "I captured number of German generals but you are the lowest. Really should turn you over to French." Dunckern protested. "Under Geneva Convention, not allowed. Am American prisoner." Patton—"How come you surrender. Why not die for Führer as he forced troops to swear they would do?" Dunckern— "No chance. Door opened and gun pointed at my stomach." (Real story— he was hiding in Sample Room of Brewery. Two GIs, looking for liquor, stumbled on him. One was asked why he didn't kill him, and replied, "Would have if I'd known who the bastard was. Thought just some Bosche officer.") Patton—"Record shows some very grave offenses." Dunckern—"Done nothing to be ashamed of. May have made some mistakes, but only those of human judgment." Patton—"Maybe according to Nazi code but not according to tenets of decent and civilized people. What about hostages?" Dunckern—"Times when that is necessary." Nothing arrogant about this hog-faced rat. Obviously scared and ready to talk. Patton dismissed him curtly.

Meyer treated very differently. Offered seat, cigar; courteously as officer and gentleman. Said he was anti Nazi and that why not made a General. Brought from East Prussia to organize Metz defense. Shocked at type of troops. Had urged withdrawal to three lines of defense, but Hitler ordered him to make fortress stand at Metz. Asked as personal favor not to be sent back in same car with Dunckern—which Patton personally ordered not be done. Dunckern taken to PM office, where Odom, at Patton's request, stripped him to check on reported tattoo. Dunckern stripped without question and no tattoo found on him. When asked about SS being tattooed, denied knowing anything about it.

ULTRA—reported Germans now have available for counter-offensive purposes the following:

6 Panzer Divs, rested and refitted

3 Para Divs

8/10 Inf Divs in Germany

3 Divs enroute from Norway

Sunday, November 26, 1944: Eisenhower, Bradley, [Charles H.] Bonesteel[71]—new Q/G [Quartermaster General] to Bradley, conferred with Patton. Afterward heard we have got new plan—French Army, after capture of Strasbourg, instead of trying to cross Rhine, turns South and destroys all bridges across Rhine to Basel, thus pocketing Germans and wiping them out. Seventh Army—XV and VI U.S. Corps move North East instead of East, also for purpose of cutting German troops off from Rhine and aiding our drive through Siegfried Line. We and Seventh to try to suck more troops down from North to destroy them by attrition and cut off on West side of Rhine, where bridges to be destroyed from air. Plan is to try to trap bulk of German Armies in West on West side of Rhine and destroy them so that if they don't collapse then, when crossing of Rhine effected, Germans will have nothing to fight with. (Navy making plans to handle movement of troops across Rhine. Working on bringing in boats and other craft, equipment and personnel for this purpose.) Plan makes sense—if it works and we can get British [and] First and Ninth Armies to envelop from their end.

Monday, November 27, 1944: Col Macdonald suddenly ordered to FUSA as CO of 4th Cav Gp. He is not particularly happy, I gather. Asked me if I would serve as Ex O of Group if he could arrange transfer and I told him definitely yes. Said Hodges had tried twice to get him but they wouldn't let him go here—in fact, not even told about it. Also told me Hodges asked him about me and spoke very highly of me.

Col Maddox and Muller got word they are nominated for Brig Genl. Both deserve it—especially Maddox, who is a very able and very decent person. Tough Koch didn't get it, although word is his name has gone in. I do hope he gets it and before that suckholing Nixon and some others. Patton remarked—"How are those new generals of ours. When they come through I want to put on ceremony. Give them flourishes."

Tuesday, November 28, 1944: OSS and Swiss sources report flu epidemic in South Germany and Austria. Black Forest, Nuremburg, Munich hard hit. Medical Section rushed around doses of sulpha drugs (8 pills) this evening because Col Conklin, Engr O, diagnosed as ill with a form of meningitis. PW Major Genl—242 Inf Div[72]—captured by French in Marseilles is talking. Laid out defenses for 30 km area of Siegfried Line at Zwei[b]rücken. From memory pinpointed on map over 300 pillboxes, MG and other defenses, and has 600 more. PW at Group. An IPW [interrogation prisoner of war] Capt (DI) won his confidence after a month of effort and he is talking—on ground that Germany has lost and the thing to do is to stop the war. Col Koch spent day with him and got marvelous stuff. What I saw of it, amazing. Might be the one thing that leads to beginning of end of war—as will enable us to knock off all strongpoints and cleave through Siegfried Line at this front where terrain most favorable for cross-country Armor movement. Koch so impressed, recommending PW be brought here for close work with XII Corps, PI [photo interpretation], Map and Air people.

All PW of field grade being specially screened now by IPW for possible use to contact Generals and other important people in Germany to overthrow regime and end war. Swiss source reported—Dr. [Karl] Schunne [Schnurre],[73] head of Economic Sec German Foreign Office, told Swiss the situation was hopeless and asked what to do. Told to open Western front to British and Americans. Replied—Good advice but difficult to accomplish anything owing to SS. We have picked up ten W/T [wireless telegraphy] agents, which we are now using to build up another Corps coming up on our front. Purpose to pull stuff down from North and to implement plan to trap German Armies west of Rhine so they can't get over.

87th Div—new outfit—G-2 showed up. Some guy by name of [Lieutenant Colonel John F. T.] Murray;[74] greener than grass and about as much a Div G-2 as I am a bomber pilot. How in Christ's name they make kids like them Div G-2s at this stage of the game when we have plenty of battle-experienced Intl Os (like Goolrick, Benson,[75] Cheadle, etc) is beyond me. Stupid and bungling and a goddamned outrage. Fault of that fatuous AGF; ought to be filling new Divs up with battle-tested Staff Os and using non-combats as replacements to vet outfits. Instead, make a green, untried and rather weak punk like Murray a Div G-2, and able, experienced youngsters don't get a break. Goddamned stupid and costly. For that matter, same applies to Corps. What Horner doesn't know about G-2ing is plenty. Schmuck or I would make a far better Corps G-2, or Benson of 4th Armd, or some others. But he has the Eagles—because he was or is a Reg. They stopped sending Corps CGs and 2-star Div CGs over from States. Why the hell don't they do the same on key General and special staff officers. This dundering Bixel, Ninth Army, is another instance. Pure ass and incompetent, and so is his staff.

Nothing new on promotion, except what I interpreted as hint by Koch that nothing doing on it. Remarked that Section had a new T/O but meant no change. However, friend in Army Group Sec told me my recommendation has not returned yet, a fact he considered was a good sign? However, from Pfann I got interesting hint that there are a dozen or so full Reg Colonels on Army staff, doing nothing really except being taken care of, and who are being carried apparently on the paper (T/O) of Sections like ours and thus blocking guys like me from getting deserved promotions. Thought it was limited to Gay, who is filling AA T/O BG (brigadier general] but apparently general throughout Hq. Wonder which goldbricking bastard is "filling" my T/O spot?

Wednesday, November 29, 1944: Visited Metz and observed shelling of Fort Driant and Fort St. Quentin.[76] Forts Jeanne D'Arc and Ploppenids [Plappeville][77] also holding out. We are shelling forts chiefly with captured 88 and 75 mm guns and Am[munition]. Visited Fort Privat,[78] which surrendered yesterday—however, for protection of Boche against retaliation against their families by SS, we announced the Fort fell as a result of combined Air-Ground assault. Privat built by Germans before 1914— not modern fort, and couldn't have stood up against full-blast Air attack.

ULTRA—reported Hitler Escort Brigade[79] coming into our zone South of Trier. Patton remarked—"Like to see them and Lee (Lt Genl SOS, ETO) MP fight it out. Out to be a hot show." Apropos Metz—was bypassed and encircled 19 November by 95th and 5th U.S. Infantry Divs.

Thursday, November 30, 1944: Patton has sunlamp, which may explain handsome outdoor color. Of course, he is out a lot, but color too good for this time of year. Explanation is—sunlamp supplied by Med Sec—which also de-chlorinates his water to make it palatable for him. Has foghorn-like horn on all his M[otor] Vehicles. Only one of its kind in Army. One blast and clears road. Not klaxon, but while less raucous, just as effective. Willie—Patton's English bulldog—outlawed from CP because he jumped on Bradley's lap. At least that's the story I heard. Also Patton gave Willie a shot of effedrine [ephedrine] when he had sniffles.

Friday, December 1, 1944: One of the most fantastic things we have experienced yet is that we now have a German Major General working for G-2 Section. He is General [Hans] Schafer [Schaefer],[80] CG of [244] Div that French captured at Marseilles and turned over (made available to us by 12 AG and SHAEF). We have him installed in a house in Nancy and he is turning out collated photo maps and poop on Siegfried Line defenses in area between Zweibrücken and Saarbrücken. His home in former times, and in 1940 he put in defenses for a Div Sect[or]. In 1943 during convalescence at home, he rode on horseback all over the area. Apparently has remarkable memory and picked out all defense installations on photos which checked with our collated maps. Producing immensely valuable detailed tactical information. Also, treatise on how to attack forts and strongpoints. Only thing he has asked for so far is to spare his house in Zweibrücken from Air and Arty fire. Also, that he be transferred from French to U.S. PW.

When he refers to visiting celebrities, Patton calls them VIP. After visit to front yesterday up around Merzig, Patton at special briefing said— "Pillbox not over 200 yards away directly down road ahead of us. Guess no one in it, because didn't fire on us. Admit had feeling in my stomach. Felt smaller than I know it is." Patton always attends briefings with long cigar. Apparently after-breakfast cigar. Favorite belt—handmade dark, highly polished leather, with highly polished ornamental brass buckle, eagle insignia. When he got ready to interrogate Metz PW, remarked— "Always wear boots when I talk to Germans."

Saturday, December 2, 1944: Weyland told us today that an all-Allied AF sweep of German airfields being organized for first clear weather. Idea is that every RAF, U.S. and other plane that can be put into air will descend on German airfields, dispersal bays, etc, and beat them up. Surprise ambush attack. Apparently careful planning and preparations being made and when right break comes in weather, will pull the trigger and let Boche have it. Damned good idea. Saturation surprise attack like that ought to massacre them.

Sunday, December 3, 1944: Visited 6th Cav Group—Task Force

Fickett—at Porce Letts [Porcelette], North West of St. Avold, where they have mission to clean out extensive forest in this area. Tough nut to crack, especially big coal mine and steel plant in clearing in forest in series of villages—Karlingen, Lauterback [Lauterbach], L'Hôpital, Aspenbubal, Schmalengarten. Boche dug in in buildings. Pretty bloody fighting. Tank counter-attack. Fickett took up in OP, top of steel plant—could see whole layout of area, our Arty shelling, enemy position, deep refuse and slag ditch. Coming back through woods in rain, he saw Boche positions and 3d Bn of 11th Inf Regt, 5th Inf Div, slogging along soaking wet up to nearby Creutzwald to North where they jump off tomorrow 0730A. Men well and warmly dressed, all new galoshes which they carried because too heavy to walk, but soaked. No talking or kidding but seemed good-humored. Heard one crack as we drove by in ¼-ton with armed MG—"Now we can win the war." When I smiled, he grinned mischievously back at me. Most young and husky—seemed unconcerned they were marching to combat. In woods, mud, wet, troops marching to battle, shelling going on and within a mile of enemy, family of civilians in Sunday best and wheeling go-cart going down center of mud road. Incongruous as hell—but no more so than all villages occupied in midst of battle.

At briefing—staff—Gaffey asked staff to remain and then announced he was going to duty with troops. Few minutes later band lined up, played "Auld Lang Syne" and after he exchanged salutes with Patton, dashed off in MG-armed ¼-ton. Later, heard he was taking over 4th Armd Div and [Major General John Shirley] Wood,[81] its CG, going to States for 90-day rest. (Later heard Wood got into row with little tub-of-lard Ham Haislip, CG XV Corps, who has terrific pull with WD, over moving into XV zone and as a result was eased out(?) . . . Something peculiar. Why the farewell, if Gaffey only TD [temporary duty]. Wood, burly guy, apparently considered blusterer, although Div has done outstandingly. *Editor's note: Wood was relieved because of a dispute with his corps commander, Manton Eddy, his junior. On November 22 Wood approached his old friend and West Point classmate Haislip, commanding XV Corps in Seventh Army, to move across the corps-army boundary.* This little punk Haislip must have some kind of a potent drag. Several times I've noticed Patton has gone out of his way to butter him up—while staff sniff derisively at him. Certainly Haislip has mediocre staff and Patton not anxious to get Corps back in TUSA. Army politics is rampant and as powerful as civilian life. Also as reactionary. Favorites certainly very prevalent. No doubt that Marshall's friends have the breaks—Twaddle, Haislip, Bradley, etc, are examples. Actually, we have damned few, if any, outstanding corps leaders. And outside of Patton—none of our Army commanders are really great, dashing, imaginative military leaders.

Monday, December 4, 1944: Replacement situation extremely critical. Everywhere I've been (visited 80th Div CP at St. Avold yesterday) they have ask[ed] about replacements and Ln O gets same sad tale. Some outfits down to 50 percent and less of strength. Situation so serious that Patton ordered Army Hq to be culled of EM with Inf training. G-2 allotment this month—five men. Three volunteered and other two chosen by lot. 87th Inf Div, which will take over Metz at 1600A 8 Dec, will conduct training program—not very happy about it. But we sure must be low on replacements if only way we can get riflemen is by taking from Army Hq and other Hq staffs. Coy Eklund (G-1) tells me that TUSA needs 50,000 riflemen to fill up to T/O strength. Right now need 10,000. Says we are getting practically none; that what are coming to UK going to First and Ninth Armies—same goddamned favoritism business all over again. Bradley is such a fair and square commander—in a pig's eye. Eklund says riflemen are our big need. Failure in replacements, he says, due to stupid miscalculation in WD or AGF or GHQ. Anyway, he spoke of a TWX [teletype writer exchange] that said that it was "calculated hostilities would cease in this theater by 15 Sept." If that is true, then some incompetent SOBs ought to be shot. How could such calculations have been made when plans were then in the works for the Belgium-Holland operation and we'd been sat down—for lack of supplies so that goddamned show could be put on. If they hadn't sat us down, it was possible that hostilities might have ceased by 15 Sept. Nothing in our way except chaos and confusion. Siegfried Line and other defenses unorganized, undermanned and location unknown. We could have roared into Germany and into Saar and been on the Rhine before they knew what had happened—if they had given us gas, Ammo, couple more Armd and Inf Divs, and a little more Air. Instead directed them to British, First [Army] and Brest and sat us down and still fighting. Lack of soaring, imaginative leadership. Dull and dumb command—in my opinion. Now we are paying for it. *Editor's note: Here Allen raises the debate over whether Patton could have reached the Rhine if he had not been halted by Eisenhower at the beginning of September. It is widely believed that fuel was diverted from Third Army to support Montgomery's attempt to cross the Rhine and reach the Ruhr industrial area—Operation Market Garden.*[82]

Winter offensive sapped Divs and same old game goes on, with FUSA getting all the breaks and TUSA the only one getting anywhere. We are only outfit in West—outside Sixth Army Group, and they now mopping up since breakthrough—that are doing anything and going anywhere. XV Corps now entirely in Germany and with several bridgeheads across Saar bucking Siegfried Line while XII is in Germany in North part of its zone and within a few miles in South.

Really astounding what Patton has accomplished with the little he has had in four weeks. Rushed across Moselle, took Metz and into Germany, and 90th Inf [Div] has big wedge through first line of Siegfried defenses. This with two Corps—3 Armd and 5 Inf Divs, with practically no Inf replacements, few tank replacements and very sketchy Air—in contrast to First with three full corps, and Ninth with two corps and a tiny Div sector and neither has done a damned thing or gone anywhere, and got all the Air and replacements available. TUSA is the only Army that has done things, and Patton has had to fight for everything to help carry him on. Irony—we print PR [public relations] stories of the desperate plight the Boche are in on replacements. Got nothing on us. We about as bad off as they are.

ULTRA briefing—Msg complaint CG Army Group G[83] on no replacements or relief for troops. Patton snorted and cracked, "That SOB is as bad off as we are."

Tuesday, December 5, 1944: Boche commanding generals in West—Rundstedt [age] 64, [Kurt] Student[84]—opposite British—airman, no quiet sector [age] 53, [Field Marshal Walter] Model[85]—Tanker—opposite FUSA and Ninth where most Armor concentrated—[age] 54, [Hermann] Balck—Cavalry—opposite Third—[age] 58. Patton commented (59)—"Goddamn good man, although a bit young."

1st U.S. Inf [Div] in Res[erve], now in FUSA zone, has had 4,600 casualties since start of this campaign—10 Nov.

Wednesday, December 6, 1944: OSS report from Swiss source—North East section of Berlin, where number of the largest plants are—little damaged and production little affected in plants. Also Tempelhof-Nenkohr freight station operating—26 Nov.

Thursday, December 7, 1944: Pfann told me this amazing story about Bradley—Big war council on Air employment held this week at SHAEF—attended by Eisenhower, Bradley, Spaatz, Doolittle, Vandenberg and Weyland—the only one-starrer present. It developed that Bradley had arranged to get all bomber forces for First and Ninth this month. The great and impartial Gp Cmdr was totally disregarding TUSA and throwing full weight of Air power to First and Ninth, actually the same as Ninth holding zone about size of small Corps. Air generals offered no objection as they accepted ground Cmdr's views, and Bradley, the non-political, honorable and earnest Gp Cmdr, had earmarked all the Bomber Air for his pet—FUSA/Ninth, which after a month has gone nowhere and given no sign of going anywhere, despite having 5 Armd and 15 Inf Divs, getting all replacements that are available and having had all the Air day after day. While TUSA, which has really gone somewhere, knocked off Metz and has driven a wedge into the Siegfried Line—only with leavings of Air—was to get again only leavings. Weyland, youngster and only one-starrer, but blew up and, according to story, sounded off to this effect: "Not fair. TUSA only Army [that has] really done something and going places, yet under this plan gets no help, except what FUSA/Ninth can't use. Not right and not sound tactically." Could hear pin drop for moment and then Eisenhower broke silence with brisk crack—"Think Weyland is absolutely right. Plan needs revision to share where can do most good." Then Air generals began climbing aboard—Spaatz, "We can give you 1,000 Heavies." Doolittle—"I can give you a thousand and we'll get the RAF to do a night job for you." In a few minutes, Weyland had completely upset Bradley's carefully set applecart and had promises of full weight of Bomber forces to aid TUSA in hammering way through line between Zweibrücken and Saarbrücken. Meeting broke up by Air generals deciding to hop down and visit Patton—*which explains their presence here this afternoon.* Reason for their being here is above amazing story.[86]

Friday, December 8, 1944: Patton walked into ULTRA briefing, saying to Colonel [Roger J.] Browne,[87] Weyland's C/S—"Bring my gun." Browne handed him pearl-handled 45-cal[iber] in waist holder. Patton—"You can see it was quite a party if I forgot my gun." Party at Weyland's house for visiting Air group. Congressional group visited CP—part of House Military Affairs Committee, but none of top rankers. Bitch Clare Luce[88] among them. Also Joe Farrington[89] of Honolulu. I kept in the background and out of their way so they wouldn't see me. Patton put on special abridged-version briefing for them, after which they ask[ed] some very stupid questions—like "Where is Rhine River? Is it East or West of Saar River?" At regular briefing—dry run for special—Patton told Murray, G-3 Air, not to repeat the fact that around Merzig the day before, we shot at several of our planes, including Colonel [James] Ferguson,[90] A-3, XIX TAC, up to direct smoke for Med Bombers. Patton—"Don't want them to know we are doing that. Make them jittery." Later in day at Metz, MG Millikin, III Corps CG, let Luce and another of the group fire 105mm Howitzer and then gave fact out to press. Subsequently created big ruckus as it was in violation of Geneva Convention. Thing being shush-shushed, but I heard Eisenhower issued statement. Plays into Nazi hands in our cracking down on *Volksturm*[91]—civilians with armbands.

Saturday, December 9, 1944: Gay announced preparing to move Fwd [Forward] CP to St. Avold. Was up there last Sunday when I visited TF [Task Force] Fickett. Beat up pretty flat and also five time-bombs blew there this week, one killing 22 O and EM and wounding 16. Some casernes around that make a pretty good CP if fixed up. Very dirty. Patton called up Major-General Manton Eddy, CG XII Corps, at ULTRA briefing: "Hello Manton. Congratulations on fine work yesterday. (4th Armored made very good progress. About 5 miles). Very good. But got to keep going. I want a hole in the line. Our future depends on it (might indicate threat to take away one of our Div. Were to get 12 Armored Div and that went to FUSA. Might grab for 4th Armored, which Haislip wants, or 87th Inf, which we got first). So kick somebody in the pants and get them going."

Rumor around that Eddy may be due to be replaced. Terrible worry wart; always fretting. Heard he called up around 2300 last night and wouldn't talk to anyone but Patton. Told story that when first up against Moselle, when he was counter-attacked one night when Patton was away and Boche drove in a wedge, Eddy strongly recommended withdrawal. Gaffey rushed down and agreed with him. Finally got hold of Patton who blew up. "Withdraw, hell. No U.S. division has withdrawn yet in this Theater and certainly none under my command will be the first to do so. Goddamn you hold and counter-attack. To hell with your flanks. Flanks is something to keep moving and not worry about." Maybe that incident is the reason why Gaffey shipped out from C/S. One thing is sure: Patton certainly has no shakes as Corps commanders have and never has had. Always had to be the sparkplug—to push, prod and boot them. Div CGs in most cases are better than Corps CGs. *Editor's note: Allen is referring to Eddy's decision on September 30 to withdraw Major General Paul W. Baade's 35th Infantry Division from the Forêt de Grémecey because he considered the forward position untenable, as it was under pressure from the 553rd, 559th, and 19th Volksgrenadier Divisions and the 15th Panzergrenadier Division. Patton was furious because Eddy had failed to commit the 6th Armored Division to reinforce Baade, as he had been instructed to do the day before. According to Eddy, Patton "gave everyone hell over the situation" when he arrived. Eddy had not sent in the*

6th Armored Division because he feared it might get trapped east of the Seille River.

Sunday, December 10, 1944: Prepared special Estimate on the Enemy Situation in adjoining VIII U.S. Corps zone to North that revealed equivalent of 7 Divs (60,000) [and] 2 Armd [Divs] up there. Four in contact; two in Immediate Reserve and three U[nknown]. Koch rushed it over for delivery at ULTRA briefing. Made no mention that I got it up. All very impressed by mysterious build-up, which could mean plans for counter-attack in Luxembourg area, where terrain is favorable for that; thus force diversion of troops from us and slow us down or stop us. Patton asked number of questions. *Editor's note: Allen observed that there were nine panzer divisions in reserve, five of which were "available for speedy employment against First and Ninth U.S. Armies." Although the initiative still rested with the Allies, the "massive" armored reserve gave the Germans "the definite capability of launching a spoiling (diversionary) offensive to disrupt the Allied drive."*[92]

Bradley conferred with Patton today; arriving around 1100. Patton remarked at ULTRA briefing that he expected him in next few days. At regular briefing when G-3 reported that "British continuing to regroup" (been doing that for couple weeks now), Patton snorted sotto voce, "Using a hell of a lot of gasoline doing nothing." Heard some dope about this Col [Phillip C.] Clayton,[93] who took over as PM in place of Macdonald. Was bounced as Regimental Commander when Div CG found him and his staff far to the rear when an attack was supposed to be on. Big, weak-faced Reg. Discard for whom a place was found. Ran PW cages after the Buzz-bomb was axed.

Monday, December 11, 1944: Patton referred at ULTRA briefing to VIII Corps Sit[uation] I brought to light yesterday with the special Estimate that Koch presented. Said that Walker, CG XX Corps, another tub of lard, had expressed concern that when he got through Siegfried Line, might be hit on North flank by powerful force. TAC/R[econnaissance] shows that bridges of Moselle are in and with what Boche have in VIII Corps zone they have that capability.

ULTRA reports Germans flying carrier planes at night to forces holding out at La Rochelle, St. Nazaire, Lorient, Channel Islands and Pas de Calais—with supplies and mail. One message inquired if Channel Islands had bombs for planes to dump on way back. Reported NO. Some planes shot down; some forced to jettison loads in sea. Also, indication planes going to Spain secretly with agents and funds.

Arty Sec reported we are now facing heaviest concentration of enemy

Arty since Operation began last August. 300 guns, all calibers, and fired 6,000 rounds ammo one day. Our expenditure one day last week was 45,000 rounds. Germans also using a salt-like agent to eliminate flash and sound. We captured a lot and have been experimenting with it in firing at Metz forts with our own and Boche guns. We have one Bn formerly PWE [prisoners of war, European] guard duty, equipped entirely with captured enemy guns.

Patton gave Maddox and Muller ceremony this morning on their promotions to BG. Ruffles and inspection MP Guard of Honor.

Heard from 12 Army Group Ln O that Russian plans are—To continue to contain two German armies in North Latvia. To do same in Yugoslavia by swinging to North and cutting Germans off from escape. And then to launch giant power drives to take Warsaw and smash across East Poland and into heart of Germany with 6 Army Groups. Russians have in action on Eastern Front—64 Armies, 562 Divisions. Allies have in West, as of this date—66 Divisions—of which 47 Divisions are in line. Third Army has 7 Infantry, 5th, 90th, 95th, 26th, 35th, 80th, and 87th. Three armored—4th, 6th, 10th—of which 4th, 10th Armored and 5th and 87th Infantry and portions of 80th not in line.

Visited German General working for us. Housed in very nice house on Rue Verdun. CIC linguist acts as orderly. General attired in U.S. uniform—officer shirt, brass buckle, tie, but own shoes, black, NO insignia. About 5 7/8—wavy black haired streaked with gray. Soldier stance. Served us tea and apple pie. Noted he had nervous habit of wringing fingers of his hand, which are reddish as a result. Very grateful for pleasant surroundings and food. Rhapsodized over cornflakes and tomato juice and abundance and excellence of food. Greeted us very cordially but remarked about feeling he was a "traitor" to his country. Koch soothed him by remarking for a common effort to end the war and also his stuff might not be needed. In the morning he gave senior officers of XII Corps, including Col [John H.] Jake Claybrook,[94] G-2, an exposition in ENGLISH on how and what to attack in Siegfried Line between Zweibrücken and Saarbrücken—where Corps' main effort is going to be made in 5–7 days. Taught himself English since he has been in captivity—obviously has excellent mind for concentrated detailed work that requires good memory. He finished work here and is being sent back to 12 Army Group. (With exposition prepared overlay showing how and where to attack.) Expressed hope he would be released from French and turned over to us and be sent to U.S. Asked about getting a suitcase to carry all the stuff—clothes—he had acquired. Worried about his wife, who lived in Saarbrücken, his home. Talked about drinking wine with her when home last year convalescing from wound on Eastern front.

At morning briefing Patton *always* carefully looks over our leaving [evening] PW and K[illed] and W[ounded] figures. Have special chart and always examines figures. Very proud of them. We prepare them for G-1, pack of dumb and incompetent asses, and I boot the K and W up every now and then as Duty Os [are] inclined to be too conservative.

Patton remarked that when Averell Harriman,[95] Ambassador to Russia, visited him recently, said that Russian Army discipline [is] very stern and better than ours. Also that Russians have developed a "new nobility" based on ability and achievements.

Tuesday, December 12, 1944: One thing Patton never fails to do at daily briefings is to closely check Enemy Casualty figures. Watches them very closely and proudly. When visitors present, always turns to them when figures are read by G-2 briefer and by a look says, in effect, "Pretty damn good, eh." Every now and then I give Enemy Killed and Wounded figures a boot to hoist them up [to capture] Air and other late reports.

A report [received that the] Boche have moved large shipment of gas shells from interior Germany to dumps at various points along the Western Front.

Visited TF Fickett at Carlsbrunn [Karlsbrunn], North West [of] St. Avold,[96] our proposed new CP, which has been under fire from Red guns last couple of nights. Went with Colonel Fickett to OP overlooking Saar River and Siegfried Line front; 6th CP in Germany, my first visit there in this war. Lots of Arty shelling. St. Avold badly beat up during fighting and since then, number of time-bombs, 12, exploded—one killing 22 and wounding [unknown].

Amusing incident—Sign put up one morning that all former soldiers in *Wehrmacht* were to report at 1400 hours. On the hour, 67 showed up. At 0905 last Metz fort, Jeanne D'Arc, surrendered. A Major [Hans] Voss,[97] CO [of] *Scorpion*,[98] formerly put out by Boche for their troops and discontinued, now put out recently by us and used by us to plant counter-propaganda. One story to effect that soldiers had right to shoot officers who order retreat—"but privilege not to be abused."

At briefing, PRO read that Patton has been awarded Oak Leaves to DSC [Distinguished Service Cross] for leadership across France. Afterwards rose and said solemnly, "This wasn't awarded to me. I am merely the peg. What was done could not [have] been done without outstanding work of this staff. You made it possible and in decorating, we honor all of you. I am merely the symbol."

Wednesday, December 13, 1944: Replacement problem becoming truly desperate. Told today another 10 percent to be pulled out of Hq. With our surplus, which will also have to go, plus 10 percent, means we lose 16 Enlisted Men. Means sock [some] for Sit Sec—5 and possibly 6. Cut us to the bone and will really be tough, especially on verge of big breakthrough attempt. Heard some more about WD reply several months ago that "it presumed that organized hostilities cease in Germany 15 November." What a laugh—the goddamned asses. Patton got up after briefing, very solemn. Said—"This Army has got to stew its own grease. No replacements and won't be any for some time. We licked lack of gas and lack of Armor and we are not going to be stopped for lack of replacements. Dig up our own. If Infantry can make attacks with 50 percent T/O strength, then this Hq can function with 90 percent. Be one draft of 5 percent. Be another and perhaps others. There will be no squawks." It's tough listing my EM for availability. Nice kids and not built for doughs. All over 30 years out of list. Wish I had lot of them now.

ULTRA—Hitler told Jap Ambassador impossible to make peace with U.S. and Britain and would be "very difficult" with Russia. Japs repeatedly urged separate peace be offered Russians.

Thursday, December 14, 1944: Air plan to crack through Siegfried Line between Saarbrücken and Zweibrücken really stupendous. 4,700 Heavy, Medium and Fighter bombers. First day concentrate all on line defenses. Troops move back 4,000 yards for this purpose. Move up first to gain familiarity with ground, then back for Air assault. First night RAF hammer selected points behind line. Second and third day same programs—minus RAF at night. Great concentrated Air attack of the war and should flatten defenses, what's in them and what's behind them. *Editor's note: The operation was code-named Tink and was initially scheduled for December 19.*

Friday, December 15, 1944: Air attack plan so super-secret that not over 8–10 officers in Hq know about it. Yet despite this, BG Sibert, the great mastermind G-2 of 12 Army Group, sends us a letter through Msg Center about the plan and desire to question PW on effect on them of bombing. That's that two-bit punk's idea of secrecy discipline. He jumped us on ULTRA and is always ready to yap about dissemination. But he doesn't function as a G-2 and I suspect doesn't know how. Practically never gives up spot Info. Repeated instances of failure to inform us of movements. Plays ULTRA practically entirely and for the rest just operates as recording and research agency. Just don't operate as a G-2 and I don't believe he is set up for that or knows how. Sibert is a mediocrity and another instance of the damnable system of putting in misfits and morons in key staff jobs—like G-2—because of drag, being a Reg, or friendships. Sibert—ex-ADC, military attaché and a social climber and glad-hander. One thing he is *not*—a two-fisted G-2.

5

The Battle of the Bulge

Saturday, December 16, 1944: German offensive cracked today. Got first word around 1330—opened with heavy Arty fire along entire FUSA front, followed by Armor-spearheaded attacks in North and South of VIII Corps zone. Six new Divisions identified in VIII Corps zone. Captured Dog [document]—Order of Day—Von Rundstedt and others that this is the great effort of the Germans. "Great hour has arrived. Strong armies are attacking the Anglo-Americans. We gamble everything on this Operation." St. Vith first objective. Evidence that VIII Corps caught napping despite plenty of previous warning and reprinting on page #1—G-2 Periodic Report, 15 Dec, our Significant Facts OB, 9 December, warning about enemy capability to launch offensive in VIII Corps area and with what.

Sunday, December 17, 1944: Enemy penetrations expand. Additional identifications increase number of Divisions in VIII Corps zone to 16 with equivalent strength of 14 Divs and 350 tanks. VIII Corps apparently widely and thinly spread out over 88-mile front. Merely outposted. 106th Infantry Division that just took over position in North badly cut up. One Regimental CP overrun and two regiments cut off. 10th Armored Division pulled from our Reserve and rushed up. 7th Armored Division rushed down from North reported "bounced off." Begins to look like our attack and great Air assault is finis. *Editor's note: By 2000 hours, the lines of Major General Alan Jones's 106th Infantry Division were still generally intact, even though he had committed his last infantry reserve, the 2nd Battalion/423rd RCT, three hours earlier. The 14th Cavalry Group had been pushed back on his left flank, but Middleton had attached CCB/9th Armored Division to Jones at 1120, and it was moving up. However, the situation deteriorated rapidly. Jones and Middleton spoke over the phone twice that evening. During the first call, Middleton stressed the importance of holding in place. When Jones called back later, indicating that he might have to withdraw, Middleton apparently gave him no definitive verbal order otherwise, leaving it to Jones's discretion as the commander on the spot. Jones believed that he was supposed to hold in place, perhaps because Middleton had not given him an unequivocal order to withdraw, even though an VIII Corps order received later stated that positions were to be held at all costs on the west bank of the Our River. All three of Jones's RCTs were east of the Our. Middleton therefore expected the 106th to pull back at least to the west bank, but Jones never moved, perhaps confident that CCB/9th Armored Division and 7th Armored Division could help.*

Monday, December 18, 1944: Enemy penetrations astride V and VIII Corps boundary continue. Elements approaching Malmedy [Malmédy] and Bastogne, VIII Corps CP. Big gas dump, 10,000 gallons, destroyed by Air attack. Enemy apparently heading for Liege [Liège], great Allied supply center. 2 Million gallons of gas, food, ammo, etc. Reports indicate VIII Corps lost at least half [of its troops]. We are very concerned about the V formed by Saar-Moselle[1] in Trier-Merzig area, when we have only 3d Cavalry Gp (Polk)[2] and the terrain is good for drive to South West towards Metz. *Editor's note: Patton had planned to reduce the Saar-Moselle Triangle in September by employing the 83rd Infantry Division, but Bradley refused to let the division participate. The 3rd Cavalry Group and CCA of the 10th Armored Division tried to penetrate the Orscholz Switch Line covering the base of the triangle later in November, but they were halted by the German 416th Division and remnants of the 25th Panzergrenadier Division.*

Big conference held at Luxembourg—Bradley, Patton—but not Hodges. Apparently he is in a blue funk and calling up Bradley constantly. Clear that First Army and 12 Army Group, despite all warning and poop put out about danger, were caught with pants down. Dixon, FUSA G-2, issued a very lurid Estimate a week ago, [while] in Paris.[3] Sibert admitted he was surprised.[4] Plan for TUSA is to take over VIII Corps and war from FUSA. *Editor's note: Sibert's last weekly intelligence summary before the attack, No. 18 issued on December 12, stated that "attrition is steadily sapping the strength of German forces on the Western Front and . . . the crust of defense is thinner, more brittle and more vulnerable than it appears on our G-2 maps. . . . The enemy's primary capabilities continue to relate to the employment of the Sixth SS Panzer Army. . . . All of the enemy's major capabilities . . . depend on the balance between the rate of attrition imposed by the Allied offensives and the rate of [German] infantry reinforcements. The balance at present is in favour of the Allies."*

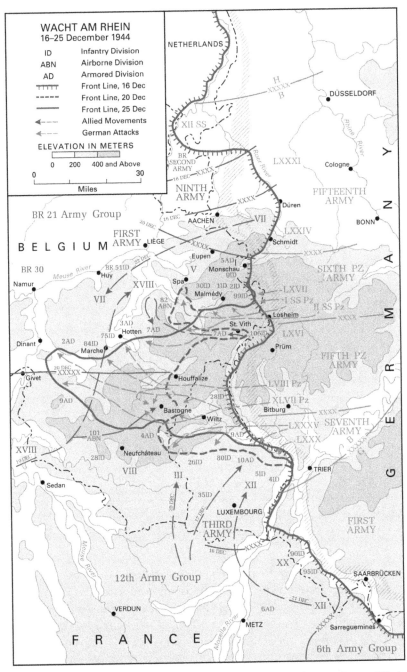

Wacht am Rhein, December 16–25, 1944 (Center for Military History, Washington, DC)

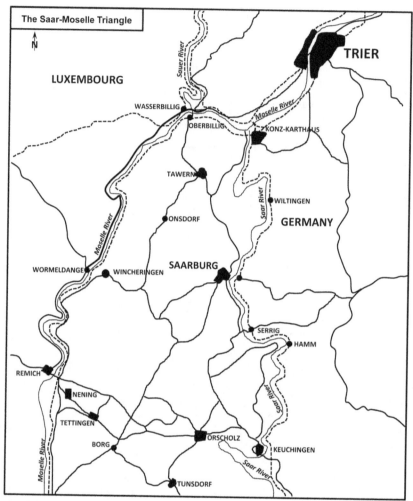

The Saar-Moselle Triangle

Tuesday, December 19, 1944: Staff conference at 0730 presided over by Patton—"Meeting with General Eisenhower yesterday and Third Army has been given a chance to go down in history as the greatest Army of this war." *Editor's note: Allen is mistaken here. Patton met with Bradley, not Eisenhower, the day before. Patton would see Eisenhower later on December 19 at Verdun.* "We are going to attack the enemy on his exposed flank and end the war this side of the Siegfried Line. That is going to kill the Germans coming at us, instead of going after the bastards

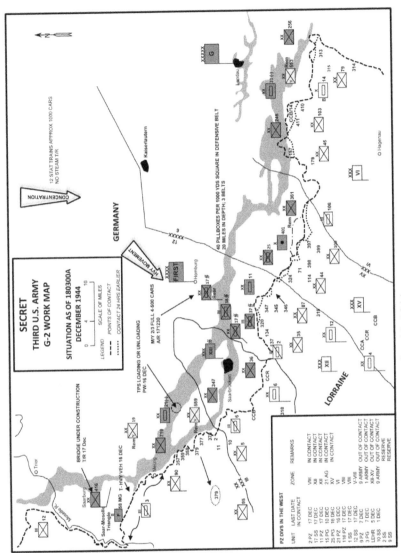

Third Army G-2 Work Map, December 18, 1944

holed up in bunkers and pillboxes." (Stood up in front of the G-3 Operational Map in Maddox's office. Tall, straight, half boots, zoot suit, brass belt, revolver—not pearled handled.) "Again want to caution you about getting excited. Excitement is a highly contagious disease that spreads with rapacious virulence. Must remain cool, calm, and collected, because if we don't, it spreads to others below. Attitude of Army Hq makes itself felt very quickly to those below it. Friends up North have their wind up and we don't want any of that. We can do this because you have always done it better. Third Army is what it is because you have always done the impossible as of yesterday. We are going to do it again. Sorry big Air show apparently off, but we'll kill Germans up North instead of down here. There will be no prisoners taken from SS." (This statement apparently prompted by FUSA report that 200 U.S. soldiers taken PW, were lined up by SS, searched and then shot. Story according to PW, based on Info from MP who was in group but not killed.)

Sunday morning (17th), day after offensive broke, Patton rose at conclusion of briefing and very solemnly said, "What has occurred is no occasion for excitement. Must keep calm because alarm communicates itself very quickly from top downward. Plans we have been working on may change, but whatever happens, we'll keep going right along as we always have done. Killing Germans wherever we can find them."

In discussion after his statement at early morning conference, Patton remarked that Eisenhower had said "I want to put as many troops as possible under Patton." Patton also intimated that Hodges was all aflutter; had called up Bradley frequently during the conference [Verdun] and asked what he should do about this and do about that. All information we get is that First Army staff is in a stew and terribly dismayed. *Editor's note: During the night before the attack, Hodges showed signs of illness. Members of his staff have recorded conflicting views of his physical and mental condition. Some claimed he was suffering from influenza, while another declared that he was confined to bed, barely conscious, with viral pneumonia. One observer noted that throughout the morning of December 17, Hodges was leaning on his desk with his head in his arms. It seems that he was incapacitated in some way for at least two days.*[5] Dixon in Paris when this broke. Very significant that in topside conference, *Hodges* apparently not present. If that presages that he was on the way out, good omen, because he certainly does not have what is required to lead an Army, especially in this kind of a situation he would never have been given the command. At best a run-of-mine Div Cmdr. Man who really made him an Army CG is Macdonald—who left recently to take over 4th Cavalry Group after being TUSA PM. At another time during discussion Patton remarked caustically apropos the idea that it might be a wise plan to carry out our attack in XII Corps zone and pin-wheel the Boche. As they strike West through our lines, we cut through to the East and hit them in rear. "Great plan—only they don't think that way up there. Not made that way." Certainly not as far as G-2ing goes, either. They G-2 from top down and not from down up. They mastermind, deal in crystal-ball thumbsucking, enemy intentions, eyewash and editorializing, and not on identification, indications and capabilities. Same as down-to-earth reporter and thumbsucking columnist.

Wednesday, December 20, 1944: Moved to Luxembourg—with advance CP. Big staff conference at 2230 held by Colonel Harkins. Three Corps brought up—VIII, III, XII—for attack to North West. VIII jumps off on 22nd, XII on 23rd. All together, 10 Divisions in attack. *Editor's note: III Corps, not VIII Corps, was scheduled to jump off on December 22. Only 4th Armored and 26th and 80th Infantry Divisions attacked on the twenty-second. The 5th Infantry and part of the 10th Armored Division attacked on the twenty-third.* Replacements coming in—at last. 800 tomorrow—800 next day plus 4,000 in two days and 2,800 in Metz Replacement & Training Center. Patton and Bradley apparently conferred most of the day—without Hodges. Wondering if he is still commanding FUSA? *Editor's note: Hodges's First Army passed to Montgomery's operational command at 1200 hours.* Simultaneous with our attack, FUSA makes one from North. Ours North West, theirs South. Question if we got enough punch to power-drive them. Captured German soldiers in GI attire and props who revealed 60 or more have been put behind our lines to assassinate VIP—Eisenhower, Bradley, Patton, etc,—and blow up dumps, cut lines, etc. Numerous reports [indicate] Germans are using Sherman tanks that were captured in earlier battles, probably Russia.

Offensive still continuing—Westward pressure unabated. Panzer and Infantry teamed; same tactics we used. Weather filthy and our Air of only reduced effectiveness. Our new Ammo—Posit [POZIT][6]—radar-type—was scheduled to be released along entire front 25 December—Xmas present to Adolf. Apparently to be used in attack tomorrow. We are extremely worried about Trier-Merzig area. Anything busting out of there would catch us right now while we are building up for our counterattack and raise hell. Nail us on our right flank at extremely critical point and time.

Thursday, December 21, 1944: Published G-2 Estimate No. 11[7]— and my eleventh. I've written many G-2 Estimates for this Army. The extent of the criminal negligence, or incompetence, or over-confidence that led to effectiveness of German drive is shown by stuff they captured in first few days—FUSA map depot—got all FUSA map supplies and we've had to furnish all units going into attack with maps. Practically all VIII Corps Artillery. Also that [artillery] of 106 and 28 Divisions and considerable gas, Ammo and rations. So Germans, who are desperately short [of] fuel and other equipment, may be fighting us with stuff they captured from us. We shelled them at Metz with their guns and ammo; they have now spearheaded their offensive with Sherman tanks, guns, Ammo and maybe gas captured from us. Wonder if they captured any new Pozit Ammo—which we haven't used against them yet. That would be the height of irony—if *they* introduced its use in the West.

Regarding 28th Inf Div, plastered in first attack—heard today interesting and characteristic story regarding Brigadier General George Davis, former C/S of Third Army under Hodges. He was put in command of a unit called TASK FORCE DAVIS[8] and in course of its conduct lost 5,000 men and several hundred officers. This terrible toll led to an investigation—in which Davis attempted to place the blame on a Captain—his G-3. Accused him of messing things up which led to the disaster. Knowing Davis as I do, that is too funny for words—Davis runs everything himself. He is his own whole staff, and a charge that a staff officer bulled like that is absurd. What probably happened is that the kid either didn't have a chance to function as G-3 or his recommendations were disregarded. Davis is a ruthless, high-handed and incompetent son-of-a-bitch. The investigation is still on, the G-3 gang tell me, but bet he escapes. He's a Reg and a general officer, and they'll whitewash him.

What has been done by Patton and this staff in last few days is fabulous. One of the greatest logistical and tactical feats of the war. Extraordinary and epic—TURNED an entire Army around as it was poised for a major effort to the East, and in two days' time assembled it—two Corps of three Divs each—125 miles to North. From Saarbrücken-Zweibrücken area to assembly areas in the Luxembourg-Arlon area. This involved not only moving half a dozen Divs in a matter of a few hours, a titanic job in itself in coordinating routes and supplies, but also unpoising the East attack, disengaging from contact with the enemy—35th Div had to delay its movement because of sharp fighting on Wednesday; and finally, adjusting boundaries between Divs, Corps, and Third Army and Sixth Army Group. Truly epic feat in *staff work* and leadership. British couldn't have done it, and Germans apparently don't think we can.

Editor's note: Although Third Army's turn north was impressive, Allen underestimates the scale of the movements carried out by First Army.[9]

ULTRA message [indicated] that they realize the danger of an attack by us, but didn't think it existed, that we could organize it as yet. If that is true, got a big surprise in store for themselves, as III Corps—4th Armored, 80th and 35th Infantry Divisions—jump off tomorrow mor-

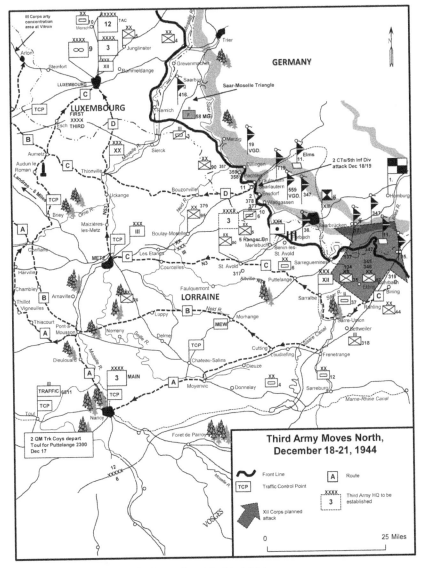

Third Army's Turn North, December 18–21, 1944

ning directly North. *Editor's note: The 26th Infantry Division, not the 35th, was in III Corps at this time. The 35th Infantry Division was at Metz, and Patton would not order it up until December 26.*

Another encouraging ULTRA report that some outfits reported out of gas. If that is true, that means we can nail them. Some of the feats in movement are sensational. At midnight on the 18th, Patton called Gaffey and told him to move 4th Armored to the vicinity of Arlon at once. 4th was out of the line in vicinity of Moyenvic, in South portion of XII Corps's zone. Despite lateness of hour, the 4th cleared Nancy by 0915 the next morning—that is the entire Division—with its hundreds of tanks and vehicles—had been routed out, mounted and in blackout moved out and had gone 50 miles in a period of nine hours. That is an example of the sort of miracles performed and all under inspiration of Patton. No wonder Eisenhower said as soon as offensive developed—"I want to put as many troops as I can under Patton's command." Patton has been his own G-3. He gets on the phone, tells this, that and other Div, Arty, TDs, to move here and there by such and such time, and then gets his G-3 to work out details—roads, etc. Given them apoplexy—but the outfits *move* and get there. Illustration of how Patton operates. He told XII Corps Hq to move up here to Luxembourg. Gave this order in telephone conversation with Eddy in morning. Corps Hq left at once and was half way to Luxembourg—without the slightest idea where CP would be—when Patton casually said to Maddox—"Hallie, just remembered. I told Eddy to bring his Corps up here. Fix them up when they get here." They were—by moving in with us until their phones could be put in, etc. Ate us out of food—sleep in our bunks and offices; we functioned for them—but they are here and we'll be set up to operate during the night.

Moved since 19 [December]—Tuesday:

TUSA—Adv CP
XII Corps Hq
III Corps Hq
4th Armored
10th Armored—moved in past Sunday
80th Infantry
26th [Infantry]
5th [Infantry]
101st AB from Reins [Rheims]
82nd AB [from Rheims]
90th Infantry

Editor's note: The 90th Infantry Division did not move north at this time. By the time III Corps launched its assault on December 22, the 90th Infantry Division had withdrawn across the Saar in the Dillingen-Pachten area and destroyed its ferry. XX Corps issued a warning order for movement north on January 5, and early the next morning the division began to move.

More and more as this unfolds—clear that there was a scandalous failure of topside G-2ing. Great "hot" SHAEF G-2 mastermind—Genl [Kenneth] Strong[10]—on down to Sibert and Dixon. All had plenty of Info. No lack of that. Absolutely NO. Definitely no failure on that score. Had dope. Even issued warnings. Dixon's lurid estimate. Sibert's and others. But did nothing about them—that goes for Eisenhower, Bradley, Hodges—right down the line. Took attitude was capability based, but the Germans just couldn't do it. Lulled with false sense of security, but reports of shortage of oil, ammo, manpower, overwhelming superiority of Air and the fact that we had them constantly on the run. Also, sticking to and concentrating everything on Kolen [Köln] drive. Bradley bent on giving breaks to TUSA (the Weyland Air plan incident). The British were playing their game and all of them were disregarding numerous indications and reports that revealed the whole picture of what was in the works. All very clear now that through Ultra and ground and Air sources they had plenty of intelligence to forewarn them and in plenty of time to do something about it. A couple of Armored Divs, of which TUSA had more than enough, along VIII-V Corps boundary—put in VIII [VIII] Corps in St. Vith area would either have stopped this putsch dead in its tracks or blunted it to some effect. In either case, it would have taken the heart out of the offensive and rocked them to the core. As it was, VIII was caught with pants down—heavily overrun—lost most of [its] Artillery—2 Regts of 106th Div cut off and still cut off. 38th badly beat up and Boche got running start. *Editor's note: Allen means the 28th, not the 38th Infantry Division.* The whole thing is terrible and a vicious indictment of top leadership from Eisenhower on down to include Bradley, Hodges and their be-starred G-2s. Col Koch was the only one who grasped the implications of the VIII Corps buildup and spoke up about it. My estimate on [December] 9th and next one the 15th.[11] Also OB Sig[nificant] Facts which VIII Corps reprinted on first page of G-2 PR [periodic report] on 15th. We told them—but they didn't do anything about it. If counterattack goes off, means greater glory than ever for Patton and Third Army Hq. Be great hero of the war on this side. All through this—clear Eisenhower and Bradley are leaning very heavily on him. He is the only great pile-driver. Hodges is disregarded. Simpson of Ninth, never a factor. Patton is the pinch-hitter and pile-driver. He is called on to pull chestnuts out of fire. German Rcn planes over Luxembourg. 15—one Sq[uadron]. Very thick. AA claims three—found one plane and got three pilots (25% not bad score) tonight.

Friday, December 22, 1944: Counter-offensive jumped off on time.

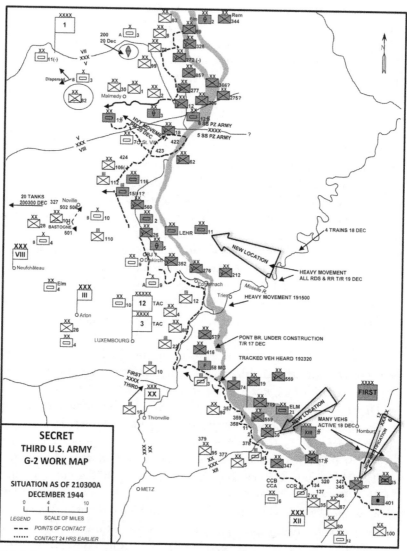

Third Army G-2 Work Map, December 21, 1944

Initially very little resistance. Only one tank working with 26th Inf Div lost up to 1000A. By 1100A—80 Inf had gone 5 miles. 26 Inf—4 miles. 4th Armd—5 mi[les].

Snowed during night and layer of damned stuff over area. No Air up, but around noon cleared some but still overcast.

At 1100A—Patton held conference in Maddox's office. Present—Maddox, Harkins, Koch, Williams, Murray, Jim Goodwin,[12] [David H.] Tull[e]y,[13] myself. In battle dress—chatty and good humor. Remarked—looking at lowering skies, snowy landscape—"Lord kind of played me a dirty trick. (Smile) But maybe He knows better. But we sure could have used some good flying weather. Killed lot of Germans." Apropos report [on] captured paratroops, of which one killed. "Why didn't they kill the others? We don't want any of that kind of PW. Of course don't kill them in cold blood like they have done to our men. Give them a chance. Take them out in brush and give them three-foot head start."

Apropos msg General Millikin—III Corps CG—reported at Advance Post observing attack—"Be tough for him if [he] got shot on his first day in battle. This big day for him. Make him or break him." In midst of the meeting, Patton suddenly said to Maddox, sitting at desk with phone—"Get me Eagle 6 (Bradley's phone)." Took phone and when told Bradley [was] in the War Room, Patton said—"Tell him I phoned and said we have a serious Arty problem. Only got 101 Arty bns. Be sure to put on long face when you tell him that. Give him idea I'm serious." Patton always loves to kid and jest—when feeling good and things rolling right. When he got up, he said—"I'm going up to III Corps—at Arlon—and maybe one op[erational] Div."

Col "Mollie" Williams, Arty O, told me we have 101 Arty Bns—about 1,250 guns—supporting VIII, III and XII Corps. Plenty of Armor and other Bns that could be called on with XX Corps. Holding Pozit for opportune use, though can use it when we want to.

Patton *started* conference by observing—"I think we achieved complete surprise. No Arty preparation. Just moved off and caught them cold. Tit for tat." With III Corps attack—1 Regt of 5th Div, 1 Regt of 4th Div. Attacks at noon in Echternach area to seize high ground in preparation for XII [Corps attack] in that section tomorrow. Patton—"Wish I could conjure up just one more good Div. Shove through hole XII makes, and we go through straight to Cologne." Harkins—"What about 42d Inf Div going to Seventh Army?" Patton—"Green, untrained recruits. Those new Divs are no good for this kind of fighting. Need tough, battle-tested units."

GAS—increasing concern over enemy use of gas. ULTRA reports indicate [Germans] may use it.[14] Bradley expressed belief that if they do, they will use it in S[outhern] shoulder of V Corps area where there is a heavy concentration of our troops and not going anywhere. All troops ordered to carry masks beyond Div rear boundary. Bradley said—"If desperate enough to send assassins behind our lines, they will use gas."

Continue to capture agents and Boche in U.S. and British uniforms. From them get Info—Wear pink or blue scarfs. Top button open. C or D on left side of vehicle or tank hood. Two knocks on helmet.

In addition to fighting Boche, also got to fight SHAEF and 12 Army Group for billets and office space. SHAEF got a number of buildings and hotels reserved for their use when they come here—planned for 1 January—laugh—not using them and we are crowded in layers and sleeping six officers in tiny room and using WC for washroom, can't get billets. In addition to working day and night and fighting Germans, got to do so in frightfully cramped and limited quarters and offices, while SHAEF has plenty of space not being used at all and 12 Army Group sprawled out all over the place. They mess up the detail, have to get us to pull them out of the fire—but they won't give an inch on their comforts—the lousy bastards.

ULTRA—GAS—Boche got one Air squadron under orders not to fly over our lines, so as to be sure not to be captured. Suspect—Gas operation. Also moved over 1,000 carloads of gas shells to North and West—probably lot more. Very SINISTER. One thing stands out on every offensive—not Advanced as fast as surprised by forces employed and we had opposing them should have none. *Editor's note: It is possible that this confusing sentence could mean: "The Germans did not advance as fast as they should have, given the forces they committed and what we had opposing them."*

Last August, with less than they have now in Divisions and in move against us, we cut them to ribbons. Of course, we had Air—but they have little against them now because of weather—so that is equalized. May be one of three reasons why they made so little an advance—(1) Really haven't got it, in equipment, fuel and troops. (2) Heavy losses too much for them. (3) Holding back another punch after we show our hand and react. Time will tell. In the meantime, they have not done as well as it looked like they could and would. One reason—another epic. Fight of 101 Airborne Division to hold Bastogne. Patton asked to hold it in order to slow up attack until III Corps jumped off today. Terrific fighting around town all day yesterday—town completely encircled, but

101 still holding it. But despite identification of 5 Boche Div—116 [Pz],[15] 130 [Pz], 11 Pz and 560 Inf[16] and 5 Para—yesterday the Germans got nowhere and town is still in Div hands. Only request—Ammo and supplies. Knocked out by count 58 tanks and possibly a number of others—all by little light Div without any heavy weapons or inf training. THAT IS AN EPIC.

SMASH DEVELOPMENT OF DAY

First and Ninth U.S. Armies placed under jurisdiction 21 Army Group, which now makes Field Marshal Montgomery CG of four Armies—1st Canadian, 2d British, First U.S. and Ninth U.S. All this leaves 12 Army Group with only one Army—Third, made up of four Corps—III, VIII, XII and XX. So Bradley becomes a Group Cmdr of Group that consists of one Army—or as I put it—a Group made up of General Patton and Third Army. Hodges and Simpson completely subordinated. Ninth actually an Army in name only. Really not even a strong Corps. First—once so proud, cocky and all-important—now an attachment to the British. Division apparently due to split between First and Third by St. Vith–Bastogne salients, which are rapidly becoming one salient. Difficulty maintaining communications and control makes regrouping necessary. International boundary between Armies East-West through St. Vith. Not a hint of this made public. Wonder what reaction will be back home—placing two U.S. Armies under British CG—who is universally and strongly disliked throughout U.S. forces as a prize punk and slow-moving muddler. Public picture of him is far different from U.S. soldiers'. He is no hero to us. Far from it, and quite contrary. He is despised and disliked, and the British are making a grave mistake in pressing him and boosting him. Building up backlog of veteran antipathy that will cost England dear in the future. This is definitely not pro-German or pro-French feeling. Germans fiercely hated and French despised. It is pure and simple anti-British—based on their bungling, arrogance, snootiness, grabbiness and bumbling and muddling. Their constant regrouping, pivoting on CAEN and sitting around doing nothing while we do the fighting aroused widespread hostility. Very bad situation that I honestly feel is largely the fault of the British.

Saturday, December 23, 1944: Clear, bright, cloudless day—best in weeks, and literally a miracle for us. GAF out in force, but so are we, and that means really blunting the German advance. Every day like this is worth three divisions in slowing them down and inflicting losses. A few more days like this and we can smash the power out of their drive.

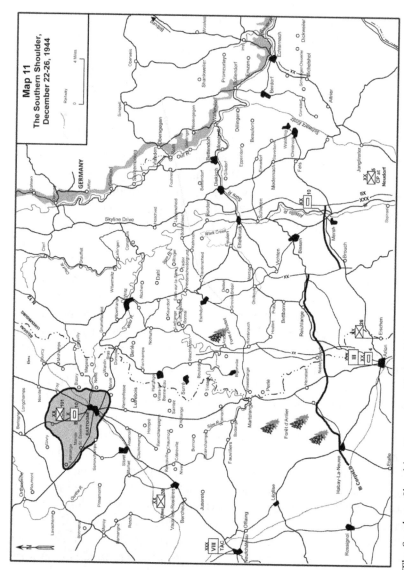

The Southern Shoulder, December 22–26, 1944

Some GAF stuff over Lux[embourg] last night and lot of AA. Paratroops dropped 5/6 miles East of Luxembourg. 101 AB grimly holding out in Bastogne. Magnificent fight with aid of CCB of 10th Armored Div and Arty, 101 AB today knocked out 35 enemy tanks by actual count—equivalent to ½ a Panzer Div. 101's fight blunted and stunted German advance—completely upset timetable plans and I believe time will prove they busted the whole scheme. This, plus miraculously fast reaction of Third Army and unexpectedly good weather. That made possible the great fight of 101, as we were able to supply them by air. Two hundred carriers brought in Ammo, fuel, medical, etc, supplies today—completely saving situation. Without this, they would have been unable to hold out as *Patton asked them to do.* 4th Armored—CCB under General [Holmes E.] Dager,[17] fighting up from South to Bastogne. About _____ miles to go and resistance very tough. Germans realize importance of the point and are fighting furiously—130 [Pz Lehr], 5 Para, 2 Panzer in battle.

Overall general Tactical Situation not good—but not bad. One attack that jumped off yesterday—III Corps—made good progress—average 7 mile advance—but not as much as hoped for. On other hand, German offensive definitely slowed up. Bastogne definitely held them up. Some sign that they realize it is too costly to take and have begun to bypass it. Trend to West and North West, but not to South—which is good, as it indicates that they are not contemplating envelopment of our West flank—a very serious capability. If we push them North, it may force Monty to fight—the stalling SOB. Whole VII Corps concentrated to North West but doing nothing. If they would attack to South East in force while Germans in movement, could throw them completely off balance and roll them back. But Monty is regrouping and VII Corps is sitting on its butt doing nothing—while we are carrying the whole brunt of enemy resistance. VII is a very good corps and if under Patton, would be killing Germans and raising hell in big way.

Patton came into briefing sober and silent this morning. Asked eagerly about weather and results of Air yesterday. Several hours later he stalked into the Situation Room with Eddy and said—"Allen, show General Eddy enemy movements." I gave the Estimate of the Situation on the map, while Eddy stood with back to big windows and Patton sat on edge of field tables we used for duty desk. I stressed capabilities to launch diversionary attack in Trier area and to envelop West flank—although trend now to North West. Afternoon Squadron of the Squadron forts flew over town on way to Trier to pound it and bridges over Saar and Moselle—about 30 Air miles. *Editor's note: This sentence could mean:*

"In the afternoon a squadron of Flying Fortresses flew over town. . . ."
Army and Navy squadrons passed each other going in and coming out.
Vivid spectacle—great planes silvery in sunlight.

Sunday, December 24, 1944: Patton bustled into briefing exclaiming—
"Got two more Regts of Engrs. Makes four. Want to use them in that
Trier area." Later, turned to Maddox and said—"Hallie, want Situation
Report by 0300 for General Bradley. Future of this Army depends on the
impression we make regarding it. Be sure to emphasize the various danger spots—Trier, exposed flank on west, Echternach and others." Around
1100A, Patton called and said he wanted Colonel Koch or me to come to
his office immediately to give General Bradley a report on the enemy situation. Ran into Koch in corridor and we both went into vast room at head
of steps. Only Bradley and Patton were there before small Situation Map.
Koch, primed by me on significant developments, gave brief outline and
then asked me for details, which I gave on the map. Bradley asked some
questions on enemy reserves which I answered. After discussion by Patton and Bradley on dangerous Trier situation, Bradley turned to me and
said—"Haven't seen you since Louisiana over two years ago." I replied,
"Yes Sir, lots of water and terrain have been passed over since then." He
commanded 38th Infantry Division in maneuvers—now badly cut up after
being overrun in first drive of offensive and badly cut up. *Editor's note:
Allen means the 28th Infantry Division.* Patton asked Koch his opinion
of moving a RCT of 35th Infantry Division down South to the Trier area,
and Koch said okay if the vacated area was buttressed with Arty. *Editor's
note: Allen's orientation is wrong here. Trier was north of XX Corps, and
the 35th Infantry Division was at Metz.* He and Bradley and Patton looked
at me, and I nodded my head in concurrence. (Later, learned Bradley told
Patton to go ahead on plan. We have been warning about Trier sector for
days. Very menacing capability.) About 5 p.m., Patton came in as I was
looking over Situation Map and I gave him a briefing as he stood moving
back and forth on heels and chewing a cigar. Then sitting down on edge of
Duty Desk field table, tensely studied map; finally remarked:

"Wish I had another two Divs. Could wipe them out."

"How about from below?" (Six Army Group)

"Gave us all basics from two Divs. Two thousand replacements."

"How about up North?"

"They wouldn't be much good if we could get them. But can't get
them. They are trying to get some of ours."

Allen—"One thing very reassuring in this situation is that we have
101 bn of Arty now on line."

Patton—"108 Bn now and really got into full action today. 101 AB doing great job. They can't wipe them out. We can supply now with this good weather and the Hun can't overrun them. They are better men and better fighters than the Hun. If we can only have a few more days of good weather like today. Then the war will be over."

Another bright, clear day—really miraculous. A truly heavenly Xmas gift. Every day like this is worth two Armd Divs to us. Weather has had tremendous effect on German offensive, definitely slowing it up and causing very heavy losses that are bound to count in long run. Has cost them at least one Div a day in personnel and equipment losses. Today, for instance, Air claimed over 600 vehicles destroyed, number of trains, gun positions, etc. No question Germans counted on bad weather and just didn't work out that way. Their Air is very active, but absolutely no effect on our operations, while our overwhelming Air superiority is really hurting them and whittling them down. Reason for this miraculously clear weather, according to Weather Det, is a freak bank of some kind over the North Sea that is keeping out cloud fog banks from this area. Further, the cold is firming the ground and giving good footing for tanks. Greatly reduced mud. Viciousness of Germans is limitless. In addition to paratroops, agents, patrols and troops in U.S. uniforms, vehicles and tanks they also have groups of assassins and are using P-47s that are shooting up our columns. Every day brings a number of reports of the latter. Yesterday, one of them strafed an ambulance, killing the driver and six wounded. Only escapee—assistant driver.

As Patton left CP in the evening, he was challenged by an MP, and after giving the password, said jovially—"Merry Xmas. Noel, Noel, this looks like a good night to give the Germans hell." I spent the night working because Cheadle came down sick with a sore throat. I was dead tired, but dragged it out somehow to the accompaniment most of night of AA fire and a goddamn siren that kept sounding alarm and all-clear—a few minutes after which AA guns would open up again. AA reported 90 planes over Luxembourg during the night, with 13 shot down. Except for noise, didn't bother us at all.

Monday, December 25, 1944: Another clear day—another priceless miracle. Air out again in force—day's claims were over 1,400 vehicles, 23 tanks, a number of RR engines, cars, guns, etc. Lord, if this will only keep up for another few days—until the 30th, as Weather Detachment says it may, due to freak formation over North Sea. As Patton remarked when that was reported by Murray at the briefing—"If it does, we'll win this war." Lot in that. Lord give us that break. Patton stalked into briefing snappily in his tight battle dress, saying "Merry Xmas to you all. Here's hoping we spend the next one in Tokyo." Few minutes after briefing began, he broke in—"Maddox, the CO of that Combat Team of 80th Div isn't sittin on his ass, is he? I want him up on that line." Maddox reported the unit moving, but was not sure how far it had gone. Patton— "Get hold of him and tell him to get up there. I want every sonofabitch to be fighting. There are to be no reserves. Everybody fights. Tell him I'm coming out there to see what the hell is going on." Maddox—"Yes Sir, I'll tell him!" Patton—"I want everyone to understand we are not fighting this battle in any half-assed way. It's either whole hog or die. Shoot the works. If those Hun bastards can do it, so can we. If those SOBs want war in the raw, we'll give it to them." Thereupon he ordered a number of shifts in troops to bring more up to the line. However, while talking tough, Patton moves with care. Acts boldly, but not as recklessly as he talks. Day after we opened the corridor to Bastogne and put in 40 trucks of supplies, he demanded and got Air supply. When Air Force cut plan in half, he personally telephoned General [Leven C.] Allen,[18] Bradley's C/S, and insisted on the full lift. "We got a corridor, but it's under fire and pressure, and I don't want to take any chances. Better be sure than sorry. Tomorrow we will do all trucking, maybe, but today need Air supply to avoid any slips." When Murray reported that we could expect possibly another couple days of clear weather, Patton beamed and said—"Print another 200,000 prayers. The Lord is on our side. Got to tell him what we need." Printing prayers [was a] reference to the little attached Xmas greetings Patton had distributed to all personnel in TUSA this morning. Lot of amusement over fact that he pleads for secession of rain. This relates to our previous Saar basin front, when record rains nearly flooded out offensive. Re above prayers, one side of card read:

HEADQUARTERS
THIRD UNITED STATES ARMY
  To each officer and soldier in the Third United States Army, I wish a Merry Christmas. I have full confidence in your courage, devotion to duty, and skill in battle. We march in our might to complete victory. May God's blessing rest upon each of you on this Christmas Day.
G. S. PATTON, JR.
Lieutenant General
Commanding, Third United States Army

The reverse side of card read:

> Almighty and most merciful Father, we humbly beseech Thee, of Thy great goodness, to restrain these immoderate rains with which we have had to contend. Grant us fair weather for Battle. Graciously hearken to us as soldiers who call upon Thee that armed with Thy power, we may advance from victory to victory, and crush the oppression and wickedness of our enemies, and establish Thy justice among men and nations. Amen.

101 AB Div, with CCB of 10th Armd and CCR of 9th Armd Divs, still holding out heroically in Bastogne. Very tight and tough squeeze, owing to supply situation. Not able to hold out if they hadn't received Air supplies that saved the battle—which is now becoming clear may be one of the decisive—if not the decisive—struggle of this mad, desperate Hun offensive. It slowed them up and also inflicted terrific losses on 130 and 116 Panzer Divs, also 2 Panzer Div. 5 Para Div whittled down to about one-third and others beat up. German efforts to take Bastogne not only slowed up sweep toward Liège and the capture of our supplies—on which they counted to move—but sapped punch out of drive. We estimate that Bastogne and other counter drives, plus good Air weather, wiped out equivalent of 3 Divs in a week. This epic defense of Bastogne saved the bacon of First Army and the British. Gave them time to regroup and get set for Germans' next punch toward North West. Also gave them time to get over their *panic*. Now it will be interesting to see how well set they get. If they don't this time—ought to be a lot of head-busting, beginning with Eisenhower, Montgomery and Hodges. Hodges, incidentally, finally condescended to visit Patton. Drove in today in a big sedan. First time he's been to our Hq. Took a beating and kick in teeth by Germans to bring him to heel. The incompetent bastard ought to be relieved and sent home. For that matter, so should Eisenhower and Montgomery. They were surprised and caught with pants down—when absolutely no reason for it. Had all the information [from] ULTRA—but paid no heed. They were criminally negligent and should be relieved and busted. If [Lieutenant General Walter C.] Short[19] and that stupid Admiral [Husband E. Kimmel][20] were guilty at Pearl Harbor—so are Eisenhower, Montgomery, Bradley and Hodges. Patton saved their bacon by moving fast and decisively—at the cost of throwing away an attack that [would] probably win the war and which cost thousands of lives to prepare for. This is the

second time they "sat him down" and the second time he is pulling their irons out of the fire.

No word of us in this situation still has been released. Germans announced it—but we are still under wraps. Meanwhile, FUSA still making extravagant claims about its zone and operations. This great Air day—knocked off over 1,500 vehicles and claimed 25 tanks! Lots of AA shooting during night. Been over every night. Lots of stuff pouring through town all night up to the line.

Tuesday, December 26, 1944: Koch told me Sibert asked him for a recommendation for G-2 to replace [Henry M.] Zeller,[21] XX Corps. Koch told Sibert he could recommend me but wouldn't because "can't do without you." Told me [he] didn't want to stand in my way for promotion, but didn't want me to go. Said [he] was working on my promotion.

Another good Air day—our rare luck still holds outs. As a result, we are taking a terrific toll of the Boche, both on ground and in the Air. Estimates place Boche Air losses at around 1,100 planes since offensive began 10 days ago. Another week at this rate and they won't have anything to put into the Air. Their great gamble in the Air got even less results than on the ground.

Murray told me stomach-sickening story about the criminal sogginess and negligence of SHAEF. A mission was asked to provide Air medical lift for some 100-plus non-transportable casualty cases of the heroic holders of Bastogne. Had to be laid on by SHAEF in UK because they don't have drop equipment on Continent. This shows their vicious goddamned incompetence and lack of foresight. So fixed on knocking off Germans easily that they did nothing to meet another contingency. So, when bases in UK were weathered in this morning, they casually scrubbed the mission—made utterly no effort to provide a substitute plan. Just cancelled the mission and went on with their pleasant holidaying. By extremist measures, Murray and XIX TAC worked out a small substitute plan. Got LI [liaison] plane, and with fighter cover of 4 P-47s, brought in one surgeon and some medical supplies. (Next day, number of others by gliders and fighter cover.) But if it hadn't been for the efforts made here, nothing would have been done for these heroic lads, while those goddamned sons-of-bitches at SHAEF revelled and whored around in comfort and with joy in Paris and UK.

At 1615 some Armored Inf of 4th Armored punched [through] finally and made a junction with the Bastogne garrison. Great and possibly decisive incident of this offensive. By night, a narrow corridor was opened to the strong point and within a few hours, a convoy of trucks carrying ammo, gas, supplies, was organized and underway. Forty truckloads put through narrow corridor during night—under fire and constant efforts by Boche to cut the thin artery. As soon as the corridor was established, Patton ordered the remainder of 4th Armored Division up to widen and strengthen it. 101 Airborne Division is cocky and tough and astoundingly not badly hurt. Remarkably few losses, considering terrific attacks faced and huge losses they inflicted on enemy. Sent word to Patton—Losses light, morale high, awaiting order to continue the offensive. When Boche sent long ultimatum to the Commander[22] of U.S. Forces in encircled Bastogne, reply signed by American Commander came back—"NUTS."

Wednesday, December 27, 1944: Another marvelously and miraculously clear day after a spectacularly clear moonlight night. Nights have been as brilliantly light and clear as the days. Full blue-white moon high in sky almost with the fall of early night. With snow covering the landscape, everything stands out with vivid brightness and our night fighters have been up roaring all over the battle area. Patton came into the briefing very jovial—brick-tight battle dress and boots—cracked to Colonel [Frederick R.] Chamberlain,[23] AA—"How many Germans did you kill last night?" "Our count shows 48 pilots and crews." "What! Hot dog." Shook Chamberlains's hand very heartily. At 1115 hours got word to assemble in Maddox's office. Koch was at Army Group, so I went. Present: Maddox, Tulley, Murray, Brown[e] (C/S XIX TAC), Jim Goodwin, [Elton F.] Hammond.[24] Before meeting started, Koch came in and I stayed. Patton came in with Harkins. Very serious, smoking and rolling cigar nervously as he always does when under tension. "Asked you to meet to give me your frank and independent view on a proposal that [has] been made by General Montgomery. Don't want you to be affected by anything you might think I want or would want you to say. Absolutely your own opinion. General Eisenhower asked for it, and after I outline General Montgomery's plan, I want you to talk it over and give me your point of view on two-page report. General Montgomery holds that FUSA has no offensive capacity and won't have for three months. Only offensive possible is from south and he says we lack the troops to do it. So he proposes that we—abandon the Colmar pocket and pull back to the Saar or Moselle. He favors that on the ground that it would shorten our lines and while it would do the same for the Germans, we would benefit most as it would make available several or more divisions to hold them off while we regroup and build up for a spring offensive."[25] Group listened in growing horror and astonishment as Patton outlined this fantastically yellow and disastrous proposal. It summarized the whole course of British operations over here. Regroup and move forward inch by inch. Let us take the chances, the losses and do the hammering. And this great, mighty military genius—newly-made Field Marshal—just a goddamned phony and scarebelly. I heard they were scared pantless, but really didn't believe it. But this was pure murder—a scheme so impossibly stupid and ruinous that it was literally traitorous. For it meant absolute defeat. The American public wouldn't take it. The Russians would wash their hands of us—as they should, and I don't think the U.S. Army over here would take it. Further—TUSA just wasn't made for that kind of operation—as Patton pointed out. And then all the terrible and bitter losses and sacrifices of the Saar offensive—against floods, mud, cold, endless fortifications—Metz, Koenigsmacher,[26] Maginot Line,[27] Saar—all to be tossed overboard at one casual flip. It has been bitter and bad enough to have all our great plans to crack the Siegfried Line junked by this colossal blundering and bungling up there—but on top of that, to give up all we won at such fearful cost in Lorraine—goddamn that filthy son-of-a-bitch— that is too much. He is a yellow bastard, and it's an outrage he can't be fully exposed as such by the disclosure of this traitorous plan. I am sure public reaction in the U.S.—and perhaps even England—would drive him into the oblivion he deserves. Really, he ought to be shot—and I mean that seriously. And Eisenhower doesn't deserve much less for even entertaining the idea. He should have relieved that SOB when he abandoned those two regts of 106th Regt [Division] that were encircled but holding out gamely East of St. Vith. If it had been Patton, he would have relieved them, just as he hammered through to relieve Bastogne. Those encircled Regiments could have been relieved and the Hun badly beat up in the process if bastardly FUSA had a General with guts and ability instead of a goddamned old puque.

Also, if Eisenhower had any guts and decency to stand up against Montgomery and make him come to heel; that yellow poseur not only threw those two American Regts to death or captivity, but forced 2d Armored Division to withdraw West from St. Vith, after the Hun took it, when 2d said it could hold high ground nearby and wanted to. If they had made a fight for it, it would have held the German drive to two prongs instead of full-bellied salient. (See sketch on page 137.)

Patton kept pretty much to his statement not to say anything to influence us. Only when Maddox remarked that the psychological effect of such a jackal plan would be catastrophic in U.S.—Patton replied, "That goes for Third Army, too. We are just not trained. We don't know how to retreat. Our Divs fight by attacking, not retreating. As I see it, if we

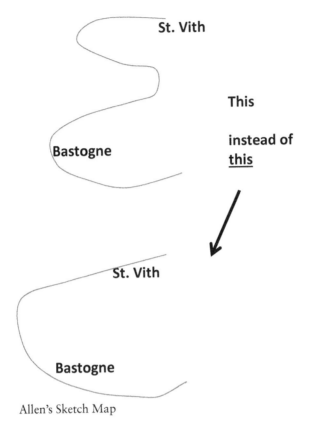

Allen's Sketch Map

do this, the war is over and the Germans will win." "As regards FUSA. Hell, all those sons-a-bitches need to fight is an order to attack. But of course, they won't if the British won't give the order. Been tied up with them so long that all they know what to do is to sit on their asses and regroup and pivot on somebody else." Patton left after that. Meeting was short. Opinion was unanimous that it would be catastrophic to adopt the plan. I helped Koch draft G-2 views. (See copies in my files.) This nefarious and traitorous plan is a complete unfoldment of sitting us down in Sept. We could have won the war in a month if Eisenhower, and Bradley had brains, flexibility, imagination, guts, and no envy of Patton. Now Montgomery proposes to lose it by running like a yellow dog—the filthy bastard.

It now develops that the Germans did capture some gas—in addition to the bulk of VIII Corps Arty. At *Houffalize,* captured 10,000 gallons in 5-gallon cans—an outrageous indictment on security and discipline, as a few shots would have set whole dump afire. Total gas "take" between 50–75,000 gallons—not great deal, but plenty when they don't have any at all.

Moved our CP to large Old People's Home on edge of big ravine that divides Luxembourg. Best CP we've had yet. Handsome stone turreted building with numerous rooms that make nice offices. What was apparently JU-88 roared over our CP in École Industry and Commerce last night around 2000A at rooftop level and did a bit of strafing but no damage or casualties.

Thursday, December 28, 1944: Clouded up today and Air activity cut down very greatly. First bad day since good weather started. Heavies and some fighter-bombers up but no great deal. *New Plan of Attack formulated* and sent to Eisenhower for approval. *VIII Corps* to attack to North West with Houffalize as objective. Houffalize about 5 miles North of Bastogne and center of road net. Set in deep value [valley] and its capture would cut German lines of communication and force him to either attempt a break [out] North/North West or envelopment of our West flank South & East or conduct a withdrawal. *III Corps* up valley of Roer to North East—sort of to right of VIII Corps. *XII Corps* to North East through Echternach in direction of Bonn. That is, we'd follow them through the hole in the Siegfried Line that they presumably had gone through. *XX Corps* to mop up V-shape area South of Trier where Moselle and Saar join—this attack to jump off after III and XII get underway. Plan indicates Monty's yellow and dastardly withdrawal scheme apparently overridden or rejected or dropped. Bradley to take this plan to Eisenhower for approval. Big pow-wow at Verdun. From hints dropped by Gay and Harkins, I gather impression that the separation of FUSA and TUSA is not the only reason Bradley was relieved from command of 12 Army Group. From their remarks, possible to deduce that Bradley was removed from command—perhaps even only temporarily—because of the German breakthrough. *Editor's note: Bradley was not relieved of command of Twelfth Army Group. He continued to command, but with only one army, Patton's Third, rather than two.* Also strong hints and a lot of gossip that Hodges is slated for the axe—I hope so—and his G-2 and G-3. The former, "Monk" Dickson certainly was all aflutter during the attack. He jittered like a dry leaf in a gale. One thing is certain: From the great and mighty General Strong, SHAEF G-3 [G-2], on down to Sibert and Dickson, all were caught by surprise and with their pants down. They all blatted about Germans' capability to attack, had all sorts of tell-tale indications that [he] was getting ready—ULTRA, radio silence, heavy movements, PW statements—but didn't do a goddamned thing about it. When the record is written, Eisenhower, Strong and others right down the line will get their nuts clipped. They bulled fearfully, and instead of getting a fifth star, Eisenhower should be getting the gate. Patton was the only one whose nose is clean and the only one they got who had drive, guts and ability to pull their bacon out of the fire and save the situation from a rout. Hodges and his fancy-pants pact just went to pieces and SHAEF and Monty were no better—and that goes for Strong, too. A lot of brass hatted bastards should—and will—burn for this shambles when the record is written. And this tragedy is not the only one there will have to be an accounting for when history writes the cold and truthful story— Why we were sat down in Sept when there was no Siegfried Line as an organized defense and there were no organized German forces between us and the Rhine. Why Patton was not allowed to close the Falaise pocket when XV Corps was only 8 miles from FUSA. Why all the weight [was] concentrated in the Aachen drive, when a few more divisions given to us would have speeded up offensive through Saar and breakthrough of Siegfried Line to Rhine, thus completely upsetting German offensive plans. Yes—a lot of things will have to be accounted for, and I'll wager a dollar to a donut that the brassy bastards who should be on the accounting end will be alibi-ing, explaining and justifying as soon as they reset their scared Adam's apples and their upset stomachs.

Friday, December 29, 1944: Good day again; clear, bright and Air out in full force. That forecast that this extraordinary and miraculous weather break might last to 30th is really coming to pass. Yesterday on an exception so far. The effect the weather is having is terrific. Making the difference between literally defeat of Germans and possible great tactical and strategical gains by them—conceivably cutting our North and South Armies apart and slashing back to the Channel again. Certainly as far as TUSA is concerned, Air is the Army's reserve. XIX TAC—and with this weather, it is worth on the ground in the line 5 Divs every day like this. Literally.

Replacement problem continues desperate. Coy Eklund told me we shipped out today about 3,500—the last that he knows will be available until 10 January when "an issue" from the States is due. Told me a peculiar thing—that Eisenhower had to send his G-1—[Brigadier] General [Joseph J.] O'Hare[28]—as a "delegation to Washington to plead urgency and need for steady flow of replacements." That certainly is extraordinary. It would seem that with his power and prestige, all Eisenhower would have to do is to declare his wants and requirements and they would be met—without sending a "delegation." Well, the German attack should have helped O'Hare a lot. It certainly gave point to his pleas for more men. Eklund told me that TUSA replacement needs at minimum are 1,000 per day. That we are now about 11,000 short and the total increases 1,000 daily—with no new men in sight. That 28th and 87th Divs are little more than divisions in name only. He remarked cryptically—"Patton is a great fighter and we need that type, but his kind of fighting eats up men." Eklund said that within two weeks, 43 percent of replacements are either dead, wounded or missing. Also was very bitter about our handling of replacements—jam them in freight cars, trucks (as I have seen), shove them up to line and into battle. No ceremony and no comforts—but that's the way it always is. Our methods, incidentally, are no better or different essentially than Germans'. We too are shoving men into battle who lack training as doughboys. We have replacements we produced from our Hq and went to units in line after only a few days' refresher training—although only men with Inf training taken. This *replacement* matter is another bungle some bastards should be called to account for.

Saturday, December 30, 1944: Visited III Corps at Arlon and VIII Corps at Floreville. Cold, wintry, snow-covered countryside. Few planes up, but very soupy over *Bastogne* area. [Lieutenant Colonel Herbert H.] Hauge at VIII Corps gave me insight on why they were caught napping. Said they considered the sector a rest and refit area; had apartment house for Os of Corps in Luxembourg and spent weekends there. However, he also told me that General Middleton, CG VIII Corps, was not worrying because he had a letter on record which he had written to FUSA pointing out the Corps was covering an over-extended front—88 miles—and had only one good Div in Corps. According to Hauge, letter received no consideration; Hodges and Bradley concentrated on Aachen attack and paid no attention to the VIII Corps situation. VIII printed our PR warning on the situation in their 15 Dec PR—one day before offensive broke.

Build-up against Bastogne continues. As I forecast in our capabilities, 2 Panzer and 1 Inf [Divisions] shoved up against wedge—9 SS and 12 SS and 26 Inf Divs.[29] Makes total of 10 Divs—5 Panzer-type surrounding wedge and trying to knock it off. III Corps jumped off on its attack. If it goes, it will be the decisive phase. One major drawback is lack of pressure by FUSA and British on North. Bastards sitting on their butts letting us take the pounding. Even a little pressure would help us enormously. Why the hell Bradley can't get that over, I don't know, unless he is in the doghouse, or Monty—the phony—is forcing them to wait until we draw as much as possible and then attack. Be just like the cautious punk. At briefing, Gay related that Millikin, III Corps, had called him yesterday and wailed that his Reserve consisted of 2 Bns. "I told him that those 2 Bns are not only III Corps Reserve, but also the Army Res." Harkins—"I suggested he better not let General Patton know he had two uncommitted bns or he would grab them." Patton laughed.

Sunday, December 31, 1944: Luxembourg being shelled by some kind of mystery rocket or Arty. Seven of the things plastered RR Depot last night—about one mile from our CP. No known casualties. Arty recovered tail part of missile—indicates some kind of rocket about the size of a 155mm shell. Our CP in handsome, turretted, stone Old People's Home in big park on edge of big ravine that splits town into two parts. 40 miles of subterranean passages all over the place. Pascators [Pescatore] Foundation[30] that SHAEF earmarked and after a week of prodding, finally released to us. Very comfortable and handy place to work. Our Sit Room in a light, roomy sun parlor.

Fair Air day—started out good but souped up in afternoon. Anything helps. It's the days that Air can't get off at all that hurt. III Corps jumped off today on time—but very slow going. Extremely heavy resistance. ORD[NANCE] report—in G-4 PR shows that between 23–30 December our tank losses were—15 Light and 93 Medium. That is no mean loss, and shows what it cost to stop and contain enemy surprise offensive.

On duty tonight. Last year this time I was at A Clark;[31] attended 2d Cav Div New Year's Party. Following night, after party in Mexico, I returned to learn that TUSA had finally been alerted. A lot of water, and terrain, and a hell of a lot of other things have passed over the dam since then.

Monday, January 1, 1945: Borders showed me a SHAEF memo on ETO demobilization and occupation schedule—1 Army (unnamed) of 2 Corps consisting of 5 Inf and 3 Armored Divs. Other Army Hq to return to States—2 every 3 months, and of them one (unnamed) to go to CIB [China-India-Burma] Theater. Our troops taking very few PW from 12 SS—which murdered 150 U.S. PW in FUSA zone.[32] Matter of fact, our men taking practically no Panzer PW. Kill them on sound theory that only good German tanker or SSer is a dead one.

Total occupation force—U.S.—to be 275,000 Ground Troops. 83,000 Air.

Met a Med[ical] Major of 28th Div who knew Cy Long and spoke with great bitterness about Gen George Davis. Inferred that Cy was sent on very risky mission and deliberately, perhaps to get rid of him. Contrary to original story that he was killed in CP by Arty, the Major indicated he was sent on the mission through uncleared terrain to establish liaison with a regt and was killed and not found for six days. Borders told me that the reason why we are not going to get 66 Inf Div is the delay in filling up its losses as a result of the sinking of its transport with 1,600 men of Div, and much of its records and equipment, a few miles off Cherbourg by enemy sub or mines a few weeks ago.[33] No word of this leaked out anywhere yet. As a result of this disaster, 66th being reorganized, and 94th, which is full strength and has been at St. Nazaire and Lorient, containing Nazi garrison there, is coming to us instead. *Editor's note: Interestingly, Allen does not refer to Operation Nordwind, a major German offensive aimed at the Saverne Gap twenty miles northwest of Strasbourg to regain the Zabern Rise, destroy Allied forces in northern Alsace, and regain contact with Nineteenth Army. It was also an attempt to deflect Third Army from Fifth Panzer Army in order to restart the drive to the Meuse. The operation used reserves that could not be effectively employed in the Ardennes due to road and logistical limitations. If Nordwind was successful, Hitler envisioned another series of operations, Zahnartz (Dentist), from the Saare valley–Saverne area toward Metz and the rear of Third Army.[34] The Luftwaffe reemerged with a vengeance on January 1 to support Nordwind. Operation Bodenplatte (Baseplate) was a coordinated attack with perhaps up to 1,000 aircraft intended to cripple Allied airpower in a single stroke by striking sixteen airfields in Belgium, Holland, and France. Fifteen to twenty-five Bf-109s attacked the Metz airfield, the forwardmost of Weyland's bases, destroying twenty aircraft and damaging eleven others. The Metz air defense battery claimed twelve of the German aircraft. Gay called the Luftwaffe offensive on January 1 the "heaviest German air attacks" ever experienced by Third Army. At 0945 Third Army phoned XIX TAC to report that Luxembourg had been strafed by approximately twenty-five FW-190s.[35]*

Tuesday, January 2, 1945: Told today that Montgomery is vigorously opposing a VII Corps jump-off. FUSA (Bradley) wanted attack from North to jump off today. Monty insisted on holding off until 6th or later—in order that more stuff can go down against us. In other words, to let us pull them down and take the edge off them. Typical Montgomery strategy—let Yanks do it. Feeling throughout Third Army very bitter against Monty and FUSA. We carried the ball and saved the situation—when they were surprised and dismayed—and now they are sitting on the North flank doing nothing, not even applying pressure. I took a crack at that in Discussion [paragraph] under capabilities, and Koch left it in without a word.

Borders told me how unhappy he is among the full colonels. Pointed out a significant fact—he and Kelley are the only non-Regs who are full colonels. Said that when he sits down with them at mess, a sort of cold chill descends and he is made to feel like he is an outsider. Schmuck finally got his promotion to Lt Col, but no hint about my recommendation—other than Koch's remark at time of the conversation of XX Corps vacancy that he was still trying to get me promoted. He may be trying, but obviously not getting anywhere—and that goes for the Legion of Merit recommendation. Patton talks a lot about his Staff being responsible for his victories—and it is. But outside of Regs, nobody gets anything. I've carried the Operations loan [load] in this Section and have received exactly ZERO to date in tangible recognition. I charge it all to Gay and Patton's failure to check and watch such things. It's all part of the vicious and damnable Reg clique business.

Heard that apparently a compromise has been reached on Monty's demand that FUSA jump off on the 6th and Bradley's that it be today. Date fixed for [January] 3d.

Wednesday, January 3, 1945: VII Corps jumped off this morning, after patrols went off yesterday 1,500 yards without contact. V Corps on left jumps off tomorrow. XXX Corps[36] on right, British, to hold its attack to go at some yet unspecified day—a fact very caustically commented on by all in the U.S. Army. At 1130 conference in Maddox's office, our plan of attack was outlined. 17 AB Div[37] goes to VIII Corps to take high ground South of Houffalize—our objective as well as FUSA's.

Apparently top brass hats practicing up on their alibis on the penetration bungle. Koch told me today that Bradley now says that our Ardennes dispositions were a calculated risk. If he is saying that, it's an outright—and not very bright—lie. In a calculated risk you don't get surprised, and certainly he won't deny FUSA was surprised. In a calculated risk you take a chance on the enemy's strength and operations, but do not get caught with pants down as we so tragically were. It was no risk—it was a plain case of incompetent G-2ing beginning with the great British mastermind General Strong, Eisenhower's G-2, and including glad-handing Sibert, the Rotarian, and Dixon, the FUSA burper. They all knew the facts, had croaked about them—but had done nothing about the matter. Also a plain case of bungling command leadership from Eisenhower to Bradley and stodgy, dull, mediocre Hodges. Eisenhower ought to can Strong and Hodges at least, and he could do a lot better than Bradley, too. Patton—for one. Shelled by mystery rocket on gun again. Eight or ten shells during night.

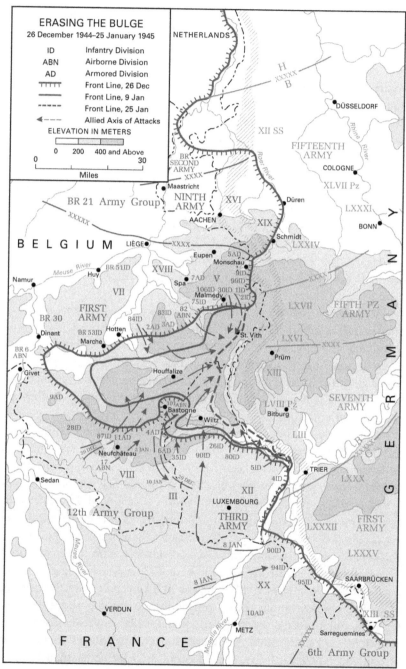

NETHERLANDS

DÜSSELDORF

H
XXXXX
B

XII SS

FIFTEENTH
ARMY

COLOGNE

XLVII Pz

BR
SECOND
ARMY
XXXX

Roer River

Rhine River

Maastricht

NINTH
ARMY

XVI

Düren

BR 21 Army Group

AACHEN

XIX

LXXXI

BONN

BELGIUM

LIÈGE

XXXX

Schmidt

LXXIV

Eupen

Meuse River

Huy

BR 51ID

XVIII

Spa

5AD
Monschau

9ID

V

99ID

Namur

VII

7AD

106ID 30ID 1ID
Malmédy
75ID

2ID

LXVII

FIFTH PZ
ARMY

FIRST
ARMY

84ID

83ID

82
ABN

XXXX

BR 30

Dinant

BR 53ID

Hotten

2AD 3AD

St. Vith

LXVI

XXXX

BR 6
ABN

Marche

Prüm

G

E

R

M

A

N

Y

Givet

Houffalize

XIII

9AD

101ABN
Bastogne

Wiltz

LVIII Pz

Bitburg

SEVENTH
ARMY

28ID

87ID 11AD
29 DEC
Neufchâteau
17
ABN

4AD

3 JAN 6AD

351ID

26ID

90ID 80ID

LIII

TRIER

LXXX

VIII

10 JAN

29 DEC

5ID

4ID

Sedan

III

XII
LUXEMBOURG

12th Army Group

THIRD
ARMY

FIRST
ARMY

8 JAN

90ID

LXXXII

LXXXV

Meuse River

8 JAN

94ID

XX

95ID

SAARBRÜCKEN

VERDUN

10AD

XIII SS

Moselle River

METZ

Sarreguemines

XXXX

6th Army Group

FRANCE

Erasing the Bulge, December 26, 1944–January 25, 1945 (Center for Military History, Washington, DC)

Thursday, January 4, 1945: Bad weather. Snow, heavy mist. No Air. Patton—looking out of window—remarked glumly, "Well, devil helping his own again." V Corps jumped off. VII Corps made fair progress against vanguard action yesterday. British still sitting on their butts doing nothing.

Friday, January 5, 1945: Patton asked what British were doing and when told XXX Corps still sitting and no word when they would jump off, remarked very soberly—"Can't understand why they don't attack. They'll have a hard time to explain their failure." And they sure will. Situation creating very bad feeling throughout our forces. Feeling widespread that British—Monty—never move until the way is cleared for him to do so cheaply. Not doing British any good—in fact, creating background of contempt and ill-feeling that will hurt the British very greatly in the future. Feeling also that they have too great a say in running of the war for what they got in it now. Our troops outnumber them about 4 to 1, and our leaders are better than theirs—Monty doesn't hold a candle to Patton. Yet SHAEF about run by the British—certainly all G-2 poop is Limey.

Sibert breezed in around noon today in a very cheerio temper. Told me Zeller is finally being rolled as XX Corps G-2, and [Lieutenant Colonel James Owen] Jimmy Curtis,[38] formally 1st U.S. Inf Div and now in SHAEF G-2 Section, to take his place. Zeller is a buzz bomb but a Reg—so he was made a Corps G-2 when he got in everyone's hair at Group in the UK. A non-Reg would have been busted, but being one of the clique, he was made a Corps G-2 by Sibert—as he admitted to me in course of conversation. But most interesting *ADMISSION* was—"Don't let anyone kid you that we weren't surprised. We were. All of us. We were caught cold. Every one of us. The only question was who blew up and who didn't. Dickson was definitely one of those who did blow." Which was another interesting *ADMISSION*. The high and mighty Dickson certainly showed all the signs of being all atwitter. And he has been grinding out daily G-2 Estimates like columnists do copy—and about as coherently. The more he writes the more of an ass he makes of himself, because he can't help contradicting himself. Sibert is certainly poor stuff as a Group G-2. A mediocrity to begin with, and without experience or background for the job. Would make a run-of-mine Asst Corps G-2; yet here he is, a BG and Group G-2. We have a number of Div G-2s,—[Lieutenant Colonel Harry E.] Brown,[39] 4th Armd Div; [Lieutenant Colonel James O.] Boswell,[40] 90th Div—who are better G-2s than he is, and Koch is so far above him that there is literally no comparison. That's the way it is all through the Army. Regs with friends or pull—like [Lieutenant Colonel Charles P.] Bixel[41]—an utter bust—get high staff jobs, and non-Regs carry pick-and-shovel load and get nowhere.

At press conference in evening, Patton came in late in field attire with gun outside. Didn't take off weather-beaten topcoat. Related story of epic turning around of TUSA in Saar and hurtling it against Ardennes penetration. "Purpose of the operation was to hit the SOBs in the flank, and we damn well did it. That stopped them cold. That may sound like George Patton is a great man, but actually he had very little to do with it. All I did was to give the order. It was the staff of this Hq and the troops that performed this unbelievable feat. When I think of what they did, you will realize it was one of the epic feats in military history. I want to repeat that because you can get an idea what was accomplished in a matter of hours when not one unit went astray and all were in position and ready for their jump-offs at the set hours." Asked about failure of British and First Army to apply pressure and he replied with smile, "I am not my brother's keeper." Characterized Bastogne as the Gettysburg of the war and gave full and unqualified credit to Bradley for insisting it be held and relieved. "He grasped its full tactical implications and was solely responsible for that. I was more than happy to command the attack because the only way to win wars is to attack and then attack again and again." This remark was over the head of the press, but was obvious crack at Monty and his unpublicized plan to run and withdraw to the Meuse.

Great deal of commotion over numerous reports of U.S. planes with German markings strafing and bombing our troops. For days these reports have been coming in. Air people getting very sensitive and finally blew up. Col. Browne, C/S XIX [TAC], told Patton there has not been one case of a plane shot down which had German markings. All German planes—FW-190 looks very much like P-51[42] and another like our P-38.[43] TWX to all Corps to report all instances of planes strafing and not to fire at any planes unless they shoot, and then to shoot them down. Action taken because of fear it might undermine confidence of Air. Situation really critical. No question our planes shooting up our troops—due to incompetent and faulty briefing and poor target fixing. Not serious but could be if not acted on.

Saturday, January 6, 1945: Germans beginning to back out of salient. Still pounding away at Bastogne, but greatly reduced scale. Tide of battle definitely turning and the enemy offensive finis-finis now. Patton—at briefing remarked—"We may go back to the Saarlautern plan. Good plan then and is still good." Interesting commentary on Ninth Army Staff.

Whole Staff from Class of 1926—and one of lousiest and most incompetent. G-2 Periodic Report a joke. Bixel is no more a G-2 than he has brains. Is an ass of the first nature—but a Reg. And classmate of [Brigadier General James E.] Moore,[44] the C/S, and the boys always take care of the group. Take our Hq. We have two full colonels as Hq Comdt. Three full colonels, all Regs of course, as PM. Two or more full colonels in Ord, Engr, etc., *all Regs.* Men really car[ry]ing the load, real burden bearers, have no chance for promotion. Eklund told me today my recommendation is still on Gay's desk—two months now. Meanwhile, I bat along with no sign of recognition except a word now and then from Koch, like his remark today that he had put me up for a Bronze Star for my work during this operation. Very nice—but: I have been twice recommended for promotion, once for Croix de Guerre, once for Legion of Merit, once for Bronze Star and I still have nothing. Meanwhile, Staff cluttered up with full Reg Colonels, all discards and holding down jobs that a competent captain from civil life could do, and do a lot better.

Sunday, January 7, 1945: British making great and stupid mistake. Press and BBC hailing Monty as the great leader who is saving the situation. Not only untrue, but doubly false because he wanted to run and fall back. When that comes out, it is going to raise unshirted hell and hurt Britain bitterly. Monty clearly a grandstanding SOB and a liability to the British, as sowing seeds of ill-will that will hurt them in the future. (Several days later BBC repudiated its burp—with snide crack at U.S. confusion by claiming Germans used same wave length. Obvious and stupid lie because that same day, *The Daily Mail* had front-page editorial saying exactly the same thing. Surely Germans didn't sneak that into the paper. Some influence in Britain is deliberately pot-shooting at U.S., and it's not only stupid but criminally vicious as playing directly into German hands.) Fact is British and Monty have far greater influence in the conduct of the war and SHAEF than their contribution to the ETO warrants. Have only a few Divs, compared to our several score. Even so-called 2d British Army is part Polish, Norwegian, Dutch and Belgian—to say nothing of First Canadian Army. Becoming clearer all the time that the reason Eisenhower is Supreme Commander is due to his willingness to kow-tow to the British. They will rue that because they are piling up a backlog of resentment and ill-will that will cost them dear in future—and us, too, possibly. Attitude of U.S. Army over here summed up by Patton's crack at briefing when told XXX British Corps advanced 1,000 yards yesterday—"Germans must have withdrawn. Only way they would have advanced."

Patton also related that he had told "Walker yesterday to make careful study of his right flank (Saarlautern-Saarbrücken area) as may be hightailing it down there soon to resume our offensive down there. That is the real strategy that should be followed. We ought to thin out up here and sneak back down there in force and hit them right between the eyes. We'd go through them like a dose of salts and be on the Rhine before the British could regroup for another 1,000-yard advance. If we can come up here in three days, we can go back in two before Germans know it. We know the country better."

Monday, January 8, 1945: Beginning to get some replacements from the States. Eklund told me 26,000 are due on 26th of the month for TUSA. Meanwhile getting several hundred to 1,500 every few days. Particularly important that we got 600 tankers today, which enable us to fill up all Armored Divs. Several had to lay up tanks for lack of crews. This supply will fill all Armd Divs up, with few to spare. However, while replacements finally beginning to come, replacement centers remain filthy, horrible messes. [Lieutenant Colonel Melvin C.] Helfers[45] told me of going down to visit his younger brother in Replacement Center of Seventh Army at Épinal. Crowded into barren factory; no heat; messes filthy; latrines horrible; and keep men confined to compound doing nothing. Could bring in combat veterans to give them valuable orientation talks and tips—but nothing done or even thought of. All part of incompetence of G-1s—apparently universally the punks and incompetents of the Army. Ours is certainly one of the worst, but all must be the same. Pack of worthless bastards.

Tuesday, January 9, 1944: Patton has apparently stopped smoking cigars. Comes to briefing without cigar and is chewing gum [instead], which he does with great vigour. Grinds away at it at great pace. Odom probably put him under ban. Heavy cigar smoker before. Must be tough. I've cut down on cigarettes and it is not easy. 83d jumped off today in attack toward Houffalize. *Editor's note: Allen means the 87th Infantry Division, not the 83rd.* Progress being made, but no walk-away. Germans fighting to keep corridors open to avoid being trapped in the pocket. Few main roads, and they are trying to keep us from them. 17 AB Div learning war the hard way. Very anxious to measure up to veteran 82d and 101st, with result it is too impetuous and has been taking needless heavy losses. First day in the line, 2 companies got out too far and were cut off—or remainder of Bn withdrew. Result, heavy loss. Yesterday a whole Bn suffered the same way. Got out in advance, there was a withdrawal and the Bn was cut off. Result, over 300 casualties. Men are game and hard fighters, but over-eager and inexperienced. Result, heavy losses. (On

18 Jan, Eklund showed me report showing the Div has had over 4,000 casualties—about one-third of its strength. That's a terribly high rate, but it's still in there slugging. Shows the outfit basically has good stuff.) 11th Armored Div also sour—rather it is sour. Apparently due to poor command leadership and not personnel. Top officers not very hot, and staff also poor. G-2 rolled and [Lieutenant Colonel William M.] Slayden,[46] VIII Corps, has gone over. This was [Edward H.] Brooks'[47] outfit in Louisiana and at times looked like a good Div.

90th Inf Div jumped off in a surprise attack in the East section of III Corps's zone to ease German pressure against the VIII Corps drive on Houffalize. Div brought up secretly from XX Corps and its attack was a big surprise. Made considerable progress in initial advance, cleaning up pocket at Eastern base of Bastogne wedge. Plan definitely a big help in helping VIII Corps. *Editor's note: Patton launched a large-scale attack across the front on this date. The 90th Infantry Division played a major role in eliminating the Harlange pocket.*

Wednesday, January 10, 1945: Much concern over situation in Saarbrücken area, where enemy has a bridgehead. Prepared Special Estimate and Terrain Study of both that area and later area covered by XX Corps on enemy capability to launch an offensive. Presented this before Patton at special briefing. *Editor's note: Patton was concerned about threats against XX Corps. Koch and Allen prepared a study of the probability of German attacks against VIII Corps and Saarbrücken, and the latter was deemed more probable. Patton had already taken steps to build up a strong defensive area between Saarbrücken and Metz. Koch's identification of Saarbrücken as the most likely place for a new German attack was not supported by Sibert's assessment of German capabilities. Only the day before, Sibert had declared that there was "no satisfactory evidence" that the Germans possessed the ability to turn a threat there into a major attack. Just as Third Army was gaining some momentum on January 10, however, Bradley telephoned Patton at 1030, described a threat to Saarbrücken, and instructed him to withdraw divisions out of contact and move to XX Corps. On January 7 German Nineteenth Army launched Operation Sonnenwende (Winter Solstice) out of the northern part of the Colmar pocket against the northern flank of VI Corps; at the same time, XXXIX Panzer Corps, along with 21st Panzer and 25th Panzergrenadier Divisions, attacked the center of VI Corps in the Hagenau Forest.[48] (See sketch on page 150.)*

Alibis beginning to shape up on Ardennes fiasco. Eisenhower had press conference yesterday—in the safe confines of Paris—at which he

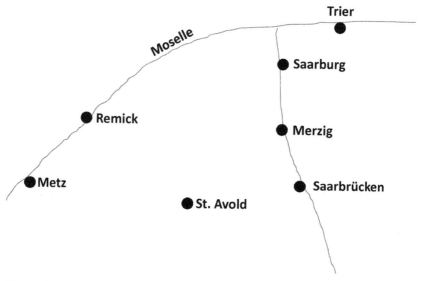

Allen's Sketch Map

announced award of BRONZE STAR (?!!) to Bradley, and claimed he knew all about the Germans' plan to launch an offensive. Staff had made a study of the Ardennes. Only surprise was weight of the operation. All a lot of hogwash. Only surprise was that they were surprised, and he can thank for that his great British G-2 mastermind Strong and little Eddie Sibert, the hoppity G-2 of Group. Both muffed the ball badly—although they had ample information of German regrouping and the Panzer Armies' plan. They just couldn't imagine the Germans would attempt a drive and they guessed wrong. Further, were criminally negligent—Bradley and Hodges—in not making a strong defensive zone out of the VIII Corps area, where four depleted Divs were sat down in a rest area. Simple fact is that from Top down, there was neglect and incompetence. The G-2s for not adding the clearly evident indications correctly, and the CGs for not taking proper precautionary measures against surprise. Wouldn't have taken much, and would have paid colossal dividends. There is going to be a great deal of arguing, explaining and ruckusing over this tragedy from now on for years and more to come. Books will be written over, about and on the subject—but it can all be summed up in a few words—We were surprised and got one hell of a beating.

Signs point to Germans beginning to withdraw. They've taken some terrific losses in personnel and equipment. Those 108 Battalions of Arty and unlimited ammo have decimated them. No general withdrawal yet—but indications are pretty definite that they have gone on the defensive and the offensive has been taken out of them. From now on they'll defend and delay, withdrawing under our pressure, and again playing for time—selling space for time in the hope of tying down our striking power while they build up a new offensive force to take another poke at us in the spring. Time is the only hope for the Nazi thugs keeping Germany in the war to escape destruction. *Editor's note: The wholesale withdrawal of German forces from the Bulge was precipitated by the eruption of the Russian front on January 12, but the SS divisions began to withdraw on January 9.*

Friday, January 12, 1945: ECLIPSE[49] is the code name for the Allied plan for military occupation of Germany. Same 12 Army Group plan as put out by them. According to it, requires 15 months from V-Day to complete occupation set-up. Calls for First Allied Airborne Army[50] to prepare plans for airborne operation to seize Berlin, Kiel and Hamburg to assist occupation—provided Russians haven't got there already. Berlin is shown on maps as in the area to be occupied by the Soviets. They have Eastern Germany; U.S., Central and South; British, North East. Plan also mentions two operations in Norway—APOSTLE[51] and ALADIN—and third on Channel Islands—NEST EGG.[52]

Prepared Terrain Study showing enemy capabilities in XX Corps zone—from Trier-Metz-Saarlautern—and presented it to Patton at special briefing. Mysterious V-rocket shelling [has] been underway for couple of days now. Last night, hit corner building occupied by U.S. Legation directly across from our billet—CONTINENTAL—and broke all the windows. 18 tossed into Luxembourg last night. Ten this morning—first daylight shelling. Arty thinks they are coming from Trier area, and in retaliation we're shelling hell out of the town. On East front lines, only about 10 miles away. At night, can hear shelling very clearly. When I submitted XII Corps report about considerable enemy movement in [on] their front, indicating possible build-up, to Patton, he remarked, "Hope they do attack in Saarlautern-Saarbrücken area. We could really massacre them there."

Sunday, January 14, 1945: Eklund told me today that Koch's recommendation in November for my promotion (2d) still was on Gay's desk. Attended conference on plan for XII Corps to attack to North in Echternach area—with 5th Inf Div, initially, and after it loses momentum, 4th Armored, under wraps in Thionville area, to reinforce with a combat command at a time. On basis of what we estimate Boche has on

XII Corps front now, attack scheduled for 18th ought to go well. Patton asked for recommendations on plan he proposes to submit apparently to Eisenhower for return to our initial plan for major offensive drive to Mainz and Rhine in the Saarlautern area. As explained, we would, under Patton's proposal, set up a defensive zone North of the Moselle in the Ardennes—from St. Vith to confluence of Moselle and Saar, South East of Echternach, and then launch drive in Saarlautern area. Koch asked me for my ideas on the number of troops needed. I submitted plan for 4 Inf Divs to hold North sector, with 1 Armd Div in reserve in Thionville area, and 2 Corps of 4 Divs each, 1 of 3 Inf and 1 Armd and another of 2 Inf and 2 Armd, to crack the Siegfried Line and rush for the Rhine.

At 1500 hours, few minutes after I left my office to go to Col Koch's, a terrific explosion occurred that shook the CP and broke all the windows on our side of the building—including those in my office. Capt [James C.] Chamberlain,[53] Arty expert on V stuff, who was sitting in my chair, got cut by hunk of glass across bridge of nose. Whatever it was landed about a block away in Ord motor pool and beat up things and wounded a number of people—including several civilians. This is the second one to land near our CP. Yesterday one landed a block away on the roof of a house facing our entrance. Today's was toward rear of CP. This sounded much louder and more powerful than any others that have hit in Lux[embourg]. May have been air bomb. Apparently not shooting at anything in particular; just harassing the city, doubtless in hope that with all Hqs here now, bound to hit something.

Now CP'd here:

12 Army Group—Spitfire
TUSA—Gangway
XII Corps—Elem[ents] of SHAEF (Shipmate)
Number of Evacuation & General Hospitals, missions, etc.

Monday, January 15, 1945: More revelations coming out on losses in offensive—FUSA lost one Ammo depot containing 1,700 tons of Ammo of all kinds—very nice for Boche—to go with all Arty he overran and captured. 20,000 mines. Nice pickings—and Hodges gets the DSM [Distinguished Service Medal] for his sterling work in causing the disaster— I suppose?

Meeting in Maddox's office to consider the plan Patton is trying to sell what he derisively calls "the Supreme Command." His idea is to keep on hammering Germans; not to give them a chance to recoup, to regain the initiative and hold onto it. Ironic that Patton has to go around constantly hawking offensive plans, but that is exactly what he has to do and is constantly doing. He started meeting—attended by Maddox, Koch, myself, Engr, Arty—by saying, "Only way to keep Germans from attacking is to attack him, instead of sitting around wondering where and when he is going to attack us. We should be kicking him in the teeth. I sure would like to attack in the Saarlautern area if I could. That would jar the bastards and set him on his rear end. But the Supreme Command isn't sold on the idea, yet." Plan as explained by Maddox—to set up defensive zone from St. Vith to Saar-Moselle gateway and secretly mount offensive in Saarlautern area.

Discussing various units, Gay remarked, "Trouble with 11th Armd Div." Patton broke in, "Is [Brigadier General Willard A.] Holbrook[54] (CO of a combat command)." Patton talked to Middleton (CG VIII Corps) yesterday and said that if Holbrook didn't get in there and fight, he'd be a colonel again damned quick. Middleton said he also told the Div CG to tell Holbrook that, too.

Patton disclosed that Bradley wants to "turn First Army around and go after Cologne again. But Supreme Command is all heated up on cleaning up what we are working on. Prestige, I guess. Doesn't make sense any other way." I presented a terrain study of the Ardennes. 11th Armd is not the only new Div that is sourish. 17th AB also learning how to fight the hard way. So far, had over 4,000 casualties. Good outfit, but trouble seems to be—too eager, too anxious to equal the record of experienced and suave 101st and 82d AB Divs. Result, taking hundreds of needless losses. On first day, jumped off 2 Coys [companies] out in front; rest of regt pulled back and most of Coys were lost. Four days ago same thing happened with Bn. It was left unsupported and surrounded and had some 600 casualties. That's plain hell. Outfit is learning but not easy. Already lost half its Inf strength.

All G-2 big-shots now pouring out potent PR and others pieces on how and why Germans did it. Trying to explain away the importance of their surprise and criminal incompetence and negligence that allowed them to get away with it. No one can ever explain that away—regardless of how much gum-rubbing and teeth-clicking is done to pooh-pooh the effect of the German drive. Two facts remain that are indisputable— (1) They surprised us. (2) They captured the initiative and unhitched our offensive just as TUSA was about to launch a great attack on the Siegfried Line in the Saarlautern-Saarbrücken area. They took the initiative away from us; captured and killed 40–50,000 of our men, large [quantities] of Arty, AMMO, food, clothing, gas and other supplies, and completely put us on the defensive. They can all talk all they want, the brass hats, but the Germans surprised us and beat the hell out of us because they SURPRISED US—and for that great crime, six men are responsible—Eisenhower and his (British) G-2; Bradley and his put-put, incompetent, ex–G-4, whirly G-2; Hodges, an old dodo and mediocrity and his G-2. They are the ones to bear the guilt, and I hope time sees to it that they do.

Tuesday, January 16, 1945: First and Third US Army forces made contact at 0930 today at Houffalize. The salient has begun to shrink markedly and ceased being a salient. It is no longer a salient but a bulge. Attack continues to North East. XII Corps is being readied to jump off on Thursday straight to St. Vith, with First Army pushing to East to capture (re) the town. 8th Armored Division,[55] latest to join us, to be assembled in U.S. XX Corps zone. Patton directed—at special briefing— "Employ them by Combat Command to assist 94th Inf Div in its attack in the Saar-Moselle triangle. Let them tackle limited objective attacks. Give them some good experience without a lot of killing. Won't cost much and teach them a lot." ULTRA—Reports indicate Germans definitely short of gas, ammo, and rations.

Wednesday, January 17, 1945: Memo from Army Group today stated some 32,000,000 letters from U.S., mailed between 4 Dec and 6 Jan, held up for various reasons; a ship having engine trouble and having to go to an out-of-the-way port, ships being routed to UK, the offensive, etc.

Thursday, January 18, 1945: XII U.S. Corps jumped off to north, with 5th U.S. Inf Div. 4th U.S. Inf Div to follow in a couple days. Diekirch, on the Sauer [River], one of the first objectives. Big "junior" rocket day here today. 18 smacked in, most of them on outskirts of town. From 5 upwards have been coming in practically every day. Go slow, don't even notice them. Still no real clue what they are.

At press conference this evening, Patton was asked what he thought was the best way to end the war quickly. Quick as a flash he barked back—with obvious reference to Montgomery and others—"By attacking the sons-of-bitches. Go after them. Find them and kill them. That's the way to end this war."

From Eklund—(Replacements). Third Army as of today is 17,000 short. By 1 Feb, supposed to get 16,000. But by that time battle losses will reduce us another 15,000. So that replacements we get just about make up daily losses and not existing deficit at all. Our losses still averaging about 1,000 a day—killed, wounded and missing. But at that, still improvement of what situation was a month ago when we were "stewing our own grease" and making replacements by pulling them from our clerks, steno[graphers] and draftsmen. At least now we are getting some with regularity. Eklund said that the plan set up a couple months ago by Washington provided 75,000 replacements a month, of which ETO was to get 45,000. That is for all U.S. Armies—Third, First, Ninth, Seventh, Fifteenth. Third Army's losses alone are two-thirds that amount a month. Plan now to set up training centers over here. Ship replacements over here after basic training in U.S. and give them final training here. Excellent idea if [we] use combat-experienced instructors, instead of gold-bricks and wire-pullers.

Friday, January 19, 1945: Got wind today of an amazing story about *Montgomery,* the great "fighting" hero of the *Ardennes.* According to story—On 15/16 Dec, he issued over his own name an official pronouncement of some kind asserting that the Germans did not have any offensive power—that is, were not capable of an offensive—and that the best thing that could be asked for would be for them to resume mobile warfare as that would enable their being quickly and easily destroyed. In other words, if this story is true, MONTGOMERY, who presumably has posed recently as a great military mastermind and whom certain British papers have played up as such, actually a day or so before the ARDENNES disaster pooh-poohed the Germans' capacity to take the offensive. At 12 Army Group, when I asked for the file, they admitted seeing a copy but strangely their 21 Army Group file was blank from 3 Dec to 21 Dec _____ and others said they saw the statement but no one knew what had become of it. If it is true that he said that—then his conduct and that of the BBC and British papers—[DAILY] MAIL particularly—is an unspeakable, and outrageous scandal. A gross insult to U.S., Bradley and also a dirty piece of bootlicking by Eisenhower to let him get away with it without public rebuke.

Saturday, January 20, 1945: British jet-propelled planes—METEOR[56] —began operating in ETO today. XIX TAC inclined to be casual about them. May have only 20-minute flying range and a speed of only 450 miles per hour. Say P-80[57]—jet we [are] producing—much faster, better and greater range, about two hours.

The inadequate clothing we are using for our front-line troops up here is a goddamn outrage—and another example of doing things late. After all our experience in Alaska and Northern woods this country and Army ought to know what kind of winter clothes to turn out for troops—

light, yet warm. Instead, our kids are fighting and living in clothing designed not only for milder climate, but garrison duty. Instead of shoe pacs, quilted clothing, Arctic gloves and mittens and hoods, they have bulky overcoats, galoshes that weigh you down. No hoods—except what they improvise. No quilted clothing. The one article that approximates practicability, Armor combat suit, jacket and overalls, has been abolished as an item of issue. It is comfortable, easy to operate in, and warm; yet they cut it out—while still continuing to issue the so-called field jacket, a cheesy, valueless garment that is neither warm nor rainproof. It never was any good, yet they continue to put it out. This weather here is murderous. Constant snow and bitterly cold. As tough and rigorous as the Northern states, and yet no intelligent effort was made beforehand to prepare for it. All part of the stupid and grossly fatuous belief that the war would be over by now—just as they bungled the replacement problem for some reason. Now belatedly rushing to get better attire. Col [Everett] Bus[c]h,[58] our QM, told me today we had 125,000 shoe pacs, but "characteristically," as he put it, "Com Z shipped shoes in one lot and felt inner liners in another." Until they arrive, he is going to try to improvise by cutting up blankets and using them. Also, ground and other rear AF personnel running around in pelt-lined and fur-collared jackets, while line troops that could really use them do not have them. Same with snow suits—our men are improvising them out of sheets and stuff found in towns—but Germans have them.

Sunday, January 21, 1945: After ULTRA briefing, Patton took us into his office and on his map explained new offensive plan to crack the Siegfried Line and drive to the Rhine on Bonn. VIII Corps, on narrow 12-mile front, with five Divs, four Inf and 1 Armor, to attack East in the vicinity of St. Vith. III and XII Corps to follow after VIII makes penetration with holding attacks. XX Corps to clean up Saar-Moselle triangle. (See sketch on page 157.)

FUSA to jump off simultaneously with us and head, again, for Cologne. "What about Ninth Army?" Patton—"Nobody loves them. Remain under 21 Army Group (Montgomery)." Gay—"Good reason for no one loving them. They're a joke."

Russian offensive pouring ahead. Today—200 miles from Berlin. Lt. Col. Murray, G-3 Air, drew big laugh at briefing today when he concluded his remarks with crack, "No Russian planes were sighted on WESTERN FRONT." Today is D+30 in the Operation, our third since August 1, when we officially became operational way back in the Cotentin.

The following is the G-1 Report for today:

Casualty Report to 2400—20 Jan '45								
	Our Own Troops				Enemy Troops			
	20 Jan	Cumulative from 1 Aug	Present Op			20 Jan	Cumulative from 1 Aug	Present Ops
Killed	64	14,104	3,953	PW		553	157,803	18,024
Wounded	358	67,376	17,970	En[emy] Buried		161	17,223	2,281
Missing	47	13,509	4,360	TOTAL		719	175,026	20,305
TOTAL	489	94,991	26,295	Killed		300	89,000	25,200
Non-battle	590	64,478	18,535	Wounded		1,000	246,700	68,500
Total	1,039	182,459	44,830	PW		500	150,100	18,100
Repl[acements]	689	140,739	37,351			1,900	433,800	109,800
Material Lost, Captured and Destroyed								
Unit Losses				Enemy Material Captured or Destroyed				
Tanks, L[ight]	0	270	72	Tanks, Mark III & IV		0	1,243	297
Tanks M[edium]	0	755	259	Tanks, Mark VI		0	702	217
Arty, 75mm & over	0	142	46	Arty, 75mm & over		0	2,489	273
Veh[icles], all types	5	3,156	279	Veh[icles], all types		1	5,971	540
				[Total]		1	10,405	1,327

Editor's note: Some of Allen's totals do not add up.

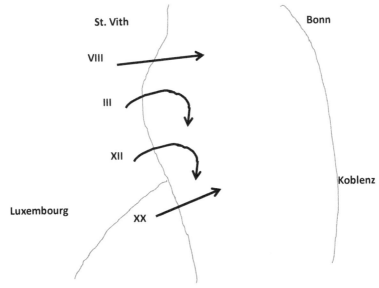

St. Vith

Bonn

VIII

III

XII

Koblenz

Luxembourg

XX

Allen's Sketch Map

Monday, January 22, 1945: More apparent chicanery and petty glory-grabbing by the British. XXX British Corps—on VIII Corps's left—claimed some days ago that it knocked out 81 tanks and a larger number of other vehicles of 2 Panzer Div. Now develops—according to 2d U.S. Armored Div—that it knocked out this stuff and administered this smashing defeat to 2 Panzer. 2d claims it destroyed the tanks and vehicles and left them while it went on with its attack, and that—apparently—the British who followed 2d Armored claimed the stuff as its handiwork. A very goddamned stinking affair, if true.

The past two days have been phenomenally successful for our Air—best days of the war in the ETO. Better even than the Falaise pocket and other smash days last summer. And all unexpected. Weather indications were not good and actually not the best, but with roads clogged, squadrons got in some remarkable killing. What a difference it would make if we had a couple days of good flying weather a week. It made the difference between victory and possible costly deadlock just a month ago at the height of the Ardennes offensive, and is making a world of difference now with the Boche pulling out. Really burning them up and killing them in masses the last two days. Went over to General Weyland's office in ABCD Bldg this afternoon and listened to radio chatter of pilots going after the Boche. Fabulous show. Claims of XIX TAC alone for today are—

1,177 vehicles destroyed
536 damaged
31 Armored vehicles & tanks destroyed
5 damaged

For Ninth AF three TACs—

2,700 vehicles
75 tanks

Tuesday, January 23, 1945: Patton not smoking. In one of his "off tobacco" periods and chewing gum like a Machine Gun. When he is on "off the wagon" mood on cigars, his temper is short and snappish. Goes around on edge and flies off the handle on the slightest provocation. Result—they keep cigars handy and encourage him to go back to smoking.

Weyland pranced into ULTRA briefing and joyfully announced—

"Biggest day for us yesterday since Falaise. Lot of killing." Patton—
"That's fine. Get any pictures of it?" Weyland explained he hadn't had
time yet to look them over. After briefing, Patton got Eddy (CG XII
Corps) on the phone. "Say, get move on. Little 6th Cav Group showing
all your outfits up. Way ahead of them. Get out there, and get them moving. What the hell's the matter with them? Keep up the attack." After
this call, Patton ordered Walker (CG XX) and got on the phone with this
remark: "I've eaten out the pants of two Corps CGs; might as well take
on another. "Johnny, what's going on down there? You're not going pac-
ifist on me are you? Get those Divs of yours going. Tell them to attack
on the right where they got hit. That's the place to go after the bastards.
If you can't get action, do some relieving. It's vital we keep on attacking
everywhere at this time. No let-up. Keep going."

The utter incompetence and crime of having a man like Sibert as
G-2 of Group stands out more and more glaringly. Almost every day
brings forth new evidence of not only his incompetence and mediocrity
and unfitness, but the danger of his being where he is. Here are two latest examples: An ULTRA message 24 hours old came in that 47 Panzer
Corps[59] had been ordered to take up a certain position in XII Corps's
zone. Not only was the message 24 hours late, but we had overrun the
position. Without stopping to check these facts, he burst out with a hot
warning of danger and of threat of counterattack, and advised Bradley
to order us to rush up an Armored Div to a place to guard against the
danger. Clear case of unfounded jumping to a conclusion and an outrageous example of incompetence. When he should have been on guard last
month, he pooh-poohed the danger. Now he sees a threat behind every
bush.

Other example: TAC/R reported bridges along Saar showed signs of
heavy use. Again, without stopping to check what kind of bridges and
where they were, he burst out with a frenzied warning that the Saar-
Moselle triangle was being reinforced and ought to be reinforced by us.
What report really showed was that the bridges were highway—not RR—
bridges, and were *along* the R[ight] bank of the river and not *over* the
river. A great deal of difference—which he later admitted, at dinner this
noon. Only to come up with another screwy idea—to attack the triangle
with an airborne landing at the apex. Apparently he hasn't the slightest
idea of the rugged terrain of the area or the uselessness of such an operation. Even if we seized it, we still could go nowhere. Bitburg and Prüm
are keys to that section—not Trier. All this is part of the whole affair of
his unfitness and incompetence—and that of the staff he has. Why Brad-

ley keeps him, I can't understand. Sibert holds major guilt for Ardennes bust. He and Strong, Eisenhower's British G-2, ought to be busted and relieved for their criminal incompetence. Instead, apparently as strong as ever and little Rotary—in more ways than one—It's all part of the outrageous Army system of [or] theory [that] any punk who once was a Military Attaché or ADC can be a G-2. Sibert hasn't any real comprehension of what being a G-2 means or how to function as one. Neither he nor his section functions as G-2 section. Never get spot reports from them, and instead of functioning through them to get stuff from other Armies, as we should, we operate direct. All due to his incompetence, unfitness and lack of background and experience—plus lack of ability. I'll wager he couldn't handle a platoon and I know none of the numerous Lt Cols and Colonels on his staff can. They probably never saw a company or Bn deployed on the ground.

Meanwhile, the Russians keep rolling along—thank God. 175 miles from Berlin.

Wednesday, January 24, 1945: Four more Divs have been shifted to "Jakie" Devers,[60] 6 Army Group, making eight sent down there in three days. First FUSA was sent four, two Inf and two Armored, and now we contribute the same dose. And they don't begin to have against them by half what the Germans had in the Ardennes. Only 3 Panzer Divs, and there were ten up here. Also, he has two Armies under him—Seventh and First French. Only Third Army did the stopping and whittling down in the Ardennes! All this must have a political basis—as so goddamn much does in this theater. Doubtless the French are raising hell about the possible loss of Strasbourg, so "Ike" sends what amounts to a whole new Army to reinforce "Jakie"—despite the fact the Germans have had no new reinforcements for days. If those eight divisions were kept up here, they could have greatly speeded up the finale of the Ardennes and the drive against the Siegfried Line. By pulling them out it reduced our punch greatly. No real danger in 6 Army Group zone because Germans didn't have enough to go far, and further, no place to go even if they went into Alsace. All a matter of stupid prestige.

After staff briefing, Gay rose and while Patton listened said—"A new offensive operation being planned. Want to emphasize importance of three things—secrecy, radio silence, speed. All vital for success of attack and also for another reason. *There are other enemies besides the Germans.* It is essential that this attack be pressed with utmost vigor because we must realize that we may lose VIII Corps and some of our best divisions." Gay said nothing more, and neither did anyone else. At first I thought his strange reference to "other enemies" meant the Russians. But subsequently learned he was referring to Montgomery and "the Supreme Command." It develops they have a scheme on to launch an offensive from the North, commanded by Montgomery, with 2 British Army and our completely complaisant and moribund Ninth Army. With FUSA, 6 Army Group and us holding Germans everywhere else and they thinned out like water, Monty will pop in with a bunch of divisions from us and FUSA and break to the Rhine. That's what happened last September, when we with a clear way open to the Rhine were sat down so the ball could be passed to him—for prestige sake. Now that goddamned bitchery all over again. When Patton was all set to break through Saarlautern last month and rush to the Rhine, everything was messed up with Eisenhower, Montgomery, Strong, and Sibert's scandalous blunder in permitting the Ardennes offensive. Now when a massing of forces in our area—or Saarlautern—they do the trick again; plug pulled from under us once more. All apparently because of prestige. Monty, the British, bearing down for sake of prestige, so sound tactics and strategy are shortchanged and the deal clipped to fit the political and personal situation. A goddamned vicious scheme and scandal—at the cost of human lives—but the brass hats and big-shots got to have their prestige.

Heard that Monty has never forgiven the fact that he wasn't in on the taking of Paris. He and British government are very sore over that fact. Meanwhile, to keep Monty from grabbing some of our divisions, Patton is cooking up men-devouring attacks. Poking away at positions and areas, like 94th Inf Div and a combat command of 8th Armored Div in the Saar-Moselle triangle, that are utterly useless. Troops and effort concentrated on one spot give breakthroughs. Someday someone should be called to account on this constant frittering away of our forces—this constant piecemeal commitment of our strength, this constant playing politics, mixing politics and prestige with tactics and strategy. If Eisenhower is a real Supreme Commander and it is responsible for letting Monty and the British do this, then he should be burned in oil. If Churchill-Roosevelt are at the bottom, then they should be scarified.

Thursday, January 25, 1945: Patton commenting on 12 Army Group staff: "Allen, C/S, only one of staff who is any good. All others dead from neck up. All they can say is 'It can't be done.'" Patton told Gay to phone Allen at Group about shifting a division. During talk with Allen, Gay said something that enraged Patton and he burst out at Gay, "Goddamn it, don't say that. Do what I tell you. None of you have any Machiavelli in you. I don't want him to know what we're doing. If he knows we're taking that RCT, they are as liable as not to send it in the opposite direction."

Russians not in on ULTRA. Fact is, we get more Info about Russians from German sources than from Russians. Plan of attack in new TUSA offensive—our next D-day—

VIII Corps—
2 Inf Divs abreast
2 Inf Divs in reserve
Armored Division on narrow front 12 miles due East, with
    PRÜM intermediate objective, and Bonn the objective

Tentative line-up—subsequently changed:

VIII Corps	III Corps	XII Corps	XX Corps
4 Inf	17 AB	80 Inf	94 Inf
87 Inf	1 RCT of 35 Inf	5 Inf	26 Inf
90 Inf	6 Armored	76 Inf	8 Armored—conditionally
95 Inf		4 Armored	

Major General Hugh J. Gaffey, chief of staff, and Lieutenant General George S. Patton in France, 1944. (National Archives)

Colonel Oscar W. Koch, assistant chief of staff, G-2. (National Archives)

Lieutenant Colonel Robert S. Allen in the field with Third Army. (Courtesy Wisconsin Historical Society)

Colonel Robert S. Allen, Washington, DC, November 1945. (Courtesy Wisconsin Historical Society)

Colonel Robert S. Allen (right) with Colonel Oscar W. Koch (left) and Colonel Harold M. Forde (middle). Forde served in the G-2 (Air) Section. (Courtesy Wisconsin Historical Society)

Major General John Millikin, commanding general, III Corps. (National Archives)

Major General Manton S. Eddy (left), commanding general, XII Corps. (National Archives)

SC 194530

G. C. U.S. ARMY

Brigadier General Otto P. Weyland, commanding general, XIX Tactical Air Command. (National Archives)

Lieutenant General Courtney Hodges, commanding general, First Army. (National Archives)

Patton (center) with his dog Willie. Major General Walton Walker, commander of XX Corps, is in the right foreground. (National Archives)

Eisenhower, Bradley, and Patton in Bastogne. (National Archives)

6

Into Germany

Saturday, January 27, 1945: Patton started smoking again. Result—much better humor. From Eklund—replacements. 55,000 due per month from States for 3 months. In addition, 10,000 from Air Force, SOS and other sources. 15,000 returned casualties. Out of 55,000—for all U.S. Armies in ETO—TUSA gets perhaps 20,000—based on number of divisions we have. With returnees from hospitals gives us approximately what we need. Currently all Inf Divs up to strength, except for some specialists airborne furnished by Airborne Command from States.

Sunday, January 28, 1945: Patton at ULTRA briefing indignant over the fact that FUSA put in an AT[TAC]K FO [Field Order] a statement that TUSA was supporting FUSA. Half-jokingly said to Maddox—"In next FO put in paragraph 'after recapturing ground lost by FUSA, TUSA will continue the attack.' Bastards wrote that FO as if we lost the ground. No mention of fact they lost it and we recaptured it for them." During discussion of Air attacks on oil plants of Germans, Patton said— "General Marshall told me oil would win the war." Maddox—"We ought to know. Lack of it prevented us from winning it last September." Patton—"Combination of lack of gas and a very stupid decision to throw weight to North. That accomplished practically nothing and kept us from reaching the Rhine, which we could have done in a couple of weeks if [Eisenhower] hadn't sat us down."

Monday, January 29, 1945: VIII Corps jumped off on new offensive to crack Siegfried Line in St. Vith area and capture Prüm. Today marks beginning of new Army operation—the fourth. *Editor's note: Third Army's role in this larger Twelfth Army Group operation was to protect First Army's right flank. Middleton's VIII Corps was the army's main effort. The northernmost division, the 87th Infantry, advanced abreast of XVIII Airborne Corps to the vicinity of Losheim. To the south, the 4th Armored and 90th Infantry Divisions were to attack the West Wall along and just south of the Schnee Eifel. These two divisions were then sup-posed to block to the southeast.*

The casualty report as of 2400 yesterday—28th—upon conclusion of last operation—Ardennes counteroffensive—as follows:

OUR TROOPS	28 Jan	Cumulative from 1 Aug	Present Op
Killed	30	14,778	1,639
Wounded	293	70,685	24,277
Missing	27	14,074	4,925
Total	350	99,537	30,841
Non-battle	548	72,248	23,305
Grand Total	898	171,785	54,146
ENEMY TROOPS			
PW	501	162,387	22,608
Enemy Buried	55	17,666	2,724
Total	556	180,053	23,332 [25,332]
Estimated			
PW	200	162,500	22,500
Killed	200	95,600	31,800
Wounded	700	267,200	87,000
Total	1,100	525,300	141,300
This is the story of the cost to TUSA of the Ardennes.			
MATERIAL LOST, CAPTURED AND DESTROYED			
OUR LOSSES			
Tks, Light	0	270	72
Tks, Medium	0	771	264
Arty, 75mm & over	0	144	28
Veh[icles], all types	2	3,185	1,008
Totals	2	4,370	1,372
ENEMY LOSSES			
Tks, Mark III & IV	0	1,264	318
Tks, Mark VI	0	710	225
Arty, 75mm & over	0	2,509	293
Veh[icles], all types	0	6,202	771
Totals	0	10,685	1,607
ENEMY AIRCRAFT DESTROYED			
Cat #1	0	510	168
Cat #2	0	254	90
[Total]	0	764	258
XIX TAC			

Allies have in WEST as of this date—74 Divs as compared to 52 Divs in Nov. Germans have nominal 73 with value of about 25.

Tuesday, January 30, 1945: New Operation being planned. XII

Corps to attack North to capture Bitburg. Actually is a sneak offensive that Patton is secretly scheming in order to prevent SHAEF (Monty) from grabbing more TUSA Divs for his offensive. Such is the path to glory—and politics—for Generals.

Wednesday, January 31, 1945: Major Marechal,[1] IRW [IPW], story—CIC asked him to work out on an agent who they said wouldn't talk. "Vat you dink. I beat up on him all night and then gottam, the bastard is innocent. Those SOB CIC make me work all night for noiding [nothing]."

Thursday, February 1, 1945: Houffalize, Wiltz—whole area battered; lacerated appearance of battlefield. Great many other tanks all over the area, knocked out and burned out. Number of Germans, too, but not as many. 17 AB Div, sourish outfit, G-2 Section had no work map. In CG office where both G-2 & G-3 maps, combined, [are] kept. Puny little map. 94th Inf Div—in Saar-Moselle triangle—apparently also very sour. Lousy staff work and same for Command line units.

Saturday, February 3, 1945: Patton returned from big War Council yesterday, apparently at Namur, 12 Army Group CP, and with great gusto related this story at ULTRA briefing—"Monty said to Eisenhower, 'I shall dispose a division on the flank and lie in wait for the Hun and at the proper moment leap on him like a *savage rabbit*.'" Patton snorted and everyone roared. Commenting on overall WEST situation, Patton remarked, "If I were in command, I'd have every division on the line attacking. Can attack a little and raise hell with the Germans." Later—"Got to get a new CG for the 4th Infantry Div. He is too much of a gentleman. 4th needs prodding and he is too nice to boot it."[2]

At 1030 hours, Patton held a conference in General Maddox's office attended by all Corps CGs—Middleton, VIII; Millikin, III; Eddy, XII; Walker, XX—general staff chiefs of staff of TUSA and I, who prepared a terrain map of our zone of advance. In battledress uniform and slacks, with pointer in hand, Patton stated—He had attended a conference held by Bradley yesterday; also present, Hodges, Simpson. Bradley told them that Eisenhower had been *ordered* by the *Combined Chiefs of Staff* [CCS][3] to make an attack from the North under command of Montgomery, who was to get for this purpose 10 U.S. Inf Divs and 3 U.S. Armd Divs that were to be commanded by Ninth U.S. Army—one of the lousiest we've got over here, but manageable by British. Eisenhower received this order to subordinate this huge U.S. force to Monty at a meeting with Marshall and some members of Combined Chiefs of Staff in Southern France. When the meeting took place, Patton did not indicate. Also, if Monty was present—nothing said. Only names mentioned—Marshall and Eisenhower. Anyway, what did happen was that Marshall—as spokesman of Combined Chiefs of Staff—told Eisenhower where next Allied offensive would be made, what with and who was to command it—Monty. Whether Marshall got his orders from still higher up, or he acted on decision of CCS, is conjecture. But CCS now directly running the war in the WEST and Eisenhower is merely, in effect, a figurehead and/or sort of brass-plated Ln O. Whether all this is due to Ardennes debacle is also a guess. Certainly it happened after that tragedy. *Editor's note: On January 10 the CCS had requested from Eisenhower a report on the progress he had made in achieving the end state envisioned in his directive of October 28, 1944.*[4]

Patton stated that there was not enough Replacements and Ammo to support more than one major effort. He said that was what he was told. He said nothing about his personal views—very strongly held—that Saarlautern-Saarbrücken area was the place to attack, or about putting the drive under Monty, whom he despises as a cautious bungler and grandstander. All he said was—"Ninth is an American Army and we must do everything we can to help it." He stated that the present plan was for Monty to jump off between 10–12 February "if he can complete regrouping by that time, which I doubt." Up to 10th, TUSA can make an all-out attack against the Siegfried Line. Also, FUSA was to get Roer River dams[5] (2) to prevent Germans from blowing them and flooding the area. After 10th, FUSA and TUSA, in effect, were to sit down. He made no direct statement, but left it very clear that he had no intention of sitting if he could help it. That was the reason for the conference—to decide on what attack to make—VIII to Prüm, or XII to Bitburg—or both. Middleton explained desperate communications problem due to snow, mud, limited good roads. Eddy, as per usual, smiled and worried about not having enough forces, Arty, etc. He is a big tub of lard, if there ever was one. Middleton made the best impression, quiet voiced, earnest and deliberate. Wasn't being rushed into anything by Patton or anyone else. After lots of discussion, during which Patton gave them totals of enemy on their fronts, he carefully concluded by pumping up III Corps—VIII—11,500; III—4,500 which he pumped to 8,000; XII—9,000; XV—15,000 and some backing and filling on whether only VIII or XII attack, finally decided both would.

Conference concluded with Patton sternly admonishing great secrecy. No reference to be made in any manner to XII Corps attack which was to get off as soon as possible. "Eddy, if you don't get going soon, they'll take some more of our units." (Monty gets four divisions from FUSA and 1 Infantry (95th) and 6 Arty Bns from us.) In other words, Patton up to his old tricks. XII Corps is to be [launched on a] sneak offensive on the hope that if it really gets going they'll let him keep on. He obviously would give a right arm to be first on the Rhine and to beat Monty there. Such is the way to fame and glory for generals—and agony, hell and death for the guys in the line.

Sunday, February 4, 1945: More on big North offensive plan—First Canadian Army jumps off on 8th. Ninth U.S. Army on 10th, and last— 2d British Army—which initially will hold line of the Maas River and cross river and advance to East—after Canadian and Ninth Armies have cleared the way. The British can always depend on "Savage Rabbit" Monty to take care of their interest. *Editor's note: First Canadian Army was to launch Operation Veritable on February 8, while Ninth U.S. Army was to launch Operation Grenade on February 10 from the Düren-Oberbruch area north toward Düsseldorf and Wesel, with the intention of meeting First Canadian Army to clear the west bank of the Rhine.*

Monday, February 5, 1945: Attack of VIII Corps going along all right. Number of penetrations through Siegfried Line but terrain is murderous. As Middleton expressed it at the conference the other day—"Not enemy holding us up but roads. We can't keep up with ourselves." Supplies are being carried in by hand—roads so difficult, and the thaw that set in making conditions even worse. Be much better if it freezes. As it is, muck and mud terrible.

Tuesday, February 6, 1945: XII Corps jumped off early this morning after heavy Arty concentration. By night, 87th Inf Div had no bridgeheads over Sauer River; 5th Inf Div only a few men over. Lost 38 out of 38 assault boats due to flood-tide and swiftness of current, estimated at 12 mph. High water covers wire Germans put in on East bank and MG fire 6 inches above water raising murderous hell. 5th Div is a good outfit but having very tough time getting over. VIII Corps also made little progress toward Prüm, which they thought they could take today.

Wednesday, February 7, 1945: Patton at it again. At ULTRA briefing, directed Maddox to prepare plans for employment of 6th, 4th, 11th Armored Divs in rush for Rhine in event we get Prüm and Bitburg and there is a breakthrough. "If that happens, be time to take some chances. We could afford to do that. They'll be on the run and we'll keep right on their heels. With any kind of a break in weather, it ought to be a cinch." Harkins—"Matter of national prestige that we should take the chance to get to the Rhine first." We begin digging up stuff on Rhine River crossings.

Thursday, February 8, 1945: Canadians jumped off—made 3–5,000 yard gains.[6] Took 1,000 PW. VIII Corps still has not got Prüm. 5th Inf Div still has no bridgehead over Sauer. 87th Inf Div has about 3 bns over and 2 foot bridges. Germans are definitely not what is holding them back, although both had a number of counterattacks. Terrain, floods, mud holding them down.

Monty's operation is titled *"VERITABLE"*—bet he personally picked that one. Ninth Army's is *GRENADE*. TUSA's operations are called "probing attacks" in 12 Army Group Letter of Instruction No. 15, 7 Feb, which ought to be burning up the old man plenty. XII Corps considers it's making a major offensive and it is. But, officially, to keep it a secret drive from Monty, and presumably the Combined Chiefs of Staff—and Eisenhower (?), it is called a "probing attack."

Big time—Topside—Stuff. Hot Dog. FUSA not doing so well getting those two Roer River dams. Only got part of one and other still in hands of Germans. Up against vicious terrain. In contrast to the complete secrecy the Germans preserved on their massing of troops for Ardennes offensive, over 12 Divisions assembled over a period of weeks, they have learned all about the concentration of troops for Monty's offensive. From ULTRA, they knew all units which had been moved and the general area. Peculiar thing is they claim it is due to RI but orders impose radio silence on units that are moving, while their traffic is being maintained where they were.

During ULTRA briefing on 5 Feb, Bradley telephoned Patton and asked him to meet him at rear CP of VIII Corps, still in Bastogne. Gay—"Shall I tell Middleton?" Patton—"No, less he knows about it the better. Ike and Bradley will be there and personally I think a certain personage wants his picture taken in Bastogne. Cost me 1½ hour road trip over miserable roads." When Patton finished on the phone and turned around, found [he was] holding up crossed fingers and hands on testicles. He laughed—and said, "No, it's all right. He didn't say anything about calling off XII Corps attack or taking any more units from us." During talk with Bradley, Patton told him 4th Inf Div was __ of a mile from Prüm and "should get there today or tomorrow." Still not there today, because of impassable terrain and roads, making supply a man-carrying condition.

The reckless and berserking [that the] Regs indulge in is unbelievable. Doesn't make rhyme or reason—but they do it and there is no arguing with them. Our PR [photo reconnaissance] is outstanding. Most interesting, competent, and best appearing in ETO. We can't fill all requests for it. Despite this, Patton, apparently in one of his berserk moods—not having enough to do to keep him busy—called in Koch and told him PR was too voluminous and to cut it down. Just like that. No discussion, no reason—blunt, flat, categoric order. Koch said "yessir" and rushed to me completely and utterly stunned and hurt to the heart. PR has been his great pride, and now ordered to massacre it without a word in his defense. Everyone of the Section is crushed, but orders are orders. That's efficiency in the Army.

Friday, February 9, 1945: Some more high-powered Army rhyme and reason. Just got word that Conklin, our Engr O, and Eugene L. Harrison,[7] G-2, 6 Army Group, have been nominated for BG. Conklin is a joke around Hq. Mediocre and grandstander. Got several good men who carry the section, but section very low grade. Never produce any original ideas, and time and again we had to turn back lousy and incorrect work—like terrain studies—or do them over ourselves. Yet, he gets a star, because of T/O vacancy, but Koch, the ablest member of the staff, doesn't; and we Lt Col wheel horses, also despite T/O authorization, get even less. Big stuff. All this is true of Harrison, who'd never done a day of G-2ing in his life before he became G-2 a few months ago of 6 Army Group, and who is notorious as a bust. But he has a big drag somewhere. Dope is he was a Military Aide at the White House and used to ride with Mrs. R[oosevelt].[8] Must be one of Pa Watson's pals. Kee-rist. Incidentally, regarding promotions here. Pfann told me today that Gay has been trying to push some recommendations for Colonel, but Patton is the one who is balking. Reason, the Hq is so cluttered up with surplus discarded full Reg Colonels, have no vacancies on paper for us guys who are really doing T/O jobs. Provost Marshal with three full Reg colonels, while all G Sections only one or two. That's an illustration of other cases. Meanwhile, we do the work and get nothing; and every time Patton gets a new decoration, he poops out with blat about how it really was in honor of our work. Horse-radish. He has the authority to promote and decorate but except for piddling stuff, he is goddamned selfish and niggardly.

Saturday, February 10, 1945: Several nights ago at about 0300, awakened by heavy AA fire from Btrys near my billet. Today learned a lesson. It was a B-17,[9] captured by Germans in Ardennes offensive. They got six in FUSA zone, and from ULTRA learned they are now using them to fly mail and supplies to La Rochelle, Lorient, St. Nazaire, Channel Islands. This Fort[ress] finally dropped proper signals and flares, and AA stopped. They, of course, didn't know they were right first time and that it was a hostile plane. Later, Btrys in the vicinity of Esch shot it down. German plane on this night service. Hit with Prosit [Pozit] shell and it blew up in the air. The B-17 that wasn't hit actually was not on night carrier service to the fortresses. It was engaged in more dramatic operations. It dropped nine Para agents—whose drop was arranged by an agent whom we captured some time ago and have been using to get Info from Bosche. Using him and his radio. Fixed up messages containing a certain amount of real Info—not real value, but definitely Intelligence to them. Double agents have been used so effectively that he was recently notified by radio that he had been *awarded Iron Cross Second Class*. Through him the drop of agents arranged. Nine dropped and so far eight picked up—all Frenchmen. Some had considerable money on them of all kinds, including greenbacks U.S. Also EEI what to find out—units, movements, dumps, etc. Also strips of acetate in sort of lipstick tubes—of maps, overlays, return routes through Saarbrücken. Also, poison pills and dope that would change color of skin. Very Hollywoodish. Also lists of names of Nazi sympathizers behind our lines.

Monday, February 12, 1945: Prüm finally taken today by 4th U.S. Inf Div. Also 5th and 80th Divisions have established firm bridgeheads over Sauer River in XII Corps zone and getting good bridges in for further attack toward Bitburg. Patton said this morning he wants to establish a line on Prüm River from Prüm to Bitburg as LD for rush to Rhine with Armored Div, as soon as he can work it or get permission. Meanwhile, we are definitely on the semi-sitdown again—and Ninth U.S. Army attack delayed pending subsiding of Roer, flooded by Germans blowing parts of dams, which had FUSA or Group blown months ago would have been over with. That's what Patton did South of St. Avold, but these goddamned incompetents didn't up here. Got copy of Monty's "No offensive power" statement on 15 Dec and sent it to Ruth[10] by private letter through [Lieutenant Colonel Walter E.] Bligh,[11] Assistant A-2, who is going home to Syracuse because of "ulcers." Ought to make interesting reading sometime in the future. Monty['s] statement [was] recalled, which explains why when I tried to get it from Group when they were here, they said they couldn't find it. (Mandel[12] got me the copy from Group files.)

Thursday, February 15, 1945: With Lt Col Charles Hallet[t],[13] A-2, XIX TAC, at P-47 airfield at Metz and with night fighter squadron at Étain. On basis of PW statements, took 1,050 trains to bring in German forces that launched Ardennes offensive; 21 trains per day for 50 days. All this in addition to other traffic. Shows extent of German skill in operating their railroads and concealing vast movement—thanks to non-flying weather and stupid G-2ing topside.

Friday, February 16, 1945: Koch told me today that my promotion to full Colonel has been approved by Patton and is to go forward to SHAEF for execution. Be interesting to see what happens in light of what happened to the recommendation for a Legion of Merit [LM] decoration for me. This was passed by TUSA Decorations Board and approved by Patton on 12 November. Now, hear from G-1, it was returned couple of days ago for "more details" in narrative portion of recommendation; the real reason for the return, though, G-1, Wing, says, is that it got held up so long at Group, for some unexplained reason, that ashamed to put it through and going through motions of asking for details so as to give the thing some currency—that pack of incompetent, diddling bastards. Nothing to do and plenty of time to do it in, and my LM gets lost in some pigeonhole—the goddamned sons-of-bitches. My instinctive dislike and distrust of them has been borne out time and again. They are just no goddamned good. Sibert is a graphic illustration of that, with his glaring incompetence as a G-2 and this small but striking piece of bitchery.

Sunday, February 18, 1944: Lubin[14] visited CP. Told me that there are 68 general officers on SHAEF rolls. That's more, I believe, than on the rolls of all the Armies in ETO.

Wednesday, February 21, 1945: Patton held a meeting of Planning Group TUSA in Maddox's office at 1530 hours for a conference with General Bradley. Present were Bradley, Patton, Gay, Harkins, Maddox, Muller, G-4, Col Tulley, Engr, Koch, Jim Goodwin, G-3 Operations, and I. (At preliminary conference, Patton looked at me and said, "Thought you were a Colonel." Gay said, "Just sent in the recommendation. Not returned yet." Patton smiled at me.) Patton's plan was to sell Bradley, or rather SHAEF through him, on allowing TUSA to keep going and not sit down. Right after lunch, we were thrown into a hectic whirl getting, or rather digging up, stuff on old Saarlautern plan offensive. Patton bent on not being sat down. Good basis for that, aside from his own restlessness, because nothing really in front of us. 18,000 for whole TUSA front and 50 tanks is a generous estimate. Only thing really stopping us—terrain and fearful roads and soggy weather. If we had a week of mild, dry weather, our Armd Divs to make a run for the Rhine, and they couldn't be stopped. But when Bradley arrived, he did the talking. Said plans called for three-phase operation—(1) Canadian—British—Ninth Army attack on Rhur [Ruhr]; (2) then FUSA turns South and strikes toward Moselle and Koblenz; (3) then TUSA makes run for Rhine either North or South of Moselle. I got the impression that Bradley was just talking to placate Patton and paint some grandiose operation for him in the future. Also, I got the impression that Patton quickly grasped the situation, didn't argue and "rode with the punch." In other words, he very smartly did not butt his head against a wall by sputtering and arguing, or fighting the problem. He listened very courteously to Bradley, went through some motions of discussing problems of a strike North or South of the Moselle and then quietly insinuated a guess that [it would] be all right for him to keep going if [he] could force a breakthrough in Trier area, where XX Corps, with 94th Inf, CC of 10th Armd, are in SHAEF Res[erve], but [could be] released for that purpose. 2d Cav Gp [has] cleaned up [the] Saar-Moselle triangle, and in XII and VIII Corps zone they are through most Siegfried defenses in the North and South on the Prüm River. Bradley said of course he could keep on going in event of a breakthrough, and Patton grinned quietly. That was enough. That was all he wanted. And I'll bet a dollar to a donut that he'll make a run for the Rhine within a couple of weeks, with our Armored Divisions—4th, 6th, 11th and any other he can lay his hands on, plus new Infantry outfits. Bradley said he wanted our Divs given rest periods and Patton agreed—saying 80th and 90th most in need. Bradley also said TUSA will get one or several new Divs, but had to be broken into combat slowly as had not completed training. Said wanted special emphasis on night attacks, with every platoon in Divs to go out on at least one operational night patrol. Patton had idea to make a run for the Rhine with Armored Divs as far back as two weeks ago. He is convinced it can be done and so fast he might even grab a crossing. Bradley remarked, "If you do that, give you another Corps to exploit it." Patton would give his right arm to do that, and given the slightest chance he will do it.

Thursday, February 22, 1945: Today is 2 weeks since Ninth Army was supposed to have jumped off and is still sitting. Dope now is tomorrow. No flooded rivers ever stopped Patton, but the Roer, blown up by dams that Germans blasted, sure sat down "Ninth British Army," as Patton derisively calls it. Dope we got is that Simpson wanted to jump off last week, but Monty would not allow it. Lt Col [Richard J.] Stillman,[15] TUSA Ln O to FUSA, brought back story today as follows: Monty made statement that [he was] "not displeased at enemy build-up against British and that Ninth Army had not attacked. Views enemy build-up against British as a much welcomed opportunity to enable *Montgomery* once and for all to decisively defeat the Germans." Hogwash and horse manure! The pussyfooting poseur and phony has never licked them before. Always U.S. forces that have really won the victory—in Africa, in Sicily and in France. And if Patton gets half a chance, he will do it again.

All in turn owe it to Russians who cut Germans down to our size and containing the bulk of his forces in the East.

Friday, February 23, 1945: Ninth Army jumped off, initially against little opposition, at 0330 hours. By noon had 10 Bns over Roer. XX Corps cleared Saarburg and has high ground overlooking Konz-Karthaus, northern tip of Saar-Moselle triangle, cleared finally after five months. From high ground, we can dominate the Siegfried Line defense and can look into and shell Trier. Patton sore as boil at 10th Armd Div, because it sat down when it got on its objective yesterday against very little opposition and when enemy obviously disorganized. He is convinced the combat command could have boiled through the Siegfried Line and possibly broken into Trier. He has been raising hell with Corps, and presumably 10th Armd, plenty. Morris, one-time CG of a corps in Texas, now CG of 10th Armd. Patton felt so strongly about the matter that after the briefing this morning, rose and said, "What happened in triangle yesterday a perfect example of the need to follow through when you are given a mission. 10th Armored sat on its ass for ten hours when it had nothing in front of it and could have effected a breakthrough. If I had been there I wouldn't have done that, and I told the Corps Comdr (Walker) that. It just goes to show you can't trust anyone. You've got to be on the alert yourself all the time (the last with great disgust)."

Yesterday—up in St. Vith, overlooking skyline drive, Vielsalm—utter desolation and unbelievably impossible roads. Main supply route into lines in area [is] a railroad bed that is stripped of rails and ties and filled out with rock, slate, corduroy (logs). Up on front with Brig Genl Ernest, who is slated to take over 90th Infantry Div shortly. Through Siegfried Line, dragon's teeth, lines of German PW returning carrying own wounded. Bright, mild, sunny day—with Arty breaking all over area—all ours.

Sunday, February 25, 1945: At 1030A, told to be prepared to give Estimate of Enemy Situation on our front at a conference to be attended by Bradley at 1330A in War Room. Koch in Paris, so I got set. Purpose of conference is to sell Bradley on allowing TUSA to continue to employ 10th Armored Div to take Trier. We have two bridgeheads over Saar at Saarburg and would be in Trier now, if 10th hadn't sat down for 12 hours when we got over river. Bad boner on part of Morris, CG of 10th, and Walker, CG XX Corps. Now Patton has to go through elaborate song and dance to get permission to continue to employ 10th Armd to take this vital communications center and anchor of enemy's defensive line North and South of Moselle. We have been aiming for 5 months to get Trier, oldest city in Germany. Once, last September, when Patton had Germans on the run and Metz had been evacuated, we could have had it without cost. From ULTRA, we knew they had nothing to man it with.[16] Now, when it is again in our grasp, Patton has to literally fight to retain the 10th to take the place, because the 10th is in SHAEF Reserve—on order of Combined C/S—5,000 miles away in Washington. The whole affair is fantastic—from start to finish; from Patton's careful dry run where he primed Corps CGs on what to say to Bradley's frank admission that Eisenhower is really not running the war—mere figurehead; that strategy and orders have been laid down and issued by Combined Chiefs of Staff—5,000 miles away.

The dry run took place unexpectedly. We were told to be there at 1115A. But after waiting, finally decided not to come down to War Room, where Jimmy Goodwin and I set up G-3 and G-2 maps and terrain studies. At 1155A, got word that Patton was in the War Room and we rushed back there. He had three corps CGs—Middleton, VIII, Gaffey, acting for Eddy, XII, and Walker, XX, standing before War Map and was priming them on what they were to tell Bradley in order, as he put it, "so this Army, the only one that really wants to fight, can fight." Then he took them to dinner and we adjourned until 1530A, when Bradley arrived with Major-General Lev Allen, his sharp-faced Chief of Staff. Patton started proceedings by saying Third Army wanted to fight and could, if allowed to do so. Then called on Middleton to present situation on his front—which he did in slow monotone, very dull. Then Gaffey gave situation on XII Corps's front, very well done, surprising for his usual diffidence, also lying a little, as told to do so at dry run by Patton that 4th Armd Div was wholly committed, which it wasn't; and then Walker, pouter-pigeonish, concluded. He carefully avoided any mention of fact that if he had been on the job, 10th Armored would have overrun Trier, but said if given two more days he could take the town. Patton strongly backed up this plan and in midst, Gay turned to me and said, "G-2, how much enemy is there in that section?" I got up and said I estimated about 2,000 remnants of 256 and 416 VG Divs[17]— in bad morale state and poor control. Then M[ajor] General Weyland, CG, XIX TAC, added that Trier had an excellent airfield with concrete runways that he wanted to begin developing as soon as possible for future operations to the east when drive to cross Rhine begins. Pointed out it would give big extension to range of his planes over fields from which they now operate—St. Dizier, Metz, Étain. This argument obviously made a strong impression on Bradley, and as we learned later, was a decisive factor in getting approval from Eisenhower on deal finally agreed on.

Bradley then took the floor and, pointer in hand and standing before Map, said, in effect, that Eisenhower was under categoric orders from Combined C/S to have so many units in SHAEF reserves and had to report every day on that—this is an obvious result of Ardennes fiasco, when caught with no reserve, and Third Army had to be pulled up from Moselle-Saar zone and its drive to Mainz called off. Bradley stated in so many words that Eisenhower was not his own complete boss and that actual conduct of operations was now being run by Combined C/S—5,000 miles away. In other words, Washington was really directing the strategy. Combined C/S decided on offensive in North and putting Third Army—and 6 Army Group—on the defensive. The latter, lacking Patton's drive and initiative, are taking the directive to go on the defensive literally and are sitting in place doing nothing—although have few Germans—estimate 3 Divs—in front of them and could break through Siegfried Line at little cost. Stupidity of this strategy is seen by the fact that due to Devers' sitting, Germans able to shift some of their divisions from this sector to fight against us—2 Mtn Div[18] in Trier area—and others against Ninth and First Armies, and also resting and rebuilding the others. That's what comes of trying to generate a 450-mile front [from] 5,000 miles away. And as far as we are concerned—if we were given a couple of Devers' unused divisions or the replacements allotted 6 Army Group, we could break through to Koblenz in a week. There is nothing but difficult terrain, and some beat-up divisions—equivalent 2 divisions—in front of us. By 6 Army Group and TUSA continuing to press forward, it would nail down German forces so they couldn't shift them back and forth, and exhaust their reserves, thus making it far easier for the northern main effort. Also cut down their losses and losses all the way down the line. Now, as it is, Germans able to mass all but two of their Panzers and all their best Inf Divs in North. Bradley left no doubt he disagreed with the strategy and personally favored pressure all down the line. Inferred that Eisenhower probably also held this view. But Bradley said that ammo and replacements are not sufficient for offensive operations all the way down the line and therefore 21 Army Group and FUSA had the green light. It all sounded like an excuse or alibi to me—because we'd need no more Ammo or replacements to hammer for Rhine outright and openly than doing it as part of "sneak" offensive as Patton is doing it. Clearly, intention of Combined C/S is for Patton to sit and do nothing as Devers is so complaisantly doing. But as Patton caustically remarked to Bradley—"Third Army is the only Army that wants to fight." But the Combined C/S—5,000 miles away—with no real grasp of ground situation and possibilities—has put binders and blinkers on Eisenhower, and Patton, with the way wide open to the Rhine, has to finagle and chisel, argue and scheme to do the obvious and sound thing—fight and kill Germans.

Bradley explained that the big strategic plan consisted of three phases—(1) the offensive to envelop the Ruhr, (2) FUSA then to turn South along the Rhine, (3) TUSA then to advance astride Moselle on Koblenz, thus creating pocket to capture or destroy the bulk of the German Armies in West on West side of Rhine so Nazis will be without forces to continue the war East of Rhine. That was his story, and as he concluded, Patton said bitterly from his seat, "That's fine, General, but it's a hell of a note to have this war run 5,000 miles from here. The Third Army wants to fight. It can fight and if allowed to fight we'll be in Koblenz in a week. There is nothing in front of us. But of course, if somebody 5,000 miles away, who has no idea of the real situation, is deciding what should and should not be done, then that's the way it is." However, although apparently acceding, Patton didn't relinquish his efforts to get permission to continue to use 10th Armored to take Trier. Pointed out it would take almost two days to disengage it and by that time, it could take Trier. Also, by taking Trier, it would give TUSA a good jumping off point for drive on Koblenz. Not have to take time out then for that. Bradley, with grin, slyly suggested that maybe by that time Army boundaries would be changed and 6 Army Group could get XX Corps's area. Patton was startled for a moment by this idea, but only for a moment. "Well, even so," he said, "then Jackie [Devers] will be in a good position for a jump off, damn him."

Then ensued a hot deal of horse trading over what to substitute for 10th Armored as it is SHAEF reserve. Practically every division in TUSA was wrestled over. Final proposal was to offer 90th Inf Div, in North part of Army zone, VIII Corps. Bradley agreed to submit proposition to Eisenhower—obviously was all for Patton, and I got the best impression I ever had of him. Kindly, solid, able—no Patton, but a very capable commander. That was the show, and what an amazing and revealing one. Eisenhower, in effect, is only a figurehead. Patton having to fight for the opportunity to fight Germans, and the war being run by a conglomeration of "masterminds" 5,000 miles away, without any real concept of the true ground situation. No wonder the Germans, although groggy and on the ropes, can continue to defend and delay the combined forces of U.S., British, French, etc, with about 200,000 combat effectives and 200 tanks—against our 70–80 divisions and 2,500–3,000 tanks. We are fighting the war to their best advantage—at a cost to us of thousands of casualties daily.

This evening, Patton received word from Bradley that Eisenhower had approved 90th Infantry as a substitute for 10th Armored for SHAEF reserve—and also that the 10th was available for continued commitment for only 48 hours. All of which caused wide grins around here, because 90th was due to come out of the line for some rest and everybody was willing to wager that if it was necessary, 10th Armd would stay in line until Trier was captured—which is exactly what happened.

Monday, February 26, 1945: Read semi-monthly secret survey on mail from ETO, based on what censors read. It's a secret report on trends and sentiments contained in soldier, Red X and civilian mail. This report covered 1–15 February, during which time—38,265,528 letters were processed through censors. Of this number, 52,421 officer, 287,140 EM and 16,586 civilian—9 percent—were screened for purposes of this report. According to report—the announcement that there is to be a beer ration was enthusiastically approved; writers complained they had too many cigarettes—very interesting in light of hullabaloo over cigarette shortage—and preferred less cigarettes and more candy. One of the most interesting items of the report was a complaint by the war correspondent of LONDON DAILY MAIL that his rag had gone anti-American and was cutting his American stuff. This is a quote in the report of statement in letter—"I'm having a bit of a go in about my stories with the office. It seems the MAIL has gone all anti-American and has been tossing some of my stories about which I have given honest praise to the Yanks in the (Ardennes) Bulge. 16 Jan 45." MAIL is one of Beaverbrook's[19] rags and is some more light on the little bastard's antics in playing up Montgomery and deliberately creating ill will and dissension. In a sensible country like Russia the son-of-a-bitch would be shot as a traitor—which he is, because creating ill-feeling is exactly what Nazis are striving and hoping for. Beaverbrook's conduct is sinisterly vicious—not only currently but for future, as creating an undercurrent of dissension and hatred between us and British that some time in future will cost both bitterly. It's a damnable outrage and the little rat should be exposed and denounced and punished. It also is not unusual for him—after all, he dabbled [in] Moseleyism,[20] Hitlerism and fascism before the war. A sewer rat is always a sewer rat.

Tuesday, February 27, 1945: Trier not yet taken, but key roads controlling area cut. Not Germans that are holding us up, but vicious terrain and a very deep mine field. At midnight when 10th Armored supposed to revert to SHAEF reserve, Patton got an extension, with 90th Div again as substitute—thus killing two birds with one stone. Giving 90th a rest, and continuing to employ 10th where it can do most good. Old Patton pulled slick one when he got two-day extension on 10th, as he knew they couldn't pull it out at end of that time if it hadn't yet taken Trier. He just couldn't lose on the deal—wise old guy and a marvelous horse trader—for a chance to lick the Germans. But if he were another Devers, or Hodges or Simpson, or Monty, we'd be sitting on our pants—as others have done—and be doing nothing.

Wednesday, February 28, 1945: PW pouring in on all fronts—except 6 Army Group, which did nothing. For last three days TUSA, supposed to be on the defensive, has captured from 1,800 to 2,000 daily—leading Ninth, First and British-Canadians. For each of these days the total for the West has been 4–6,000—equivalent in PW alone of a German Div of present size.

Friday, March 2, 1945: Trier, oldest city in Germany, founded by Romans and with oldest church in Germany, was captured today at 1620A. In the process, 10th Armd took 2,000 PW in city, and 94th Div another 1,000 in pocket to the West. Total PW bag for Third Army for the day—4,600. Total for entire WEST, 10,600. Since 25th Feb, that makes over 16,000 PW, equivalent to two full-strength German divisions and four of present strength. In fact, there is not a German division in the West today that has 4,000 combat effectives. [Harold Sydney Harmsworth, 1st Viscount] Rothemere[21]—not Beaverbrook—owner of DAILY MAIL, I'm told. To be checked.

Saturday, March 3, 1945: Bixel, tall, stupid, stone-faced G-2 of Ninth Army, finally rolled. And it's about time. An utter incompetent and ass. Only got job because he was a classmate of C/S of '26. Only surprise is how they put up with him this long. Question now is whether the equally moronic staff he had will be rolled. They are just as stupid as he is.

PW score for day—8,800. Astoundingly large number of officers—Regtl and Bn CP being overrun, and Os being nabbed in batches. VIII Corps grabbed 14 in a Regtl CP.

Sunday, March 4, 1945: This happened on 2 March. Around 1100A, Harkins called and asked me to bring map showing roads to Rhine North of Moselle. I grabbed maps and terrain studies from our files and ran to Gay's office—where I found Patton and Walker, CG XX Corps. Maddox came in later. Patton asked me about routes of advance and after

I explained them, Patton told Walker to grab a bridge over the Moselle North of Trier [near] Schweich. Walker then phoned his C/S—[William A.] Collier[22]—and in a few words told him to have 10th Armd go after the bridge—we still have 10th committed. Then Patton, sitting edgewise on a chair and leaning on back said, "Don't mention one word of this to anyone. It's not to go out in any Sitreps, Issues or any other reports. This is strictly between us in this room. We want to fight, but they don't want to let us, so what they don't know won't hurt them."

Heard today that only American BG left on SHAEF G-2 staff is ill, with result that Eisenhower is getting all his G-2 information and recommendations from Strong and the other Brits that fill up the G-2 staff. No wonder we have to fight for a chance to fight and why possibilities for striking a death blow to the Germans in our zone are being disregarded. Total PW bag for the week—45,000. Equivalent of 4½ full-strength divisions and about 10 of present strength. Was told to stand by for another Bradley conference, like one last Sunday, but he didn't show up. Heard later he went to SHAEF and didn't get back in time to get here.

Monday, March 5, 1945: 4th Armored Div has bridgehead over Kyll. That is, 5th Inf Div made a bridgehead several days ago and put in tread bridges, and 4th jumped off on breakthrough today. Very little resistance and made 12-mile advance. Another 6,400 PW yesterday—of which TUSA's share is 1,800. Prince Felix,[23] consort of Grand Duchess of Luxembourg, doing quite a bit of hanging around our CP, mooching cigarettes and trips to the front. Gay took him to Trier. Felix rather a handsome guy, very pleasant and proudly wears on his uniform of a British brigadier a TUSA shoulder patch. Today's PW bag 6,500—TUSA 1,700.

Tuesday, March 6, 1945: Heard interesting story today on inner topside machinations. According to tale, Major [Thomas S.] Bigland,[24] 21 Army Group Ln O to 12 Army Group, made very enthusiastic report on what Third Army was doing and had done in capturing Trier. Monty was greatly interested and said he would have to talk to Eisenhower and get him to take wraps off of Patton so he could launch full-scale drive on Rhine. If story is true, Monty is wasting his breath because Patton is driving for Rhine anyway. 4th Armored has broken out of bridgehead over Kyll and is rolling hell-bent for the Rhine. Advanced about 12 miles today—CCA. PW bag today 8,300 for West—2,500 TUSA.

Heard that reason Bradley didn't show up yesterday was because he was called to SHAEF to sit in on a conference to give TUSA its head. Maybe this story about Monty is correct and something to it. Further indication—Bradley telephoned Patton this evening and when found he was out, told Harkins for him to "tell your boss" that he would call him tomorrow and thought he would be able to give him the green light.

According to SHAEF—PW from D-Day to 28 Feb '45—943,038. Doesn't include French figures, not fully available. Visited Trier, Saarburg, Cerf, while counterattack in progress, Remick, Moselle and Saar, [and] vineyards. All area a shambles of beat-up villages and towns. Trier is complete devastation in center of town. Only thing unmarred, Porta Negra,[25] old Roman ruin, and hotel nearby.

Wednesday, March 7, 1945: General d. Cavalrie (Lt Genl Enrs. Georg Edwin Graf von Rothkirch und Trach,[26] CG LIII (53) Corps) captured by CCA of 4th Armored, when he was out visiting what he thought were his lines. Saw a long column of German troops and vehicles and drove over to see who they were. They were PW and he arrived in time to join the procession. Was brought to Luxembourg and put up under guard at Brasseur Hotel. Patton received him next day and after few minutes' talk, PW was sent on way to Group.

4th Armored going like bat out of hell. Few miles West of Mayen and should be on Rhine tomorrow. III U.S. Corps, First Army, grabbed railroad bridge intact at Remagen South of Bonn and have five bns of Infantry over. Complete surprise (or some fancy sabotage) to Germans—also to FUSA, SHAEF and Monty. Wasn't in plan at all. FUSA (III Corps) was to come down West bank of Rhine and envelop with us and then try for bridgehead, while 21 Army Group enveloped Ruhr from the North and we, in conjunction with 6 Army Group, made bridgehead in the vicinity of Worms.

The III Corps bridgehead apparently has SHAEF all aflutter and atwitter. Completely disrupted their nicely fitted plan, whereby Monty would win the war—after U.S. Armies opened the way for him. Evidence of this perturbation is the fact that in morning papers London carried stories, obviously all from SHAEF, that no bridgehead over Rhine contemplated at this time. Regroup and reorganize and then cross Rhine. But the Patton-thrusted III Corps messed all these plans up by taking the Remagen bridge, and it has thrown the SHAEF cookie-pushers into a tailspin.

Meanwhile, Patton making hay by pounding ahead and trying to get VIII Corps (Middleton) off its dead bottom and join XII Corps in rush to the river. Middleton is as slow and pokey as British. The Ardennes bust apparently had terrific shock on him. Made him crawlingly cautious and scary. Patton has to constantly needle him, and prod and coax him to get a move on. 90th Inf Div people complaining bitterly about being held back when not a thing in front of them. Patton definitely made mistake when he shifted III Corps to FUSA and kept VIII. III Corps is hot and with them holding VIII Corps's present sector, we'd have been on the river days ago and might even have a bridgehead. Patton made bum choice on that deal. 9th Armored Div captured Remagen bridge—significant [that it is] 2 Armored Divs that [are] spearheading drive to and along the Rhine.

From 3 March TUSA bag of PW to 10 March—10,000 for total for this operation of 53,115. Not bad for an Army that is supposed to be on the *DEFENSIVE*. Out of seven Armies in the West—TUSA captured about 40 percent of PW while being on the Defensive and stripped of a number of divisions that were given to NUSA and SUSA [Seventh U.S. Army] for their offensives.

Thursday, March 8, 1945: Remagen bridgehead has been given a terrain limitation—8 miles deep and 20 miles long. Apparently, III Corps CG decision to grab bridge has not been received with jubilation topside.[27] 9th Inf Div, 78th Div, 9th Armored Div being put into bridgehead, which is drawing all the weight the enemy can mass against it. 130 Panzer, 116 Panzer, 106 Panzer B[rigade],[28] 11 Panzer and various Recn units of Inf Divs being massed against it. In first three days German air attacks totaled about 66 planes, as follows: 4 first day, 4 shot down, 6 shot down second day, 26 shot down out of 43 third day. Good shooting.

Friday, March 9, 1945: Lot of excitement for while over report that XII Corps captured bridge over Moselle at Lochem [Losheim]. Had bridge all right, but either failed to remove charges or couldn't find them in time, [so] Enemy blew bridge—after Patton, who was up at Group conferring with Bradley, was told we had it.

Saturday, March 10, 1945: At ULTRA briefing, Patton telephoned Gay and told him we are not to attempt crossing of Rhine at this time. Concentrate on Moselle—into Palatinate. XII Corps to cross Moselle, XX to attack to South East to Kaiserlautern, in conjunction with Seventh Army. 4th Armored to attempt bridgehead over Moselle South of Koblenz.

Around 1 AM this morning (11th) Luxembourg shelled by 380mm RR gun. 16 rounds landed. One hit directly in front of our CP, about 20 yards from the building. Shattered all windows and killed two men in AG's office on ground floor. Also killed 9 civilians, 7 in displaced persons camp, and wounded 16.

Sunday, March 11, 1945: Decorated with Croix de Guerre with Gold Star this morning and in afternoon notified that my promotion to full

Colonel had come through. Col Koch pinned on Eagles at ceremony in front of Sit Sec War Room in presence of all Os of Section. Mine is the only Colonel promotion that came through. Harrison[29] of G-4, sent at same time as mine, strangely not received.

Heard today that recently Germans pulled two Air attacks on UK. One, followed in RAF night bombers, on their tail, and destroyed 25 as they landed and got away scot clean. Other, night bomber raid of over 60 AC. Conjecture whether the last was not a trial (dry) run for possible later gas attack. Much concern developing over danger the enemy may resort to CM [CW—chemical warfare]. Not positive information indicating that, but enough suspicious indications to give rise to fears. Due to these, Bradley issued order warning about danger of enemy resort to CW, due to desperation, and directing every precaution and preparation be taken.

Monday, March 12, 1945: SHAEF has 88 divisions—of which—

62 U.S.
10 British
5 Canadian
11 French

6 Army Group—

First French Army 6 Div
Seventh U.S. Army 16 [Div]—and not doing a goddamned thing except sitting on tails

12 Army Group—30 divisions—

FUSA—12
TUSA—12
Fifteenth Army—5—and not in line and doing nothing

21 Army Group—26 divisions—and doing nothing, except regrouping, which the British do most of the time.

Dope now is they won't jump off on attack to envelop Ruhr from North until 24 March. Keerist—the great and mighty Monty sitting on bottom, doing nothing, while TUSA cleaning up Eifel (while on the defensive) and getting set tomorrow to jump off on new operation to cross Moselle and envelop whole German Army and Siegfried positions from the rear. It's fantastic—but Patton really is the only Army that is fighting on West Front. British, 6 Army Group sitting, doing absolutely nothing with some 48 divisions (over 700,000 troops)—and Patton, with 10 divisions, about 150,000, doing all the fighting and space winning, except FUSA, which is maintaining Remagen bridgehead—

First Canadian Army 5
Second British Army 8
Ninth U.S. Army 12
First AB Artillery [First Allied Airborne Army]—6 Div
1 British Airborne Corps—2 Div
XVIII Airborne Corps—4 Div

Re AB outfits, Patton at ULTRA briefing remarked: "They are fighting sons-of-bitches all right, but takes them to hell and gone to get ready. They are organized wrong. Should only be Bns. Divisions too cumbersome. Should be organized as Bns and then can be employed as needed." Patton also observed—"You remember that widow of 'blowhard' Bailey. How inconsolable she was over his death. Was going to commit suicide and all that. Well, she got married again. Married some little bastard with lots of money. George, my son, wrote me about it. Very indignant. Said 'These *women*' and underlined it." Patton laughed uproariously.

7

The Palatinate Campaign

Tuesday, March 13, 1945: Start today our fifth major operation. 4th Armored Div jumped off, got bridgehead over Moselle, and started rolling like hell. Simmers [Simmern], first objective (reached by nightfall today) and Bad Kreuznach, on Nahe River and about half the distance across the Palatinate triangle to Worms and Mainz. It's the only wide-end run again, only this time it's across the enemy's rear. Seventh Army still sitting; their jump-off date is tomorrow. They better jump off or they will be pinched out by TUSA.

Was summoned to Gay's office with Koch this afternoon and told to prepare a terrain study and enemy estimate of area East of Rhine between Andernach North of Koblenz and Mainz-Worms South of Koblenz. Purpose was to determine whether to make a crossing of the Rhine above or below Koblenz. Submitted my terrain estimate—recommending Mainz-Worms area as affording the best route of advance through historic Rhine or Frankfurt corridor by 1700A.

Patton has relieved Brigadier-General Charles Kilburn,[1] twitchy little CG of 11th Armd Div, and it's about time. Scrawny, bullying and incompetent little punk. Patton [has] been raising hell with him from way back at Bastogne. Threatened then to bounce him, and he finally did. Sent him to 4th Armored to learn how to command Armor. What they should have done with him is bust him and send him home as a Lt Col. But he's a cavalryman and an old friend of Gay's and Patton, so they are taking care of him.

Wednesday, March 14, 1945: 6 Army Group finally jumped off—using our old Saarlautern attack plan—that was set for 21 December, but which we did not get the chance to put into effect because of being rushed up to Luxembourg to counterattack the German Ardennes offensive. 6 Army Group even using all the data we got from that German General PW, who worked for G-2 Section when we were down in Nancy. We turned stuff he gave us on Siegfried defenses and how and where it

185

was best to attack them in Saarlautern area over to Seventh Army, and they are using it in their attack. That PW was [an] astounding affair. He briefed our Corps and Division CGs, who were to make the attack, dressed in his field uniform and medals and [spoke] in English. Talked for 1½ hours. Then in the afternoon our guards took him out walking dressed in GI attire.

4th Armored rolling and wound up day in Simmern, half way to Bad Kreuznach. Put on briefing for Patton in War Room on crossing question. I opened with terrain analysis, which I conducted on layered overlay I prepared. Koch followed with enemy strength estimate. Maddox next with G-3 proposals. Then Muller on G-4, concluding with Gay with recommendation that nothing be done on a decision pending tactical developments. No question but that the best place to cross for an advance into Central Germany (to Kassel, our objective) is between Mainz and Worms. But that is right across the path of advance of 6 Army Group and in their zone. Obviously, some topside maneuvering has got to be finagled to do that. Means we would pinch out 6 Army Group. Patton rose after presentation and complimented it as a superior presentation. Then with smile said, "Got to get the lead out of certain people's asses, and I'm going to do that right now—by phone." Then as he got to the door, turned and said, "One thing you want to remember. Roads don't matter, terrain doesn't matter, and neither do exposed flanks. The only thing that counts is to come to grips with the Germans and to kill lots of them. That is the only thing that should decide any decision."

Flew in P-47 with Col Ferguson, A-3 XIX TAC, over Trier, Bitburg, Wittlich, Mayen, the last terrifically beat up, up Moselle to Rhine, skirting Koblenz. Saw number of contrails of enemy planes, many fires on East bank of Rhine. Ferguson fired his guns at some vehicles on East bank of Rhine, but didn't see any results. Exciting trip.

Thursday, March 15, 1945: Heard several marvelous stories on Patton. [Lieutenant General Alexander M.] Patch,[2] CG Seventh Army, telephoned him and jocularly chided, "George, let me congratulate you on being the last Army to reach the Rhine." Quick as a flash, Patton shot back—"Thanks, and let me congratulate you on being the first and only Army to be kicked off the Rhine."

Patton likes to load up his soup with catsup, mustard, horse-radish, almost everything on the table. General Alexander, Brit, visiting him, watched him with interest, and finally asked if it was good. Patton assured him it was delicious, only way to eat soup, and ordering another plate, put everything on the table in it, including jam, and solemnly offered it to Alexander. He partook some and then remarked, "Very extraordinary, indeed. First time I ever ate jam in my soup. Most unusual combination." Patton assured him he ate it that way all the time.

Seventh Army is having heavy going in attack against Siegfried positions. Made couple mile gains on entire front, but slow and little progress compared to our sweep across Germany's rear. 4th Armored still pounding ahead. Bad Kreuznach entered by 4th Armd columns today and its capture is a cinch. Seventh Army has 16 divisions—to our 12 divisions. Word now is that British drive to envelop Ruhr from North now set for 24th March. I Canadian Corps being brought from Italy to reinforce British for operation.[3] Meanwhile, we are sweeping ahead. And we are the only ones doing so.

Pressure against FUSA Remagen bridgehead easing, although enemy massed most of his panzers against it. But they are not containing extension of the bridgehead and it is steadily expanding. When Patton [was] told at ULTRA briefing that the British planned to jump off on the 24th, he snorted "What month?"

Friday, March 16, 1945: At 1100A got word that 4th Armored Div had captured Bad Kreuznach on the Nahe River, and on our boundary with Seventh Army. Next move now up to Eisenhower, who suddenly appeared here. We briefed him and Lt. General [Walter] Beedle Smith,[4] his C/S, at noon in the War Room. Only leading staff section chiefs present. I was the only non-section chief asked to attend. He appeared in very jovial humor. Slouches in chair. Keeps hands in pockets. Had on new five-star insignia and some other brass thing that looked like a British job. Slacks and shoes, low-cuts. When the briefing was over, got up, hands in pocket, waggled around in front of War Map and said, "George, be sure to take a shot for me at that statue of that Kaiser Wilhelm or something that sticks up at Koblenz." Patton—"Delighted. We'll take care of that for you without trouble." Eisenhower asked what was to be done with 6th Armored Div, one of the crack TUSA tank units, that was loaned to Seventh Army. Told they still had it, and he asked Smith to call Patch on the matter. Smith left with Gay to go to the phone. Eisenhower asked Patton to help get out favorable press stories about our tanks. "Just got a cable from George Marshall on matter today. Seems men go home and say German Panther tanks outshoot us. Someone got us in Congress and said Germans had better equipment and winter clothing than we had. That 75 percent of our stuff was inferior to Germans. Old Man worried about public reaction." Patton—"Hell, Panther['s] not as good as our tank. One basic factor behind the German defeat was that they went to the Panther. I couldn't have done what Third Army has accomplished if we had Panthers. Not as fast, as durable, or as mobile. Our tanks are far more effective all around. Look at these figures (pointing to our daily casualty chart showing over 800 enemy medium tanks destroyed). That tells the story." Eisenhower—"I know they do. You know it and I know it, but people back home don't know it. And strange as it may seem, they'll believe some sergeant before they'll believe you or me. What I want you to do is get your PRO to get hold of some correspondent you can trust and arrange to have men all the way down the line, from division commanders to GI, give him stories on how good our tanks are. You have to handle it carefully. Those PRO are stupid. They have no imagination. You have to arrange it all for them. Wish you would take care of this and get out some good stories. The Old Man needs some help on this and we want to do it up right." Patton told Col Koch to handle the matter at once.

Koch's recommendation for a Bronze Star for me on my work during Ardennes offensive returned today—G-1 claimed we had no more allotment for that decoration, and Gay approved the rejection on that ground. So my outstanding work counted for nothing and my chief's recommendation turned down on ground the G-2 Section had used up its allotment of Bronze Stars—which is very ironic because I recommended and got for my subordinates most of them.

Heard today that Millikin, CG III Corps, relieved for grabbing Remagen bridge and establishing bridgehead. Report unconfirmed, but personally don't doubt it. Am certain it threw SHAEF and Dear Old Monty into a terrible flap. Patton would have decorated Millikin. SHAEF busts him. Well, if he was relieved, he can have no fears of being assailed by the public or history. On the other hand, some of the iron-headed mediocrities topside can have much to fear on what history will say about their antics.

Saturday, March 17, 1945: Eisenhower attended 11 a.m. and regular briefing. ULTRA message revealed that Hitler ordered Palatinate defended to the last and all resources directed to destruction of Remagen bridgehead.[5] Silly, because attacks on Remagen are puny, and our sweep across the rear of the Palatinate positions made them hopelessly untenable. Ordering troops not to withdraw is right down our alley and ensures our trapping and capturing them. After regular briefing, Eisenhower rose, hands in pocket and slouching around, made his second pep talk before Staff Hq TUSA. The first was in Nancy. Put on a spiel he obviously uses on such occasions. Has all mannerisms of a gum rubber, including hail-fellow-well-met ebullience and glibness. His line was,

"If I have one criticism to make it is that you are too modest. (Everyone smiled at that because all other outfits consider us the brassiest and cockiest on the Continent. They['re] always derisive about our blowing our horn.) You don't boast enough about your great achievements. You put it matter of factly that enemy resistance is crumbling, but say nothing about brilliant operations that caused that collapse. I want you to talk more about yourselves. Let the world know how good you are. (I could hardly contain myself.) Give stories about yourselves and your work to the press. Call in the reporters and feed the right kind of stories to them. They'll use them and the folks back home will eat it up. We need the right kind of publicity right now." Eisenhower's constant preoccupation with the press and "right kind" of publicity is one of the most pronounced things about him. Twice in two days he talked about this, and the same when [he] was at the CP in Nancy.

Ludenberg [Ludendorff] bridge over the Rhine at Remagen bridgehead collapsed shortly after 1500—indirect due to damage from our bombing, several German Arty hits and terrific strain of tanks. However, not serious as we have two other pontoon bridges and a number of Navy ferries in operation. Over 150 men on bridge at time of collapse—over 50 lost.

Around 1600A—called to Gay's office to discuss radio deception plan, and found Patton on scrambler phone. Patton—"Connie (C/S XX Corps), what's the matter with the 11th Armored? Get them going. General Eisenhower is here today and is greatly disappointed over failure of 11th to roll. Utmost importance it gets to Rhine without delay. High political considerations involved, and he wants us to put on extra steam. Get going and get them going." After he hung up the phone, leaned back in chair and grinning mischievously said, "Eisenhower didn't say that, but they don't know it and if it will boot them along, I'm sure Ike won't mind my using his name. It's been used for a lot worse purposes."

Patton lost no time taking Eisenhower at his word about publicity. Called special press conference this evening and after he got through coking them up, they filed 20,000 words of cable and radio copy. (For next week, TUSA had top billing on radio and press—including BBC.) Eisenhower didn't know what he is starting when he urged Patton to boast more about TUSA. Patton can do that better than any other big shot in the West, just as he is a better field commander than any others—including Eisenhower.

Sunday, March 18, 1945: Col Nick Campanole,[6] our G-5, departed today. Going home because of kidney trouble. Patton staged formal ceremony for him and decorated him with Bronze Star. Old Nick is a genial old faker and bungler. His successor, another mediocre Reg Colonel, who was rolled from combat post and given G-5 sinecure—which he probably will mess up to the hilt.

TUSA took 4,500 PW today—big swoops resuming again. 60,000 to 75,000 in Palatinate triangle to be captured and/or destroyed, and in coming days we'll get them wholesale. Our sweep across and around rear of Boche positions in Palatinate sure tough from publicity angle on Seventh Army. We are getting all the press breaks by our spectacular smashing advances, and Seventh is getting the toughest kind of resistance and going cracking toughest position in the Siegfried Line. Also TUSA literally pinching them out. We've overrun the Army boundary and are racing for the Rhine right across Seventh Army's zone of advance. Patton is sure having the last laugh on Patch in a big way. Remagen plastered with 11 V-2 yesterday. Ten laid in during the week and then yesterday they threw in 11 in one day. That is not funny in that small area. Also Marble Arch got one V-2 the same day and blew all the windows out of nearby Cumberland and other hotels.

Monday, March 19, 1945: Middleton, CG VIII Corps, called up during ULTRA briefing to tell Patton he now was "Mayor of Koblenz." Also, that the statue Eisenhower wanted a shot taken at, was kaput. Had been blasted into river. Also, that [they] had dropped leaflets notifying Boche that for every shell they fired across the river, ten would be fired back.

11th and 12th Armored Divs joined and close[d] pocket West of Kaiserlautern—trapping at least 10,000 Boche. Germans are great military organizers, but they have their great weaknesses. One of them currently is costing them dear. When they overran Europe, in line with their sound doctrine of mobility, they built airfields all over—except in Germany. Outside of a few major fields, they have very limited net of fields of good operational value—especially fields with extra-long runways needed for jets. Result, now being driven East of Rhine, they are hard-put for good fighter and bomber fields—which is very ironic in view of the hundreds of fields they built in all the occupied countries.

Around 1430 General Bradley arrived and we were summoned to the War Room where all Gs, Arty, Engineer present. With Bradley was Hodges, CG FUSA—first time I've seen him since we left San Antonio that sunny day in February 1944. Bradley neatly dressed, mild, and hair tousled as usual. Hodges also in battle suit, with pants fitting him like a sack. From rear he looked like one of one-time Mack Sennett[7] comedians. Patton was most extraordinary of all—had on skin-tight pair of riding breeches, tailored battle jacket with brass buttons, leather belt with brass buckle, and 2 buckle pair of issue cavalry boots—that came up to his calves—leaving the rest of his legs unbooted. Looked funny as hell—like he was in slippers. All gathered around 1/100,000 map of Rhine front, and Gay began by saying seriously, "Hate to say this, because its unconfirmed, but got word that Commander of Worms is offering to negotiate surrender of town." (Report was untrue and arose out of an Officer PW who surrendered and who turned out to be quite a prize). Bradley grinned broadly and Patton, beaming widely, hugged Hodges, who smiled belatedly and weakly. Gay continued that 10th and 11th Armored Divs were converging on the city and only a matter of hours before it was taken. Bradley then took pointer and standing before big War Map said, "Ike has to make the main effort in North. That's the decision (didn't say whose) and that is what will have to be done. I will try to persuade SHAEF not to take any divisions from Third Army. Have to have 10 divisions for the main effort, and I'll try to get them to take them from Jake (Devers, 6th Army Group, who has 16 divisions, including the crack 6th Armored from us). The question is whether to attempt a breakout of Remagen bridgehead or an assault crossing of Rhine in Mainz-Worms area. That raises question, does TUSA have equipment for an assault in that area?" Gay—"We have the equipment. Absolutely. We can get the equipment up in time without any trouble." Bradley—"Then you feel, George, that you would rather cross down here than North." Patton—"Oh, yes (hurriedly). Logistically much sounder, and terrain far better. Here we have straight, open route to Kassel." (Also, down South no danger of his crossing being snagged by FUSA.) Bradley—"I told Ike FUSA can break out of Remagen bridgehead and extend South to Koblenz without any trouble at any time. I'm inclined to think that should be done after you go across. You will keep Germans from reinforcing North and that will help FUSA. I'm afraid if they start first they'll run into full weight of Boche, whereas if you cross first, you will tend to pull some of the Boche to your area and thus split them. How do you feel about that, Courtney?" Hodges—"I'd like to jump off about three days after George." Bradley—"My thought is that you will come down the Autobahn to Gissen and by that time George can prove whether he can go to Kassel." Patton—breaking in—"Don't have to prove it. We'll just go ahead and do it. Nothing to it." Bradley—"All right. Then you cross first, FUSA will break out of Remagen and bridgehead South and meet you around Limburg. The Seventh (Army) will come up from South and then we can go up and help out . . ." (Bradley didn't finish; just grinned and everyone laughed. Knew exactly what he meant—Montgomery.) That ended the conference. Bradley, Patton and Hodges clustered around the map and discussed details of the operation among themselves for awhile. During this chat, Bradley remarked, "General Marshall very anxious to get lot of favorable publicity for ETO." Wonder what that is all about. Overshadow [General Douglas] MacArthur[8] to put someone else in command over there, or what? Something behind it all. First Eisenhower bears down on publicity angle as coming from Marshall, now Bradley. Must be a lot of heat over something—and it's clearly big topside inner politics. Of course, this all meat for Patton. If they want publicity, he's the guy to give it to them. (Wednesday afternoon he called me up and directed I compile total number of square miles and towns TUSA has liberated from Kyll River to Rhine North of Moselle and from Saar to Rhine South of Moselle. When I submitted figures hours later, he directed they go to PRO for immediate release to press.)

Heard today that Brig General Davis, former rat C/S [of] TUSA and Assistant CG 28th Div, has been relieved and is either at or running some Replenishment Training Center. According to story, was going to be tried but Hodges saved him. But when Div went to Seventh Army, Div had no one to save his bacon and he was rolled. Whether had anything to do with the loss of a Signal truck with all code equipment, [I] don't know. Too bad rat bastard isn't busted and sent home as Lt Col.

Took over 17,000 PW yesterday. First Army—1,500. Pretty certain now Kesselring has been brought up from Italy and made C-in-C [commander in chief] West. Well, he's fighting different guys than Mark Clark here. Patton is horse of another color. Road to Worms jammed with MT and horse-drawn vehicles, and XIX TAC had a field day. Weather has been grand for about a week straight now and it helps like hell—and plays hell with the Hun. Isolation of Ruhr by Air has begun. Plot of yesterday's heavy bombing surrounds Ruhr and shows clearly design of attacks to "isolate battlefield" up there in preparation of Monty's ME [main effort] that is scheduled to jump off on Sat—24th. Following meeting with Bradley, word was received that 4th Armored entered Worms at 1800A. *Editor's note: This happened the following day, March 20. The notes are mixed up.*

Tuesday, March 20, 1945: Third Army PW bag yesterday over 17,000. FUSA—1,500. Major General Millikin, former CG III Corps, appeared at CP today and I heard he was not relieved because of grabbing Remagen bridge. Story now is that he personally requested relief in order to command a division in combat and that he is to get 4th Armored. Gaffey has gone to XXIII Corps, replacing [James A.] Van Fleet,[9] former CG of 90th Inf Div, who took over III Corps. So Gaffey gets his wish to command a Corps, Van Fleet takes over a crack Corps Hq, and Millikin gets the 4th Armd.

4th Armored produced an unusual PW today, whom we rushed up to CP here blindfolded for special interrogation. He wanted to talk to Patton, but was presented to Gay, whom he thought was Patton. Tall, slender, blond Junker, GSC Oberleutenant. Junker by name of Ardut.[10] Arrogant bastard who deserted and had gall to propose he not be classed as ordinary PW, but put in category of sort of German military advisor to Allies. Was Adjutant to Chief of Signal Section of OKW and through that connection claims he was implicated in 20 July putsch. General, he says, was hung as conspirator. PW deserted in the vicinity of Worms, and from this fact arose report he was emissary from Worms commandant to negotiate surrender. He may have put out that story when he turned himself in to get attention to himself, because that was the report from S-2. The interrogation with Gay was short. Only long enough to indicate Boche had considerable information that was of value topside, so he was shipped forward to Group. PW talked fair English and gave us—Exact pinpointed location of Hitler's Hq in Berlin—Fact that Zozzen about 25 km from Berlin, has been set up as new OKW Hq if Berlin has to be evacuated—That Hitler is personally running the war and generals are merely technical advisors and fronts—That if Ruhr is isolated, mass war production in Germany [will] have to end in 2 weeks as [they] have no coal reserves—That the Huns will not use CW as they fear retaliatory effect would be too great—That "the secret weapon," which he says he doesn't know what it is, will be used against Remagen bridgehead when our concentration of troops there has reached a point where it indicates we are going to launch a breakthrough offensive.

Later Sibert called and thanked me for finding PW and exploiting him. Sibert said he is proving a very valuable find and was being sent North to aid in plans up there—I presume Monty's long-delayed offensive to envelop the Ruhr. That is scheduled for jump-off Saturday 24, but already rumors seeping around that there is to be a delay—Keerist! More regrouping and pivoting on Caen, I suppose. Meanwhile, looks like we got another Kraut bastard working for us—the great master race—of traitors to holy Germany!!!

Word today is that FUSA due to jump off [on] 23d—Friday—in breakout of Remagen bridgehead to South East to Giessen to join up with us in our drive through Frankfurt corridor to Kassel. We'll see whether they really jump on 23d, or delay—until we make assault crossing of Rhine and pull enemy down in front of us. That's what Monty is waiting for. Story is that he is supposed to have remarked, "By Jove, I've got to call up George and congratulate him on fine job he is going and urge him to keep it up so he will keep the Boche from building up against me." Also heard Simpson, CG Ninth Army, held powwow of his Corps and Div CGs, and after briefing them on exploits of TUSA, directed that they emulate them in their forthcoming operation. 80th Inf Div captured Kaiserlautern—our objective just three months ago when we were fighting across Moselle Valley. Now we are in Kaiserlautern by the longest and hardest route—via the Ardennes, the Eifel, the Hunsruck [Hunsrück] and the Palatinate—what a goddamn blundering mess it all has been.

Wednesday, March 21, 1945: ULTRA—Jap Military Attachés in Germany sending back very sour reports. Reason for pessimism is that they were told to give 30 days' warning of German collapse and apparently they are not taking any chances. Also, Japs greatly worried over 25 April, last date for Russian notice of continuance or abrogation of non-aggression treaty. Patton bustled into ULTRA briefing and asked, "Where is Landau?" When pointed out on the map, he said, "Patch just called me up and asked for help by sending 4th Armored down there. Harkins, put that in the diary. Time was 10 minutes to 9." After briefing, Patton shook Major Al Stiller, one of his aides, by the hand and said, "You go down there (to Rhine) and don't get killed (Worms) but tell them to get something over that son-of-a-bitching river. Anything, anywhere, anyhow; a squadron, platoon, company or anything, but get it over. Any way they can, by swimming, driving, cub plane, ferry, canoe, no matter how, but tell them I want them to get over and establish a bridgehead. Tell them there isn't a thing over there and that, goddammit, that's what I want, and not to let anything stop them." Stiller wanted me to go with him and I'd have given anything to do so, but Koch wouldn't approve because of ULTRA, and also Forde was away and I was only Executive Officer present—goddammit.

XIX TAC had an especially good day yesterday—destroyed over 550 MT of all kinds, damaged over 350 others, and burned up jammed roads into Worms. Around 1600A, Gay came in and at map asked what was on East side of the Rhine. I told him, "Nothing. Not a damn thing that can stop us if we get a bridgehead, and nothing to stop us from doing that. It's an administrative march, a promenade to Kassel from here on." He grinned and said, "I'll tell that to the General. He'll like to hear that."

Another German weapon on which they expended great production efforts, materials and based great hopes—and which is a bust—is MIDGET U-boats—the BIBER. Been popping them around futilely since early phases of invasion. Recently intensified operations with equally unavailing results. From 11–14 March, launched a number against shipping in the Scheldt—17 destroyed *without any loss to Allied shipping*. On 21 February, learned from PW, that 14 of the doddle bugs were destroyed on land, when train carrying them to coast was bombed in vicinity of Zeist.

Today, processed over 11,000 PW, and Army cage and corps and div cages so jammed with them we can't move them for lack of equipment—trucks. So far this week, processed 36,000 through cages, including hundreds of officers, large proposition [proportion of] staff and regimental COs. Indications another 25,000, or more, waiting to be processed. Looks like our Palatinate bag will run 60 to 75,000 for one week's operation.

Thursday, March 22, 1945: Just a year ago we landed up in Scotland, the second leg on the way to the Continent and all we have gone through so far—and it has been quite a bit. Processed over 11,000 PW at Trier PWE cage today, for total so far of over 45,000. Know that corps have at least another 20,000, which brings the total up to around 70,000. With 20,000 or so that Seventh Army captured the overall Palatinate bag will be well within our estimate of 80 to 90,000—all in one week's time, and all due to TUSA sweep across and around rear of Boche Army Group G (First and Seventh Armies). Entire Group of some 25 normal divisions completely destroyed. Total casualties, killed, wounded and PW, not less than 125,000—at least 40 percent of Hun's combat strength in West. And all done in one week.

At ULTRA briefing this morning, Patton said, "We've got to get a bridgehead over the Rhine. Every day we save doing that means saving hundreds of American lives. The Germans are smashed and in chaos right now in our front. But if we delay, 72 hours from now they will have reorganized. We must not give them that chance—and I don't give a goddamn what other plans may be. I don't propose to give the sons-of-bitches a chance to recover from the killing we gave them in the Palatinate. We destroyed two armies there in one week with very little losses to ourselves, and we are now going to finish them off for good East of the Rhine. We are going to make a crossing of the river immediately. I don't care where or how we get the necessary equipment, but get it. Steal it, beg it, or make it, but I want it and it better be there right now. We are going to cross the Rhine and do it today."

Around 2000A, the kettle began to boil around G-3 Operations and this is what unfolded: At 2200 tonight, 5th Inf Div would make an assault crossing of Rhine in vicinity Oppenheim—by assault boat, ferry, raft, LCVP [landing craft, vehicles and personnel] or what-have-you. At dawn, 90 L/5 planes would start an air transport of a bn or more on a bridgehead established during night. Cubs assembled during afternoon from various Arty bns, and a dry run yesterday showed that a bn could be flown across the river, about 400 feet wide at Oppenheim, with all its weapons in about 6 hours. Col Molly Williams, TUSA's able Arty chief, was the originator of the idea, and Patton seized on it jubilantly. Crossing tonight to be dead secret from everyone. Only our topside G-3 Operations and I in on it. Blackout to last from 24 to 48 hours. No mention of assault to be contained in any reports, nor to be shown on any maps. All this grew out of directive issued by Group today on SHAEF orders on plan that clearly is designed to give British play for rest of the war. Obviously the plan by Bradley he outlined the other day was modified to ensure that British were in on the glory march—even if they had to be dragged in by scruff of the neck—and we, First and Seventh sat down. In fact, plan clearly designed to keep Patton from running away with the show and to ensure the British are in on it and other Armies get share of final glory.

Under plan, as given to Gay at Group, British (21 Army Group) to envelop Ruhr from North and presumably advance East to meet Russians around Berlin. For FUSA, TUSA and NUSA, a bridgehead area set up extending on huge convex into central Germany from Giessen-Hanau-Aschaffenburg-Miltenburg, on South. Within this circle, FUSA to jump off a day after British who jump on the 24th. FUSA to advance to South East on Giessen. TUSA boundary fixed on very narrow front from just South of Koblenz to Mainz—25 miles. However, through Group, Gay arranged a temporary boundary to South of Worms to give us plenty of crossing sites. So, although Patton cleaned out Palatinate, except for narrow strip that includes the great Blingen-Koblenz gorge of Rhine 4/5 of distance of our front, he was robbed of whole area. Not only that, but adding injury to insult, they rubbed it in by giving him the Rhine gorge. However, if the intention was to crimp him, they missed as widely as before. Patton promptly ordered a crossing tonight—any way, from swimming to LCVP or cub planes. When we get our bridgehead, Seventh Army will use it to make its crossing—after clearing up its still uncleared South East portion of Palatinate and regrouping. So that was the buggery—the British deliberately given the ball after sitting on their rear ends regrouping for six weeks during which time III Corps grabbed the Remagen bridgehead and Patton—on the defensive—cleared out the Eifel, swept through the Palatinate, destroying entire Army Group G (First and Seventh Armies), and capturing over 135,000 PW—around 100,000 in Palatinate since 13 March; plus capturing Koblenz, Mainz and Worms, and dominating half the distance of West bank of Rhine. Inconceivable that Eisenhower did this alone. Clearly high politics involved. This is Combined Chiefs of Staff job—has all the earmarks of that—plus fingerprints of FDR and Winnie. Undoubtedly Eisenhower offered no objection to binders being put on Patton, so it all worked out nicely for all concerned, except Patton. However, he is not being stopped, and clearly with Bradley's approval and backing, is pulling another sneak offensive. It's a cinch and the sound and logical thing to do. The enemy is completely shattered in our section of the West; there isn't a damn thing in front of us now and if he is hit now, he won't have a chance to rush anything in and regain his balance. By Monday he would be back off the ropes if we gave him the time. If socked now, he can't regain full balance again. Hasn't the available reserves, equipment or transport. So with Bradley's full blessing and knowledge—Patton is cracking the Rhine secretly—with a blackout on it to SHAEF and Eisenhower for at least 24 hours.

Friday, March 23, 1945: Crossing was a cinch. As I told Patton and Gay, not a damned thing over there and what was there—very few scattered and miscellaneous elements—caught completely napping. Most of them asleep. Not even small arms fire encountered by first waves. Crossing made in brilliant moonlight, balmy springish night. By 0700—6 bns of Inf—10 and 11 Inf Regts and their weapons over, a tread pontoon bridge started, and ferrying on pontoon rafts of TDs and Arty and tanks begun. Quietist and easiest river crossing in TUSA experience. By night our bridgehead was 6 miles deep and 7 miles long—in contrast to 21 Army Group's, preceded by 3,000 planes and terrific Arty bombardment, of 1 mile deep. Also, by 1600A, tread pontoon bridge completed and 4th Armored Div assembled nearby to move over during night. Had wonderful day at crossing with Cols Charles Hallet, A-2, and Paul Ferguson, A-3, XIX TAC. Flew there, across Palatinate, in L/5s and, under some desultory enemy Arty fire that landed a couple hundred yards away, watched show for hours. A very memorable occasion because just one year ago today we landed in UK and I reported to Col Koch at Peover. One year from Peover to the Rhine—much time and space, and much has happened. The original crowd mostly scattered—some gone for good. Anyway, nice way to mark the occasion. Crossing the Rhine. Big day for

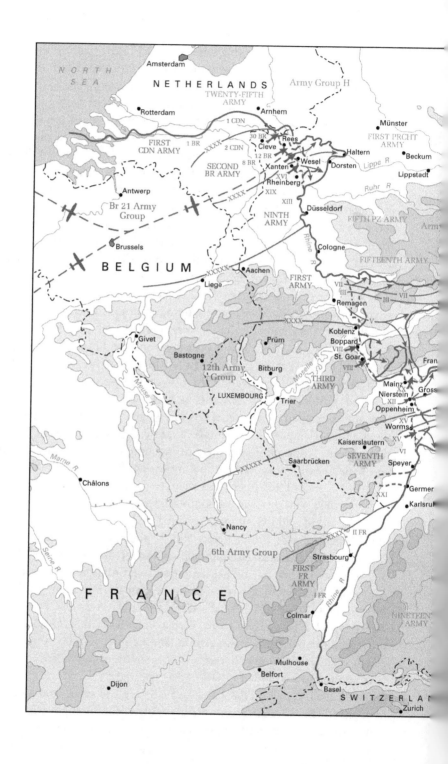

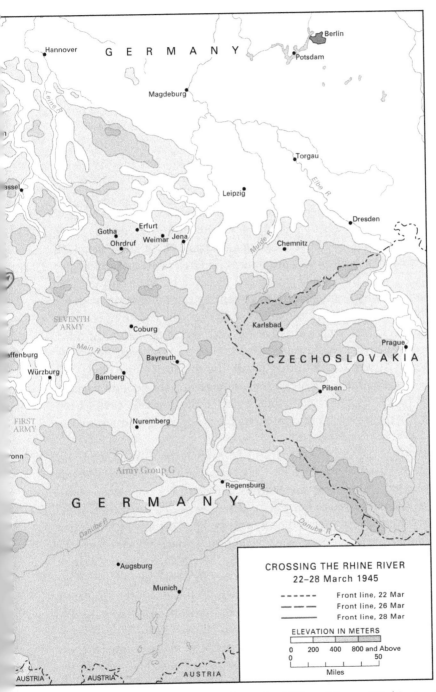

Crossing the Rhine, March 22–28, 1945 (Center for Military History, Washington, DC)

XIX TAC. Concentrated over bridgehead, giving top cover. Huns came out in some force—to their bloody loss. XIX TAC knocked down 22 and 1 probable for biggest day in months of aerial fighting. In one encounter, eight P-51s pounced on 50 JU-88s and got 11. In another, P-47s jumped flock of FW-190 and got 8 out of 9. These German planes are as good if not better than ours, but pilots are apparently untrained and unfit to equal our by now battle-tested youngsters. Another toll the enemy is paying for employing GAF as infantry.

Bradley "tidied up" scores with Monty tonight and did it so deftly British can't squawk. Skinned them with a tooth-edged drill and they had to take it. Although a regular Friday AM press conference in the War Room, Gay told correspondents about crossing under strictest secrecy. Around 2200 we were told blackout was lifted and event was being released as of 2400 by SHAEF, Group and Army. Don't know details of what transpired, but has all appearances on basis of what happened of being something that Bradley arranged. Because he went on the air at 2400 and personally announced the crossing and followed it up with the very pointed and deftly searing observation that now the Rhine could be breached anywhere with a massive Air and Arty preparation. In other words, he quietly served notice that the 3,000-plane and great Arty bombardment that was scheduled to prepare the way for Monty's long-prepared offensive was a lot of wasted commotion. Don't know whether listening public got the point, but wasn't lost in service circles here. 11,699 PW processed at cage yesterday. Clear now our PW total will run over 75,000 for the Palatinate.

Saturday, March 24, 1945: Up to 16 March, total PW in West was 1,042,415. Visited Army cage on top of hill overlooking Trier, and was an astounding sight. Cage was a former German PW camp, where thousands of Russians lived in horrible squalor and deadly starvation. Some left there were so emaciated they had to be lifted with vehicles. Today over 18,000 men processed—old, young, kids that said they were 17 and looked 15, cripples, literally, officers, the whole goddamn German Army—getting the works as PW in a former hell hole they ran for their PW and still bearing their sign. And no less fantastic was the Displaced Persons [DP] camp we are operating directly across the road from the PW cage. Thousands of men and women from all over Europe, the dispossessed, the slave workers, the victims of the Nazi mania—now living in the big wooden barracks crowded by dozens in rooms and using furniture, bedding and what-have-you they looted in deserted Trier, a mile or so in the valley below. Poles, Russians, Greeks, everything—free at last and having the time of their lives watching the long convoy of German PW pouring in, and pillaging Trier. Good pickings, too. Wine in cellars, bedding, furniture, clothing—a fitting interlude in their bitter and torturous travails. I'll be god-damned.

Col Matthews, our drooling and incompetent G-1, has hung another decoration on himself. Few weeks ago, he got Legion of Merit, and today the Bronze Star. It's the goddamnedest display of shameless gall; that bastardly crew messed up my recommendation for L of M, and turned down my recommendation for Bronze Star on grounds that our quota was exhausted. But the hoppety droolhead hangs both decorations on himself, while the only first-class man he has in the section, Coy Eklund, has nothing. But all the other swillpusses in that section—complete morons like Thomas[11] and Wing[12]—they have Bronze Stars! It sure pays to be a Reg with a low serial number. 4th Armored broke loose and breezing like fury again. Headed for Darmstadt, which it captured without a fight. Found only 40 PW in town.

Sunday, March 25, 1945: Made air trip over lower Saar area to St. Wendel, Kaiserlautern, Bad Dirkheim, Saarbrücken, Saarlautern, Neunkirchen, Remick, etc. Fabulous site the air destruction of these cities and scores of other smaller towns, marshalling yards, rail lines, bridges, autobahn highway and plants devastated by explosives, ravaged by fire. Looked like evacuations of ancient volcano-destroyed craters. Fitting finale, indeed, for the Saarlanders' pro-Nazi plebiscite. They asked for it and they got it. Silliest spectacle was miles of futile dragon's teeth—that didn't stop anything, and Arty-pocked miles of crawl and fire trenches running along crests overlooking Saar River. Very absorbing junket, climaxed by seeing a flame-damaged B-26 make a beautiful emergency landing at emergency field at Luxembourg.

Under 12 Army Group directive dated today, 12 Army Group bridgehead boundaries given as Hanau–Giessen–Siegen–Sieg River to juncture with Rhine. Our PW total East of the Rhine in three days of operation already over 5,000 mark. 5,400. 4th Armored captured Aschaffenberg and one bridge intact South of Hanau.

VIII Corps jumped off and established a two-mile bridgehead over the Rhine gorge South of Koblenz. Tougher going than at Oppenheim, but making better progress than 21 Army Group, that claims it is having very "strong" resistance—although have taken, they say, 3,000 PW.

Monday, March 26, 1945: Packed today to move CP into Germany—Oberstein—about halfway between Trier and Bad Kreuznach, and 80 miles from Luxembourg. Been highly eventful three months since we first lighted here in a snow-sleet storm, with Arlon railroad only 12 miles away and 12 Army Group all set to pull out on the run. Now they are moving back in.

6th Armored Division well into Frankfurt with one bridge intact over Main River. 9th Armored Div, FUSA, also running free and has taken Limburg on the Lahn River. Another big pocket shaping up, but bag doesn't look very big. Not much in this area—other than the big towns Wiesbaden, Darmstadt, Frankfurt—which are undefended and unarmed. Plan now is to put XX Corps over our bridge South at Oppenheim to envelop Mainz and establish a bridge there. XX Corps jumps off tomorrow. Sure to be a cinch.

XV Corps, Seventh Army, finally going to hump itself and make an assault crossing in the Worms area tomorrow. Pudgy little "Ham" Haislip, about as much a Corps CG as I am a bomber pilot, going to go over—after everything, including the kitchen stove, is over already. That ought to be worth a cluster on his DSM—at least—the hayheaded politico.

Third Army PW total topped 300,000 today—over 1,000 more than FUSA, although we became operational 55 days later and were robbed of 20,000 in Elster capture South of the Loire by a change of boundary. Over 75,000 of total captured in Palatinate since 13 March.

Notes: Our lack of an adequate winter uniform another glaring instance of criminal failure in planning. Claim is that we didn't expect winter warfare. (1) Obvious as early as Sept when 21 Army Group offensive failed, that we couldn't defeat Germany before next spring or summer. (2) Lack of gas and Ammo for more than one major effort in September also clear evidence that we expected the war to continue. There was enough gas and Ammo on Continent, but the question was who got it. Gave it to 21 Army Group, which busted; while TUSA, with patrols in Metz, evacuated, Siegfried Line unorganized and way clear to Rhine, was sat down. That colossal blunder, followed by Ardennes disaster and lack of winter equipment. Three great failures—and leaders responsible not only not removed but made 4 and 5-star generals and Monty a Marshal.

Tuesday, March 27, 1945: Oberstein on the Nahe—our first CP in Germany. In modern barracks on hill overlooking city in valley below—narrow and long. 7th and 9th Armd Divs—FUSA—staged a TUSA-like sweep today—9th driving to vicinity of Wiesbaden, and 7th all the way to Giessen. We received today very elaborate and detailed graphic study of Rhine crossings—just about one week too late—from ETOUSA Engineer. At that, study [was] early. Usual stuff from them [is] months old. Two weeks ago, when preparing for crossing, this job would have been priceless. As it is, it's worse than useless because it is now just so much excess paper we have to lug. TUSA PW total 5,600—others 8,800. Total for yesterday 14,400.

Patton embarked on secret project that sure will be a sensational story if it works out. Sent Task Force of two companies of tanks and two companies of Armd Inf from 4th Armored Div to Hammelburg[13]—about 60 miles East of Aschaffenburg—to rescue 800 or so Allied Officer PW reported in camp in this area. Major Al Stiller, Patton's driver and ADC, went over the roads with me. Affair very shush-shush. Patton very concerned about it, and we sent a number of TAC/R missions to check on movement. Plan is to rescue PW and return to Aschaffenburg.

Wednesday, March 28, 1945: Accompanied CIC in raid through Oberstein to round up local Nazi leaders. MG [military government] (civil affairs) has been here a couple of weeks but has done nothing about matter. Still allowing police to wear bright green Nazi uniform and have given them an MG armband, compounding an outrage and stupidity, in keeping with MG antics. MG probably most incompetent branch in Army. Made up primarily of incompetents, politicians and broken down or inept lawyers. While downtown, I saw an interesting spectacle—long convoy of 2½-ton trucks, driven by negroes, roared by jammed to gunwales with German PW, the sight being observed in wide-eyed astonishment by local populace. Quite a satisfying sight.

Still no word from the Task Force sent to Hammelburg. One TAC/R mission late in afternoon reported what pilot thought was a column of our tanks and MT moving East about 40 miles from Frankfurt.

New Army boundaries and change of direction. Our South boundary moved from Mainz to Hanau and North to Kassel. This permits us to go North and East. Also given three new divisions—70th and 71st Inf and 13th Armored. Apparently Patton given the ball and wherewithal to carry it. His plan tonight is to first grab Kassel and then swing East for Dresden—to meet Russians. Meanwhile, 4th Armd Div doing its share by breaking loose and reaching Bad Nauheim by noon, about halfway to Kassel. At this rate, should be there by tomorrow, and we should be in Dresden by 7 April. Here's hoping. PW total for day in West—22,800, of which TUSA got 6,800.

This occurred 24 March at ULTRA briefing. Patton in high good humor said was going across Rhine (by L plane to XX Corps CP at Bad Kreuznach, then by ¼ ton) and was taking camera. "I'm going to take a picture of myself pissing in the goddamned river," he said grinning. "If Churchill can have himself photographed pissing on dragon's teeth, I can do same pissing in the goddamned Rhine." Next morning [when] asked about it, replied he had picture and wished he had taken along Willie, his English bull, so could have got picture of dog pissing in river. "Hell," Patton observed, "not much of a river. Doesn't begin to compare with our big ones. It reminded me of the Red River in Louisiana."

Thursday, March 29, 1945: Still no word from Hammelburg expedition. Germans claim it was attacked and destroyed. They say they knocked out 20 tanks and capture[d] 9 Med, 3 Lts and 20 halftracks and 250 PW. ULTRA reports that a column was bombed on 27th—believe it to be one of our Armored spearheads. No hint from German sources of any knowledge of its true nature. Stiller, Patton's driver ADC, was with Task Force, which explains why he declined to ask to have me go with them when I asked him to.

TUSA total PW bag for Palatinate operation 80,396—from 13 to 25 March. Interesting that our estimate was right on the nose. We put figure—when Patton asked us—at 80,000. He shook his head disbelievingly, but that is the official PWE count. Included in total is over 1,600 officers, of which 40 are from corps and Army Hq.

More about Major General Millikin, former CG of III Corps that grabbed Remagen bridge. Latest story from Lt Col Mandel, liaison officer from 12 Army Group, is that Millikin was relieved. He did not voluntarily step out in order to take command of a line division—as last story went. According to Mandel, Hodges summoned Millikin and told him he was relieved because of lack of aggressiveness in exploiting the seized bridge. That is a scream—Hodges relieving anyone for lack of aggressiveness. He is about as aggressive as a flabby hamburger; a soggy dishrag. Mandel was of the opinion that Hodges was ordered to bounce Millikin by SHAEF, and the lack-of-aggressiveness line was cooked up as an excuse. Makes sense. Mandel said Millikin went to Paris to see what he could do for himself after talking to Patton, who told him if [he] was allowed to do so, would give him a division.

Little, incompetent pipsqueak Kilburn, bounced CG of 11th Armd Div, has got himself into a hospital for an exam, doubtless to get himself either sent home or fixed up with a rear job—the yellow little bastard. Pfann says he ducked Patton's offer to make him a CC Cmdr in 4th Armd to learn how to lead an Armd Div, and sneaked for cover to a hospital. Of course, he was able to get away with that because he is wearing a star, is a Reg, and had friends on Army topside. What should have happened is—he should not only have been relieved, but busted to permanent grade and sent home for reclassification. Utter incompetent and total loss to the country. Arty reported today that in 12 Army Group offensive to cross Rhine last week XVI U.S. Corps alone fired 165,000 R[oun]ds in preparation. And we never fired one round, and within 24 hours had 6 x 7 mile bridgehead. Theirs still isn't much more than that.

Friday, March 30, 1945: Patton very depressed over Hammelburg expedition. Remarked at ULTRA briefing, "Guess that was a mistake on me. My first one over here. But guess 500 is good exchange for 22,000." 22,400 was total PW TUSA rolled up yesterday, compared to 350 for Ninth Army, 5,000 FUSA, 1,550 Seventh. Total for West for the day was 30,000. FUSA's 3d Armored Div broke loose yesterday and raced 60 miles to Paderborn, about 25 miles North West of Kassel. Civil authorities reported attempting to negotiate surrender of Heidelberg, reported bypassed by XXI Corps of Seventh Army in the South. Even 21 Army Group got move on and advanced about 20 miles against sporadic and disorganized resistance.

Began work today on terrain study for area Fulda-Kassel-Halle-Leipzig-Dresden-Erfurt-Eisenach—our next zone of advance. Hope this is last terrain job I have to do.

At press conference this evening Patton, indirectly explaining his picaresque attire—elastique riding breeches and calf-length boots—remarked, "I was reading Caesar's writings the other night—not in the original—and was interested to note that he wore a Red Robe so the Huns would know where he was. He also used to serve notice on them where he was going and what he was going to do. Occurred to me in the present situation that might be a good idea for us. Tell present-day Huns what we propose to do so they can get out of our way or come there and surrender." Patton—"Third Army up to today has made 24 assault crossings over rivers since 1 August '44. It has got so that the Army's theme song is 'One More River to Cross.' Hope that one won't be the Jordan." Patton—"When war ends? My opinion is it won't end over here, just peter out."

Patton interrogated Genl Maj Dr. Hans Boehlen [Boelsen],[14] former CG 18 Inf Div, captured by XII Corps in the vicinity of Rothges yesterday and brought here to CP blindfolded. A former utility lawyer in Frankfurt, PW is reserve officer and was relieved from command of division after destruction in the East. Was Defense Cmdr of the Rothges area when captured. He tried to escape by tagging a fast advance 4th Armd Div column but ruse failed and he was nabbed. Among his comments after meeting Patton was that latter looked like, dressed and talked like a German general. Also, that PW had no qualms about surrendering as family lived in

Frankfurt and couldn't be harmed by SS. Also that as more German territory was overrun, more Germans would be free to surrender as families would be safe from retaliation. (This certainly borne out by huge daily PW totals.) In response to Patton's question why the war was continuing, PW replied soldierly duty and fear of Nazi reprisal. Said Germans had no strength left for large-scale counterattack. Nazis keeping war going because couldn't afford to quit. Did not believe they would use gas now that Rhine crossed. Boelsen is the sixth General captured in the West this week. FUSA got one; Seventh a couple; and 21 Army Group a couple.

PW captured yesterday—TUSA 10,000, FUSA 5,850, Seventh 4,000, Ninth 800. Estimate total West—22,000.

Sunday, April 1, 1945: Patton at ULTRA briefing said to Gay—"I want Kassel taken today. Been fiddling around two days now. Tell Walker the town must be captured today and to use a whole division, or whatever necessary to do that."

Monday, April 2, 1945: PW captured yesterday—TUSA—7,100, FUSA—4,800, [total] 11,900. But, enemy command is still resisting. PW captured today from 6 SS Mountain Div[15] claim 6 SS Panzer Army has been withdrawn from line in southeastern front; sent to Frankfurt/Oder for refit preparatory for employment in the West. Possible, but so far no confirmation. Meanwhile, strong indications of better organized resistance in our zone of advance as we move into Kassel-Eisenach area. What may be happening is that we have compressed enemy to such an extent that we are now up against inner core of resistance. Further evidence from PW that Ohrdruf is a major OKW CP installation, confirming information from PW Lt Arndtz a week ago.

2d and 3d Armored Divs of FUSA and Ninth Army closed pocket in West. Estimate 30,000 combat effectives and 50,000 overall trapped. ULTRA reports Seventh German Army Hq trapped and trying to fight its way out.[16] Also hot exchange between Kesselring and Model over tactics; former ordering West and South flanks be held and attack launched against East flank, and Model caustically pointing out inconsistency of the directive owing to lack of troops. This is very ironic, because Model is one of the most inconsistent directive issuers in OKW.

French enlarged their bridgehead in Baden sector to 8–10 miles. 80th Div fighting in outskirts of Kassel.

Patton received letter from Marlene Dietrich[17] saying she served with number of U.S. Armies and wanted to come back to TUSA. "I am entirely at your service. I could act as an interpreter or in any other capacity you wish to use me." Harkins related this one—Patton remarked to him this evening, "Well, guess I'll call up Bradley and recharge *his* batteries."

PW total—TUSA—5,300, FUSA—4,500.

Sibert around today and one of the things he talked to Koch about was trying to find a post for Bixel, incompetent ex-NUSA G-2 who was rolled. Now in a Replenishment Depot and should be reclassified, but little Eddy [Sibert] is so little occupied, despite great operations and multitudinous problems with *ECLIPSE*, which his section is NOT handling, that he can take time out to try and find a job for one of the old-tie boys. That's the Reg Army for you. No wonder it's so cluttered up with incompetents and misfits.

Three more Generals captured today. Gen Maj Heurich Hoffmann,[18] in Fulda, where he was on leave from Eastern front. Gen der Inf Edgar Roehricht [Röhricht],[19] former CG of LIX Corps in the East, was sent to the West to command either a Corps or an Army, but was captured instead. Gen der Arty Graf von Oriola,[20] CG of XIII Corps.

Tuesday, April 3, 1945: PW totals—TUSA—5,000, FUSA—3,500, Seventh—2,800, Ninth—4,800, [total] 16,100.

80th Infantry drove through center of Kassel from West to East, captured two bridges intact and broke the back of enemy resistance in town. 4th Armored Div swept to outskirts of Gotha, about a third of the distance to Dresden. TUSA now farthest Allied Army in Germany—about 190 miles from Russians. ULTRA reports Kesselring and Model still trying to break out to East out of Ruhr pocket. Not getting anywhere. Patton commenting on U.S. equipment—C-47 (carrier plane) and 2½ ton truck our "secret weapon." Done more to win war than any other equipment. Our advance columns being supplied largely with oil and rations by C-47s. One day they transported 526,000 gallons of gas and over 150,000 rations.

PW Lt Genl Röhricht stated today that Hitler personally ordered Ardennes offensive because [Joseph] Goebbels[21] and Himmler demanded a victory to bolster flagging morale. Von Rundstedt was against the offensive; wanted to organize in depth, but Hitler overruled him.

Ninth U.S. Army reverted back to 12 Army Group today, giving Bradley four armies—1, 3, 9 and 15. Talk about that Third Army will be hooked up with Seventh under 6 Army Group—commanded by Jackie Devers, Patton's classmate whom he strongly dislikes and who is a thorough mediocrity. CP moved to Frankfurt. Crossed Rhine on 1800-foot tread-bridge. Road packed with displaced persons, hundreds of them, all heading West; walking, riding horses, bicycles, pulling carts, everything and anything—soldiers, men, women, children—the chaff of Europe, tragic, homeless, helpless—but all heading West out of Germany. Frankfurt, about the size of Baltimore, is devastated in city proper. Heart of town completely destroyed. Yet, streets are cleaner than most of our towns. Debris piled neatly on sidewalks behind walls made of debris. Incongruous touches. In financial district, near Bourse, a battered shell, four white little streetcars untouched on tracks, blinds pulled down and apparently ready to move out as soon as the power is turned on. On another corner, handsome full-length statue of [Friedrich] Schiller,[22] the Jewish poet, unscarred, while everything around battered and burned out.

Wednesday, April 4, 1945: PW total—TUSA—4,000, FUSA—2,900, Seventh—3,000.

Gotha cleared. Small, unsuccessful counterattack North of Kassel. 13 counterattacks in FUSA zone along North East perimeter of Ruhr pocket, but none successful as estimate 35,000 combat effectives trying to break out to East on orders of Hitler. Hq Army Group B and Seventh Army in pocket. Model, who commands Group, also has control [of] Kassel sector, and according to ULTRA, is complaining bitterly about inability to direct these except by radio. French clear Karlsruhe. Another General, Gen Maj Krxleben,[23] Signals Officer, captured by XX Corps.

ETOUSA, Engineer, came through again today—in big way, as usual. Got batch of elaborate studies on crossings of Fulda, Werrs [Werra], and Eder Rivers, which we crossed several or more days ago. This is typical of the way topside has worked all the way through our operations. Never furnish us with a single, effective thing yet. Either never get it or get it after we [are] long past the place. Example: Weeks ago when we were on Kyll River, requisitioned from our burping Engineer a terrain model of Germany. They went to ETOUSA Engineer, and told us we would get it middle of March. Still has not showed up and we are two-thirds the way across Germany. That's an illustration of the way they work.

Another German general working for us—Genlmajor Ludwig Heilmann,[24] CG of 5 Para Div, captured 12 March, in special DIC (MIS [Military Intelligence Service]) Interrogation report, outlined in detail plan of offensive by Allied Armies into central Germany. Detailed what each U.S. Army should do and where and how to go. The great German Officer Corps and its honor (?).

Bradley came to CP for conference with Patton and stated the following: "SHAEF will issue a directive on a new plan but until it's issued he would give a fill-in on the situation. It is expected to take a week to

10 days to clean out the Ruhr pocket. An SS Div at Paderborn is trying to break out to the East but can't do it because it lacks the power. After the pocket is cleaned out, it will take Hodges a couple of days to get up on line with TUSA. 21 Army Group will also move up on line but it will take them a couple of days to regroup." (Everybody laughed, although Bradley said this without conscious humor.) Patton tried to urge to be allowed to keep going on the ground [and warned] that if the Germans are given time they would mine and organize defensive positions. Bradley—"I don't think they'll mine because they have nothing to mine with." Bradley asked Weyland to lay off of bombing German barracks. "We'll have to live in this country for some time, perhaps years. Our people have got to have places to live, so don't bomb any of their casernes as we will need them." Patton asked Bradley when they expected to meet the Russians, and Bradley replied he didn't know. Quick as a flash, Patton retorted: "Just get me off from a telephone connection with SHAEF and I'll meet them for you in two days."

Thursday, April 5, 1945: Visited Frankfurt. Practically completely devastated. Vast I. G. Farben plant and offices, unbombed, being used to house thousands of DP's. Cross-section of the dispossessed of Europe, living in their own dirt and squalor.

Sunday, April 7, 1945: On mission to Ohrdruff yesterday, by Patton, I saw atrocity camp and on return from Gotha, ran into a roadblock at Apfelstadt, about 20 km South West of Erfurt, and in ensuing firefight, I was wounded and captured. Right forearm amputated in German military hospital in Erfurt.

Wednesday, April 11, 1945: Rescued by troops of 80th Inf Div and taken to 39th Evacuation Hospital in cub plane by Colonel Odom, personal physician of Patton's. Evacuation Hospital located within 500 yards of TUSA CP at Hersfeld on autobahn.

Thursday, April 12, 1945: Decorated with Purple Heart by Patton, who visited me in hospital accompanied by Gay and other members of his staff.

Tuesday, April 17, 1945: Returned to full duty. Patton got personal permission to allow me to do this from Eisenhower who was at the CP the day Odom brought me back.

Monday, April 23, 1945: CP moved to Erlangen. An officer of the 86th Inf Div, commanded by Maj Gen Malinowski [Harris M. Melasky],[25] was captured by the Germans with an overlay showing all our dispositions for the forthcoming operation, from the Army right down to the bns of Divs. Lot of hell being raised about the matter, but too late to do

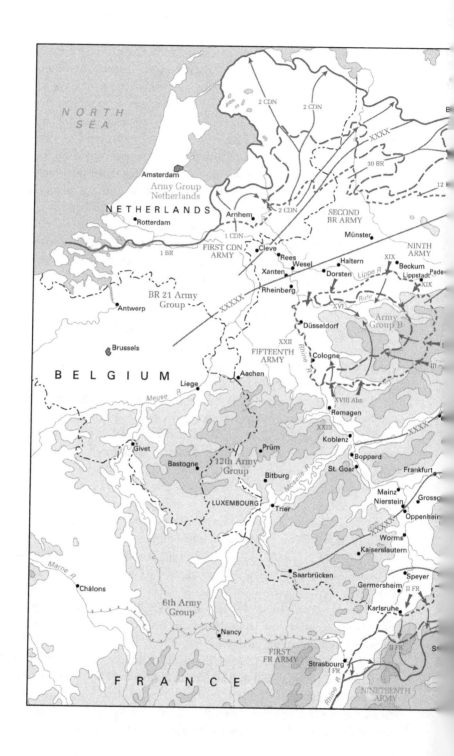

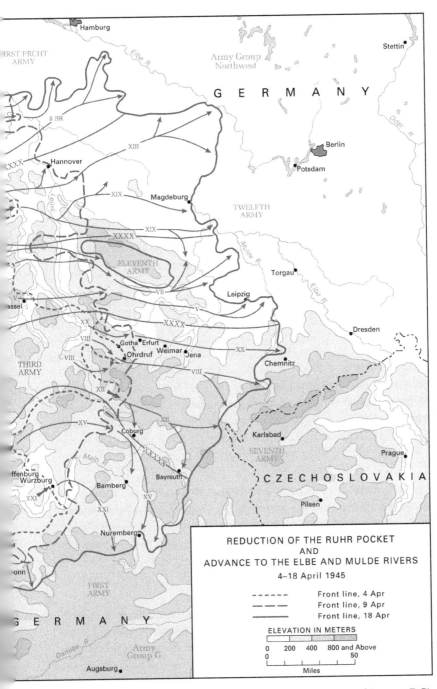

Hamburg

FIRST PRCHT
ARMY

Elbe R.

Stettin

Army Group
Northwest

G E R M A N Y

Oder R.

8 BR

XIII

Berlin

XXXX

Hannover

Potsdam

Leine R.

XIX

Magdeburg

TWELFTH
ARMY

XXXX

XIX

Mulde R.

ELEVENTH
ARMY

VII

Torgau

Elbe R.

Kassel

Leipzig

V

Dresden

XX

VIII

XXXX

Gotha Erfurt

XX

THIRD
ARMY

VIII

Ohrdruf

Weimar Jena

Chemnitz

XII

VIII

XV

XII

Coburg

Karlsbad

SEVENTH
ARMY

Prague

Offenburg
Würzburg

Main R.

XXXII

Bamberg

Bayreuth

C Z E C H O S L O V A K I A

XXI

XXI

XV

Pilsen

Nuremberg

Bonn

FIRST
ARMY

REDUCTION OF THE RUHR POCKET
AND
ADVANCE TO THE ELBE AND MULDE RIVERS

4–18 April 1945

- - - - - Front line, 4 Apr
— — — Front line, 9 Apr
———— Front line, 18 Apr

G E R M A N Y

Danube R.

Army
Group G

ELEVATION IN METERS

0   200   400   800 and Above
0   50
Miles

Augsburg

Drive to the Elbe, April 4–18, 1945 (Center for Military History, Washington, DC) anything about it as the jump-off is set for tomorrow. Also, chances are the Germans can't do anything about it either, as they don't have anything to do it with, but this could be a great disaster if they did have.

Tuesday, April 24, 1945: Our Army Surgeon, Hurley, was made a brigadier-general a week ago and today got himself evacuated back to the States as a medical disability. The real reason was alcoholism. He's been an incompetent drunk for months and should have been relieved a long time ago. But because he was a Reg, the system protected him and he was able to hang on until he got his T/O star, after which he beat it back home. Now there is a big scramble on to fill his vacancy, with even Eisenhower and Bradley sticking in an oar on behalf of friends of theirs. Patton would appoint Odom, brilliant young civilian medic from New Orleans, if he had his way, but the pressure is too strong from topside to give the place to a Reg. (A Reg got it, presumably a better man than Hurley but not in the same class in any sense, either as a medic or as an administrator, with Odom.)

Wednesday, April 25, 1945: 40,000 of our PW stacked up in cages and not moving because ADSEC refused to take any more for evacuation to the rear. Claims they can't handle them. Visited Nurnberg [Nuremburg], 90 percent destroyed. Visited Stadium where Nazi annual conclaves were held and other points of interest in city. All thoroughly beat-up by bombing and Arty shelling.

Marlene Dietrich showed up at mess tonight, putting on very coy act of gushing young babe adoring brave generals and senior colonels—all of them too old to do her any good. She apparently has some personal reason for wanting to be with us in Germany. My hunch is that she is trying to find relatives.

Thursday, April 26, 1945: Emil Ludwig,[26] shyster author, showed up at CP today in civilian clothes and wearing a cap. Claims he is writing a book on Allied war leaders and interviewed Patton. My hunch is that he too is prowling around trying to locate relatives and friends. Russians contacted by troops of First Army but it's not being announced. News is being withheld until official announcement is made simultaneously from Washington, London and Moscow.

Monday, April 30, 1945: Patton very restless because of a lack of enough to do. Is talking about resuming flying his own plane. Patton summoned me to help him write a VE Day statement that the WD is having all Army commanders prepare in preparation for use when Germans finally surrender. Over 1,000,000 PW were captured by the Allies in the first 21 days of April.

8

The End of the War in the European Theater of Operations

Tuesday, May 1, 1945: PW captured yesterday—TUSA—17,000, FUSA—5,000, SUSA—27,000, [total] 49,000. Our casualties for day— Killed—30, Wounded—226, Non-battle casualties—338.

Wednesday, May 2, 1945: CP moved to Regensburg. German Armies in Italy surrender. This has all [the] earmarks of the beginning of the final collapse.

Thursday, May 3, 1945: [Guenther] Blumentritt[1] surrendered all German forces in northern Germany. This is the final throe. It can only be a matter of days now before the bastards quit. Our PW bag yesterday was over 20,000, with 8–10 Generals. Our casualties—4 killed, 61 wounded, 50 missing.

Friday, May 4, 1945: Got word today that FUSA is being pulled out of the line for shipment to States preparatory to being sent to CIB [Theater]. Only reason I can see that it was picked for this is that it's Bradley's old Army. Certainly TUSA is a far better outfit and would have far greater effect on the Japs when an announcement is made about the matter. Another instance of favoritism that we have suffered under for so long. We always have got the short end of the deal, and this is just another instance of it. Our old enemy, 11 Panzer Div that we beat up a number of times since the breakthrough at Avranches, surrendered today. More final throes.

Saturday, May 5, 1945: Despite all the Nazi claptrap about racial purity and drastic measures to preserve it, including the hanging and torturing of many DP's for shacking up with Germans, a captured OKW report, as of 1 Jan '45, discloses that there was plenty of intermingling. According to this official report, there were—

500,000 children born of Russian mothers and German fathers

190,000 children of French mothers and German fathers
156,000 children of *German* mothers and *foreign laborers* (DP's)

Monday, May 7, 1945: TWX from SHAEF—TOP SEC[RET]—reported final German surrender would be as of 2400, 8 May.

Tuesday, May 8, 1945: War over in ETO. At conclusion of morning briefing, Patton rose and said: "This will be the last briefing of this Staff in Europe. I want to thank you for all you have done. It has been an outstanding job from start to finish. There probably is no Army commander who did less work than I did. You did it all, and the historic record of the Third U.S. Army is due largely to your outstanding efforts." First manifestation of peace—Gay announced that steel helmets would be dispensed with and liners worn.

Wednesday, May 9, 1945: Top Secret TWX from Sibert requesting the collection of all possible Order of Battle data on Russians. Stated neither we nor British had very much information regarding Red Army and higher HQ wanted it. However, strongly cautioned that the info was to be gathered very discretely and transmitted under the strictest secrecy—only by Top Secret. Estimates indicate that over 100,000 German troops who were fighting the Russians are trying to surrender to us. Some 35 German planes, carrying officers, women and children, landed in our area and surrendered in order to avoid giving up to the Russians. Front line troops report roads in Czechoslovakia and Austria leading into our area literally jammed with thousands of German troops and civilians on foot and in every type of vehicle.

Visited PW camp outside Regensburg where over 40,000 PW, including thousands of Hungarians, several hundred women, and SS generals are incarcerated, and thousands more pouring in every few hours. Generals living in a beat-up wooden barracks, but all other PW out in open corrals. Women have a wooden shed.

Thursday, May 10, 1945: Visited Pilsen. While in MG office in Rathaus five U.S. PWX's [Prisoner of War Executive Branch, under SHAEF G-1 Division] came in, having walked from a Lager miles away where they had been liberated by Russians. Men were walking skeletons, but typically American, each had around his waist ½ dozen Lugers and other guns, and from neck, field glasses and cameras they had stripped from Germans while hiking to our lines.

Saturday, May 12, 1945: Patton and senior members of Staff went to Linz where in a hunting lodge [of] Emperor Franz Josef[2] [they] were entertained by Russians, among them Marshal [Fedor] Tolbokin [Tolbukhin].[3] Russian show was very elaborate, including numerous entertainers and lavish food and drinks. In striking contrast to reception given by Patton to them several days ago on our side of Linz. At this party, Russians served sandwiches, peanuts, sardines (captured) and whiskey.

Tuesday, May 15, 1945: Illustration of the way the Reg Army mind works. Gay drove downtown and noticing two GI's from an Engineer bn, guarding PW cleaning away debris, [the GIs] did not salute him. He stopped and ordered them tried by summary court at once and fined. This was done and it cost them $10 apiece. A block further on, he saw another GI from the same outfit also guarding a bunch of working PW. This boy not only gave Gay a big highball but very smartly answered some questions he put to him about his outfit and the work they were doing. Gay ordered his aide to prepare a citation giving this soldier a Bronze Star. Two GI's fined $10 for not saluting, and the third given a Bronze Star for saluting. Various G-2 recommendations for outstanding and unceasing work during 10 months of major operations have been turned down by Gay on the ground that our allotment was exhausted.

Friday, May 18, 1945: Great deal of excitement around HQ over numerous wild rumors and reports of possible difficulties with Russians. Patton called back from a week's leave in London for conference with Bradley on movement of Third Army troops into Yugoslavia.[4] Conference took place in the War Room at 1330B with Bradley and some Seventh Army Staff members present. Also his tubby G-3, who gets fatter by the day and apparently also dumber. Today he fitted his battle suit like a sack of lard.[5] Bradley—"Tito[6] is causing considerable concern in the Trieste area. He has moved into the British part of Austria and the British don't think they have enough troops to deal with the situation. SHAEF wants to move five divisions to the Enns River. We don't know how far the Russians will back Tito up. We don't think they will [put] on a showdown but in the meanwhile, SHAEF wants to make a show of force." Patton—"The point we want to stress is an ostentatious closing on the river and the bringing up of Bridging. Whole purpose of the operation is to determine how far the Russians will go in backing up Tito." Bradley—"Two things we want to keep in mind: (1) Do nothing to violate the terms of our agreement with the Russians. Must meticulously observe all terms with them so as not to give them an excuse to raise any issues in some other place on some other ground. We must keep situation strictly to this question in order to determine their position as regards Tito. (2) Plenty of publicity regarding our move to the river. If TUSA does have to cross river it would come under 15 Army

Group operationally but continue under 12 Army Group administratively. Want to stress necessity not to give Russians excuse for doing anything anywhere else. SHAEF wants to make them show their hand squarely on Tito."

Sunday, May 20, 1945: With Patton, flew over Alps, Salzburg, Berchtesgarden, Venice, Bolzano, Brenner Pass, Munich. After several days of waiting for the SHAEF directive, it finally arrived and plan set in motion against Tito. III Corps in Western portion of our ECLIPSE area shifted to Seventh Army, and we are to take over XV Corps from Seventh Army. Divisions start moving South at 0600B tomorrow.

Tuesday, May 22, 1945: Captured 2½ truckloads of German Order of Battle material on Russian Armies, including 1944 Red-covered Order of Battle book on Soviet Armies. This OKW document estimates Russian strength as of 1 Jan '45 as follows:

> 513 Inf Divs as against 482 a year ago
> 223 Tk Brigs as against 209 a year ago
> 19 Arty Divs—13 a year ago
> 96 Mtz & Mczd [Motorized & Mechanized] Brigs—82 a year ago
> 72 Armies—5–10 Inf Divs, Tk Brigs, etc, per Army; 10 airborne
>   Divs listed; Inf Divs reduced from 12,800 to 10,800 and
>   currently to 9,500 in 1944
> Total mobilized strength (male) 1 Jan '45—11,500,000, as
>   follows—
> Army—7,500,000
> Air—1,500,000
> Navy—200,000
> Training—1,200,000
> Strategic Reserve—1,500,000 (150 Divs)
> Also 1–2 million women in Armed Services
> Of these numbers, according to OKW book, 10,700,000 in West;
>   800,000 in East.

Wednesday, May 23, 1945: CP moved to Bad Tolz. Nineteenth CP location of TUSA on Continent. Total distance of CP moves: 1,375 miles. Enroute, visited Munich. Center of town completely destroyed. South of Munich, on Autobahn, over 100 different types of German planes dispersed along highway in adjoining woods. CP located in SS Junkerschule. Very modern commodious installation.

Thursday, May 24, 1945: Patton billeted in elaborate villa owned by

Max Amann,[7] Nazi big-shot and head of big Nazi publishing firm, on lake about 10 miles from CP. Told by Odom today that Patton is returning to States early in June on war bond selling tour of Pacific Coast. Also that Patton asked him about me and suggested that I be taken along with them when they returned.

Saturday, May 26, 1945: Published last Periodic Report today—# 351, 14 short of a full year. A Monsignor Carroll (?) accompanied by 4–5 other civilians and traveling in a huge blue sedan, new, with American flags painted on hood and rear, appeared in our office today to get clearance for pass to travel about our area. [Lieutenant Colonel Horace] Franklin[8] took him in tow. He told me the priest had Vatican papers and also that he was violently anti-Russian and anti-nonfraternization policy. According to Franklin, the priest voiced far bitterer sentiments against the Russians than the Germans. Priest is fat, well dressed and smoking a big cigar and members of his party the same.

Sunday, May 27, 1945: Patton—learning that Von Rundstedt, captured in Bad Tolz several weeks ago by troops of Seventh Army, had been paroled by SUSA contrary to ECLIPSE directive—ordered him evacuated after physical exam to make sure he was in traveling condition. Odom found Von Rundstedt in sound health, despite claims of latter's personal doctor that he was a sick man. Von Rundstedt is living in town in a small hotel with wife, his son, acting as his aide, and a couple of adjutants. Wearing plus-fours. When Group asked where they wanted Von Rundstedt sent, they became very much agitated. Seems they didn't know he was down here. Ordered him sent to their interrogation center alone; wife and others to remain behind. Gay sent him off with his son and one adjutant on grounds that Geneva Convention required that.

Monday, May 28, 1945: Duchess of Luxembourg's summer castle, about 5 miles from CP, discovered filled with art treasures from Alte and Neue Pinopetak [Pinakothek] museums of Munich, both destroyed by our air bombing. Apparently Germans used castle for this purpose in belief we wouldn't bomb the place. Actually we didn't know it existed until her consort, Prince Felix, asked Codman, Patton's aide, to check up on the place and he discovered it was being used as an art preserve. Priceless paintings stacked one against the other in rooms and corridors under guard of a small detail of GI's.

Thursday, May 31, 1945: [Lieutenant Colonel] Louis Hout [Huot][9] story—Beautiful, blonde, blue-eyed American girl in Paris, Gay Orloff [Orlova].[10] Married to White Russian, enamored [with] handsome, dashing U.S. major. Brussels. Arrested by MPs. She suspected WAC, he a Canadian Private. AWOL 18 months. She once was Lucky Luciano's[11] girl.

Sunday, June 3, 1945: Decorated by Patton in his office with Silver Star and Bronze Star awards. Scheduled to leave for home tomorrow with Patton, Odom, Pfann.

Appendix A

Selected Ultra Messages

Legend:
ZE represents Third Army
NX represents Twelfth Army Group
Zs reflect importance of message—Z to ZZZZZ

REF: CX/MSS/T387/1   HP 8448
                                   ZZZZ

((HP 8448 £ 8448 YKA YK ZE FZ GU 80 £ 80 TGA TG 35 £ 35 WM 3
£ 3 NX 54 £ 54 LF 92 £ 92 SHA 32 £ 32 SH 64 £ 64 %
ADVANCE EXTRACT TRANSPORT MOVEMENTS ACCORD-
ING GAF £ GAF LIAISON)) DETACHMENT WITH CHARLIE IN
CHARLIE WEST £ WEST ON SECOND. THREE TWO SIX VIC-
TOR GEORGE DIVISION COLON DESTINATION GEROLSTEIN £
GEROLSTEIN (LOVE TWO EIGHT)—BITBURG £ BITBURG (LOVE
ONE FIVE). OF THREE EIGHT TRAINS TWO NINE UNLOADED
IN AREA BETWEEN GEROLSTEIN £ GEROLSTEIN AND TRIER
£ TRIER. FUEHRER ESCORT BRIGADE (COMMENT, COUNTS
AS PANZER TROOPS) COLON DESTINATION AREA TRABEN-
TRARBACH £ TRABENTRARBACH (LOVE FIVE FIVE)—KIRN
£ KIRN (LOVE THREE EIGHT). OF TWO FIVE TRAINS ONE
FIVE UNLOADED AREA KOCHEM £ KOCHEM—OBERSTEIN £
OBERSTEIN. (STRONG INDICATIONS FOUR) SIX TWO VICTOR
GEORGE DIVISION COLON DESTINATION AREA WITTLICH £
WITTLICH—KOCHEM £ KOCHEM. OF THREE FOUR TRAINS
TWO THREE UNLOADED AREA KOCHEM £ KOCHEM—WEN-
GEROHR £ WENGEROHR. FULL DETAILS FOLLOW AS HOW
PETER EIGHT FOUR FOUR NINE.
TRLB/RFB/JB   030842Z/12/44

219

REF. CX/MSS/T411/16   BT 479
                              ZZZZ
((BT 479 £ 479 ONA ON QX YKA YK ZE GU 94 £ 94 TGA TG 43 £
43 WM 10 £ 10 NX 43 £ 43 LF 96 £ 96 DL 25 £ 25 STA 22 £ 22 ST 11
£ 11 SH 55 £ 55 %
(FAIR INDICATIONS AOK £ AOK SEVEN NOUGHT ONE HOURS
TWENTYSEVENTH COLON ON ENTIRE)) WIDTH OF ARMY
FRONT, HEAVY DEFENSIVE FIGHTING AGAINST ALLIES WHO
HAD MATERIAL SUPERIORITY. INTENTIONS COLON DECISIVE
DEFENCE ON NORTH BANK SAUER £ SAUER WHERE SITUA-
TION MIGHT MAKE IT POSSIBLE TO GO OVER TO OFFENSIVE
AGAIN. SITUATION ESPECIALLY CRITICAL ON BOTH WINGS
GELC/WM   271656Z/12/44.
FB

REF: 949, CX/MSS/T412/20   BT 674
                               Z
((BT 674 £ 674 CR FZ TG 92 £ 92 LF 45 £ 45 SH 21 £ 21 %
SUMIT (BAKER TARE FIVE SEVEN EIGHT) INTENTIONS UNSPECI-
FIED)) AUTHORITY TWENTY SEVENTH INCLUDED COLON ONE
SIX SEVEN VG £ VG DIVISION AND THREE PANZER DIVISION
(COMMENT PRESUMABLY THREE PG £ PG) TO TAKE BASTOGNE
£ BASTOGNE
RS/HYD/IFF   291741Z/12/44

REF: CX/MSS/T413/77   BT 708
                              ZZZZZ
((BT 708 £ 708 ONA ON QX YKA YK ZE TG 15 £ 15 WM 78 £ 78 NX
9 £ 9 LF 68 £ 68 AD 26 £ 26 EFR 47 £ 47 SH 48 £ 48 %
ACCORDING JAGDKORPS TWO AT TWO ONE FOUR FIVE HOURS
TWENTY NINTH SECOND ATTACK)) ON BASTOGNE £ BAS-
TOGNE ORDERED AT NOUGHT SIX THREE NOUGHT HOURS.
PANZER ARMY FIVE TO REPORT BY NOUGHT FOUR HOURS
WHETHER ATTACK CAN STILL BE CARRIED OUT.
NH/RFB/
EVB   292318Z/12/44

REF. CX/MSS/T414/34   BT 752

ZZZZZ

((BT 752 £ 752 ONA ON QX YKA YK ZE GU 92 £ 92 TGA TG 49 £ 49 WM 12 £ 12 NX 41 £ 41 LF 3 £ 3 DL 49 £ 49 STA 78 £ 78 ST 67 £ 67 SH 85 85%
INTENTIONS ONE REPEAT ONE SUGAR SUGAR DIVISION ACCORDING)) FLIVO ONE ONE THREE NOUGHT HOURS THIR-TIETH COLON THRUST SOUTH OF BASTOGNE £ BASTOGNE (PETER FIVE FIVE) TO WEST WEST, AGAIN ENCIRCLED ALLIES IN BASTOGNE £ BASTOGNE.

CAZ/HYD   301642Z/12/44

FB

Appendix B

Third Army G-2 Estimates

Koch and Allen did not prepare estimates according to a cycle. Instead, they prepared them to address significant changes in the situation. The dates of Third Army's G-2 estimates for 1944 are as follows.

No. 1	April 23
No. 2	May 14
No. 3	May 19
No. 4	June 5
No. 5	June 17
No. 6	August 10
No. 7	August 18
No. 8	August 24
No. 9	August 28
No. 10	November 1
No. 11	December 21

G-2 ESTIMATE NO. 9
28 August 1944
Maps: GSGS 4249, FRANCE, Scale 1/100,000
    1. <u>SUMMARY OF THE ENEMY SITUATION</u>
    a. <u>General</u>.
    (1) The Battle for Germany has begun. It started when Third US Army columns forced the SEINE N and S of PARIS and followed this up with armor-spearheaded penetrations that, as of this date, have reached a N-S line extending from REIMS-VITRY-TROYES, approximately 100 miles from the German border. That the enemy is fully aware that the Battle for Germany is underway is evident from numerous indications. Units of every variety and concoction are being scraped together from every available source in a desperate effort to reinforce the crumpling

forces and lines of defense between the onsweeping Third US Army columns and the REICH border.

(2) The futility of these frantic efforts is strikingly revealed by numerous PW statements and captured documents, disclosing plans for concentrations and dispositions at locations already overrun before the enemy could organize them.

(3) While unable to contain Third US Army thrusts, the enemy still has strong ground forces in France and the capability of considerably reinforcing them. His lines of communication are extensively disrupted and his movements are tortuous and laborious. Also there are numerous indications of widespread confusion and disorganization among the constantly retreating enemy units. It appears probable that Elm [elements] of the 158 Tng [Training] Div (upgraded to 16 Inf Div) were in process of moving N across the LOIRE and found themselves in a pocket S of ORLEANS. It also appears probable that with the landing of the Seventh US Army in MEDITERRANEAN FRANCE that other Elm of enemy forces now S of the LOIRE and generally W of the RHÔNE (notable 159 Tng Div) find themselves blocked, except to the NE between Third US Army's S flank, and the N Elm of the Seventh US Army, and that a general exodus may be anticipated in that direction.

(4) As a sidelight of what remains in S France the following is based on official reports received to date as to identifications of enemy units opposing Seventh US Army or in S France exclusive of 16 Inf and 159 Tng Divs.

Division	General Location	Bns Identified in Combat Either W or S France	Bns to Be Accounted For
189	TOULOUSE Gap	4	2 to 5
198	BEZIERS	6	0 to 3
338	SETTE	3	3 to 6
244	MARSEILLES	8	1 to 1
242	TOULON	6	0 to 3
148	NICE-CANNES	6	0 to 3
157	GRENOBLE	6	0 to 3
716	SPANISH Border	None	6 to 6?
Ost	LYON	None	6 to 6?
11 Pz	RHÔNE Valley	3?	3 to 3
?	Unlocated	Total 21 to 39	(Equivalent of 4 Divs)

Note: The last column gives alternate figures for Bn strength due to insufficient reports on present strength of Divs contacted in South.

(5) The value of any of these units, though they must be considered in the S, is practically negated as a threat during movement to the N because of Maquis activities, lack of transportation, and disorganization and confusion which must exist due to chaotic communications and control. Definitely then, these units, in addition to delaying the advance of Seventh US Army Northward, have to escape through the narrowing gap between Third US Army troops and the SWISS border as an immediate objective.

(6) Despite the crippling factors of shattered communications, disorganization and tremendous losses in personnel and equipment, the enemy has nevertheless been able to maintain a sufficiently cohesive front to exercise an overall control of his tactical situation. His withdrawal, though continuous, has not been a rout of mass collapse. Numerous new identifications in contact in recent days have demonstrated clearly that, despite the enormous difficulties under which he is operating, the enemy still is capable of bringing new elements into the battle area and transferring some from other fronts, as the newly identified in contact, 3, 15 and 90 Pz Gren[adier] Div from Italy.

(7) These reinforcements will not give the enemy any new offensive power. His immediate attitude will continue to be wholly defensive in every sector. But in the execution of his defensive operations the reinforcements will give the enemy the capability of small-scale local counterattacks designed to stem the rate and scope of our advance. This capability is particularly indicated against the shoulders and exposed flanks of our thrusts.

(8) It is clear from all indications that the fixed determination of the Nazis is to wage a last-ditch struggle in the field at all costs. It must be constantly kept in mind that fundamentally the enemy is playing for time. Weather will soon be one of his most potent Allies, as well as terrain, as we move E to narrowing corridors. What the recently announced "total mobilization" portends is impractical to forecast at this time. But barring internal upheaval in the homeland, and the remoter possibility of insurrection within the Wehrmacht, it can be expected that the German Armies will continue to fight until destroyed or captured. PW statements, captured documents, and other ground reports indicate that plans contemplate this last-ditch battle for Germany to [be] wage[d] on three main river lines: (1) SOMME-AISNE; (2) MEUSE-MOSELLE; and (3) RHINE–SIEGFRIED LINE. (The SOMME-MARNE has been turned by our forces on the East.) A number of reports have also been received the last few days of intensified construction activity to strengthen and re-equip the largely dismantled SIEGFRIED Line.

(9) For the opening round of the Battle of Germany, indications point to a concentration by the enemy of the bulk of the Armor he has left in the West N of the line ROUEN-SENLIS-REIMS. This would be borne out by favorable operating terrain. Further, PW and captured documents indicate that the enemy's armor has been reinforced by a series of desperate expedients; cannibalism, in which whole brigades have been infused into battle-depleted divisions (17 SS, 9 SS, 130 Pz), hasty formation of entirely new units, and drawing upon low-category reserves in Denmark, Germany, and from the Italian Front. It is estimated that, as of this date, the enemy has the equivalent of five full Panzer divisions (75,000 troops) 600 tanks E of the SEINE, and the equivalent of one full Panzer division and 100 tanks S of the LOIRE. This means that E of SEINE the Panzer force defends a 300 mile battle front and S of the LOIRE a sector extending from ST. NAZAIRE-TOURS-ORLEANS-TROYES-SWISS Border.

(10) It is estimated that in 14 days, the enemy has the capability of still further piecemeal reinforcement of the Panzer force E of the SEINE with Elm equivalent to 3 additional divisions, a total of 40,000 troops and 250 tanks, from Denmark, Germany, and the Italian Front.

(11) The bulk of enemy infantry E of the SEINE is currently in the PAS DE CALAIS area. This force is made up of the remnants of the units that escaped across the SEINE plus three divisions (49, 47 and 18 GAF) committed E of the SEINE and three divisions (345, 245, 182) not yet identified in contact from the PAS DE CALAIS. The strength of this force is estimated as equivalent to ten divisions, 60 Bns. The enemy has the capability of piecemeal reinforcement of the PAS DE CALAIS sector in seven days with the equivalent of five additional Infantry divisions, 30 Bns, and in fourteen days, four more divisions, 24 Bns.

(12) The enemy's Infantry strength in the First and Third US Army zones of advance is estimated as equivalent to five divisions, 30 Bns. The enemy has the capability in this sector of reinforcing in seven days with the equivalent of three Infantry divisions, 18 Bns, and in fourteen days with the equivalent of six Infantry divisions, 36 Bns.

(13) Also in the First and Third US Army zones of advance (in the Third Army front) is one Pz Gren Div (3 from Italy), and the enemy has the capability of employing two additional Pz Gren Div (15 and 90) from Italy.

  b. <u>Enemy Situation in the WEST</u>.

CLASSIFICATION	PANZER	INFANTRY					TOTAL
		Field Type		Limited Employment		Training	
FRANCE	*1 SS	*3 Para	*271	*16 GAF	*343	#148	
	*2 SS	*5 Para	*272	*17 GAF	*344	#157	
	*9 SS	*6 Para	*275	*18 GAF	*345	159	
	*10 SS	16	*276	#242	348	182	
	*12 SS	*48	*277	*243	*708	#189*	
	*17 SS	*49	*331	*244	*709		
	*20 SS	*77	*352	245	*711		
	*2	*84	*353	*265	*716		
	*9	*85	*2 Para	*266			
	#11*	*89	*363	319 Elms			
	*21	*91	*198	*326			
	*116	*47		*338			
	*130						
	*15 PG						
	* 3 PG						
	*90 PG						64 (Equivalent strength—40)
BELGIUM				712–? Div			2
HOLLAND				347–719		165	3
TOTALS	16 (*15)	23 (*22)		24 (*15)		6	69

* Divisions committed in battle—51.
# Divisions committed against Seventh US Army. Equivalent strength—20.

c. Third US Army Zones.

(1) BRITTANY. The enemy situation in BRITTANY remains unchanged. (See G-2 Estimate No. 8, Hq Third US Army, dated 24 August 1944.) The enemy is continuing defense of the major ports of BREST, LORIENT and ST. NAZAIRE in order to deny them to us as long as possible for tactical as well as logistical reasons.

(2) S of LOIRE River—From ANGERS-FOURS-ORLEANS. FFI and Tac/R indicate the presence in this area of the equivalent of two enemy divisions. While a few small-scale forays have been made N of the river, the enemy's attitude throughout the sector has been wholly defensive. Lack of any substantial bases of supply precludes a large scale operation. Indications point to the enemy's use of this area as a corridor of escape Eastward for remnants from BRITTANY and units from the BAY OF BISCAY (159 Inf Tng Div, GHQ Bns and miscellaneous Elms).

(3) Third US Army Zone of Advance.

(a) Of the total shown in Subpars (9), (12), and (13) above, the enemy's strength in contact in the Third US Army Zone of Advance is estimated as equivalent to three and one-half Inf and one-half Pz divisions, 23 Inf and 1 Tk Bns. In immediate reserve the enemy is estimated to have an additional three Inf and one Pz divisions, 22 Inf and 2 Tk Bns. The enemy has the capability of piecemeal reinforcement of this sector in seven days with the equivalent of another two Inf and one Pz Divs, 16 Inf and 2 Tk Bns, making a combined total of six and one-half Inf and two and one-half Pz divisions, 49 Inf and 5 Tk Bns.

(b) On the Southeastern flank of the Third US Army, in the TROYES-CHAUMONT area, the enemy has the capability of assembling from the area S of the LOIRE, Upper RHÔNE Valley, Italy, Germany, and elsewhere, in three days the equivalent of three Inf divisions, 18 Bns, and in seven days the equivalent of four Inf divisions and 1 Tk Bn. This force could be employed to attack our exposed Southern flank, or as reinforcement against our frontal advances.

2. CONCLUSIONS.

a. Enemy Capabilities.

(1) BRITTANY. The enemy is capable of continuing the defense of the major ports of BREST, LORIENT and ST. NAZAIRE in order to deny them to us as long as possible for tactical as well as logistical reasons.

(2) S of LOIRE River–From ANGERS–FOURS–ORLEANS. In this area the enemy has the capability of attempting a Northward thrust to disrupt our lines of communication and force us to employ troops that might otherwise be used in exerting pressure against him in our zone of advance.

(3) Third US Army Zone of Advance.

(a) The enemy is capable of delaying and defending to the E and counterattacking from the S.

(b) The enemy is capable of withdrawing troops from the S to NE as [and] using them as reinforcements or replacements across our Eastward line of advance.

(c) The enemy is capable of mounting small-scale local counterattacks, spearheaded by Tks, in the REIMS-CHALONS-TROYES area to cover his withdrawal behind the AISNE-MEUSE Rivers.

(d) The enemy is capable of attacking our exposed SE flank with the equivalent of three Inf divisions in three days and four Infantry divisions and 1 or 2 Tk Bns in seven days.

(e) The enemy is capable of establishing a defensive position based on the AISNE-MEUSE Rivers and undertaking to hold this position with the equivalent of six and one-half Inf and two and one-half Pz divisions, while bringing in reserves from Germany, Norway, Italy and more distant fronts.

(f) The enemy is capable of holding on the AISNE-MEUSE Rivers, and attacking our exposed SE flank with the equivalent of three Inf divisions in three days and 1 or 2 Tk Bns in seven days.

b. <u>Conclusions</u>.

Capabilities (a), (b), and (c) are favored in that order.

G-2 ESTIMATE NO. 10

1 November 1944

Maps: GSGS 4249, FRANCE; GSGS 4416, GERMANY AND FRANCE; Scale 1/100,000

1. <u>SUMMARY OF THE ENEMY SITUATION</u>.

a. <u>General</u>.

Tightly ringed on the EAST and WEST by the Allied and Russian Armies, and defending and delaying on the NORTH and on the SOUTH, the enemy is confronted with the desperate dilemma of deciding where to employ the depleted reserves he is frantically trying to scrape together to avert complete collapse before winter sets in. The enemy's only hope to stave off complete destruction this year is to deadlock the battlefronts long enough to permit the approaching cold and wet weather to engulf them in bogs of mud, and freezing temperatures. If he can accomplish this he will win the precious time he needs to muster his resources to organize, equip and train a new Army and Air Force. If he can gain it and secure the winter months to refurbish his combat resources, the enemy will have the capability of prolonging the war to costly lengths. If he does not win this time, he faces early annihilation.

b. <u>Overall Capabilities</u>.

(1) In this desperate struggle for time the enemy has a number of favorable factors of vital tactical advantage to him. One, is the increasingly inclement weather limiting Allied air operations. Another, is short interior lines of communication and the fact that . . . are under the control of forces friendly to him and hostile to us. Third, is terrain favorable for defense and delay in successive positions, powerfully reinforced with extensive field fortifications and organized positions. A fourth, is detailed knowledge of this terrain, plus the time to sow it with mines and prepared demolitions. Still another important advantage is time and personnel to establish a network of agents, spies and saboteurs to operate in our rear when we overrun this terrain. Finally, the enemy has the powerful advantage of friendly population on whom we not only can place no reli-

ance for either support or information, but which may be actively subversive and hostile in attitude and act.

(2) Developments in the last few weeks have repeatedly demonstrated the great value of these favorable factors to the enemy. As a result of weather-restricted Allied air operations, the enemy has been able both to effect a considerable build-up in the strength and capabilities of the GAF and to execute troop movements of considerable length with relative speed and effectiveness. He has also been able to infiltrate agents and spies behind our lines. And, by the use of the favorable terrain and his extensive fortified and organized defensive positions, the enemy has been able to block catastrophic breakthroughs into GERMANY proper by utilizing low-quality makeshift reserves. Further, he has been able to secure the maximum employment out of these reserves by being able to shuttle them quickly from one threatened sector to another, thus allowing him to husband the better quality forces he is endeavoring to build up into a mobile strategic reserve for possible greater future threats.

(3) As of this date the enemy's overall pool of potential reinforcements against the EAST and/or WEST is estimated as follows:

GERMANY	13 divisions
DENMARK	2 divisions
NORWAY	16 divisions
FINLAND	5 divisions
ITALY	5 divisions
Western Front	<u>10</u> divisions (reforming)
Total	51 divisions

The above figure of fifty-one divisions does not include an estimate equivalent of five divisions in independent battalions Kampfgruppen and other miscellaneous units that could be employed as replacements and reinforcements.

(4) The total of fifty-one divisions is only a nominal capability. No divisions from the Italian Front have appeared on either the EAST or WEST in over a month, and there are no reports of large troop movements from that Theater. Also, only one division (269 Inf) has so far been identified on the WEST from SCANDANAVIA, although considerable troop movements from there have been reported. Similarly, although the enemy is making strenuous efforts to evacuate troops from FINLAND, so far none have been identified from that sector. The probabilities favor the enemy succeeding in withdrawing some of his beleaguered forces

from SCANDANAVIA, but it also is likely that these withdrawals will be increments rather than complete divisions, as was the case in BRITTANY when movement difficulties to NORMANDY forced the enemy to commit portions of divisions from battalion upward in size.

(5)For the purpose of this estimate it is assumed that the enemy's current major dispositions will remain unchanged for the present. On the basis of the above enumerated considerations it is therefore estimated, that the enemy's actual capability of reinforcing the EAST or WEST within the next thirty days is as follows:

GERMANY	13 divisions
DENMARK	2 divisions
NORWAY	4 divisions
FINLAND	2 divisions
ITALY	3 divisions
Western Front	10 divisions (reforming)
Total	34 divisions

(6) While possessing the capability of withdrawing the equivalent of six divisions from NORWAY and FINLAND and three from ITALY in the next thirty days, the enemy faces numerous difficulties in accomplishing that. Russian thrusts into NORWAY and mounting Allied Naval and Air operations in that area confront the enemy with increasing hazards to effective evacuations. In Southeastern EUROPE the situation is similarly precarious for the enemy as regards withdrawals from ITALY. Russian and Partisan advances in HUNGARY and the BALKANS confront him with the possibility of his main routes of egress from ITALY being cut off. By withdrawing to the Italian ALPS the enemy could maintain this Southwestern flank with relatively small forces, not over six of the equivalent of fourteen divisions he is now estimated to have in ITALY. Such a withdrawal at this time would enable him to evacuate the bulk of his Italian forces. But if he delays doing this, and the BALKANS are overrun by the Soviets and the Partisans, the enemy is likely to be unable to extricate more than a small portion of his Italian garrison.

(7) The above estimated thirty-four divisions (250,000 troops) give the enemy the capability of piecemeal reinforcement against either the EAST or the WEST with the equivalent of four divisions the first week, eight divisions the second week, ten divisions the third week, and twelve divisions the fourth week. This capability, however, is confined strictly to one of these two crucial Fronts. The enemy cannot maintain such a

flow of reinforcements to both Fronts at the same time. If tactical developments force him to make a choice between the two Fronts, the enemy will be compelled to decide which confronts him with the most critical menace.

(8) So far the enemy has repeatedly demonstrated his dexterity in improvising makeshift reinforcements, and it can be expected that he will continue to display this ingenuity. Further, powerfully operating in his favor in the WEST in meeting this dilemma are two massive barriers to offensive operations: (1) the heavily fortified SIEGFRIED Line and supplementary organized positions, and (2) terrain unfavorable to mechanized cross-country movement, particularly in the prevailing inclement weather. These natural and man-made obstacles permit the enemy to strongly defend and delay with a minimum of troops, and he can be counted on to employ these two [to] great advantage to the utmost to enable him to meet commitments in the EAST with a maximum [of] reinforcements while endeavoring to contain the WEST with a minimum build-up. However, there is one factor as regards the Eastern Front that may prove decisive in the situation. This is the Russians' historic capability for effective winter warfare. This is a very distinctive capability not possessed by either the enemy or the Allies. In this war, as in others in the past, the Russians have smashingly demonstrated their great offensive power in the winter. This capability in the coming months is a threat of the gravest moment to the enemy.

(9) On the basis of the above assumption, that the enemy will defend and delay in the WEST with a minimum of reinforcements in order to be able to bolster the EAST with a maximum of reserves, it is estimated that the enemy has the capability in the next thirty days of reinforcing the WEST with the equivalent of three divisions the first week and thereafter four divisions a week for the next three weeks. It is further estimated that the bulk of these reinforcements will come from the ten divisions (seven Panzer and three Para) currently withdrawn from the line and undergoing reforming in GERMANY, plus the thirteen new divisions estimated being organized in GERMANY. The seven Panzer and three Para divisions undergoing reconstruction are actually in immediate reserve in the WEST and, with the enemy's short interior lines of communication and favorable weather conditions, can be committed relatively quickly on any sector of this Front. Also, being predominantly Panzer they would appreciably increase his artillery strength, thus giving him a double advantage in these reinforcements. Mobile artillery would greatly complement the favorable terrain and numerous fortified and organized

defensive positions that constitute the backbone of the enemy's defenses in the WEST. Further, he also possesses the capability of employing these mobile reserves according to the danger of the offensive threat versus terrain; e.g., where the Allies have to fight terrain he will use these mobile reserves in small increments, and where the terrain is favorable and the Allies must overcome defensive positions, he will use his Panzers for local containing counterattacks or for a general counteroffensive.

2. THIRD US ARMY FRONT.

a. General.

(1) Operations in the WEST the past month indicate that the enemy's priority of threats there are as follows:

(a) First US ARMY zone aimed at the great RHUR [RUHR] industrial center.

(b) 21 Army Group zone that would outflank the SIEGFRIED Line on the North and open the way for envelopment of the RUHR.

(c) Sixth Army Group zone that would outflank the SIEGFRIED Line on the South through the BELFORT Pass.

(d) The relatively lightly fortified sector East of LUXEMBOURG.

(2) In view of the terrain and other enumerated favorable factors, it is indicated that the resumption of large scale offensive operations in any of these sectors may be met initially by a wait-and-see policy by the enemy. In the zone facing the densely populated RUHR Valley, the enemy might confine himself to defending and delaying pending a break-through. This sector lends itself readily to effective defense with a minimum of forces because of its heavy congestion which makes a rapid break-through difficult. The area would permit the enemy to resort to house to house warfare, in which he excels from a background of extensive experience.

(3) The zone occupied by the Third US Army is one of the quiescent sectors. It includes the strongest fortified portions of the SIEGFRIED Line and also some of the most difficult cross-country movement terrain in the WEST. However, the Third US Army's historic record of crushing break-through assaults must be deeply imbedded in the enemy's mind. A successful break-through in this sector would not only lay him open to an envelopment of the RUHR on the South but also would prevent effective reinforcement of the BELFORT Pass area in the event of an offensive thrust by the Sixth Army Group. Such a successful thrust would crumple the enemy's whole Southern wall of defense and place two powerful hostile Armies in a strategic position to strike directly at the heart of GERMANY itself.

b. Conclusions.

(1) On the basis of the above assumption it is estimated that the enemy has the capability of:

(a) D+1—reinforcing against the Third US Army with the equivalent of one Panzer division; 11 Pz now in immediate reserve in the Third US Army zone.

(b) D+3—reinforcing against the Third US Army with the equivalent of two Infantry divisions from GERMANY.

(c) D+6—reinforcing the SIEGFRIED Line and supplementary organized positions in Third US Army zone of advance with Fortress and other miscellaneous units from GERMANY equivalent to one Infantry division.

(d) D+14—reinforcing with two Panzer and two Infantry divisions; the Panzer divisions drawn from the seven now undergoing reforming in GERMANY, one Infantry division from SCANDANAVIA and one from GERMANY.

(e) D+21—reinforcing with one Panzer and three Infantry divisions; the Panzer from the seven now undergoing reorganization in GERMANY, one Infantry division from GERMANY, one from SCANDANAVIA and one from ITALY.

(f) D+30—reinforcing with two Panzer and two Infantry divisions; one Panzer division from another sector in the WEST, second Panzer from the seven undergoing reforming in GERMANY, one division from the three Para divisions undergoing reorganization and the second Infantry division from GERMANY.

(2) With a strength estimated the equivalent of five and one-half divisions in the Third US Army zone as of this date, on the basis of the above enumerated capability, it is indicated that the enemy has the potentiality of a build-up to a total of nine and one-half divisions by D+6. Further, that by D+14 the enemy has the capability of a 150% build-up for a total of thirteen and one-half divisions. And, in the third and fourth weeks, the enemy has the capability of still further increasing his build-up 100% weekly for a total, by the end of thirty days, equivalent to twenty-one and one-half divisions against the Third US Army.

(3) It is considered probable that the enemy's build-up against a Third US Army offensive would be restricted by similar operations on other zones of the Western Front. The extent to which the capability of build-up against the Third US Army would be obstructed by this factor would depend on the situation at the time. Developments in other sectors might very well prevent the enemy from fulfilling his estimated reinforcement capability against the Third US Army, but, on the assumption that

his major dispositions will remain unchanged, the enemy has the capability of reinforcing against the Third US Army as outlined above.

3. <u>ESTIMATE OF ENEMY STRENGTH IN THE THIRD US ARMY ZONE.</u>

a. The estimated enemy strength in the Third US Army zones as of 1 November is as follows:

CORPS ZONE	IDENTIFIED IN CONTACT		EST AVAILABLE AS IMMEDIATE RESERVES	
	UNITS	EST EFFECTIVE COMBAT STRENGTH	UNITS	EST EFFECTIVE COMBAT STRENGTH
XX Corps	17 SS Pz Gren Div (Elm)	1,500 (10 A[ssault] G[uns] or Tks)	416 Inf Div (Elm)	6,000
	19 Inf Div (Elm)	4,000	353 Inf Div 50 Inf Div (Rem) 91 Inf Div (Elm) 2 SS Pz Div (Elm)	6,000 (30 Tks)
	416 Inf Div (Elm)	2,000		
	462 Inf Div	4,500		
	Misc	6,500	Misc	5,000 (25 AG or Tks)
Total Effective Combat Strength		18,500 (10 AG or Tks)		17,000 (55 AG or Tks)
III Corps	17 SS Pz Gren Div (Elm)	1,500 (15 AG or Tks)	11 Pz Div*	4,500 (65 Tks)
			111 Pz Brig (Rem)	
	48 Inf Div (Elm)	2,500	19 Inf Div	1,500
			48 Inf Div (Elm)	4,500
	361 Gren Div	7,000	553 Gren Div	3,000
	559 Gren Div	4,000	21 Pz Div 113 Pz Brig 106 Pz Brig 405 Adm Div 1 GAF Tng Div	6,000 (50 Tks)
	Misc	6,000	Misc	7,000
Total Effective Combat Strength		21,000 (15 AG or Tks)		26,500 (115 Tks)
TOTAL EFFECTIVE COMBAT STRENGTH	Equivalent to: 5 Divs 36 Inf Bns 32 Misc Bns 65 Bns	39,500 (25 AG or Tks)	Equivalent to: 5½ Divs 37 Inf Bns 5 Tk Bns 32 Misc Bns 72 Bns	43,500 (170 AG or Tks)

*If 11 Pz, estimated to be in immediate reserve, is counted in the Zone total, the enemy's strength is estimated at 5½ Divs.

b. <u>Estimate of Enemy Strength in the METZ Area—Bridgehead and METZ Forts.</u>

(1) Enemy strength in the METZ area as of this date is estimated as follows:

(a) In METZ bridgehead—4,500

(b) METZ forts—2,000

Total—6,500*

*(Not included in this estimate are an undetermined number of troops impressed into combat units from the large local German civilian population.)

(2) Artillery definitely established to be in METZ forts:

(a) 88mm pieces—12

(b) 105mm pieces—40

(c) 150mm pieces—18

Total—70*

* (In addition, the enemy has an undetermined number of artillery pieces of various calibers in and around the forts.)

4. <u>ENEMY CAPABILITIES ON THE BASIS OF THE ENEMY'S CURRENT DISPOSITIONS IN THE THIRD US ARMY ZONE.</u>

a. <u>Capabilities—as of 1 November:</u>

(1) The enemy is capable of defending and delaying in our zone of advance, counterattacking locally with Infantry and Armor in an attempt to block and contain Eastward thrusts.

(2) The enemy is capable of making a fortress stand at METZ to impede our Eastward advance by the diversion of troops, artillery, ammunition and aviation.

(3) The enemy is capable of pivoting on METZ to establish a general defensive line paralleling the SIEGFRIED Line to gain time to bring in reserves from other fronts, to man the SIEGFRIED Line and supplementary defensive position, and to secure the powerful tactical advantage of the crippling wet and cold winter weather.

(4) The enemy is capable of taking advantage of favorable terrain in our zone of advance to construct new organized defensive positions and create inundations for employment in conjunction with the inclement weather, to defend and delay against our Eastward thrust.

b. <u>Conclusions.</u>

Capabilities (1) and (2) are favored, executed in combination with (3) and (4).

Allen's Recommendation for Promotion, November 9, 1944

HEADQUARTERS
THIRD UNITED STATES ARMY
Office of the Assistant Chief of Staff, G-2
APO 403

9 November 1944
Memorandum

To: Chief of Staff.

1. The attached recommendation for the promotion of Lt Colonel Robert S. Allen, 0-481033, to the rank of Colonel, Cavalry, dated 13 August 1944, is resubmitted for consideration in view of the continued outstanding achievements of this officer during the additional period.

2. In addition to the outstanding and weighty responsibilities performed by this officer since in the G-2 Section, Third US Army, as now constituted the following additional data is informally submitted for consideration of this recommendation:

a. Lt Col Allen was commissioned:

2d Lieutenant, Cavalry—May, 1918
1st Lieutenant, Cavalry—September 1921
Captain, Cavalry—March 1925
Major, Cavalry—July, 1941
Lt Colonel, Cavalry—May, 1943

and will have on 1 January 1945 completed approximately 26 years of commissioned service.

b. During World War I, he was in active commissioned service from May, 1918 to April 1919; was then commissioned 2d Lieutenant, Cavalry, Wisconsin National Guard about December 1920, from which he was discharged as a Captain in December 1928. At that time he was commissioned a Captain, Cavalry Reserve, which grade he held until commissioned a Major and called to active duty in July, 1941 [1942].

c. He is a graduate of the National Guard Troop Officers course at Cavalry School, 1924; served two or three tours of fifteen days each while a reserve officer and has been on continued active duty since July, 1941 [1942]. He graduated from Special Course No. 10 (G-2), Command and General Staff School in February, 1943, with an academic rating of "excellent"; he was Corps G-2 of XXI Provisional Corps in Louisiana Maneuver Area October and November, 1943; and organized, directed and conducted three schools for G-2/S-2's of the Third Army which extended over a period from July to November, 1943.

3. Since joining Headquarters Third Army in March, 1943, all of the services of Lt Colonel Allen have been outstanding. Great reliance has been placed on him and his professional skill and ability. He is eminently qualified to be a Corps or Army G-2 with emphasis on Operational intelligence and is so capable that I would not hesitate to recommend him a Corps G-2 replacement without the necessity of a period of indoctrination for more thorough familiarization of the auxiliary agencies with which he would more intimately be in contact than he has since working on duty as the operational executive of this section.

4. Informal request to G-1 as to Lt Colonel Allen's relative standing on the list of Lt Colonels of this headquarters indicates that he is about No. 20. It is further my opinion that this officer could assume any duties, commensurate with his recommended rank, with a Cavalry organization and give a good account of himself in combat in such capacity.

OSCAR W. KOCH
Colonel, GSC,
AC of S, G-2

Abbreviations

AA	antiaircraft
AAs	auxiliary agencies
AB	Airborne
AC	aircraft
actg	acting
ADC	aide-de-camp
ADSEC	Advanced Section
adv	advance
AEAF	Allied Expeditionary Air Force
AEF	Allied Expeditionary Force
AF	Air Force
AG	adjutant general; Army Group; assault gun
AGF	Army Ground Forces
AL	Air Landing
APO	Army Post Office
ARCO	air reconnaissance coordinating officer
Armd	Armored
Arty	Artillery
asst	assistant
AT	antitank
AWOL	absent without leave
BBC	British Broadcasting Corporation
BG	brigadier general
bn	battalion
brig	brigade
bty or btry	battery
C	captured
Cav	Cavalry
CC	Combat Command
CCS	Combined Chiefs of Staff
CE	chief engineer
C/G	commanding general
CI	counterintelligence

CIA	Central Intelligence Agency (U.S.)
CIB	China-India-Burma
CIC	Counter Intelligence Corps
C-in-C	commander in chief
CIS	Combined Intelligence Section
Cmd	command
Cmdr	commander
Cmdt	commandant
CO	commanding officer
COI	Coordinator of Information
Com Z or COMZ	communications zone
Cositintrep	Combined Situation Intelligence Report
COSSAC	Chief of Staff to the Supreme Allied Commander
Coys	companies
CP	command post
C/S	chief of staff
CW	chemical warfare
Det	detachment
Div	Division
DP	displaced person(s)
DSC	Distinguished Service Cross
DSM	Distinguished Service Medal
EAM-ELAS	Ethnikón Apeleftherotikón Métopon–Ethnikós Laïkós Apeleftherotikós Strátos (Greek National Liberation Front–National Popular Liberation Army)
EDES	Ellínikos Dímokratikos Ethnikós Strátos (Greek Democratic National Army)
EEI	essential elements of information
Elm	element(s)
EM	enlisted man (men)
Engr	Engineer
Est	estimate(s); estimated
ETO	European Theater of Operations
ETOUSA	European Theater of Operations United States Army
Ex O	executive officer
FDR	Franklin Delano Roosevelt
FFI	French Forces of the Interior
FO	field order
F/O	flight officers
FUSA	First United States Army

FUSAG	First United States Army Group
Fwd	forward
GAF	German Air Force
Gds	Guards
GHQ	General Headquarters
GOP	Grand Old Party (Republican)
Gp	Group
GS	General Staff
GSC	General Staff Corps
HMG	heavy machine gun
Hq or HQ	headquarters
Inf	Infantry
Intl	Intelligence
IPW	interrogation prisoner of war
ISUM	intelligence summary
JCS	Joint Chiefs of Staff
K	killed
KGB	State Security Committee (Soviet)
KO	knockout
LCT	landing craft, tank
LCVP	landing craft, vehicles and personnel
LD	line of departure
L/G	lieutenant general
LM	Legion of Merit
Ln	liaison
LST	landing ship, tank
Mcz	Mechanized
ME	main effort
Med	medium (bombers); Medical
MG	machine gun; major general; military government
MII	Military Intelligence interpreter
MIS	Military Intelligence Service
Misc	miscellaneous
MP	military police
msg	message
Mt or Mtn	mountain
MT	motorized transport
NARA II	National Archives and Records Administration II, College Park, MD
NCO	noncommissioned officer

NG	National Guard
NKVD	People's Commissariat for Internal Affairs (Soviet)
NO	New Orleans
NOIC	naval officer in charge
NSA	National Security Agency
NUSA	Ninth United States Army
O	officer(s)
OB	order of battle
OCE	Office of the Chief Engineer
OKW	Oberkommando der Wehrmacht
op	operation
OP	observation post
Ord	Ordnance
OSS	Office of Strategic Services
P & PW	public relations and psychological warfare
PA	Public Affairs
para	parachute
PG	panzergrenadier
PI	photo interpretation
PM	provost marshal
POE	port of embarkation
PP	pilotless plane
PR	photo reconnaissance; periodic report; public relations
PRO	public relations officer
PW	prisoner(s) of war
PWE	prisoner(s) of war, European
PWX	Prisoner of War Executive Branch
Pz	panzer
Q/G	Quartermaster General
QM	Quartermaster
RA	Regular Army
RAF	Royal Air Force
Rcn	reconnaissance
RCT	Regimental Combat Team
Reg	Regular (Army)
regt	regiment
Rem	remnants
Res	Reserve
RG	Records Group
RI	radio interception

RM	Reichsmarks
RR	railroad
Sec	Section
SHAEF	Supreme Headquarters Allied Expeditionary Forces
SI	Special Intelligence
Sig O	signals officer
SIS	Secret Intelligence Service (Br.)
Sitrep	situation report
Sit Sec	Situation Section
SLU	Special Liaison Unit
SO	Special Operations
SOE	Special Operations Executive
SOS	Services of Supply
SOW	secretary of war
SP	self-propelled
sq	squadron
SR	short-range
SRH	Special Research History
SS	Schutzstaffel (Hitler's intelligence and security force)
S/Sgt	staff sergeant
SUSA	Seventh United States Army
TAC	Tactical Air Command
TAC/R	Tactical Reconnaissance
TAF	Tactical Air Force
TD	tank destroyer; temporary duty
TF	Task Force
TIS	Theater Intelligence Section
Tk	Tank
Tng	Training
T/O	table of organization
TTA	tactical terrain analysis
TUSA	Third United States Army
TWX	teletype writer exchange
UFO	unidentified flying object
UK	United Kingdom
USAF	United States Air Force
VE	victory in Europe
VG	Volksgrenadier
VIP	very important person (people)
W	wounded

WAC	Women's Auxiliary Corps
WD	War Department
W/O	warrant officer
W/T	wireless telegraphy

Notes

Editor's Preface

1. George F. Hofmann, *Through Mobility We Conquer: The Mechanization of U.S. Cavalry* (Lexington: University Press of Kentucky, 2006), 364–67; John Nelson Rickard, *Advance and Destroy: Patton as Commander in the Bulge* (Lexington: University Press of Kentucky, 2011).

2. Robert S. Allen, *Lucky Forward: The History of Patton's Third U.S. Army* (New York: Vanguard Press, 1947).

3. Lieutenant Colonel M. C. Helfers, "My Personal Experience with High Level Intelligence," November 1947, Melvin Helfers Papers, The Citadel Archives and Museum, Charleston, SC.

4. John F. Cheadle Oral History, interview by Edward B. Williams, June 6, 2003, Coldspring, TX, http://digital.library.shsu.edu/cdm/ref/collection/p16042c0111/id/44.

Introduction

1. Robert S. Allen 201 File, Maneuver Center of Excellence, Fort Benning, GA.

2. Samuel Nicholson, "A Most Unlikely Agent: Robert S. Allen," *Washington Decoded,* September 11, 2010, http://www.washingtondecoded.com/site/2010/09/a-most-unlikely-agent.html. See also Samuel Nicholson, "A Most Unlikely Agent: Robert S. Allen," *Intelligencer* 18, no. 1 (Fall–Winter 2010): 35–41.

3. Thomas Reed Powell, review of *Nine Old Men, Yale Law Journal* 46, no. 3 (January 1937): 561–63.

4. See http://www.authentichistory.com/1939-1945/1-war/2-PH/19411207_1830_NBC_Blue Drew_Pearson_and_Robert_S_Allen.html.

5. Oscar W. Koch, *G-2: Intelligence for Patton* (Philadelphia: Whitmore, 1971), 132.

6. See Project 1947, http://www.project1947.com/allen/index.htm.

7. See http://www.foia.cia.gov/sites/default/files/document_conversions/89801/DOC_0001451843.pdf.

8. Frank McCarthy Collection, box 13, Scripts and Screenplays, 1961–1969, George C. Marshall Foundation, Lexington, VA.

9. Ibid., box 3, Pre-Production, 1953–1970.

10. Ladislas Farago, *Patton: Ordeal and Triumph* (New York: Ivan Obolensky, 1964), 851.

11. John Earl Haynes, Harvey Klehr, and Alexander Vassiliev, *Spies: The Rise and Fall of the KGB in America* (New Haven, CT: Yale University Press, 2009), 159, 191. Vassiliev's research notes can be found at http://digitalarchive .wilsoncenter.org/collection/86/vassiliev-notebooks.

12. Memorandum for Chief, Security Research Staff, September 7, 1967, http://www.archives.gov/declassification/iscap/pdf/2011-054-doc3.pdf.

13. Adeline Sunday, *Come Live with Me and the Colonel* (Pittsburgh: Dorrance, 2009).

1. From New Jersey to England

1. Courtney Hicks Hodges (1887–1966) failed out of West Point in 1905, enlisted as a private in 1906, and was commissioned in 1909. He was promoted to lieutenant general and assumed command of Southern Defense Command, which included Third Army, in February 1943. For a recent biography of Hodges, see Stephan T. Wishnevsky, *Courtney Hicks Hodges: From Private to Four-Star General in the United States Army* (Jefferson, NC: McFarland, 2006). See also John T. Greenwood, ed., *Normandy to Victory: The War Diary of General Courtney H. Hodges and the First U.S. Army* (Lexington: University Press of Kentucky, 2008).

2. Frederick H. Kelley (1896–1986), infantry, was executive officer of the staff. The headquarters commandant was Colonel Rufus S. Bratton.

3. Beatrice Ayer Patton (1886–1953) married George S. Patton Jr. in 1910. She suffered an aortic aneurysm that caused her to fall from her horse, leading to her death.

4. George A. Davis (1892–1969) served as chief, Operations and Training Division, Headquarters, Replacement and Training Command, from February to May 1942, at which point he became chief of staff of X Corps. In January 1943 Davis was appointed chief of staff, Third Army.

5. Richard Gray McKee (1896–1986), infantry, graduated from West Point in 1918. In July 1943 he became the assistant chief of staff, G-3, of Third Army at Fort Sam Houston, TX.

6. Frederick Stone Matthews (b. 1892) began his career as an infantry officer in the 40th Infantry Regiment of the Maryland National Guard from 1914 to 1917. He joined the Regular Army in 1917 and served on the Mexican border. He graduated from the Command and General Staff College in 1932. Matthews commanded a U.S. task force and British forces in British Guiana. He was assistant chief of staff, G-1, in Second Army in 1942 and assumed the same position in Third Army. See Larry I. Bland and Sharon R. Stevens, eds., *The Papers of George Catlett Marshall*, vol. 3, *"The Right Man for the Job" December 7, 1941–May 31, 1943* (Baltimore: Johns Hopkins University Press, 1991), 406. Matthews's papers are in the Library of Congress.

7. HMS *Queen Mary,* nicknamed the "Grey Ghost," was the largest and fastest troop transport ship of World War II.

8. George Albert Hadd (1892–1962) served as adjutant general under Hodges.

9. Allen could be referring to Colonel Clell B. Perkins, chief veterinarian of Third Army.

10. This individual could not be identified.

11. No biographical information on Zwrick could be found.

12. After a refit at the Todd shipyards in New York in 1941, *Ile de France,* a luxurious cruise liner, was painted gray and became a full-fledged troopship. It sailed under the dual flags of Britain and Free France. The Third Army after-action report states that the *Ile de France* departed on March 13.

13. Borders served as executive officer of the G-3 Section.

14. No biographical information on Davis could be found.

15. Arthur Pulsifer (1895–1996), infantry, graduated from West Point in 1918. He transferred to signals in March 1925.

16. Omar Nelson Bradley (1893–1981), infantry, graduated from West Point in 1915. When Patton assumed command of II Corps in early 1943, he made Bradley his deputy commander. Bradley assumed command of the corps in the final stages of the Tunisian campaign and led it during the invasion of Sicily. He was appointed to command First U.S. Army for the Normandy invasion on October 16, 1943. See Omar N. Bradley, *A Soldier's Story* (New York: Henry Holt, 1951), and Omar N. Bradley with Clay Blair, *A General's Life* (New York: Simon & Schuster, 1983).

17. James Grafton Anding (1903–1983), field artillery, graduated from West Point in 1924. He served as assistant chief of staff, G-4, in Third Army from February 1942 to March 1944.

18. John C. Macdonald was born in Nova Scotia in 1895 and became a U.S. citizen in 1917. He received a commission in the Officers' Reserve Corps that year and graduated from Norwich University in 1920. Macdonald was Third Army's assistant chief of staff, G-3, operations, from May 1943 to March 1944. See George F. Hofmann, *Through Mobility We Conquer: The Mechanization of U.S. Cavalry* (Lexington: University Press of Kentucky, 2006), 353–54.

19. George Devers Swanson (1912–1944) served in the G-2 Section but later became executive officer of the 43rd Cavalry Reconnaissance Squadron. He was killed in action on November 5, 1944, while leading a dismounted attack into Berg.

20. McDowell served in the Provost Marshal Section.

21. John Francis Cheadle (1914–2005) graduated from the University of Oklahoma in 1939. He was the officer in charge of the staff briefings at 0900 every morning.

22. William K. Goolrick Jr. (1920–2012) graduated from the Virginia Military Institute in 1941. See William K. Goolrick and Ogden Tanner, *The Battle of the Bulge* (New York: Time-Life Books, 1979). After the war Goolrick earned a master's degree in English literature from Columbia University; he worked as a

correspondent for *Life,* as chief editorial writer for the *Saturday Evening Post,* and as an editor at Time-Life Books.

23. Oscar W. Koch (1897–1970) first met Patton while teaching at the Cavalry School at Fort Riley, KS, in the 1930s. He was promoted to colonel on January 7, 1943. See Koch, *G-2: Intelligence for Patton* (Philadelphia: Whitmore, 1971), 132; Robert Hays, *Patton's Oracle: General Oscar Koch, as I Knew Him* (Savoy, IL: Lucidus Books, 2013).

24. Franklin Delano Roosevelt (1882–1945) was the thirty-second president of the United States, serving from 1933 to his death in 1945.

25. The Theater Intelligence Section was established by the British in 1940. When Supreme Headquarters Allied Expeditionary Forces (SHAEF) was established, it took over the majority of the section's personnel and files. U.S. personnel were added in 1943. See Forrest C. Pogue, *U.S. Army in World War II: The Supreme Command* (Washington, DC: Center of Military History, 1989), 71–72.

26. Overlord was the code name given to the Allied invasion of France scheduled for May–June 1944.

27. Neptune was the amphibious cross-channel assault phase of Overlord and consisted of capturing an initial beachhead, capturing Cherbourg, and developing airfields in the Caen area.

28. Second British Army was commanded by Lieutenant General Sir Miles C. Dempsey. See Peter Rostron, *The Life and Times of General Sir Miles Dempsey: Monty's Army Commander* (Barnsley, UK: Pen & Sword, 2010).

29. First United States Army Group was a skeleton headquarters destined to command American forces in the field. The existence of this skeleton headquarters was exploited by the joint planners to flesh out the order of battle necessary to execute the large-scale deception of Fortitude South, intended to focus German attention on the Pas de Calais. See Roger Hesketh, *Fortitude: The D-Day Deception Campaign* (London: Ermin's Press, 1999), 90–93.

30. On February 13, 1944, SHAEF replaced and absorbed the planning group called the Chief of Staff to the Supreme Allied Commander (COSSAC), which had been established in April 1943. See Pogue, *Supreme Command.*

31. Dwight David Eisenhower (1890–1969) graduated from West Point in 1915. He was appointed commander in chief of Allied Expeditionary Forces for Operation Torch in August 1942 and was appointed Supreme Commander for Overlord in December 1943. See Dwight D. Eisenhower, *Crusade in Europe* (New York: Doubleday, 1948).

32. Headquarters European Theater of Operations United States Army was established in London on June 8, 1942, succeeding Headquarters U.S. Army in the British Isles, which had been established in London on January 8, 1942. Until the establishment of SHAEF on February 13, 1944, HQ ETOUSA participated in operational planning for the Allied invasion of Western Europe. HQ ETOUSA was commanded by Lieutenant General Jacob L. Devers.

33. John Clifford Hodges Lee (1887–1958), engineer, graduated from West Point in 1909. Marshall appointed him to command the Services of Supply in the

United Kingdom in May 1942. Lee was promoted to lieutenant general in February 1944 and became deputy theater commander for administration, ETOUSA. For biographical information, see Roland G. Ruppenthal, *U.S. Army in World War II: Logistical Support of the Armies,* vol. 1, *May 1941–September 1944* (Washington, DC: Center of Military History, 1989), 33–36.

34. Allen could be referring to Major Louis P. Dups.

35. Lorraine L. Manly (1907–1989) served as assistant adjutant general under Hodges.

36. This individual could not be identified.

37. Major William C. Sylvan served as Hodges's senior aide-de-camp and assisted in compiling First Army's war diary. For additional information, see Dempsey Allphin, *Two of Us Ain't Going* (Lincoln, NE: Writer's Club Press, 2001). Allphin was an administrative assistant to Hodges.

38. Bernard Law Montgomery (1887–1976) was one of the most experienced commanders of World War II. During the battle for France in 1940, he commanded the 3rd "Iron" Division in the British Expeditionary Force. After Dunkirk, Montgomery trained British and Canadian formations and units in England until he assumed command of Eighth Army in August 1942. Montgomery's greatest feat may have been rebuilding Eighth Army's morale in the Western Desert and refocusing its mind-set from a defensive to an offensive one. He won a great defensive victory over Erwin Rommel at Alam Halfa in August 1942 and decisively defeated him at El Alamein in late October and early November, driving him back to Tunisia over the next three and a half months. In Tunisia, Montgomery fought a masterful defensive battle against Rommel at Medinine and subsequently broke the Mareth Line by a well-executed assault on El Hamma. Both were key victories that led to the final collapse of Axis power in Tunisia in May 1943. Montgomery commanded Eighth Army during Operation Husky, the invasion of Sicily in July 1944, and during the early phases of the campaign on the Italian mainland. He was appointed commander in chief of Twenty-First Army Group on December 24, 1944. See B. L. Montgomery, *The Memoirs of Field Marshal Montgomery of Alamein* (London: Collins, 1958).

39. Edward Thomas Williams (1901–1973) graduated from West Point in 1920.

40. No biographical information on Brehner could be found.

41. Willis Dale Crittenberger (1890–1980), cavalry, graduated from West Point in 1913. He took XIX Corps to England in January 1944 but was transferred to command IV Corps, which was scheduled to fight in Italy. See Stephen R. Taaffe, *Marshall and His Generals: U.S. Army Commanders in World War II* (Lawrence: University Press of Kansas, 2011), 123.

42. Hugh Joseph Gaffey (1895–1946), artillery, commanded 2nd Armored Division from April 1943 to April 1944. He then became Third Army chief of staff. See the chapter on Gaffey in David T. Zabecki, ed., *Chief of Staff: The Principal Officers behind History's Greatest Commanders, II: World War II to Korea*

and Vietnam (Annapolis, MD: Naval Institute Press, 2008).

43. Hobart Raymond Gay (1894–1983), cavalry, transferred to the Quartermaster Corps on June 11, 1934. Gay served as commander of the Fourteenth Quartermaster Battalion and division quartermaster in Patton's 2nd Armored Division in January 1941. He was promoted to colonel in December 1941 and to brigadier general in June 1943. He served as Patton's chief of staff of the Western Task Force during Operation Torch. He also served as chief of staff of Seventh Army and then moved on to do the same job in Third Army starting in February 1944. See Zabecki, *Chief of Staff.*

44. Major Charles B. Odom (1909–1988) began his military service with 134th General Hospital, the Louisiana State University School of Medicine unit, which was sent to Fort Jackson, SC, in 1942 for training. He became consultant to the surgeon in Third Army. Odom wrote a short book, *General George S. Patton and Eisenhower* (New Orleans: Word Picture Productions, 1985). See also Charles M. Province, *I Was Patton's Doctor: The Reminiscences of Colonel Charles B. Odom, M.D., Third Army Surgical Consultant and General Patton's Personal Physician* (privately published, 2010). This book is based on Province's correspondence with Odom from 1983 onward.

45. Operation Axehead was to be carried out by First Canadian Army once it had entered the eastern sector of the bridgehead; it envisioned capturing the ports of Le Havre and Rouen. See C. P. Stacey, *Official History of the Canadian Army in the Second World War, III: The Victory Campaign, Operations in North-West Europe, 1944–1945* (Ottawa: Queen's Printer, 1960), 39.

46. Swordhilt was a combined amphibious-airborne operation intended to seize an area east of Brest.

47. The 2nd Infantry Division was commanded by Major General Walter E. Robertson from May 1942 onward.

48. The 2nd Infantry Division returned to Fort Sam Houston in September 1942 and thereafter began training at Camp McCoy in Sparta, WI. See Walter E. Robertson, *Combat History of the Second Infantry Division in World War II* (Nashville, TN: Battery Press, 1979).

49. See Carlo D'Este, *Fatal Decision: Anzio and the Battle for Rome* (New York: HarperCollins, 1986).

50. Allen misuses the term *Reichswehr.* The Reichswehr was the German military organization in existence from 1918 to 1935. Hitler replaced it with the Wehrmacht in 1935.

51. By late 1944, the German army was filled with *Hilfswillige,* Russian prisoners of war.

52. The term *Waffen-SS* was first introduced into the SS administrative lexicon at the beginning of November 1939. See Bernd Wegner, *The Waffen-SS: Organization, Ideology and Function,* trans. Ronald Webster (London: Basil Blackwell, 1990).

53. Neptune's initial joint plan was promulgated by the combined commanders—Montgomery, Admiral Bertram Ramsay, and Air Chief Marshal Sir Trafford

Leigh-Mallory—on February 1, 1944. See Pogue, *Supreme Command*, 173–74. This was the only written campaign plan accepted by Montgomery.

54. The Ninth Air Force was officially constituted in the United Kingdom on October 16, 1943. See Colonel William B. Reed et al., *Condensed Analysis of the Ninth Air Force in the European Theater of Operations* (1946; reprint, Washington, DC: Office of Air Force History, 1984).

55. The theater was divided into a *combat zone*, the forward area required for active operations and the immediate administration of combat forces, and a *communications zone* (COMZ), containing the area required for the administration of the theater as a whole. The combat zone extended from the rear boundary of the corps to the forward edge of the battle area, and the *army service area* extended from the corps' rear boundary to the forward edge of the COMZ. The COMZ was divided into an Advanced Section (ADSEC), an Intermediate Section, and a Base Section. COMZ headquarters was located in Paris, and ADSEC headquarters was in Namur. The Base Section was subdivided into the Channel, Brittany, Seine, and Oise Base Sections. See War Department, FM 100-10, *Field Service Regulations, Administration*, November 15, 1943, 7; Roland G. Ruppenthal, *U.S. Army in World War II: Logistical Support of the Armies*, vol. 2, *September 1944–May 1945* (Washington, DC: Center of Military History, 1989), 39.

56. Patton outlined his policy on civil affairs on April 26, 1944, stating, "The sole mission of Civil Affairs Administration is to further military objectives. The exercise of Civil Affairs control is a command responsibility." A special order issued on April 29 detailed the chief civil affairs officer to the General Staff Corps, and the next day the section was designated G-5. See *Third U.S. Army After Action Report, 1 August 1944–9 May 1945*, vol. 1, *The Operations* (1945).

57. The Special Operations Executive was authorized by the British war cabinet on July 22, 1940. See Michael R. D. Foot, *SOE in France: An Account of the Work of the British Special Operations Executive in France, 1940–1944* (London: Her Majesty's Stationery Office, 1966).

58. After the start of World War II, William J. Donovan worked with the newly created Joint Chiefs of Staff (JCS) to place the Coordinator of Information (COI) under JCS control. On June 13, 1942, the COI became the Office of Strategic Services (OSS). The OSS gathered intelligence information about practically every country in existence, but it was not allowed to conduct operations in the Pacific Theater, which General Douglas MacArthur claimed as his own. See Anthony C. Brown, ed., *The Secret War Report of the OSS* (New York: Berkeley, 1976).

59. First Canadian Army was commanded by Lieutenant General H. D. G. Crerar. See Paul D. Dickson, "The Politics of Army Expansion: General H. D. G. Crerar and the Creation of First Canadian Army, 1940–1941," *Journal of Military History* 60, no. 2 (April 1996): 271–98.

60. The Western Naval Task Force, or Task Force 22, was commanded by British Rear Admiral Alan G. Kirk. See Samuel Eliot Morrison, *History of United*

States Naval Operations in World War II, vol. 11, *The Invasion of France and Germany, 1944–1945* (Boston: Little Brown, 1957).

61. RAF Second Tactical Air Force was formed in 1943 to concentrate all the British and Commonwealth tactical airpower designated for the invasion of Europe under one command. It was commanded by Air Marshal Sir Arthur Coningham. See Air Ministry, "Report on the Air and Administrative Organization of the 2nd Tactical Air Force," August 1947; Paul Johnston, "2nd TAF and the Normandy Campaign: Controversy and Under-developed Doctrine" (master's thesis, Royal Military College of Canada, 1999).

62. The U.S. Eighth Air Force was redesignated from the Eighth Bomber Command in February 1944, which had been activated as part of the U.S. Army Air Forces on January 28, 1942, at Hunter Field in Savannah, GA. Brigadier General Ira C. Eaker took the headquarters to England the next month to prepare for its mission of conducting aerial bombardments against Nazi-occupied Europe. See Roger Freeman, *The Mighty Eighth: A History of the U.S. 8th Army Air Force* (Garden City, NY: Doubleday, 1970).

63. The Allied Expeditionary Air Force was established with the specific mission of supporting the Allied armies through the campaign in northwestern Europe. Its commander was British Air Chief Marshal Sir Trafford Leigh-Mallory. See Bill N. Dunn, *Big Wing: The Biography of Air Chief Marshal Sir Trafford Leigh-Mallory* (Shrewsbury, UK: AirLife Publications, 1992).

64. John Jay McCloy (1895–1989) graduated from Harvard Law School in 1921. He became an adviser to Secretary of War Henry Stimson in 1940 before serving as assistant secretary of war from 1941 to 1945. See Henry L. Stimson and McGeorge Bundy, *On Active Service in Peace and War* (New York: Hippocrene, 1971).

65. Joseph Taggart McNarney (1893–1972) graduated from West Point in 1915. He was a member of the Roberts Commission, led by associate justice of the Supreme Court Owen J. Roberts, which investigated the lack of readiness at Pearl Harbor.

66. No biographical information on Edwards could be found.

67. Elwood Richard "Pete" Quesada (1904–1993) entered the army as a private in 1924. He assumed command of the Twelfth Fighter Command in December 1942 and became commander of the Ninth Fighter Command in October 1943. See Thomas Alexander Hughes, *Overlord: General Pete Quesada and the Triumph of Tactical Air Power in World War II* (New York: Free Press, 1995).

68. Here Allen means the Ninth Tactical Air Command. Quesada originally established the Ninth Fighter Command in October 1943, but the name was changed in 1944.

69. The P-47 Thunderbolt, built by Republic, was a single-seat fighter and fighter-bomber. See Bernard Fitzsimons, ed., *The Illustrated Encyclopedia of 20th Century Weapons and Warfare* (New York: Columbia House, 1978), 23:2490–92.

70. Flint commanded the Signals Intelligence Section, which included Lieutenants E. A. Devine, Orsen A. Dalton, and Deverton Carpenter. In May the 118th Signal Radio Intelligence Company was assigned to Third Army. The 3254th Signal Service Company had already been activated on April 16, and three more were assembled later to complete the first block of seven corps companies. See George F. Howe, *United States Cryptographic History, Sources in Cryptographic History,* series 4, vol. 1, *American Signals Intelligence in Northwest Africa and Western Europe* (Washington, DC: National Security Agency, 2010), 126.

71. Rankin was a contingency plan for an emergency return to the Continent in the winter of 1943–1944 or the early spring of 1944, before Overlord. Case A provided for "substantial weakening of the strength and morale of the German armed forces" to the point that the Allies could invade successfully before Overlord. Case B covered a German withdrawal from occupied territories. Case C addressed a German unconditional surrender. See Pogue, *Supreme Command,* 106.

72. Bolero was the code name for the buildup of resources for the cross-Channel invasion. See Ruppenthal, *Logistical Support of the Armies,* 1:52–59.

73. Wade Hampton Haislip (1889–1971), infantry, graduated from West Point in 1912. He assumed command of XV Corps in February 1943. See his article "Corps Command in World War II," *Military Review* 70, no. 5 (May 1990): 22–32.

74. Allen is probably referring to the Third Army Maneuver Director Headquarters. He served as an assistant there from July to October 1943.

75. See Ulysses Lee, *U.S. Army in World War II: Special Studies: The Employment of Negro Troops* (Washington, DC: Center of Military History, 2001).

76. EAM-ELAS is an abbreviation of the Greek Ethnikón Apeleftherotikón Métopon Ethnikós Laïkós Apeleftherotikós Strátos, which in English is the National Liberation Front–National Popular Liberation Army. EAM-ELAS was a communist-sponsored resistance organization formed in September 1941. Its military wing was created in December 1942. EAM-ELAS fought against the Germans and the Italians, as well as against other guerrilla bands, particularly Ellínikos Dímokratikos Ethnikós Strátos (EDES)—the Greek Democratic National Army. EAM-ELAS became the most powerful guerrilla band in the country. After eliminating all its political and guerrilla rivals except the EDES in early 1944, EAM-ELAS set up a provisional government in the Greek mountains that, by implication, disowned both the Greek king and his government-in-exile. It also established an effective administrative apparatus through which it ruled liberated areas. See Ian F. W. Beckett, *Encyclopedia of Guerrilla Warfare* (Santa Barbara, CA: ABC-CLIO, 1999), 65.

77. Wright served in the G-3 Section.

78. The British Broadcasting Company (BBC) started daily transmissions on November 14, 1922. In 1927 the company was restructured as a public corporation by its founder, John Reith.

79. The battle of Tarawa occurred on November 20–23, 1943.

80. The battle of Makin Island occurred on November 20–23, 1943.

81. This individual could not be identified.

82. Jacques Le Clerc (1902–1947) was the nom de guerre of Jacques Philippe Hauteclocque; he adopted the name in 1940 to protect his family from German retribution. Le Clerc rose from the rank of captain in 1940 to major general. He commanded the 2nd French Armored Division in the U.S. First, Third, and Seventh Armies. See Mark M. Boatner III, *Biographical Dictionary of World War II* (Novato, CA: Presidio Press, 1996), 310–11.

83. The officer in question was Major General Henry J. F. Miller (1890–1949), who graduated from West Point in 1915. Miller commanded the Ninth Air Force Service Command. On April 18 he declared in the presence of British civilians in the dining room of the Claridge Hotel that the invasion would take place by mid-June. Eisenhower, a West Point classmate and friend, demoted Miller to colonel in May and sent him home.

84. Harold McClure Forde (1904–1994) graduated from West Point in 1926. He served as assistant chief of staff, G-1, and assistant chief of staff, G-2, in the 2nd Armored Division commanded by Hugh J. Gaffey in 1943. Forde served in the G-2 Air Section.

85. G-2 estimates were produced at irregular intervals to give detailed information on enemy capabilities and intentions. G-2 Estimate No. 2 was published on May 14. See *Third U.S. Army After Action Report,* vol. 2, *Staff Section Reports,* G-2, annex 7. All subsequent references to G-2 estimates can be found in annex 7.

86. No biographical information on McIntosh could be found.

87. This individual could not be identified.

88. Target Area Analysis No. 2 was issued on May 14. Section 1, prepared by the Engineer Section, comprised a "Strategical Terrain Study." Sections 2, 3, and 4 were prepared by the G-2 Section and were entitled, respectively, "Tactical Terrain Analysis," "Special Beach Studies," and "Railroad Situation in France." Target Area Analysis No. 3 was published on May 20.

89. John Birch Mayo (1919–2009) graduated from Cornell University.

90. This individual could not be identified.

91. G-2 Estimate No. 3, Operation Neptune, was issued May 19, 1944.

92. On July 14, 1943, thirty-six Italian prisoners were shot by soldiers in Patton's Seventh Army near Bascari airfield. See Carlo D'Este, *Bitter Victory: The Battle for Sicily, 1943* (New York: E. P. Dutton, 1988), 318–19.

93. The Hitler Line (or von Senger Line) ran across the Liri Valley a few miles north of Cassino.

94. Operation Anvil was the invasion of southern France. See Maurice Matloff, *U.S. Army in World War II: The War Department, Strategic Planning for Coalition Warfare, 1943–1944* (Washington DC: Center of Military History, 1994), 416–23.

95. Operation Chastity was the creation of a new port facility in Quiberon

Bay on the Brittany Peninsula. However, Roger Cirillo has argued that neither Ruppenthal's first volume of *Logistical Support of the Armies* nor Martin Blumenson's *U.S. Army in World War II: Breakout and Pursuit* (Washington, DC: Center of Military History, 1988) adequately explains the Chastity plan and its various supporting plans—Beneficiary, Hands Up, and Swordhilt—or the failure of Bradley and Patton to press for the capture of the ports. See Roger Cirillo, "The MARKET GARDEN Campaign: Allied Operational Command in Northwest Europe, 1944" (PhD diss., Cranfield University, 2001), 262 n. 484.

96. Troy H. Middleton (1889–1976) graduated from Mississippi A&M College in 1909. He commanded 45th Infantry Division in Sicily and assumed command of VIII Corps in March 1944. See Frank J. Price, *Troy H. Middleton: A Biography* (Baton Rouge: Louisiana State University Press, 1974).

97. Herbert Henry Hauge (1906–1978) graduated from Iowa State University in 1930. He was commissioned a second lieutenant in 1940 and served as VIII Corps' assistant G-2. His papers are in the archives of the State Historical Society of Iowa.

98. Daniel Isom Sultan (1885–1947) graduated from West Point in 1907. He commanded VIII Corps between 1942 and 1943 and was deputy commander in chief of the China-Burma-India Theater in 1943–1944.

99. Joseph Warren Stilwell (1883–1946) graduated from West Point in 1904. He commanded U.S. forces in the China-Burma-India Theater and served as chief of the Joint Staff under Chiang Kai-shek from February 1942 until October 1944. See Barbara Tuchman, *Stilwell and the American Experience in China, 1911–1945* (New York: Grove Press, 2001).

100. Emil Frederick Reinhart (1888–1969) graduated from West Point in 1910. He commanded VIII Corps from December 1943 to March 1944.

101. George Catlett Marshall (1880–1959) graduated from the Virginia Military Institute in 1901. He was promoted to four-star rank upon becoming army chief of staff on September 1, 1939. See Larry I. Bland, ed., *The Papers of George Catlett Marshall*, 5 vols. (Baltimore: Johns Hopkins University Press, 1981–2003).

102. Gallagher was replaced by Colonel Frederick R. Chamberlain.

103. Bricker was replaced by Colonel Thomas H. Nixon.

104. Bernard Shirley Carter (1893–1961) was the son of one of the original partners in the J. P. Morgan Bank. See "Bernard Carter, Banker, 68, Dead," *New York Times*, November 9, 1961. Carter's papers are in Special Collections, U.S. Military Academy Library.

105. Operation Sussex was implemented to keep SHAEF informed of the movement of German panzer divisions. See Anthony Cave Brown, *Bodyguard of Lies* (New York: Harper & Row, 1975), 566–67.

106. In 1909 the British created a Secret Service Bureau. The SIS represented the Foreign Section, and the Home Section would later become MI5. See F. H. Hinsley, *British Intelligence in the Second World War: Its Influence on Operations and Strategy*, vol. 1 (London: Her Majesty's Stationery Office, 1986), chaps. 1, 2.

107. The OSS Special Counter-Intelligence Unit No. 54 was withdrawn from attachment to Third Army in August and attached to Twelfth Army Group. See *Third U.S. Army After Action Report,* vol. 2, *Staff Section Reports,* G-2, XIII.

108. V-1 was an abbreviation for *Vergeltungswaffe I* (Revenge Weapon No. 1). This flying bomb, known as a "buzz bomb," was launched from a ski ramp and flew at a speed of approximately 400 miles per hour. The V-1 attacks against London commenced on June 12 and continued until March 1945.

109. I could find no reference to an aide to Hodges named Sullivan. Allen may be referring to Major William C. Sylvan.

110. Fourth U.S. Army was one of four armies created by General Douglas MacArthur, the army chief of staff, in 1932. Fourth Army moved its headquarters from the Presidio of Monterey, CA, to Fort Sam Houston, TX, on January 7, 1944, to assume the duties of headquarters, Third U.S. Army, which in turn proceeded to the European Theater. Fourth Army formed two combat armies in 1944, the Ninth and Fifteenth.

111. William Hood Simpson (1888–1980) graduated from West Point in 1909. He was promoted to lieutenant general on October 12, 1943, and assumed command of Fourth Army headquarters. In early 1944 his headquarters provided a cadre for Eighth U.S. Army, but to avoid confusion with British Eighth Army, it was redesignated Ninth Army on May 22, 1944, at Fort Sam Houston. See *Conqueror: The Story of Ninth Army, 1944–1945* (Washington, DC: Infantry Journal Press, 1947).

112. Second U.S. Army was another of the four armies created by MacArthur in 1932.

113. Harold R. Bull (1893–1976) graduated from West Point in 1914. He assumed the position of SHAEF G-3 in February 1944.

114. Coy G. Eklund (1915–2008) served in the G-1 Section.

115. Charles Pennoyer Bixel (1904–1975) graduated from West Point in 1927. He was promoted to colonel in January 1943.

116. The B-24 Liberator was a heavy bomber designed by Consolidated Aircraft of San Diego, CA.

117. Army Ground Forces was one of three new organizations created on March 9, 1942, during a major reorganization of the War Department. The other two were Army Air Forces and Services of Supply. See Kent Roberts Greenfield, Robert R. Palmer, and Bell I. Wiley, *U.S. Army in World War II: The Army Ground Forces; The Organization of Ground Combat Troops* (Washington, DC: Historical Division, 1947), chap. 10.

118. Robert McCandless Beck Jr. (1879–1970) graduated from West Point in 1901. He served as the assistant chief of staff, Operations and Training Division, War Department General Staff, in 1938–1939. Beck retired in 1939.

119. Point Blank was the code name for the strategic bombing offensive against Germany. The directive to initiate it was issued on June 10, 1943, to RAF Bomber Command and U.S. Eighth Air Force. See Max Hastings, *Bomber Com-*

mand: The Myths and Realities of the Strategic Bombing Offensive 1939–1945 (New York: Dial Press, 1979), 187–88.

120. Plan Fortitude was initiated on February 26, 1944. See Hesketh, *Fortitude*.

121. Crossbow was the code name for British air attacks against German V-1 weapons (*Vergeltungswaffen*), pilotless aircraft launched from ski ramps in the Pas de Calais and Cherbourg areas.

122. Martian reports were issued weekly by the Combined Intelligence Section (CIS) between 1942 and 1944. For the format of the reports, see F. H. Hinsley, *British Intelligence in the Second World War: Its Influence on Operations and Strategy,* vol. 3, pt. 2 (London: Her Majesty's Stationery Office, 1988), appendix 2.

123. Halley Grey Maddox (1899–1977), cavalry, graduated from West Point in 1920. Maddox came to know Patton through the U.S. Army polo team. He served as Patton's assistant chief of staff, G-3, in I Armored Corps, Seventh Army, and Third Army.

124. G-2 Section Estimate No. 4 was issued the same day, reporting a total of 60.5 enemy divisions in the west (France, Belgium, and Holland). This was an increase of 8.5 divisions since Estimate No. 1, dated April 23. The report dealt in detail with the Cherbourg (012) area. The Cotentin Peninsula was estimated to include 6.5 enemy divisions. The enemy had 45 infantry and 2 tank battalions on or in the immediate vicinity of the Cherbourg Peninsula. Rommel, with headquarters at La Roche-Guyon (R57), was reported to be in command of Army Group B, which included Seventh and Fifteenth German Armies and LXXXVIII German Corps. The report also indicated that parachute divisions were being concentrated in France.

125. Target Area Analysis No. 4 included "A Study of Northwest France and Area South of Loire River as to Suitability of Terrain for Mechanized Operations" and "German Underwater Beach Obstacles." No. 5 included four sections, the first two of which were prepared by the G-2 Section. Its subjects were: (1) "Additional Material to Supplement Tactical Study of the Terrain, Belle Isle-en-Mere (M77)"; (2) "Terrain and Defense Characteristics and Order of Battle, Quiberon Bay (M99) Area"; (3) "Study of Feasibility of Mounting a Seaborne Assault Force from Vicinity of Granville (T13)"; and (4) "Tactical Study of the Terrain, Northwest Brittany."

126. The 2nd Panzer Division, nicknamed Vienna, was a Wehrmacht formation commanded by Meinrad von Lauchert. See Franz von Steinzer, *Die 2. Panzer Division* (Freiburg, Germany: Podzun-Pallas Verlag, 1974).

2. Watching and Waiting

1. The meaning of the acronym CMA is unclear.

2. For a good description of the action at Omaha, see John C. McManus, *The Dead and Those About to Die: D-Day: The Big Red One at Omaha Beach* (New York: NAL Caliber, 2014).

3. The 21st Panzer Division was a Wehrmacht formation commanded by Edgar von Feuchtinger. It was in place in the Caen sector on D-Day, divided on either side of the Orne River. See Marc Milner, *Stopping the Panzers: The Untold Story of D-Day* (Lawrence: University Press of Kansas, 2014).

4. Walton Harris Walker (1889–1950) graduated from West Point in 1912. He assumed command of XX Corps in October 1943 when it was redesignated from 4th Armored Corps. See Wilson A. Heefner, *Patton's Bulldog: The Life and Service of General Walton H. Walker* (Shippensburg, PA: White Mane Books, 2001).

5. The 352nd Division was a static Wehrmacht division.

6. The 17th SS Panzergrenadier Division "Götz von Berlichingen" began forming in November 1943. By D-Day, it was still not combat ready and possessed no tanks. It was commanded by SS-Brigadeführer Werner Ostendorff. See Niklas Zetterling, *Normandy 1944: German Military Organization, Combat Power and Organizational Effectiveness* (Winnipeg: J. J. Fedorowicz, 2000), 363–69.

7. The 130th Panzer Lehr Division was a Wehrmacht formation commanded by Fritz Bayerlein. The division arrived opposite 3rd Canadian Infantry Division on June 8. See Helmut Ritgen, *The Western Front 1944: Memoirs of a Panzer Lehr Officer* (Winnipeg: J. J. Fedorowicz, 1995).

8. The position of G-2 Air was a formally recognized staff section responsibility for air reconnaissance and observation.

9. It is unclear what Allen means by COE. Gooseberries were shelters formed by block ships. One Gooseberry was established at each beach. The actual breakwater obstacles consisted of Bombardons and Phoenixes. See G. Hartcup, *Code Name Mulberry: The Planning, Building and Operation of the Normandy Harbours* (Newton Abbot, UK: David & Charles, 1977).

10. The 12th SS Panzer Division "Hitler Youth" arrived in the Caen sector in stages. The 25th SS-Panzergrenadier Regiment struck the 3rd Canadian Infantry Division on the morning of June 7. The rest of the 12th SS did not arrive until the next day. The division was commanded by Fritz Witt. See Hubert Meyer, *History of the 12. SS-Panzer Division "Hitlerjugend"* (Winnipeg: J. J. Fedorowicz, 1994).

11. The 3rd Parachute Division comprised three regiments of three battalions each. It was brought into Brittany in March and stationed east of Brest. Its mission was to complete its organization and at the same time train to defend against airborne attack. It was commanded by Generalleutnant Gustav Wilke. In early May the 5th Parachute Division moved into the Rennes area with a similar mission. It was commanded by Generalleutnant Richard Schimpf. In May both divisions were placed under the command of II Parachute Corps.

12. Pilotless planes refer to the V-1 flying bomb. See F. H. Hinsley, *British Intelligence in the Second World War: Its Influence on Strategy and Operations,* vol. 3, pt. 2 (London: Her Majesty's Stationery Office, 1988), chap. 25.

13. See William Manchester, *The Arms of Krupp 1587–1968* (Boston: Little, Brown, 1968).

14. Alexander C. Stiller (1893–1962) served with Patton in World War I and was wounded at St. Varennes-de-Argonne. See Joseph Sprouse, *Documentary: Gen. George Patton, Jr., 2nd Lt. Peter Bonano, and a Vanishing Cache of Nazi Gold* (Indianapolis: Dog Ear Publishing, 2010), 26.

15. Paul Hamilton (1901–1981), infantry, graduated from West Point in 1926. He was promoted to lieutenant colonel on June 16, 1942.

16. Allen's identification of the officer is in error here. Major General Ernest J. Dawley was relieved of command of VI Corps on September 20, 1943. See Mark Clark, *Calculated Risk: His Personal Story of the War in North Africa and Italy* (London: George G. Harrap, 1951), 201–2.

17. Mark Wayne Clark (1896–1984) graduated from West Point in 1917. He assumed command of Fifth Army on December 12, 1942. See Martin Blumenson, *Mark Clark: The Last of the Great World War II Commanders* (New York: Congdon & Weed, 1984).

18. Henry Cabot Lodge (1902–1985) served as an Army Reserve major in 1st Armored Division until July 1942 while also serving as a Republican senator. Lodge resigned from the Senate on February 3, 1944, and returned to active duty.

19. The Panzerkampfwagen (Mark) IV, V (Panther), and VI (Tiger) were German tank models. The Tiger mounted a powerful 88mm gun. See Walter J. Spielberger, *The Spielberger German Armor & Military Vehicle Series*, vol. 1, *Panther and Its Variants*, and vol. 4, *Panzer IV and Its Variants* (Atglen, PA: Schiffer Military, 1993); Bernard Fitzsimons, ed., *The Illustrated Encyclopedia of 20th Century Weapons and Warfare* (New York: Columbia House, 1978), 23:2496–97.

20. Gustav Bismarck Guenther (1896–1944) was killed on June 18 in London.

21. The 2nd SS Panzer Division "Das Reich" was formed in the spring of 1941 based on the former SS Verfügungs Division. It participated in the Balkan and Russian campaigns and was sent to France in the summer of 1942 to rest and refit. There, it reorganized as a panzergrenadier division. It then returned to Russia and fought at Kharkov and Kursk. Prior to the Normandy invasion, the division was stationed near Toulouse and was delayed for some fifteen days by SOE and French resistance. See Otto Weidinger, *Das Reich V, 1943–1945: 2nd SS Panzer Division* (Winnipeg: J. J. Fedorowicz, 2012); Max Hastings, *Das Reich: The March of the 2nd Panzer Division through France, 1944* (New York: Pan Books, 2010).

22. *Maquis* was a popular term for French Forces of the Interior (FFI). See George Millar, *Maquis: The French Resistance at War* (London: Cassell, 2003).

23. Charles Russell Codman (1893–1956) graduated from Harvard in 1915. He saw combat in World War I as a pilot and won the Silver Star and Croix de Guerre. Codman was assigned as a translator for Operation Torch because of his fluency in French. He became Patton's aide in early 1943. See Charles R. Codman, *Drive* (Boston: Little, Brown, 1957).

24. Robert I. Powell (1900–1963) graduated from Princeton in 1922 and worked in Manhattan as an architect. He also held a pre–World War II commission in the National Guard. See Lieutenant Colonel (Ret.) Will Irwin, *The Jedburghs: The Secret History of the Allied Special Forces, France 1944* (New York: Public Affairs, 2005), 126–27.

25. The 11th Panzer Division was a Wehrmacht formation stationed on the south coast of France. It was commanded by Wend von Wittersheim. See A. Harding Ganz, "The 11th Panzers in the Defense, 1944," *Armor* 103, no. 2 (March–April 1994): 26–37.

26. The RF circuit, or network, was established by the SOE F Section to assist General Charles de Gaulle's Free French.

27. This individual could not be identified.

28. Field Marshal Erwin Rommel (1891–1944) was one of the greatest battlefield commanders of World War II. During World War I he served in the *Württembergische* mountain battalion, and during the battle of Caporetto in late October 1917 he captured the key Italian position of Monte Matajur. In 1915 he was awarded the Iron Cross First Class and the Pour le Mérite, comparable to the Victoria Cross. In 1937 Rommel published *Infanterie Greift An* (Infantry Attacks), based on his World War I experiences. During the invasion of France in 1940 Rommel commanded the 7th Panzer Division with great energy and initiative and excelled at the deep penetration. In mid-February 1941 he assumed command of the soon to be famous Afrika Korps and immediately seized the initiative from British Eighth Army. He was forced to withdraw from Cyrenaica during Operation Crusader in November 1941, but by January 1942 he had regained the initiative from Eighth Army. Rommel's finest moment may have been the battle of Gazala in May 1942, followed by the capture of the great fortress of Tobruk on the Mediterranean coast in June. Rommel was defeated by Montgomery during the second battle of El Alamein in October–November 1942 and thereafter began a 1,500-mile retreat to Tunisia. In mid-February 1943 Rommel struck the inexperienced U.S. II Corps at Kasserine Pass and inflicted heavy casualties. When he turned east to engage the arriving Eighth Army in southeast Tunisia, however, he was decisively beaten at the battle of Medenine. On March 9, 1943, Rommel departed Africa for good. During the Normandy invasion Rommel served as commander in chief of Army Group B and waged a battle of attrition against the numerically and materially superior Allied forces. Rommel was seriously wounded by Allied aircraft on July 17, 1944, and never commanded in the field again. He subsequently committed suicide. See Basil Liddell Hart, ed., *The Rommel Papers* (London: Collins, 1958).

29. The 1st SS Panzer Division "Leibstandarte SS Adolf Hitler" began as a bodyguard regiment for Hitler in 1933. By 1941 it had expanded to division size and took part in the Balkan and Russian campaigns. It was transferred to Belgium in April 1944. See Rudolf Lehmann and Ralf Tiemann, *The Leibstandarte IV/2* (Winnipeg: J. J. Fedorowicz, 1998).

30. The 9th SS Panzer Division was formed in the west in early 1943 as the 9th SS Panzergrenadier Division and shortly thereafter was given the title "Hohenstaufen." The 10th SS Panzer Division was formed in the west in early 1943 with the title "Frundsberg." See George F. Nafziger, *The German Order of Battle: Waffen SS and Other Units in World War II* (Conshohocken, PA: Combined Publishing, 2001), 91–94, 95–97.

31. See Michael Reynolds, *Sons of the Reich: II SS Panzer Corps, Normandy, Arnhem, Ardennes, Eastern Front* (New York: Sarpedon, 2002).

32. Fifth U.S. Army was created in the spring of 1943 to conduct operations in Italy.

33. The Messerschmitt Bf-109 was a fighter produced by the Bayerische Flugzeugwerke (BFW; Bavarian Aircraft Company). See Robert Jackson and Adam Tooby, *Messerschmitt Bf 109 E-F Series* (London: Osprey, 2015).

34. The Junkers-88 was a versatile airframe capable of performing as a fast bomber, a dedicated night fighter, a torpedo bomber, and a special mission aircraft. More than 15,000 of the Ju-88 variants were produced during the war. See William A. Medcalf, *Ju88*, vol. 1, *From Snellbomber to Multi-Mission Warplane* (London: Ian Allan, 2013).

35. Operation Lucky Strike was a series of studies by Twenty-First Army Group based on the possible acceleration of the Overlord timetable. The central premise was exploiting the deterioration of the Germans' will to resist by advancing eastward. It was an outline plan that reflected the tactical situation and formalized First Army as the sword. See General Board, United States Forces, European Theater, *Strategy of the Campaign in Western Europe, 1944–1945*, Study No. 1, U.S. Army Heritage and Education Center, 21.

36. Operation Hands Up was to be executed by airborne troops and Rangers. Martin Blumenson, *U.S. Army in World War II: Breakout and Pursuit* (Washington, DC: Center of Military History, 1988), 186 n. 6.

37. Here Allen is probably referring to Beneficiary, a plan to seize the Breton ports of St. Malo. Ibid.

38. Operation Swordhilt was supposed to secure port facilities in Brittany. Ibid.

39. This individual could not be identified. Elsewhere, Allen refers to a Major Fred I. Lindau who worked in the G-3 Section.

40. Matthew Bunker Ridgway (1895–1993), infantry, graduated from West Point in 1917. He assumed command of the 82nd Airborne Division in June 1942 and led it during combat drops in Sicily and Normandy. See *Soldier: The Memoirs of Matthew B. Ridgway* (New York: Harper & Brothers, 1956).

41. Andrew R. Reeves (1893–1979?), artillery, was promoted to colonel on December 24, 1941.

42. Periodic reports provided information on the enemy situation, including his front line, defensive organization, units in contact, reserves, and additional pertinent information.

43. See Duke Shoop, "Deeds of Fiends," *Kansas City Star,* May 13, 1945, 1, 6. Shoop would become the bureau chief of the *Kansas City Star* in the postwar period.

44. Kenneth Crawford (1902–1983) was reportedly the first American war correspondent to land on D-Day.

45. This was M-510 dated July 10, 1944. For a visual description, see Nigel Hamilton, *Monty: Master of the Battlefield, 1942–1944* (London: Hamish Hamilton, 1983), 725.

46. Nelson Macy Walker (1891–1944) was promoted to brigadier general on September 11, 1942. He became assistant division commander, 8th Infantry Division, in November 1943 and was killed in Normandy on July 10, 1944.

47. Frederick William Winterbotham (1897–1990) graduated from the University of Oxford in 1920. He joined the British Secret Service in 1929. By 1938, MI6 had gained access to the German mechanical encrypting device known as Enigma, and Winterbotham was placed in charge of disseminating the top-secret translated intelligence known as Ultra. See Frederick W. Winterbotham, *Secret and Personal* (London: Kimber, 1969), *The Ultra Secret* (New York: Harper & Row, 1974), and *The Ultra Spy* (London: Macmillan, 1989).

48. Ultra was the British cover name for all high-grade signals intelligence extracted from Enigma, Fish, and hand ciphers and from Italian and Japanese codes and ciphers. The British started using the term Ultra in June 1941, and the Americans adopted it later. A high-grade code or cipher is one designed to provide a high level of security; it does not characterize the actual traffic the code or cipher carries. Fish was Bletchley Park's cover name for German non-Morse traffic enciphered on a *Schlüsselzusatz* or *Geheimschreiber* machine. F. H. Hinsley and Alan Stripp, eds., *Codebreakers: The Inside Story of Bletchley Park* (Oxford: Oxford University Press, 1993), glossary and abbreviations.

49. Winston Leonard Spencer Churchill (1874–1965) became the British prime minister on May 10, 1940. See Carlo D'Este, *Warlord: A Life of Churchill at War, 1874–1945* (New York: Harper Perennial, 2009).

50. Allen is most likely referring to Montgomery's operations at Medenine in early March 1943. He rushed up reinforcements based on Ultra messages indicating that Rommel was about to attack. Whitehall criticized Montgomery for taking insufficient precautions to protect the source of this intelligence. See F. H. Hinsley, *British Intelligence in the Second World War: Its Influence on Strategy and Operations,* vol. 2 (London: Her Majesty's Stationery Office, 1991), 596.

51. The Special Liaison Unit was established at army headquarters to process Ultra. The unit, which maintained direct liaison with higher echelons of command, was made up largely of British personnel and was attached to assistant chief of staff, G-2, headquarters, Third U.S. Army. It consisted of four officers (two U.S.) and thirteen enlisted men (all British). It was supplemented by a special communications unit.

52. Allen may or may not be correct here, depending on when members of Third Army were indoctrinated. Those officers in Third Army who were Ultra

recipients and had been indoctrinated in its use included Gay; Harkins; Halley G. Maddox, the G-3; Colonel Harold M. Forde, G-2 executive officer; Allen; Major Charles W. Flint, Third Army's signals security officer; Weyland, his chief of staff; Colonel Roger Browne; and Major Harry M. Grove, the Ultra representative at XIX Tactical Air Command. See Captain George C. Church, memorandum for Colonel Taylor: Ultra and the Third Army, May 28, 1945, 1, in SRH 023–026, "Reports by U.S. Army Ultra Representatives with Army Field Command in the European Theater of Operations," RG 457, NARA II. See also Harry M. Grove, "ULTRA and Its Use by XIX Tactical Air Command," May 30, 1945, in SRH 023, ibid., pt. 2.

53. Benjamin Abbott "Monk" Dixon (1897–1976) graduated from West Point in 1918 and from the Massachusetts Institute of Technology in 1922 with a bachelor of science degree in mechanical engineering. Dixon was called to active duty in 1940 as an intelligence officer. He was given the assignment of Counter Intelligence Corps chief of the Ground Force, which eventually led to his transfer to G-2, II Corps, then commanded by General Lloyd R. Fredendall. During a personal reconnaissance at El Guettar, Dixon was severely wounded and permanently crippled, but he continued to serve as G-2 under Bradley when the latter assumed command of First Army.

54. Theodore Roosevelt Jr. (1887–1944) was the eldest son of President Theodore Roosevelt and cousin to President Franklin Delano Roosevelt. Roosevelt was the only general to land in the first wave at Utah Beach. He died of a heart attack on July 12 and was posthumously awarded the Medal of Honor. See H. Paul Jeffers, *Theodore Roosevelt, Jr.: The Life of a War Hero* (Novato, CA: Presidio Press, 2002).

55. LXXXIV Army Korps was commanded by General of Artillery Erich Marcks. For the Ultra message, see DEFE 3/56, XL 2030, July 14, 1944, in Hinsley, *British Intelligence in the Second World War*, vol. 3, pt. 2, 214.

56. Albert Kesselring (1885–1960) was appointed commander in chief South West and commander in chief of Army Group C on November 21, 1943. See Kenneth Macksey, *Kesselring: German Master Strategist of the Second World War* (London: Greenhill Books, 1996).

57. Cobra was designed to break through the German defenses and complete Montgomery's broad concept of operations for Overlord. The plan consisted of a concentrated breakthrough by VII Corps, with the 4th, 9th, and 30th Infantry Divisions making the initial breakthrough, followed by the 2nd and 3rd Armored Divisions exploiting. The operation was to be initiated by a massive carpet bombing of German positions. See James Jay Carafano, *After D-Day: Operation Cobra and the Normandy Breakout* (Boulder, CO: Lynne Rienner, 2000).

58. Jedburg teams were a Special Forces unit made up of American, British, and French volunteers. Teams of three parachuted behind German lines in France, with the mission of conducting guerrilla warfare with the assistance of locally recruited support. See Irwin, *Jedburghs*.

59. According to available evidence, Foothorap did not command Third Army's 303rd CIC Detachment. Instead, he served in Sixth Army Group. See *Princeton Alumni Weekly,* September 28, 1945, 14. The CIC Detachments at corps level in Third Army were as follows: III Corps—203rd Detachment, XII Corps—212th Detachment, XX Corps—220th Detachment. Third Army Troop List, December 27, 1944, RG 407, box 2054, entry 427, NARA II.

60. The Corps of Intelligence Police was established in August 1917. On January 1, 1942, the name was changed to the Counter Intelligence Corps. See Ian Sayer and Douglas Botting, *America's Secret Army: The Untold Story of the Counter Intelligence Corps* (New York: Franklin Watts, 1989).

61. John James Bohn (1889–1983) was promoted to brigadier general in July 1942 and assumed command of Combat Command B, 3rd Armored Division. See Blumenson, *Breakout and Pursuit,* 104–18.

62. The chief of staff of 79th Infantry Division was Colonel Kramer Thomas. The chief of staff of 90th Infantry Division during the invasion was Colonel Robert L. Bacon. He was replaced on July 15 by Colonel John C. Whitcomb.

63. An attempt was made on Hitler's life on July 20 at Rastenburg. See Peter Hoffmann, *The History of the German Resistance 1933–1945,* trans. Richard Barry (Cambridge, MA: MIT Press, 1977), 397–411.

64. William Morris Hoge (1894–1979) graduated from West Point in 1916. In March 1944 he was given command of the Provisional Engineer Special Brigade Group, which included the 5th and 6th Engineer Special Brigades. His mission was to prepare for and conduct landing operations with the D-Day assault divisions on Omaha beach and then develop the beachhead to support the combat troops once they were ashore. On D-Day Hoge's command successfully carried out its duties and played a significant part in securing the initial foothold at Omaha beach.

65. No biographical information on Morris could be found.

66. O'Neil commanded a Special Engineer Task Force.

67. Harold Raynsford Stark (1880–1972) graduated from Annapolis in 1903 and served as chief of naval operations from 1939 to 1942. From 1942 to the end of the war he served as commander of U.S. Naval Forces Europe. See B. Mitchell Simpson, *Admiral Harold R. Stark: Architect of Victory, 1939–1945* (Columbia: University of South Carolina Press, 1989).

68. G-2 Estimate No. 6 was published on July 27.

69. Lesley James McNair (1883–1944), artillery and ordnance, graduated from West Point in 1904. He became commanding general of Army Ground Forces in March 1942 and held that position until June 1944, when he assumed command of FUSAG. See Mark T. Calhoun, *General Lesley J. McNair: Unsung Architect of the U.S. Army* (Lawrence: University Press of Kansas, 2015).

70. Fliegerkorps IX was commanded by Generalmajor Dietrich Peltz.

71. Edward Joseph Schmuck (1909–1990) graduated from Fordham University in 1932. He practiced law in New York City from 1933 to 1941.

3. Third Army Enters the Fight

1. N. S. Ives (d. 1944) was the commanding officer of the U.S. Naval Advanced Base, Cherbourg. He organized a reconnaissance into St. Malo and proceeded from Granville on August 2. See recollections of the incident in the *Massillon (OH) Evening Independent,* November 6, 1944.

2. The 2nd Parachute Division started to move east from Brest but returned to the city. See Martin Blumenson, *U.S. Army in World War II: Breakout and Pursuit* (Washington, DC: Center of Military History, 1988), 341–42.

3. John Palmer Dieter (1915–1999) graduated from the University of Kansas in 1936 and from Yale University Law School in 1939. He entered the U.S. Army in February 1941 and attended the Cavalry School, 7th Officers Candidate Course Mechanized, at Fort Riley, KS. Dieter's papers are in the Dwight D. Eisenhower Library.

4. No biographical information on Dunkerley could be found.

5. Why Allen would refer to the Germans in St. Malo as "Tommy" is unclear. It would make more sense to use the term "Jerry."

6. Herbert L. Earnest (1895–1970) was the commander of Combat Command A, 4th Armored Division. In order to secure the Brest-Rennes railroad for transportation purposes, Patton created Task Force A under Earnest's command. The headquarters element was the 1st Tank Destroyer Brigade with the 60th Tank Destroyer Group and 159th Engineer Battalion.

7. Baron Hiroshi Ôshima (1886–1975) was a general in the Imperial Japanese Army and served as military attaché and Japanese ambassador to Nazi Germany before and during World War II. He sent regular reports to Tokyo via the Japanese diplomatic machine system, which the Americans nicknamed Purple. See Nigel West, *Historical Dictionary of Signals Intelligence* (Plymouth, UK: Scarecrow Press, 2012), 166.

8. Unlike the slow-flying V-1, the V-2 was a single-stage rocket-launched ballistic missile. Upon reaching an altitude of approximately sixty miles, the V-2 reached speeds approaching Mach 5, rendering it virtually undetectable and invulnerable to interception. The V-2 was the creation of Wernher von Braun and was developed at the Peenemünde Military Test Site, Germany. See Gregory P. Kennedy, *Germany's V-2 Rocket* (Atglen, PA: Schiffer Military, 2006). For the Ultra message Allen refers to, see BAY/XL 67, July 27, 1944, in F. H. Hinsley, *British Intelligence in the Second World War: Its Influence on Strategy and Operations,* vol. 3, pt. 2 (London: Her Majesty's Stationery Office, 1988), 536.

9. Karl Doenitz (1891–1980) became commander in chief of the German navy in January 1943. See his *Memoirs: Ten Years and Twenty Days* (London: Weidenfeld & Nicolson, 1959).

10. Joachim von Ribbentrop (1893–1946) became German foreign minister in February 1938. See *The Ribbentrop Memoirs* (London: Weidenfeld & Nicolson, 1954).

11. The Franco-German Armistice of June 22, 1940, divided France into two zones. One zone was to be under German military occupation, and the other was to be left to the French in nominal sovereignty. The unoccupied zone comprised the southeastern two-fifths of the country, from the Swiss frontier near Geneva to a point 12 miles (19 km) east of Tours and thence southwest to the Spanish frontier, 30 miles (48 km) from the Bay of Biscay. From July 1940 to September 1944, France was under the regime of Marshal Philippe Pétain.

12. See DEFE 3/115, XL 5438, August 9, 1944, in Hinsley, *British Intelligence in the Second World War,* vol. 3, pt. 2, 256.

13. The 49th Infantry Division was formed in the Boulogne area in early February 1944 and was commanded by Siegfried Macholz. The 6th Parachute Division was formed in France in June 1944 and was commanded by Rüdiger von Heyking.

14. Otto Paul Weyland (1902–1979) graduated from Texas A&M in 1923. He attended the Air Corps Tactical School at Maxwell Field, AL, in 1937; graduated from the army's Command and General Staff School in 1939; and was promoted to brigadier general in September 1943. Weyland departed for Europe in November as commanding general of the 84th Fighter Wing, and by early 1944 he had assumed command of XIX Tactical Air Command. See David N. Spires, *Patton's Air Force: Forging a Legendary Air-Ground Team* (Washington, DC: Smithsonian Institution Press, 2002).

15. Hickory was the code name for XV Corps.

16. See Hinsley, *British Intelligence in the Second World War,* vol. 3, pt. 2, 260.

17. Here Allen is referring to the loss of Worthington Force during Operation Totalize. On August 9 the 28th Canadian Armored Regiment (British Columbia Regiment) and infantry of the Algonquin Regiment advanced toward their objective, Point 195, but got lost and were ultimately destroyed on Point 140. See Mike Bechthold, "Lost in Normandy: The Odyssey of Worthington Force, 9 August 1944," *Canadian Military History* 19, no. 2 (Spring 2010): 5–24.

18. Generalleutnant Karl Spang (1886–1979) was captured by elements of the 212th Armored Field Artillery Battalion.

19. The German 266th Infantry Division was in position on the northern coast of Brittany on D-Day.

20. See Hinsley, *British Intelligence in the Second World War,* vol. 3, pt. 2, 371–72.

21. Dietrich von Choltitz (1894–1966) assumed command of the Greater Paris area on August 7, 1944. See his memoir *Brennt Paris?* (Konstanz, Germany: Europa-Verlag, 1951).

4. The Lorraine Campaign

1. Heinrich "Hans" Eberbach (1895–1993) assumed command of 4th Panzer Division in April 1942 and was promoted to major general in January 1943. Eber-

bach succeeded General Leo Geyr von Schweppenburg as commander of Panzer Group West (renamed Fifth Panzer Army on August 5) on July 3, 1944, and was succeeded by Josef "Sepp" Dietrich on August 9. See Mark M. Boatner III, *Biographical Dictionary of World War II* (Novato, CA: Presidio Press, 1996), 145–46.

2. Josef "Sepp" Dietrich (1892–1966) began forming I SS Panzer Corps in July 1943. He committed the corps early in the Normandy campaign and played a major role in halting the Anglo-Canadian advance south of Caen. Dietrich assumed command of Fifth Panzer Army on August 9 and then handed over command to Hasso von Manteuffel on September 11. See Charles Messenger, *Hitler's Gladiator: The Life and Times of Oberstgruppenführer and Panzergeneral der Waffen SS Sepp Dietrich* (London: Brassey's, 1988).

3. The meanings of S and O are unclear.

4. Fort Driant was located atop a 360-meter hill southwest of Metz on the west bank of the Moselle River. It was oriented southwest and had a frontage of 1,000 yards and a depth of 700 yards. The main complex contained four artillery casements and five bunkers. A fifth artillery casement, Battery Moselle, sat just off the southeast corner. See Steven J. Zaloga, *Metz 1944: Patton's Fortified Nemesis* (Midland House, UK: Osprey, 2012), 34–43.

5. Allen most likely meant Patton here. Colonel Clarence C. Park was the inspector general.

6. Bomber Command was created in 1936 to be responsible for all RAF bombing operations. See Max Hastings, *Bomber Command: The Myths and Realities of the Strategic Bombing Offensive, 1939–1945* (New York: Dial Press/ James Wade, 1979).

7. King George VI (1895–1952).

8. The liberation of the Philippines commenced with amphibious landings on the eastern island of Leyte on October 20 by U.S. Sixth Army's X and XXIV Corps. See Robert Ross Smith, *U.S. Army in World War II: The War in the Pacific: Triumph in the Philippines* (Washington, DC: Center of Military History, 1984).

9. Manton Sprague Eddy (1892–1962) graduated from Shattuck Military School in Faribault, MN, in 1913. He was promoted to brigadier in March 1942 and became assistant division commander of 9th Infantry Division. In July he was promoted to major general and assumed command of the division. During Operation Torch, Eddy commanded the Western Task Force's Provisional Corps consisting of all the elements of 9th Infantry Division not required for the landings in Morocco. Eddy then commanded the division in Tunisia and Sicily. He assumed command of XII Corps on August 20, 1944, replacing an ill Gilbert R. Cook. See Henry G. Phillips, *The Making of a Professional: Manton S. Eddy, USA* (Westport, CT: Greenwood, 2000).

10. This was the Etang de Lindre Dam, which lay three miles southeast of Dieuze. See David N. Spires, *Patton's Air Force: Forging a Legendary Air-Ground Team* (Washington, DC: Smithsonian Institution Press, 2002), 143–44.

11. Hoyt Sanford Vandenberg (1899–1954) graduated from West Point in 1923. In April 1944 Vandenberg was designated deputy air commander in chief of the Allied Expeditionary Forces and commander of its American Air Component. In August 1944 General Vandenberg assumed command of Ninth Air Force. See Philip S. Meilinger, *Vandenberg: The Life of a General* (Bloomington: Indiana University Press, 1989).

12. John Millikin (1888–1970) graduated from West Point in 1910. He assumed command of III Corps in October 1943. See Harold R. Winton, *Corps Commanders of the Bulge: Six American Generals and Victory in the Ardennes* (Lawrence: University Press of Kansas, 2007).

13. Harry Lewis Twaddle (1888–1954) was attached to the General Staff of the War Department's Operations and Training Division from 1938 to 1941. He served as assistant chief of staff to George Marshall during 1941–1942 and assumed command of the 95th Infantry Division in March 1942. See Major General Harry L. Twaddle, "From Metz to the Saar," *Military Review* 25, no. 8 (November 1945): 4–8.

14. Carter became assistant chief of staff, G-2, in August 1944.

15. Benjamin Oliver Davis (1877–1970) was the U.S. Army's first black general. See Marvin E. Fletcher, *America's First Black General, Benjamin O. Davis, Sr., 1880–1970* (Lawrence: University Press of Kansas, 1989).

16. This individual could not be positively identified. The closest match found in Allen's book *Lucky Forward* is Lieutenant John Arcudi of the Enemy Order of Battle Section.

17. The St. Mihiel battle of September 12–13, 1918, was the first major American-led offensive of World War I. The American First Army, consisting of three corps and nine divisions, was in the front line. St. Mihiel was less than twenty miles west of Pont-à-Mousson, where XII Corps attempted to cross the Moselle on September 5. The Meuse-Argonne offensive lasted from September 26 to November 11. See John J. Pershing, *My Experiences in the World War* (New York: Frederick A. Stokes, 1931), 2:264–359.

18. This individual could not be identified.

19. The War Department ordered the activation of the 761st Tank Battalion (Light) on March 15, 1942, at Camp Claiborne, LA. On September 15, 1943, the battalion moved to Camp Hood, TX, for advanced training. See Charles W. Sasser, *Patton's Panthers: The African-American 761st Tank Battalion in World War II* (New York: Gallery Books, 2005).

20. Thomas Hay Nixon (1893–1985) graduated from West Point in 1918. He was attached to the Ordnance Department in Washington, DC, in 1932.

21. John French Conklin (1891–1973) graduated from West Point in 1915. He was promoted to colonel on June 12, 1943.

22. Hermann Goering Steel Works was a component of the larger Reichswerke Hermann Göring consortium established in 1937 to accelerate the production of steel. See Adam Tooze, *The Wages of Destruction: The Making and Breaking of the Nazi Economy* (London: Allen Lane, 2006).

23. Francisco Franco y Bahamonde (1892–1875) was named the head of state in Nationalist Spain on October 1, 1936. See Charles B. Burdick, *Germany's Military Strategy and Spain in World War II* (Syracuse, NY: Syracuse University Press, 1968).

24. Charles André Joseph Marie de Gaulle (1890–1970) was recognized by Winston Churchill as chief of the Free French on June 28, 1940.

25. The Siegfried Line, or West Wall, was a linear fortification system protecting the western border of Germany. It ran from the Swiss border to the Netherlands and followed the Rhine and Saar Rivers. See J. E. Kaufmann and Robert M. Jurga, *Fortress Europe: European Fortifications of World War II* (Conshohocken, PA: Combined Publishing, 1999).

26. Paul Donal Harkins (1904–1984), cavalry, graduated from West Point in 1929. He was deputy chief of staff of the Western Task Force in Operation Torch and later served with I Armored Corps until February 22, 1943. He was the acting chief of staff of I Armored Corps (Reinforced) during the planning for Operation Husky. On May 17, 1943, he was reassigned as deputy chief of staff (tactical) of Seventh Army during the Sicilian campaign and remained in that position until February 12, 1944. At that point, he became the deputy chief of staff (tactical) for Third Army. See Paul D. Harkins, *When the Third Cracked Europe: The Story of Patton's Incredible Army* (Harrisburg, PA: Army Times Publishing, 1969).

27. Daniel O'Madigan Kennedy (1900–2003) graduated from the Missouri School of Mines in 1926. He joined the U.S. Army Corps of Engineers in 1942 and was assigned as commander of the 1681st Engineer Survey Liaison Detachment in 1944. Allen called him "one of the greatest map experts in the United States." See Daniel O'Madigan Kennedy, *Surveying the Century: A Soldier of the Two World Wars and Topographic Engineer Remembers* (Westphalia, MO: Westphalia Publishing, 1998); D. A. Lande, *I Was with Patton: First-Person Accounts of WWII in George S. Patton's Command* (St. Paul, MN: Motor Books International, 2002), 155, 296–97.

28. G-2 Estimate No. 10 was issued on November 1. See *Third U.S. Army After Action Report,* vol. 2, *Staff Section Reports,* G-2, CIII.

29. No biographical information on Horne could be found.

30. George R. Pfann (1902–1966) graduated from Cornell University in 1924. He played quarterback for Cornell's football team and was twice named all-American. Pfann received a Rhodes scholarship in 1926.

31. Walter Joseph "Maude" Muller (1895–1967) graduated from West Point in 1918.

32. Gestapo stood for *Geheime Staatspolizie* (Secret State Police). It was formed in 1933, and by April 1934 Heinrich Himmler had assumed control.

33. Fort Jeanne D'Arc was a group of positions on the west side of the Moselle River directly opposite Metz and formed part of the outer belt of defenses.

34. Prior to becoming the military governor of Metz, André Marie François Dody (1887–1960) commanded the 2nd Moroccan Division in Italy.

35. Edwin Luther Sibert (1897–1977), field artillery, graduated from West Point in 1918. He became chief of staff of 7th Infantry Division in May 1942 and then commander of divisional artillery in 99th Infantry Division in August. Sibert became assistant chief of staff, G-2, of Twelfth Army Group in March 1944.

36. The two panzer corps were LVIII and XLVII. See DEFE 3/301, HP 5368, November 2, 1944, and HPs 5397, 5467, November 3, 1944, in F. H. Hinsley, *British Intelligence in the Second World War: Its Influence on Strategy and Operations,* vol. 3, pt. 2 (London: Her Majesty's Stationery Office, 1988), 404–5.

37. Allen is referring to the Messerschmitt Me 262, the world's first turbojet aircraft, which became operational in June 1944. It could fly at speeds in excess of 500 miles per hour.

38. The identity of this individual is unclear. Colonel Loren W. Potter served as assistant chief of staff, G-4, of the Seine Section. William E. Potter served as chief of the Plans and Operations Branch. See *Engineer Memoirs: Major-General William E. Potter* (Washington, DC: Historical Division, Office of the Chief of Engineers, 1983).

39. No biographical information on Alison could be found.

40. See Marshal de Lattre de Tassigny, *The History of the French First Army,* trans. Malcolm Barnes (London: George Allen & Unwin, 1952).

41. William Henry Harrison Morris Jr. (1890–1971) graduated from West Point in 1911. During World War II Morris commanded 6th Armored Division during its Stateside training. He was promoted to brigadier general in January 1942 and major general the following May. In 1943 and 1944 he commanded II Armored Corps, which was later reorganized as XVIII Airborne Corps. See Lester M. Nichols, *Impact: The Battle Story of the Tenth Armored Division* (Nashville, TN: Battery Press, 2000).

42. After the attack on Pearl Harbor, James Harold Doolittle (1896–1993) planned and led the air raid on Tokyo from the carrier USS *Hornet* on April 18, 1942. He was awarded the Medal of Honor, and the operation famously became known as the Doolittle Raid. Doolittle commanded the Twelfth Air Force in Operation Torch and the Northwest African Strategic Air Force before being appointed commander of Eighth Air Force in January 1944. See James H. Doolittle, *I Could Never Be so Lucky Again* (New York: Bantam Books, 1991).

43. This individual could not be identified.

44. For these critical operations, see W. Denis Whitaker, *Tug of War: The Canadian Victory that Opened Antwerp* (Toronto: Stoddart, 1984).

45. Samuel E. Anderson (1906–1982), Air Corps, graduated from West Point in 1928. He was appointed commander of IX Air Force Bomber Command (Medium) of IX in October 1943.

46. Napalm is a stable burning gel that sticks to virtually any surface. It was invented in 1942 by Harvard organic chemist Julius Fieser.

47. Carl Andrew Spaatz (1891–1974) graduated from West Point in 1914. He

was appointed commanding general, U.S. Strategic Air Forces Europe, by Eisenhower in January 1944. See Richard Davis, *Carl A. Spaatz and the Air War in Europe* (Washington, DC: Smithsonian, 2004).

48. This individual could not be identified.

49. The 25th Panzergrenadier Division fought in the central sector of the Eastern Front from June 1943 to July 1944. It was destroyed in the encirclement east of Minsk in July and was re-formed in October 1944 at Truppenübungsplatz Grafenwöhr.

50. The He 111 was a twin-engine medium bomber aircraft that first appeared in front-line service in 1937. See Bernard Fitzsimons, ed., *The Illustrated Encyclopedia of 20th Century Weapons and Warfare* (New York: Columbia House, 1978), vol. 12.

51. The *Tirpitz* was identified in its new anchorage three miles west of Tromso town by reconnaissance aircraft from HMS *Implacable* on October 18. After aborted strikes due to poor weather, thirty-two Lancaster bombers, armed with 12,000-pound bombs, sank the battleship on November 12.

52. Karl Rudolf Gerd von Rundstedt (1875–1953) commanded Army Group South during Operation Barbarossa. He was appointed commander in chief of Army Group West in early September 1944. See Charles Messenger, *The Last Prussian: A Biography of Field Marshal Gerd von Rundstedt, 1875–1953* (London: Brassey's, 1991).

53. The 36th Volksgrenadier Division was commanded by Generalmajor August Wellm. The division was mentioned in ULTRA on August 21, but not during November. See Hinsley, *British Intelligence in the Second World War*, vol. 3, pt. 2, 372.

54. Kay Summersby (1908–1975) became Eisenhower's private secretary in October 1944. See Kay Summersby Morgan, *Past Forgetting: My Love Affair with Dwight D. Eisenhower* (London: Collins, 1977).

55. Heinrich Himmler (1900–1945) became the leader of Hitler's SS bodyguard in January 1929. See Heinz Höhne, *The Order of the Death's Head: The Story of Hitler's S.S.*, trans. Richard Barry (London: Secker & Warburg, 1967).

56. Fala was the name of President Roosevelt's Scottish terrier.

57. Walter Ducloux (1913–1997) was born in Lucerne, Switzerland, and attended university in Munich, where he studied philosophy and German literature as well as composition and piano. He received his doctorate in 1935 and graduated from the Munich Music Academy in 1937. Ducloux first met Arturo Toscanini (1867–1957) at the Lucerne Music Festival. Toscanini encouraged Ducloux to follow him to New York in 1939, where he became an assistant conductor and opera coach. For more on Toscanini, see Harvey Sachs, ed., *The Letters of Arturo Toscanini* (New York: Knopf, 2002).

58. Allen Welsh Dulles (1893–1969) graduated from Princeton in 1914. See Allen W. Dulles, *Germany's Underground: The Anti-Nazi Resistance* (New York: Da Capo, 2000), and *The Secret Surrender* (New York: Harper & Row, 1966).

59. Hans Oschmann (1894–1944).

60. Hamilton Fish III (1888–1991) served in the U.S. House of Representatives from 1920 to 1945. Fish, a Republican, was a prominent opponent of U.S. intervention in foreign affairs and a critic of President Franklin D. Roosevelt. When Fish celebrated his 102nd birthday in 1990, he was the oldest living American who had served in Congress.

61. Gerald Prentice Nye (1892–1971), was a Republican senator (ND).

62. Stephen A. Day (1882–1950), a Republican, was elected to the Seventy-Seventh and Seventy-Eighth Congresses. He was an unsuccessful candidate for reelection in 1944 to the Seventy-Ninth Congress.

63. John Anthony Danaher (1899–1990) was a Republican senator (CT).

64. The meaning of this acronym is unknown.

65. Edward Maynard Fickett (1895–1973), cavalry, was promoted to colonel on December 24, 1941.

66. Charles Hancock Reed (1900–1980), cavalry, graduated from West Point in 1922. He was promoted to colonel on March 4, 1943.

67. John Boyd Coates Jr. (1928–1996) graduated from Ursinus College in 1932 and received his medical degree from the University of Pennsylvania School of Medicine in 1936.

68. See Hinsley, *British Intelligence in the Second World War*, vol. 3, pt. 2, 600.

69. Anton Leonard Dunckern (1905–1985) was a senior police official. For Patton's interrogation, see Martin Blumenson, ed., *The Patton Papers*, vol. 2, *1940–1945* (Boston: Houghton Mifflin, 1974), 577–79. See also Sergeant Saul Levitt, "Capturing a Gestapo General," *Yank*, February 16, 1945, 8.

70. No biographical information on Meyer could be found.

71. Charles Hartwell Bonesteel (1885–1964) graduated from West Point in 1908. In November and December 1944 Bonesteel served as an assistant to Bradley and then commanded the G-1 Section in SHAEF headquarters.

72. The 242nd Infantry Division was commanded by Generalleutnant Johannes Bässler.

73. Dr. Karl Schnurre (1892–1990) was counselor of legation, later minister, and head of the Eastern European and Baltic Section of the Commercial Policy Division of the German Foreign Office. Schnurre was a lawyer by profession and had joined the Foreign Ministry in 1929. By 1936, he was a counselor in the German foreign service, the youngest man ever to hold such rank. See Anthony Read and David Fisher, *The Deadly Embrace: Hitler, Stalin and the Nazi-Soviet Pact 1939–1941* (New York: W. W. Norton, 1988), 54–55.

74. John Francis Thomas Murray (1918–2012), artillery, graduated from West Point in 1941. He served from November 1941 to August 1942 as a battery officer and battery commander in the 10th Field Artillery Battalion. During World War II he served as a weapons test evaluation officer from November 1942 to March 1943 at Camp Edwards, MA, and Carabelle, FL. In March 1943

he was assigned to the 87th Infantry Division, Camp McCain, MS. In 1943 he attended the U.S. Army Command and General Staff College. Murray became G-2 of the 87th Infantry Division in October 1944. See Danny R. Ross and Earle Munns Jr., US Army JAG School oral history interview conducted with Colonel John F. T. Murray, 1987.

75. No biographical information on Benson could be found.

76. Fort St. Quentin sat across the Moselle River from Metz and was one of the positions in the inner belt. It was extensively overhauled when the Germans took possession in 1940. It was linked into a fortified group with Forts Girardin and Diou through a series of supporting bunkers, pillboxes, armored observation posts, heavily reinforced casements, minefields, and a trench system.

77. Fort Plappeville sat approximately one mile north of Fort St. Quentin.

78. Fort Privat sat just south of Metz on the east side of the Moselle River.

79. Führer Escort Brigade was an Oberkommando der Wehrmacht (OKW) reserve formation of approximately 7,000 men. It was formed in the second half of 1944 and was commanded by Otto Remer. The first reference to the brigade is in Hinsley, *British Intelligence in the Second World War,* vol. 3, pt. 2, 423.

80. Hans Schaefer (1912–1978) assumed command of the division in April 1944.

81. John Shirley Wood (1888–1966) graduated from the University of Arkansas in 1907 and then attended West Point, graduating in 1912. He served as a staff officer in World War I and as an artillery commander in Patton's 2nd Armored Division. Wood assumed command of the 4th Armored Division in May 1942. See A. Harding Ganz, "Patton's Relief of General Wood," *Journal of Military History* 53, no. 3 (July 1989): 257–73; Hanson W. Baldwin, *Tiger Jack* (Fort Collins, CO: Old Army Press, 1979).

82. On this issue, see Roger Cirillo, "The MARKET GARDEN Campaign: Allied Operational Command in Northwest Europe, 1944"(PhD diss., Cranfield University, 2001), 320–21; Dennis Showalter, "The Southern Option: A Path to Victory in 1944?" *Military Chronicles* 1, no. 1 (May–June 2005): 44–59.

83. Hermann Balck (1893–1982) assumed command of Army Group G on September 21, 1944, from Johannes Blaskowitz. See David T. Zabecki, ed., *Order in Chaos: The Memoirs of General of Panzer Troops Hermann Balck* (Lexington: University Press of Kentucky, 2015).

84. Kurt Student (1890–1978) was the principal architect of German airborne forces, serving as chief of the parachute and glider arm in 1938. He formed the 7th Flieger Division, elements of which earned fame for their success in capturing the fortress of Eben Emael on May 10, 1940. By early 1941, Student was commanding the 11th Fliegerkorps; he planned and executed Operation Mercury, the invasion of Crete in May 1941. Following the capture of Antwerp in early September 1944, Student began organizing the 1st Parachute Army to oppose Montgomery's advance through Holland. In November 1944 Student assumed command of Army Group H. See Correlli Barnett, ed., *Hitler's Generals* (London: Weidenfeld & Nicolson, 1989), chap. 20.

85. Walter Model (1891–1945) commanded 9th Army from January 1942 to January 1944 and Army Group North from January to March 1944. He was commander in chief of Army Group B from September 5, 1944. See Stephen H. Newton, *Hitler's Commander: Field Marshal Walter Model, Hitler's Favorite General* (New York: Da Capo Books, 2006).

86. The meeting in question took place on December 5 in Paris. See Spires, *Patton's Air Force*, 173–74.

87. Roger James Browne (1907–1974) graduated from West Point in 1929. In August 1942 he was assigned to the Operations Division of the War Department General Staff. See Colonel Roger J. Browne, "Eggcup was the Call Sign," *Infantry Journal* 63, no. 1 (July 1948): 29–32.

88. In 1942 Clare Booth Luce (1903–1987) won a seat in the U.S. House of Representatives representing the Fourth Congressional District in Fairfield County, CT. She filled the seat formerly held by her late stepfather, Dr. Albert Austin. Luce, a Republican, was an outspoken critic of FDR's foreign policy. With the support of isolationists and conservatives in Congress, she received an appointment to the Military Affairs Committee. However, her voting record was generally more moderate, and she sided with the administration on issues such as funding for American troops and aid to war victims. Luce won a second term in the House in 1944.

89. Joseph Rider Farrington (1897–1954), a Republican congressman, was sworn in on January 3, 1943.

90. James Ferguson (1913–2000) was born in Turkey and was promoted to colonel on August 19, 1943.

91. See David K. Yelton, *Hitler's Volkssturm: The Nazi Militia and the Fall of Germany, 1944–1945* (Lawrence: University Press of Kansas, 2002).

92. See *Third U.S. Army After Action Report*, vol. 2, *Staff Section Reports*, G-2, CXIV.

93. Phillip C. Clayton (b. 1891), cavalry, was promoted to colonel on March 4, 1943.

94. John Harold Claybrook (1898–1948) graduated from West Point in 1924. He became the G-2 of XII Corps in March 1944.

95. William Averell Harriman (1891–1986) became ambassador to Moscow in October 1943. See William Averell Harriman, *Special Envoy to Churchill and Stalin, 1941–1946* (New York: Random House, 1975).

96. Karlsbrunn is actually northeast of St. Avold.

97. This individual could not be identified.

98. *Scorpion* was a Nazi propaganda paper for the troops.

5. The Battle of the Bulge

1. The Saar-Moselle Triangle was the strip of Germany lying between the Saar and Moselle Rivers. Its apex was the confluence of the two rivers, and its

western and eastern legs were the Moselle and Saar Rivers, respectively. Its base was formed by the southern flank of a mountainous ridge running east from Sierck to Merzig. The triangle measured approximately nineteen miles long from base to apex and had a ten-mile-wide base. The terrain resembled the rugged country of the Eifel to the north.

2. James Hilliard Polk (1911–1992) graduated from West Point in 1933. See James H. Polk, *World War II Letters and Notes of Colonel James H. Polk* (Oakland, OR: Elderberry Press, 2005).

3. See First Army G-2 Estimate No. 37, December 10, 1944, in the Oscar Koch Papers, U.S. Army History and Education Center, Carlisle Barracks, PA.

4. For an analysis of this failure to interpret intelligence properly, see John Nelson Rickard, "December 1944: Eisenhower, Bradley, and the Calculated Risk in the Ardennes," *Global War Studies* 8, no. 1 (2011): 7–34.

5. David Hogan Jr., *A Command Post at War: First Army Headquarters in Europe, 1943–1945* (Washington, DC: Center of Military History, 2000), 212.

6. POZIT was the term for a proximity or variable-time fuse, designed to detonate in the close vicinity of a target instead of exploding on contact. It was a closely guarded secret American design. POZIT fuses had been prepared for some 210,000 rounds of artillery ammunition on the Continent in December.

7. G-2 Estimate No. 11 was published on December 20. See *Third U.S. Army After Action Report*, vol. 2, *Staff Section Reports*, G-2, CXXXII.

8. Task Force Davis was established by Major General Norman D. Cota, commander of 28th Infantry Division, on November 7 to recapture Schmidt. The task force consisted of one battalion from the 109th Infantry and the 112th Infantry minus one battalion.

9. See Hogan, *Command Post at War*, appendix H.

10. Kenneth William Dobson Strong (1900–1982) graduated from Sandhurst in 1920. He was appointed G-2 of Allied Force Headquarters in the Mediterranean in February 1943. Eisenhower specifically requested Strong as SHAEF G-2, and he assumed that position on May 25, 1944. See Major General Kenneth Strong, *Intelligence at the Top: The Recollections of an Intelligence Officer* (London: Cassell, 1968).

11. Allen did not write a full estimate on December 9. Estimate No. 10 was published on November 1, and he did not write Estimate No. 11 until December 21. Third Army's after-action report does contain a December 9 "Changes in Enemy Front Lines" discussion, but it offers nothing in the way of a warning about VIII Corps. Similarly, the December 15 "Changes in Enemy Front Lines" has no warning about VIII Corps.

12. James E. Goodwin (1913–?) graduated from West Point in 1936. He was promoted to lieutenant colonel on December 10, 1942.

13. David H. Tulley (1904–1975) graduated from West Point in 1925. He was the executive officer of the Engineer Section.

14. The first mention of gas stocks in Germany was revealed by Ultra on

December 11. On December 20 Oberkommando der Heeres (OKH) stressed to the commander in chief, West, the importance of capturing American mask filters in factory condition. F. H. Hinsley, *British Intelligence in the Second World War: Its Influence on Strategy and Operations,* vol. 3, pt. 2, (London: Her Majesty's Stationery Office, 1988), 581–82.

15. The 116th Panzer Division, a Wehrmacht formation, was nicknamed the Greyhound Division. See Heinz Günther Guderian, *From Normandy to the Ruhr: With the 116th Panzer Division in World War II* (Bedford, PA: Aberjona Press, 2001).

16. The 560th Volksgrenadier Division was commanded by Oberst Rudolf Bäder.

17. Holmes Ely Dager (1893–1973) was given command of Combat Command B, 4th Armored Division, in 1942. He was promoted to brigadier general on June 21, 1942.

18. Leven Cooper Allen (1894–1979) served as commandant of the Infantry School in 1942–1943. He was promoted to major general on September 8, 1942. Allen became chief of staff of First U.S. Army Group in October 1943 and stayed with Bradley when Twelfth Army Group was activated.

19. Walter Campbell Short (1880–1949) assumed command of the Hawaiian Department, U.S. Army, in February 1941. Following the attack on Pearl Harbor, Short was relieved of command. The Roberts Commission concluded in January 1942 that Short had failed to coordinate properly with Admiral Husband Kimmel, commander in chief, Pacific, and cited Short for dereliction of duty.

20. Husband Edward Kimmel (1882–1968) became commander in chief, Pacific, in February 1941. The Roberts Commission cited Kimmel for failure to coordinate with General Short and for dereliction of duty.

21. Henry Magruder Zeller Jr. (1906–1982) graduated from West Point in 1927.

22. Anthony Clement McAuliffe (1898–1975), artillery, graduated from West Point in 1919. He was the assistant division commander but served as the commanding general from December 5 to 26 in the absence of Maxwell Taylor.

23. Frederick R. Chamberlain Jr. (b. 1897) was promoted to colonel on September 8, 1942. See Colonel Frederick R. Chamberlain Jr. and Captain John G. Wynn, "Activities of Third U.S. Army AAA," *Coast Artillery Journal* 91, no. 1 (July–August 1948): 2–16. Wynn joined the Antiaircraft Artillery Section of Third Army in the spring of 1945 and remained with it until June 1946.

24. Elton Foster Hammond (1896–1990) graduated from West Point in 1918. He served as the signals officer for the Western Task Force during Operation Torch, I Armored Corps in July 1943, Seventh Army, and Third Army. See Colonel Elton F. Hammond, "Signals for Patton," *Signals* 2, no. 1 (September–October 1947): 5–11.

25. See Nigel Hamilton, *Monty: The Field Marshal, 1944–1976* (London: Hamish Hamilton, 1986), 247.

26. Fort Koenigsmacher was situated on the east bank of the Moselle River opposite Thionville, twenty miles north of Metz. Koenigsmacher formed the final part of the Metz-Thionville *Stellung* (fortress).

27. The Maginot Line was a comprehensive defensive barrier in northeast France constructed during the 1930s. It was named after its principal creator, André Maginot, France's minister of war in 1929–1931. See Alistair Horne, *To Lose a Battle: France 1940* (London: Macmillan, 1969), 26–27.

28. Joseph J. O'Hare (1893–1961) graduated from West Point in 1916. He became G-1 of Twelfth Army Group in August 1944 and was promoted to brigadier in November.

29. Allen means the 26th Volksgrenadier Division, commanded by Heinz Kokott.

30. La Fondation Jean-Pierre Pescatore was an old people's home that opened in 1892.

31. Allen's reference here is unclear.

32. The Malmédy massacre occurred on December 16, 1944, and initiated a series of atrocities committed by Battle Group Peiper of the 1st SS Panzer Regiment, commanded by Colonel Joachim Peiper. Its parent division was 1st SS Panzer Division. See Michael Reynolds, *The Devil's Adjutant: Jochen Peiper, Panzer Leader* (New York: Sarpedon, 1995). The 12th SS Panzer Division was not implicated in the massacres. See *Malmedy Massacre Investigation, Report of the Subcommittee of the Committee on Armed Services United States Senate, Eighty-First Congress, First Session,* October 3, 1949 (Washington, DC: Government Printing Office, 1949).

33. The 66th Infantry Division crossed the English Channel on Christmas Eve 1944. The majority of the infantry troops were on board the SS *Leopoldville* and HMS *Cheshire*. Just five miles offshore from Cherbourg, the *Leopoldville* was torpedoed by a German U-boat. Fourteen officers and 748 servicemen were lost.

34. MS #A-858 (Schramm), "The Course of Events of the German Offensive in the Ardennes 16 Dec 44 to 14 Jan 45," in *World War II German Military Studies,* vol. 10, pt. 4, *The OKW War Diary Series, Continued,* ed. Donald S. Detwiler, Charles B. Burdick, and Jürgen Rohwer (New York: Garland Publishing, 1979), 5–6.

35. David N. Spires, *Patton's Air Force: Forging a Legendary Air-Ground Team* (Washington, DC: Smithsonian Institution Press, 2002), 215; Adolf Galland, *The First and the Last: The German Fighter Force in World War II* (London: Methuen, 1955), 319.

36. British XXX Corps was commanded by Lieutenant General Sir Brian Horrocks. On December 19 Montgomery began to assemble the corps near Louvain–St. Trond.

37. At 1200 on December 27, command of VIII Corps' Meuse River sector was formally relinquished to 17th Airborne Division. At 0230 the division issued Field Order No. 3, directing a march from assembly areas west of the Meuse via

Charleville-Sedan-Carignan and Jamoigne to the vicinity of Neufchâteau, Belgium. Rear-echelon division headquarters remained at Rethel, France. See Don R. Pay, *Thunder from Heaven: Story of the 17th Airborne Division, 1943–1945* (Nashville, TN: Battery Press, 1980).

38. James Owen Curtis Jr. (1909–1978) graduated from West Point in 1930. He won the Silver Star for gallantry in action with the 1st Infantry Division in the Mediterranean.

39. Brown was appointed G-2 on January 11, 1944.

40. James Orr Boswell (1910–1996) graduated from West Point in 1933. He became G-2 of 90th Infantry Division in February 1944.

41. Charles Pennoyer Bixel (1904–1975), cavalry, graduated from West Point in 1927. He was the G-2 of Ninth Army.

42. The P-51 Mustang was the first single-engine plane based in Britain to penetrate Germany and reach Berlin. It accompanied heavy bombers over the Ploiesti oil fields in Romania and made an all-fighter sweep to hunt down the dwindling Luftwaffe. It replaced the P-38 Lightning because of its superior range. See Jeffrey Ethell, *P-51 Mustang* (London: Arms & Armour Press, 1990).

43. The P-38 Lightning was built by Lockheed-Martin. It was a twin-engine, single-seat fighter that lacked the capacity for long-range fighter operations. See Jeffrey Ethell, *P-38 Lightning* (New York: Random House Value Publishing, 1984).

44. James E. Moore (1902–1986), infantry, graduated from West Point in 1924. He became chief of staff of XII Corps in August 1943 and continued in the same position in Fourth Army, which became Ninth Army in May 1944.

45. Melvin C. Helfers (1913–1987) graduated from The Citadel in 1937. He was the only Regular U.S. Army officer selected for Ultra duty. Helfers received Ultra directly from Hut 3 at the Government Code and Cypher School, Bletchley Park, four times a day and signed for each message. See Melvin Helfers Papers, The Citadel Archives and Museum, A1974.5, box 1, folder 1; SRH-006, "Synthesis of Experiences in the Use of Ultra Intelligence by U.S. Army Field Commands in the European Theatre of Operations," Studies in Cryptology, NSA, 12–13, RG 457, NARA II. Paul Harkins refers to him as "Captain John J. Helfers of the super-secret 'Black Market' or SIS, Signal Intelligence Service." Paul Harkins, *When the Third Cracked Europe: The Story of Patton's Incredible Army* (Harrisburg, PA: Army Times Publishing, 1969), 39.

46. William Marshall Slayden (1911–2004) graduated from the University of Tennessee in 1932. He was appointed liaison officer to the 106th Infantry Division by Middleton.

47. Edward Hale Brooks (1893–1978) was promoted to brigadier general and assumed command of 11th Armored Division in July 1942. He commanded 2nd Armored Division from March to September 1944.

48. See John Nelson Rickard, *Advance and Destroy: Patton as Commander in the Bulge* (Lexington: University Press of Kentucky, 2011), 281.

49. Eclipse was the code name for dealing with post-hostility activities following a sudden collapse of Germany. The original code name, Talisman, was changed in November 1944 after evidence suggested that it was known to the enemy. See Walter M. Hudson, *Army Diplomacy: American Military Occupation and Foreign Policy after World War II* (Lexington: University Press of Kentucky, 2015), 163–67.

50. First Allied Airborne Army was activated on August 2, 1944, and was commanded by U.S. Army Air Force Lieutenant General Lewis H. Brereton. See Lewis H. Brereton, *The Brereton Diaries: The War in the Pacific, Middle East and Europe, 3 October 1941–8 May 1945* (New York: William Morrow, 1946).

51. There were two courses of action under Apostle: Apostle I and Apostle II.

52. Nest Egg was instituted in September 1944 in case of a German collapse or surrender.

53. No biographical information on Chamberlain could be found.

54. Willard Ames Holbrook Jr. (1898–1986) graduated from West Point in 1918.

55. The 8th Armored Division arrived in France on January 5, 1945, and assembled in the vicinity of Pont-à-Mousson to organize a counterattack against an expected enemy strike in the Metz area.

56. The Gloster Meteor was Britain's first jet fighter. It entered operational service on July 27, 1944. See Steven Bond, *Meteor: Gloster's First Jet Fighter* (London: Midland Publishing, 1985).

57. The P-80 Shooting Star was built by Lockheed-Martin but did not enter service during the war.

58. Everett Busch (1893–1985) was born in Sardis, Ohio, and graduated from the University of Virginia. He was promoted to colonel on February 1, 1942, and was appointed quartermaster of Third Army in February 1943. See Everett Busch, "Quartermaster Supply of Third Army," *Quartermaster Review* 26, no. 6 (November–December 1946): 71–72.

59. The 47th Panzer Corps was commanded by Heinrich Freiherr von Lüttwitz.

60. Jacob Loucks Devers (1887–1979) graduated from West Point in 1909. Following the invasion of southern France in August 1944, Devers became commanding general, Sixth Army Group. See John A. Adams, *General Jacob Devers: World War II's Forgotten Four Star* (Bloomington: Indiana University Press, 2015).

6. Into Germany

1. This individual could not be identified. However, a Captain Hans H. Marechal served as a courier in Third Army. See Martin Blumenson, *U.S. Army in World War II: Breakout and Pursuit* (Washington, DC: Center of Military History, 1988), 352.

2. Patton is referring to Raymond Oscar "Tubby" Barton (1889–1963), who graduated from West Point in 1912. Between 1940 and 1942, Barton successively served as chief of staff of IV Corps and commander of the 85th Infantry Division. Barton assumed command of 4th Infantry Division in July 1942 and was replaced on December 27, 1944, by Harold W. Blakeley, the division artillery commander.

3. The membership of the Combined Chiefs of Staff varied somewhat, but basically the same officers were involved throughout. The most prominent British participants included Admiral Sir Dudley Pound, Admiral Sir Charles Little, Field Marshal Sir John Dill, General Sir Alan F. Brooke, Lieutenant General Sir Colville Wemyss, Air Chief Marshal Sir Charles Portal, Air Chief Marshal Arthur T. Harris, Vice Admiral Lord Louis Mountbatten, and Admiral of the Fleet Sir Andrew Cunningham. U.S. officers included Admirals Harold R. Stark, William D. Leahy, and Ernest J. King; Rear Admirals W. R. Sexton, F. J. Horne, J. H. Towers, and Richard K. Turner; Vice Admiral R. Willson; Generals George C. Marshall and Brehon B. Somervell; Lieutenant General Harold H. Arnold; and Brigadier Generals Dwight D. Eisenhower and Leonard T. Gerow. The Combined Chiefs of Staff held their first meeting (the Arcadia conference) on December 24, 1941. See David Rigby, *Allied Master Strategists: The Combined Chiefs of Staff in World War II* (Annapolis, MD: Naval Institute Press, 2012).

4. See Alfred D. Chandler Jr., ed., *The Papers of Dwight D. Eisenhower: The War Years,* vol. 4 (Baltimore: Johns Hopkins University Press, 1970), 2444–54.

5. There was a series of seven dams near the headwaters of the Roer River. Three of the seven were on tributaries of the Roer. The two principal dams were the Urft and the Schwammenauel. The Urft dam was constructed just after the turn of the twentieth century on the Urft River between Gemuend and Ruhrberg and was capable of impounding approximately 42,000 acre-feet of water. The Schwammenauel dam—of earth construction with a concrete core—was built in the mid-1930s near Hasenfeld, about two miles downhill from Schmidt. It formed a reservoir encompassing approximately 81,000 acre-feet. Lesser dams downstream from the Schwammenauel were at Heimbach and Obermaubach. These were designed primarily to create equalizing basins in accordance with industrial needs farther downstream. The Paulushof dam, near the confluence of the Roer and the Urft at Ruhrberg, was designed primarily to regulate water levels at the headwaters of the Schwammenauel reservoir; the Kall Valley dam, on the upper reaches of the Kall River near Lammersdorf, had only a small capacity; and the Dreilaenderbach dam created the Hauptbecken reservoir near Roetgen on the headwaters of the Vicht River.

6. First Canadian Army had been preparing for Operation Veritable since November 1944. Lieutenant General H. D. G. Crerar had thirteen divisions, mostly British, for the operation to destroy the northern German armies west of the Rhine. It was the largest force ever commanded by a Canadian. Veritable began with a massive artillery preparation. First Canadian Army employed more than

1,000 guns to cover the assault, from right to left, by the 51st Highland Division, 53rd Welsh Division, 15th Scottish Division, and 2nd Canadian Infantry Division. See Paul D. Dickson, *A Thoroughly Canadian General: A Biography of General H. D. G. Crerar* (Toronto: University of Toronto Press, 2007), chap. 22.

7. Eugene Lynch Harrison (1898–1981) graduated from West Point in 1923. In 1944 he was appointed assistant chief of staff, G-3, of IV Corps, which was heavily engaged in the Italian Arno River campaign. This was followed by headquarters service in Corsica and postings as assistant chief of staff, G-2, of Sixth Army Group in France and Germany.

8. Anna Eleanor Roosevelt (1884–1962).

9. The B-17 Flying Fortress was built by Boeing. It first saw combat with the RAF in 1941. See Roger Freeman, *B 17: Flying Fortress* (New York: Crown, 1984).

10. Allen's wife, Ruth Finney Allen (1906–1979), was a journalist. See Kathleen A. Cairns, *Front-Page Women Journalists, 1920–1950* (Lincoln: University of Nebraska Press, 2003).

11. No biographical information on Bligh could be found, but he was apparently indoctrinated into Ultra. See "Holy Name Society Offers Prayer for Gen. Patton," *Syracuse Herald Journal,* December 12, 1945, 12.

12. This individual could not be identified.

13. Hallett succeeded Colonel Joseph Cella.

14. This individual could not be identified. Allen might be referring to Dr. Isador Lubin, an economist and statistician and commissioner of labor statistics, U.S. Department of Labor, 1933–1946.

15. Richard J. Stillman (1917–2008) graduated from the University of Southern California. He was the chief of Third Army's Test and Inspection Section in March 1944. See Richard J. Stillman, *General Patton's Timeless Leadership Principles: Your Practical Guide for a Successful Career and Life* (New Orleans: R. J. Stillman, 1998).

16. Ultra had revealed that the Germans considered their greatest point of weakness to be in the Metz-Trier area. See Ralph Bennett, *Ultra in the West: The Normandy Campaign of 1944–1945* (London: Hutchinson, 1979), 133.

17. The 416th Volksgrenadier Division was commanded by Generalleutnant Kurt Pflieger.

18. The 2nd Mountain Division contained only two regiments.

19. William Maxwell Aitken, Lord Beaverbrook (1879–1964), was born in Ontario and raised in New Brunswick, Canada. In 1910 he sold his business interests and moved to England. He quickly secured a seat as a conservative minister in Parliament and was knighted in 1911. Beaverbrook built a newspaper empire comprising the *London Daily Express, Sunday Express,* and *Evening Standard.* In May 1940 he became minister of aircraft production. He also served as minister of production twice and as lord privy seal. See A. J. P. Taylor, *Beaverbrook* (London: Hamish Hamilton, 1972).

20. Oswald Moseley (1896–1980), an English politician, was known principally as the founder of the British Union of Fascists. See Oswald Mosley, *My Life* (New Rochelle, NY: Arlington House, 1972).

21. Harold Sydney Harmsworth, 1st Viscount Rothemere (1868–1940).

22. As a lieutenant colonel and colonel, William Albert Collier (1896–1984) was assistant director of the Infantry Board at Fort Benning, GA. In 1942 Colonel Collier was appointed chief of staff, 78th Infantry Division, Camp Butner, NC. Soon thereafter, he was reassigned as chief of staff, IV Armored Corps (under the command of Walton H. Walker), which served in the California desert and at Fort Campbell, KY. In 1943 the IV Armored Corps was redesignated XX Corps and was stationed in England, France, and Germany during World War II. In November 1944 Collier was promoted to brigadier general.

23. Prince Félix of Bourbon-Parma (1893–1970).

24. Bigland's papers are in the Imperial War Museum in London. See Thomas S. Bigland, *Bigland's War: War Letters of Tom Bigland 1941–45* (Wirral, UK: privately published, 1990).

25. The Porta Negra was a grand Roman gateway in Trier dating to AD 180.

26. Georg Edwin Graf von Rothkirch und Trach (1888–1980) assumed command of LIII Corps on November 3, 1944.

27. See John T. Greenwood, ed., *Normandy to Victory: The War Diary of General Courtney H. Hodges and the First U.S. Army* (Lexington: University Press of Kentucky, 2008), 324–27.

28. The 106th Panzer Brigade made its first appearance against Third Army in early September 1944. It detrained its new Panther tanks at Trier and engaged the 90th Infantry Division west of Metz on September 8 but was virtually crippled in the process. See John Nelson Rickard, *Patton at Bay: The Lorraine Campaign, September to December 1944* (Westport, CT: Praeger, 1999), 88.

29. Harrison was executive officer of the G-4 Section.

7. The Palatinate Campaign

1. Charles Solomon Kilburn (1895–1978) graduated from West Point in 1917. He assumed command of 11th Armored Division in early 1943.

2. Alexander McCarrel Patch Jr. (1889–1945) graduated from West Point in 1913. He assumed command of XIV Corps, South Pacific Theater, in January 1943; the Americal Division in New Caledonia in February 1943, and Seventh Army in March 1944. See William K. Wyant, *Sandy Patch: A Biography of Lt. Gen. Alexander M. Patch* (New York: Praeger, 1991).

3. I Canadian Corps was sent to Italy as a political expedient in 1944, but the minister of national defense, James L. Ralston, expressed a desire for it to return to First Canadian Army before it had fought its first battle in the Liri Valley. Operation Goldflake saw the formations arrive in stages. The 5th Canadian Armored Division began arriving in Belgium in late February, and the 1st Canadian Tank Brigade by mid-March.

4. Walter Bedell Smith (1895–1961) was appointed Eisenhower's chief of staff for Operation Torch. See D. K. R. Crosswell, *Beetle: The Life of General Walter Bedell Smith* (Lexington: University Press of Kentucky, 2010).

5. See F. H. Hinsley, *British Intelligence in the Second World War: Its Influence on Strategy and Operations,* vol. 3, pt. 2 (London: Her Majesty's Stationery Office, 1988), 681–83.

6. Nicholas William Campanole (1881–1955) was the G-5 overseeing civil affairs.

7. Mack Sennett (1884–1960) is considered the father of film comedy.

8. Douglas MacArthur (1880–1964) graduated from West Point in 1903. He served as army chief of staff from 1930 to 1935 and retired in December 1937. From 1937 to 1941 he was a civilian adviser to the Philippine government on military matters. MacArthur was recalled to active duty on July 26, 1941, and assumed command of U.S. Army Forces in the Far East. In February 1942 Roosevelt ordered MacArthur to leave the Philippines and establish himself in Australia. In May MacArthur was appointed Supreme Allied Commander, South West Pacific Area. See William Manchester, *American Caesar: Douglas MacArthur 1880–1964* (Boston: Little, Brown, 1978).

9. James Alward Van Fleet (1892–1992) graduated from West Point in 1915. He assumed command of the 90th Infantry Division in October 1944. See Paul Braim, *The Will to Win: The Life of General James A. Van Fleet* (Annapolis, MD: Naval Institute Press, 2001).

10. This individual could not be identified.

11. No biographical information on this individual could be found.

12. No biographical information on this individual could be found.

13. Patton's Hammelburg raid is one of the most controversial episodes of his career. On March 25, 1945, Third Army had established bridgeheads over the Main River near Hanau and Aschaffenburg. Intelligence reports indicated the presence of a prisoner of war camp approximately forty miles east of Aschaffenburg, and that the Germans were killing the prisoners. The fact that Patton believed that his son-in-law, John K. Waters, was a prisoner there is usually offered as the sole reason for the raid. Patton had originally intended to send a combat command-sized force but finally settled on a task force consisting of C Company, 37th Tank Battalion, and A Company, 10th Armored Infantry Battalion, as well as some light tanks and assault guns. The force was known as Task Force Baum, after its commander, Captain Abraham J. Baum. See Richard Baron, Abe Baum, and Richard Goldhurst, *Raid: The Untold Story of Patton's Secret Mission* (New York: G. P. Putnam's Sons, 1981); Lieutenant Colonel Frederick E. Oldinsky, "Patton and the Hammelburg Mission," *Armor* 85, no. 4 (July–August 1976): 13–18.

14. Hans Boelsen (1894–1960) was a recipient of the Knight's Cross of the Iron Cross.

15. See Stephen M. Rusiecki, *In Final Defense: The Destruction of the 6th SS Mountain Division "Nord"* (Annapolis, MD: Naval Institute Press, 2010).

16. See Hinsley, *British Intelligence in the Second World War,* vol. 3, pt. 2, 683.

17. Marlene Dietrich (1901–1992) became a U.S. citizen in 1939. During World War II, she traveled extensively to entertain the Allied troops, singing "Lili Marlene" and other songs that would become staples in her cabaret act. She also participated in war-bond drives and recorded anti-Nazi messages in German for broadcast. See Steven Bach, *Marlene Dietrich: Life and Legend* (New York: William Morrow, 1992).

18. No biographical information on this individual could be found.

19. Edgar Röhricht (1892–1967) assumed command of German LIX Army Corps in March 1944 in the region of Kamenetz-Podolsk.

20. Ralph Graf von Oriola (1895–1970) assumed command of German XIII Army Corps in February 1945. He was captured on March 31, 1945.

21. Paul Joseph Goebbels (1897–1945) was the Nazi propaganda minister. See Louis P. Lochner, ed., *The Goebbels Diaries, 1942–1943* (Garden City, NY: Doubleday, 1948); Willi A. Boelcke, ed., *The Secret Conferences of Dr. Goebbels: The Nazi Propaganda War 1939–1943* (New York: Dutton, 1970).

22. Friedrich Schiller (1759–1805) was a German poet, philosopher, historian, and playwright.

23. This individual could not be identified.

24. Ludwig Heilmann (1903–1959) assumed command of the 5th Fallschirmjäger Division in November 1944.

25. Harris M. Melasky (1893–1972), infantry, graduated from West Point in 1917. He assumed command of the division in January 1943.

26. Emil Ludwig (née Cohn; 1881–1948) became a Swiss citizen in 1932 and immigrated to the United States in 1940.

8. The End of the War in the European Theater of Operations

1. Guenther Blumentritt (1896–1967) commanded the First Parachute Army from March 1945. See Mark M. Boatner III, *Biographical Dictionary of World War II* (Novato, CA: Presidio Press, 1996), 48.

2. Franz Joseph (1830–1916) was emperor of Austria (1848–1916) and king of Hungary (1867–1916). See John Van der Kiste, *Emperor Francis Joseph: Life, Death and the Fall of the Habsburg Empire* (London: Sutton, 2005).

3. Fedor Tolbukhin (1894–1949) assumed command of the Third Ukrainian Front in May 1944. See Harold Shukman, ed., *Stalin's Generals* (New York: Grove Press, 1993), 22, 120, 289, 367; Martin Blumenson, ed., *The Patton Papers,* vol. 2, *1940–1945* (Boston: Houghton Mifflin, 1974), 711–12.

4. See Blumenson, *Patton Papers,* 2:716.

5. Bradley's G-3 was Brigadier General A. Franklin Kibler (1891–1955), field artillery. Kibler graduated from the Virginia Military Institute in 1912. He became G-3 of Twelfth Army Group in October 1943.

6. Josip Brozovitch (or Broz) Tito (1892–1980) was recognized by the Western Allies as the leader of the Yugoslav resistance in 1943. See Jasper Ridley, *Tito: A Biography* (London: Constable, 1996).

7. Max Amann (1891–1957) was a German Nazi official with the honorary rank of SS-Obergruppenführer.

8. Franklin served in the G-2 Section.

9. Louis Huot (1906–?) was born in Duluth, MN. He worked in Montreal for the *Gazette* and the *Montreal Daily Herald;* he also worked for the *Chicago Tribune* and was manager of the Paris Bureau of *Press Wireless* before the war. Huot served as the psychological warfare officer in the G-2 Section. See Lieutenant Colonel Louis Huot, "Civilian Tanker," *This Week Magazine,* November 25, 1945, 4–5; "Louis Huot Named Journalism Hero," *Gazette,* June 13, 1940, 2; Leon Edel, *The Visitable Past: A Wartime Memoir* (Honolulu: University of Hawaii Press, 2001).

10. Galina Orlova was a Russian-born dancer who arrived in the United States at age sixteen. She soon began working on Broadway and met Lucky Luciano.

11. Sicilian immigrant Salvatore Lucania (1897–1962) changed his name to Charles Luciano and was nicknamed "Lucky." He was considered the most powerful crime boss in America in the 1930s.

Selected Bibliography

Archives

Armor School, Fort Benning, Georgia
Robert S. Allen Papers (typescript journal)

Combined Arms Research Library, Fort Leavenworth, Kansas
Report of Operations, Twelfth Army Group, vol. 5, G-2 Section

Wisconsin Historical Society
Robert S. Allen Papers (contains the original, handwritten journal)

Published Sources

Abell, Tyler, ed. *Drew Pearson Diaries 1949–1959.* New York: Holt, Rinehart & Winston, 1974.

Allen, Robert S. *Lucky Forward: The History of Patton's Third U.S. Army.* New York: Vanguard Press, 1947.

———. "Patton Used Fighting Words to Staff in Taking over Third Army." *Milwaukee Journal,* December 29, 1945, 13.

———. "Patton's Secret 'I Am Going to Resign from the Army. Quit Outright, Not Retire.'" *Army* 21, no. 6 (June 1971): 29–33.

Association of Graduates, U.S. Military Academy. *Register of Graduates and Former Cadets of the United States Military Academy West Point, New York, 2000.* West Point, NY: Association of Graduates, 1999.

Barron, Leo. *Patton at the Battle of the Bulge: How the General's Tanks Turned the Tide at Bastogne.* New York: NAL Caliber, 2014.

Bennett, Ralph. *Ultra in the West: The Normandy Campaign of 1944–1945.* London: Hutchinson, 1979.

Bigelow, Michael E. "Big Business: Intelligence in Patton's Third Army." *Military Intelligence* 18, no. 2 (April–June 1992): 31–36.

Blumenson, Martin. *Patton: The Man behind the Legend 1885–1945.* New York: William Morrow, 1985.

———. *U.S. Army in World War II: Breakout and Pursuit.* Washington, DC: Center of Military History, 1988.

———, ed. *The Patton Papers.* 2 vols. Boston: Houghton Mifflin, 1972, 1974.

Boatner, Mark M., III. *Biographical Dictionary of World War II*. Novato, CA: Presidio Press, 1996.

Bradley, Omar N. *A Soldier's Story*. New York: Henry Holt, 1951.

Bradley, Omar N., with Clay Blair. *A General's Life*. New York: Simon & Schuster, 1983.

Braim, Paul. *The Will to Win: The Life of General James A. Van Fleet*. Annapolis, MD: Naval Institute Press, 2001.

Brown, Anthony C., ed. *The Secret War Report of the OSS*. New York: Berkeley, 1976.

Browne, Colonel Roger J. "Eggcup Was the Call Sign." *Infantry Journal* 63, no. 1 (July 1948): 29–32.

Busch, Everett. "Quartermaster Supply of Third Army." *Quartermaster Review* 26, no. 6 (November–December 1946): 71–72.

Butcher, Harry C. *My Three Years with Eisenhower*. New York: Simon & Schuster, 1946.

Chamberlain, Colonel Frederick R., Jr., and Captain John G. Wynn. "Activities of Third U.S. Army AAA." *Coast Artillery Journal* 91, no. 1 (July–August 1948): 2–16.

Chandler, Alfred D., Jr., ed. *The Papers of Dwight D. Eisenhower: The War Years*, vols. 3 and 4. Baltimore: Johns Hopkins University Press, 1970.

Codman, Charles R. *Drive*. Boston: Little, Brown, 1957.

Colby, John. *War from the Ground Up: The 90th Division in WW II*. Austin, TX: Nortex Press, 1991.

Cole, Hugh M. *U.S. Army in World War II: The Ardennes: Battle of the Bulge*. Washington, DC: Center of Military History, 1988.

————. *U.S. Army in World War II: The Lorraine Campaign*. Washington, DC: Center of Military History, 1988.

D'Este, Carlo. *Patton: A Genius for War*. New York: HarperCollins, 1996.

Deutsch, Harold C. "Commanding Generals and the Uses of Intelligence." *Intelligence and National Security* 3, no. 3 (1988): 194–260.

Dougherty, Major Kevin. "Our MI Heritage: Oscar Koch: An Unsung Hero behind Patton's Victories." *Military Intelligence Professional Bulletin* 28, no. 1 (April–June 2002): 64–66.

Dyer, George. *XII Corps: Spearhead of Patton's Third Army*. Baton Rouge: Military Press of Louisiana, 1947.

Eisenhower, Dwight D. *Crusade in Europe*. New York: Doubleday, 1948.

Essame, H. *Patton: A Study in Command*. New York: Charles Scribner's Sons, 1974.

Farago, Ladislas. *Patton: Ordeal and Triumph*. New York: Ivan Obolensky, 1964.

Fitzharris, Joseph C., ed. *Patton's Fighting Bridge Builders: Company C, 1303rd Engineer General Service Regiment*. College Station: Texas A&M University Press, 2007.

Forty, George. *Patton's Third Army at War*. New York: Charles Scribner's Sons, 1979.

Fox, Donald M. *Patton's Vanguard: The United States Army's Fourth Armored Division*. Jefferson, NC: McFarland, 2003.

Frankel, Nat, and Larry Smith. *Patton's Best: An Informal History of the 4th Armored Division*. New York: David McKay, 1978.

Ganz, A. Harding. "Patton's Relief of General Wood." *Journal of Military History* 53, no. 3 (July 1989): 257–73.

Gawne, Jonathan. *Ghosts of the ETO: American Tactical Deception Units in the European Theater 1944–1945*. Havertown, PA: Casemate, 2002.

Greenwood, John T., ed. *Normandy to Victory: The War Diary of General Courtney H. Hodges and the First U.S. Army*. Lexington: University Press of Kentucky, 2008.

Haislip, Wade H. "Corps Command in World War II." *Military Review* 70, no. 5 (May 1990): 22–32.

Hammond, Colonel Elton F. "Signals for Patton." *Signals* 2, no. 1 (September–October 1947): 5–11.

Harkins, Paul D. *When the Third Cracked Europe: The Story of Patton's Incredible Army*. Harrisburg, PA: Army Times Publishing, 1969.

Haynes, John Earl, Harvey Klehr, and Alexander Vassiliev. *Spies: The Rise and Fall of the KGB in America*. New Haven, CT: Yale University Press, 2009.

Hays, Robert. *Patton's Oracle: General Oscar Koch, as I Knew Him*. Savoy, IL: Lucidus Books, 2013.

Hobar, Colonel Basil J. "The Ardennes 1944: Intelligence Failure or Deception Success?" *Military Intelligence* 10, no. 4 (October–December 1984): 8–16.

Hofmann, George F. *The Super Sixth: History of the 6th Armored Division in World War II and Its Post-War Association*. Nashville, TN: Battery Press, n.d.

———. *Through Mobility We Conquer: The Mechanization of U.S. Cavalry*. Lexington: University Press of Kentucky, 2006.

Huot, Lieutenant Colonel Louis. "Civilian Tanker." *This Week Magazine*, November 25, 1945, 4–5.

Hymel, Kevin M. *Patton's Photographs: War as He Saw It*. Washington, DC: Potomac Books, 2006.

Keefler, Wilson A. *Patton's Bulldog: The Life and Service of General Walton H. Walker*. Shippensburg, PA: White Mane, 2001.

Kemp, Anthony. *The Unknown Battle: Metz 1944*. London: Frederick Warne, 1981.

Kirkpatrick, Lyman B. "Combat Intelligence: A Comparative Evaluation." *Studies in Intelligence* 5, no. 4 (Fall 1960): 45–51.

Koch, Oscar W. *G-2: Intelligence for Patton*. Philadelphia: Whitmore, 1971.

Lande, D. A. *I Was with Patton: First-Person Accounts of WWII in George S. Patton's Command*. St. Paul, MN: Motor Books International, 2002.

Macdonald, Charles B. *U.S. Army in World War II: The Last Offensive*. Washington, DC: Center of Military History, 1973.

Mansoor, Peter. *The G.I. Offensive in Europe: The Triumph of American Infantry Divisions, 1944–1945*. Lawrence: University Press of Kansas, 1999.

Miller, Edward G. *Nothing Less than Full Victory: Americans at War in Europe, 1944–1945*. Annapolis, MD: Naval Institute Press, 2007.

Munch, Paul G. "Patton's Staff and the Battle of the Bulge." *Military Review* 70, no. 5 (May 1990): 46–54.

Nichols, Lester M. *Impact: The Battle Story of the Tenth Armored Division*. Nashville, TN: Battery Press, 2000.

Nye, Roger H. *The Patton Mind: The Professional Development of an Extraordinary Leader*. Garden City, NY: Avery Publishing, 1993.

Oden, Delk M. "The 4th Armored Division in the Relief of Bastogne." *Military Review* 27, no. 10 (January 1948): 39–44.

Odom, Charles B. *General George S. Patton and Eisenhower*. New Orleans: Word Picture Productions, 1985.

Ohl, John Kennedy. *Supplying the Troops: General Somervell and American Logistics in World War II*. De Kalb: Northern Illinois University Press, 1994.

Patton, George S. *War as I Knew It*. New York: Bantam, 1981.

Pay, Don R. *Thunder from Heaven: Story of the 17th Airborne Division, 1943–1945*. Nashville, TN: Battery Press, 1980.

Phillips, Henry G. *The Making of a Professional: Manton S. Eddy, USA*. Westport, CT: Greenwood, 2000.

Pogue, Forrest C. "The Ardennes Campaign: The Impact of Intelligence." Remarks to the NSA Communications Analysis Association, December 16, 1980.

———. *U.S. Army in World War II: The Supreme Command*. Washington, DC: Center of Military History, 1989.

Polk, General James K. "Patton: 'You Might as Well Die a Hero.'" *Army* 25, no. 12 (December 1975): 39–44.

Price, Frank J. *Troy H. Middleton: A Biography*. Baton Rouge: Louisiana State University Press, 1974.

Province, Charles M. *Patton's Third Army: A Daily Combat Diary*. New York: Hippocrene Books, 1992.

Rickard, John Nelson. *Advance and Destroy: Patton as Commander in the Bulge*. Lexington: University Press of Kentucky, 2011.

———. "December 1944: Eisenhower, Bradley and the Calculated Risk in the Ardennes." *Global War Studies* 8, no. 1 (2011): 7–34.

———. *Patton at Bay: The Lorraine Campaign, September to December 1944*. Westport, CT: Praeger, 1999.

Ricks, Thomas E. "Patton's Third Army Deputy Intel Officer Briefly Was on the KGB's Payroll." *Foreign Policy* (December 1, 2010). http://foreignpolicy.com/2010/12/01/pattons-third-army-deputy-intel-officer-briefly-was-on-the-kgbs-payroll/ (accessed January 24, 2017).

Rosengarten, Adolph G., Jr. "The Bulge: A Glimpse of Combat Intelligence." *Military Review* 41, no. 6 (June 1961): 29–33.

Spires, David N. *Patton's Air Force: Forging a Legendary Air-Ground Team.* Washington, DC: Smithsonian Institution Press, 2002.

Stevenson, Lieutenant Colonel Frank E. "Third Army's Planning for the Crossing of the Rhine River." *Military Review* 30, no. 12 (March 1951): 33–42.

Steward, Hal D. *Thunderbolt: The History of the Eleventh Armored Division.* Nashville, TN: Battery Press, 1981.

Stillman, Richard J. *General Patton's Timeless Leadership Principles: Your Practical Guide for a Successful Career and Life.* New Orleans: R. J. Stillman, 1998.

Sullivan, John J. *Air Support for Patton's Third Army.* Jefferson, NC: McFarland, 2003.

Sunday, Adeline. *Come Live with Me and the Colonel.* Pittsburgh: Dorrance, 2009.

Swedo, Major Bradford J. *XIX Tactical Air Command and ULTRA: Patton's Force Enhancers in the 1944 Campaign in France.* Cadre Paper No. 10. Maxwell Air Force Base, AL: Air University Press, 2001.

Twaddle, Major General Harry L. "From Metz to the Saar." *Military Review* 25, no. 8 (November 1945): 4–8.

Wallace, Brenton G. *Patton and His Third Army.* Harrisburg, PA: Military Service Publishing, 1946.

Weigley, Russell F. *Eisenhower's Lieutenants: The Campaigns of France and Germany, 1944–1945.* Bloomington: Indiana University Press, 1981.

Williams, Brigadier General Robert W. "Moving Information: The Third Army Imperative." *Army* 25, no. 4 (April 1975): 17–21.

Winton, Harold R. *Corps Commanders of the Bulge: Six American Generals and Victory in the Ardennes.* Lawrence: University Press of Kansas, 2007.

XX Corps. *The XX Corps: Its History and Service in World War II.* Osaka, Japan: Mainichi Publishing Company, n.d.

Zabecki, David T., ed. *Chief of Staff: The Principal Officers behind History's Greatest Commanders, II: World War II to Korea and Vietnam.* Annapolis, MD: Naval Institute Press, 2008.

Zaloga, Steven J. *Metz 1944: Patton's Fortified Nemesis.* Midland House, UK: Osprey, 2012.

Index

293

CPSIA information can be obtained
at www.ICGtesting.com
Printed in the USA
LVHW090016110620
656428LV00010BA/150